WMG WRITER'S GUIDES

Bundle on Marketing
Copyright © 2020 by Kristine Kathryn Rusch & Dean Wesley Smith
Published by WMG Publishing
Cover and layout copyright © 2020 by WMG Publishing
Cover design by Allyson Longueira/WMG Publishing

How to Write Fiction Sales Copy
Copyright © 2020 by Dean Wesley Smith
First published in a different form in 2015 on Dean Wesley Smith's blog at
www.deanwesleysmith.com
Published by WMG Publishing
Cover and layout copyright © 2020 by WMG Publishing
Cover design by Allyson Longueira/WMG Publishing
Cover art copyright © Madmaxer/Source

Creating Your Author Brand
Copyright © 2020 by Kristine Kathryn Rusch
First published in 2017 in a slightly different version on kristinekathrynrusch.com
Published by WMG Publishing
Layout and design © copyright 2020 WMG Publishing
Cover design by Allyson Longueira/WMG Publishing
Interior art © copyright andrewgenn/CanStockPhoto
Cover art © copyright andrewgenn/Depositphotos

Discoverability
Copyright © 2020 by Kristine Kathryn Rusch
Parts of this book have appeared as blog posts on kristinekathrynrusch.com from November 2013 to August 2014
Published by WMG Publishing
Cover and Layout copyright © 2020 by WMG Publishing
Cover design by Allyson Longueira/WMG Publishing
Cover art copyright © Davidarts/Dreamstime

ISBN: 13 - 978-1-56146-348-0
ISBN:10 - 1-56146-348-5

This book is licensed for your personal enjoyment only. All rights reserved. This book, or parts thereof, may not be reproduced in any form without permission.

BUNDLE ON MARKETING

A WMG WRITER'S GUIDE

KRISTINE KATHRYN RUSCH
& DEAN WESLEY SMITH

CONTENTS

BUNDLE ON MARKETING

USA TODAY BESTSELLING AUTHOR

DEAN WESLEY SMITH

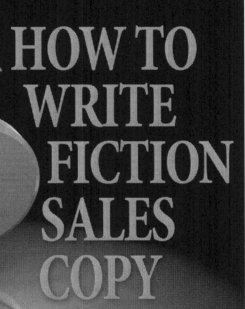

HOW TO WRITE FICTION SALES COPY

WITH 32 COVERS AND EXAMPLES TO STUDY

A WMG WRITER'S GUIDE

INTRODUCTION

In July of 2015, I managed to write one short story a day. Actually had one extra, so ended up with 32 stories.

I did a cover for all of those stories as well, usually the next day.

My goal seemed simple on the surface:

- Write 31 or 32 short stories.
- Put them all in a book titled *Stories from July*.
- Later publish all of them as standalone stories in electronic and paper.
- Also put each story in my monthly magazine (*Smith's Monthly*) one or two a month, mixed with other stories and new novels.
- Include the stories in themed collections.

In the book *Stories from July*, I wanted the blogs about writing each story, a cover, a blurb, and then the story.

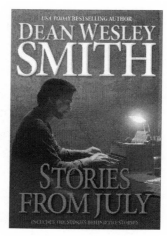

Stories from July

To do that, I needed first to write the story each day. Check. Got that done. And it was great fun, more fun than I had imagined it would be.

Second, I needed to do a cover for each story, branded to me, the author. Check. Got that done.

Also fun.

And third, each story needed some sales copy. It would need it for the blurb on all the sales sites and for the back cover on the paper versions of each story and at the start of each story in *Stories from July* and in *Smith's Monthly*.

So that's what this series is all about.

Sales copy.

I need to write the sales copy for all 32 stories. A couple people asked about how I was going to do that. So I figured why not explain some about how to write the sales copy, since I also teach doing this in a workshop, among other things.

I will include my thinking about each story as I wrote the sales copy for it and how I got out of author problems and wrote sales.

Maybe I can help a few writers with their own sales copy if I talk about this process and show examples. At least that's the hope.

So onward.

1

I figure the best way to do this is just start with the very first story I wrote on July 1st and work my way though each one. I will put the covers here with the blurbs.

A few basic thoughts about sales copy writing first off.

This is difficult for most fiction writers to do for a couple of reasons, both of which I call "The Author Problem."

I will go into this more later, but the author problem comes in basically two parts.

First: Can't see beyond the plot.

Second: Can't write anything but passive voice when talking about their own work.

Keep that in mind as I dive into these first few. In later chapters I will deal a lot with more details about "The Author Problem" in writing sales copy.

I'm going to put up two blurbs I wrote for the first two stories and then talk about them in this first chapter before moving on.

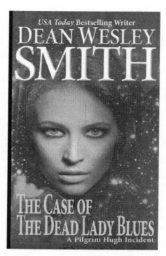

The Case of the Dead Lady Blues: A Pilgrim Hugh Incident

Private Detective Pilgrim Hugh loves solving strange cases. Very little stumps him for very long.

But a woman by the name of Deep Blue, dead in her empty apartment and dyed blue, seemed like an impossible case.

And more than Hugh knows depends on his quick solution.

Pilgrim Hugh once again rides to the rescue in his stretch limo driven by his brilliant assistant. If you love puzzle crime stories, grab "The Case of the Dead Lady Blues."

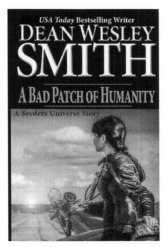

A Bad Patch of Humanity: A Seeders Universe Story

Most of humanity died one ugly day four years before. Now the survivors wanted to rebuild.

Angie Park's job consisted of telling survivors outside of Portland, Oregon, of the plans to rebuild. But some survivors wanted nothing to do with civilization.

And some thought killing worth the price to pay to stay alone.

In the galaxy-spanning Seeders Universe, "A Bad Patch of Humanity" focuses down on an early event in Angie Park's life, an event that starts her on her path to becoming a woman of legend in a hundred galaxies.

So first, let me talk about a pattern I used for these two, and that I will continue to use through a lot of these stories.

Blurb Pattern: Basic

Paragraph one: Character or world summary. Interesting. And nails genre if possible.

Paragraph two: One very short paragraph with short sentences about the first page of the plot.

Paragraph three: Plot kicker line.

Paragraph four: Why readers will want to read the story (mostly using tags).

That is a structure that works well for short stories and most novels. It isn't the only structure by a long ways, but it is a standby basic structure to fall back on.

My Thinking About Each Story

The Case of the Dead Lady Blues: A Pilgrim Hugh Incident
This is a story using a developing character. I think I have done four or five of these stories now. All strange. So when I came to write the blurb, I had a couple givens that were easy.

First, I needed to explain Pilgrim Hugh slightly and what he did. Thus, the summary paragraph about him.

That also nails the genre.

Plot opens basically with him standing in an empty apartment looking at a dead body that has been dyed blue. So I just described that since the scene was interesting enough to hook a mystery reader into wondering how a body in an empty apartment could be dyed blue.

Then I raised the stakes with a hint at something bigger in the story. (Third paragraph.) Always good to raise the stakes without giving plot away.

Then I told readers with a hint of the strangeness of Pilgrim Hugh that readers didn't want to miss this story. A form of call-to-action.

A Bad Patch of Humanity: A Seeder's Universe Story
This story presented more problems for me in a number of ways. First off, after rebranding this series recently, all Seeders novels covers have massive spaceships on them. But this story is basically an opening story of a new character. So I needed a cover to the story. (Story opens with her getting off her motorcycle.)

Then I needed the blurb to address in a fashion the questions of those who read the Seeders Universe novels.

So first paragraph set the scene.

Second paragraph introduced the character and the plot.

Third paragraph raised the stakes.

Fourth paragraph told the reader this was standalone, but also how this story fit into the larger Seeders Universe. This time the last paragraph set the genre.

And readers love start-of-legend stories.

Author Problem

Look at both sales copy for the author problem.

First off, how you know you have too much plot is if you have two or more **"and then this happens."**

I had none.

Not a one.

The plot I revealed in these two first blurbs a reader would know in the first page or so of each story.

Second, notice there is not a passive verb anywhere. Every verb is active. Sentences are short.

Easy for a buyer to read.

2

In the first chapter of this book, I touched on what I call "The Author Problem" and gave a basic formula that I sometimes use to give blurbs a structure.

One point right now before I jump down into more of these. I got a question from two people privately, wondering where I would use these blurbs exactly.

So here is exactly how I plan to use all of these:

- Introduction to each story in the book *Stories from July.*
- Introduction to each story when I late put them in *Smith's Monthly* magazine.
- Introduction to each story in a collection that contains one of these stories.
- Sales copy on all electronic and paper sales sites. Amazon, B&N, iBooks, Kobo, and so on. Including Smashwords. These are just barely over 400 characters, so shouldn't be hard to get them down a ways.
- The sales copy on the back of the paperback of each story. Yes, even the short ones will be standalone paperbacks.

So now onward to some more stories.
Then for each one I will detail out my thinking while writing the blurb.

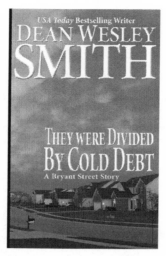

They Were Divided by Cold Debt: A Bryant Street Story

Bryant Street, a standard subdivision street, haunts us all. To escape Bryant Street often takes real courage.

Meet Neil Prendell. He made a mistake. He lost his job but avoided telling his wife. Instead, he pretended to go to work while looking for another job.

Pride? Fear? Stupidity? The reason no longer mattered. He paid the price.

A price that only made sense in the twisted logic of Bryant Street.

My Bryant Street stories are the hardest stories I have to blurb every time. Think *Twilight Zone* without Rod Serling explaining everything through a cloud of smoke.

Bryant Street is based on my complete fear of subdivisions and the trap, the prison they form for so many. So I write stories set in those homes along the street.

As Stephen King often says, "Write what scares you." Subdivisions scare hell out of me.

So I went to the form I talked about last chapter and first gave a summary of Bryant Street in general and vague terms.

Second paragraph, I played off the *Twilight Zone* pattern with the first line, then gave the plot from the first few paragraphs of the story.

Third paragraph I raised the stakes to make readers wonder what price did he pay? And from the first paragraph, did he have the courage to escape.

Fourth paragraph I went back to *Twilight Zone* rip to make sure readers understood Bryant Street is a very strange and dangerous place.

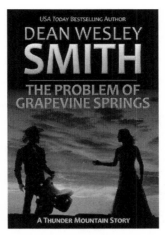

The Problem of Grapevine Springs: A Thunder Mountain Story

Duster Kendal lost an Idaho mining town called Grapevine Springs. In 2020 he knew the town, spent time there. In 1901 the valley sat empty.

The town never existed. Not possible.

Duster needed to get back to the year 2020 to solve the mystery of the lost mining town.

A standalone story that introduces a new mining town and new characters into the Thunder Mountain world of westerns and time travel.

I used what I call "The Hook" structure on this one due to the fact that Thunder Mountain novels and stories are well established. So I needed to get across to Thunder Mountain readers the idea, but also do enough to attract a non-reader of the series.

(I'll talk more about this structure later in the chapter.)

So I made the first paragraph a plot focus with the crazy plot hook of losing an entire town.

Then I punched that plot hook in the second paragraph.

Then the third paragraph established the story solidly as time travel, with a mystery element, still using the hook from the first page of the story.

The fourth paragraph made sure that I told readers of the series this was a standalone story and again punched the time travel aspect of the genre.

So in this one I stayed with four paragraphs, but focused on a plot hook. Just one element of plot. The hook of the plot actually. Never once did I put in any "and then this happens..." silliness.

Writing blurbs in established series is often a trick.

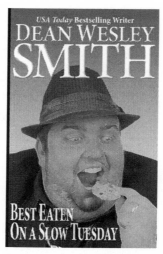

Best Eaten on a Slow Tuesday

Mark Estes flaunted his money, abused his power, cheated on his wife, and most of all loved to eat.

Warned that a dozen sugar cookies would kill him, he ate them anyway.

So how would Mark Estes deal with the ultimate diet challenge?

A story that answers the simple question: Do diets come from hell?

Between the blurb and the cover, you get a pretty good idea of the subject of this story.

I approached the story first from the idea that everyone understands the problems of weight, but tossed that. Sometimes generalizing readers helps, but other times not so much. This was a not-so-much time.

I finally went to the focus of telling what the story is about. Not the plot. Just the hook.

The story is about eating and ego. Or not eating and ego.

So first paragraph set the character. Second paragraph set the first page problem and hook.

Third paragraph hinted at something more without going into detail of what the ultimate diet challenge really was.

Last paragraph then played into what we all believe, that diets come from hell. And with luck gave the story just a hope of someone buying it.

Fighting upstream against topic with this one.

On this story, I had to fight for a moment the "Author Problem" of knowing nifty details of the story and wanting to put those nifty details in the blurb. In fact, the nifty details are what makes the story fun and cool, but if I put even one of them in the blurb, the story would be ruined for readers.

A Matter for a Future Year: A Seeders Universe Story

A single Seeder scout ship trapped on the edge of a distant, uncharted galaxy. Chairman Peter German holds the fate of the three thousand people on the Pale Light.

Main drives mysteriously not working, the ship hobbles along at sub-light speed with not enough supplies to reach the nearest Earth-like planet

The Chairman faces a hard, hard choice. He must find the solution.

Galaxy spanning ships, billions of civilizations, the Seeders Universe stories and novels cover it all. But "A Matter for a Future Year" brings it all down to a single human choice. And the price paid by those who risk to explore outward.

This was the second Seeders Universe story in the first week. This one in deep space, the other one set firmly on a devastated Earth. It's a very large universe I am writing books in, that's for sure.

And the key with large universes is always bringing the story down to a human level. An understandable level.

So on this one, I started with the first-page-of-the-story problem and the character, trying quickly to brush stroke the main character's problem.

That took three paragraphs. And it was the hook of the first page of the story. Nothing more.

Then I dropped back into giving a blurb about the entire Seeders Universe, making it crystal clear this story is on the human levels of being in space.

So the structure of blurbs I used in the first chapter of this book is not evident at all.

A Second Basic Structure

As shown in three of the blurbs in this chapter, the second basic structure is what I tend to call "The Hook" structure.

The opening page of a story, or opening chapter of a novel, has a great hook that will pull readers in.

Then, in this structure, get a character (readers always read for character) and relay the hook and nothing more in two quick, short paragraphs.

Punch with a third paragraph if possible.

Summary of the theme, why readers would want to read the story, in the last paragraph.

Again four paragraphs. All short. With punch.

Author Problem Check

Did I get into any author problem here?

Were there any passive verbs in any of the four blurbs?

Did I once go "and then this happens" with the plot I did reveal?

I think all four of them don't have any author problems, but I did have some trouble writing one. If I hadn't been paying attention, I might have tossed in too much plot.

3

In the first chapter of this book, I touched on what I call "The Author Problem" and gave a basic formula that I sometimes use to give blurbs a structure.

And in Chapter Two I laid out another formula for writing blurbs.

In this chapter, my friend, professional fiction and extraordinary comic book writer Lee Allred, put in the comments on my web site a great way of looking at blurbs to stay out of author problems.

What he uses is the first three parts of the Algis Budrys plot structure to open a blurb.

1) Character. 2) In a Setting. 3) With a Problem.

Then, as he said, if you are using the try-fail cycles that Algis Budrys talks about in his plot summary, you are deep in the weeds of plot-telling.

So Lee suggests opening with **Character in Context with a Problem,** use no passive voice, and a strong hook line for the last line.

I can only agree completely, Lee.

I have seen a bunch of Lee's blurbs, and he has written some for the upcoming Poker Boy relaunch and they are stunning.

Thanks, Lee.

Yet another way to approach these. In three chapters, that's three ways.

So now onward. Let me see what I need to do on a few more covers.

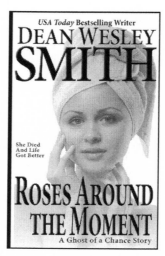

Roses Around the Moment: A Ghost of a Chance Story

Eve Bryson died so fast that she felt fine, standing on a twisting mountain road in the rain, not realizing her body lay broken in her Miata down a slope.

Then hunk-of-a-man Deputy Cascade steps into her life, arriving on the scene to investigate her death.

Wet, cold, hungry, and needing to pee, she finds herself dead and in lust. Then things really start to happen.

Eve died. And life got better.

I have written three Ghost of a Chance novels, but I think this was the first short story in that world. The story stands alone, but it is clear that these two characters, one a ghost, another a superhero, will have their own novel.

This is another tie across to my Poker Boy world. The Ghost of a Chance agents are basically a team of ghosts that run around and save the world, sometimes working with Poker Boy and his team.

However, not a bit of that could be in this blurb. Not a bit. This story stands alone and is a great introduction to a ghost and a superhero cop. So I had to focus on the story.

So I did what Lee suggested here in a way.

I also used a romance trope. (This story would be a meet cute in a romance novel.) Introduce her and setting. Then introduce the hero. (Actually a superhero, but she doesn't know that.)

Have her lust after the hero. Set her opening setting even more firmly.

Then tag line. Which is also on the cover.

With three novels, the author problem was strong in this one to try to explain all that. I refrained.

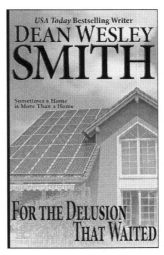

For the Delusion That Waited

Modern homes take care of themselves more and more. Called "Smart Homes," new features get added every year.

Imagine a spotless, five-bedroom home, self-cleaning, self-sustaining, and furnished with the best 2051 furniture human styles offered.

The home named Matilda also repaired itself.

A simple short story that asks a standard science fiction question: What if this goes on?

This story is the shortest of all the stories I wrote at 1,250 words. It is a biting science fiction IDEA story.

But the problem with that is I didn't dare take any of the power away from the story in the blurb or the cover. Huge author problem here. One slip and I would ruin the story completely.

So I went back to my first chapter's formula for blurbs for this story.

Paragraph one, idea set.

Paragraph two set the scene, such as it was. But I wanted to set the year to make sure this was clear that it was in the future.

Paragraph three added in that the house was an AI and had a name.

Last paragraph nails the genre and I hope gets readers interested in reading about what might just happen if smart homes went on. At least 1,200 words of reading.

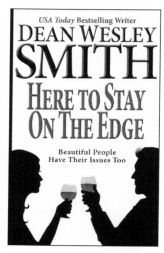

Here to Stay on the Edge

Stunningly beautiful Carol Lynn once again finds herself stood up on a blind date. A romantic patio, perfect warm evening, the smell of roasted duck in a thick cheese sauce, and a glass of red wine in her hand.

Perfect. If the bastard showed up. But the empty chair across from her spoke volumes.

Then the most handsome man she might ever dream about sat across from her. Not her date. And not in her league.

A sweet story of a romantic dinner. And a possible future.

This story is a meet cute romance short story. So I needed to set the stage first.

This I used Lee Allred's form more than any other.

Character, in a setting, with a problem.

Problem came in paragraph two.

Romance form required the male side of things to come on stage. Paragraph three.

Last paragraph punches the romance element solidly.

Again a story with a bunch of fun stuff in it that I didn't dare reveal in the blurb, so author problem caused me to write and then back up a few times on this blurb.

Author Problem Check

Did I get into any author problem on any of these three stories? All were difficult because of author problems. But I think I stayed out of them.

Were there any passive verbs in any of the three blurbs? Nope, none that I can see, but a couple on the covers of two of the books, which is fine for tag lines there.

Did I once go "and then this happens" with the plot I did reveal? Nope

I think all three of them don't have any author problems. But all three wanted to have more plot in them.

Onward to more blurbs. And thanks, Lee Allred, for adding in yet another form.

4

In the first chapter of this book, I touched on what I call "The Author Problem" and gave a basic formula that I sometimes use to give blurbs a structure.

And in Chapter Two I laid out another formula for writing blurbs. And in the third chapter I talked about a method Lee Allred uses.

This chapter I want to note that sometimes you can use varied versions of first lines from your story in your blurb. And other kicker lines from your story as well.

The first lines have to be good ones, and often you will have to alter them into sales language, meaning no passive and punchy.

But watch for those first lines.

Let me give you an example with this next story.

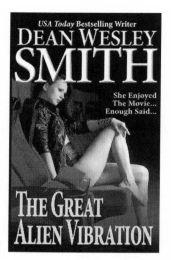

The Great Alien Vibration

As first dates go, a failure for him, a total success for her.

As first alien contacts go, he will walk funny for a few days.

Jimmy Loche asks Stephanie Peters to a special test of a new movie done with brand new technology. A first date that never reaches a second date.

Put it this way, she enjoyed the movie. Enough said...

Another story that could be ruined if I gave too much away on the cover or the blurb. And when I wrote the first two lines of the story, I knew instantly they would also be the first two lines of the blurb.

Those lines set the tone, both in reading the story and for the blurb.

Then I jumped to a plot point from the first page.

Last paragraph was back in tone.

Tone, tone, plot point, tone.

A very simple formula for blurbing really wacked-out stories like this one.

So this one was also a perfect example of being able to use the first lines of a story in the blurb. Sometimes, in the right circumstances with the right story, that really works.

A Great First Day: A Ghost of a Chance Story

Eve Bryson, ghost agent, assigned to work with Deputy Cascade, superhero cop.

Cascade rolls nice guy, handsome stud, and superhero into a tight package. What could a horny ghost of a girl do?

Before Eve suggests a ghost affair, they experience a first day on the job together. She soon learns that lust sometimes takes a side seat to saving lives.

A Ghost of a Chance story that expands the universe. Don't miss this one if you enjoy the series. Or if you want to jump into the series for the first time.

This story was the second story in the series and the second one with these two characters. I even used the same model on both covers. Both stories stand alone completely, which is darned hard to do when one follows the other, sort of.

I reverted back to the standard opening hook for two paragraphs that introduces the two characters. Critical in a romance.

Third paragraph is plot.

Last paragraph is pitch, call to action.

I thought about using the first few lines from this one as well, but the sentences are passive and they wouldn't work if I changed the verbs. So this one didn't work on today's topic at all, but at first glance I thought it would.

And like the first story in this series, the Author Problem of tossing in far, far too much plot was a nagging temptation. Really hard to keep this one on the first page or so of the story.

Super hard because there is some cool stuff in this story.

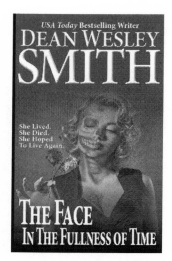

The Face in the Fullness of Time

The dream vanished with the picture.

Lena loves her life, being alone, until reminded that she killed a boyfriend in college. Self-defense, since he hit her, beat her, abused her.

What did she do?

What didn't she do?

And could she ever live in peaceful solitude again? A crime story that might just surprise you.

The first line of this blurb is also the first line of the story. So this is another instance when that really works well.

This crime story could have been totally destroyed for readers by one wrong word in the wrong place in this blurb. So with this one I went back to the standard form.

Paragraph one, hook. (First line of the story.)

Paragraph two is plot from the first two pages of the story.

Paragraphs three through five are questions about the story that a reader would be thinking after the little bit of plot, with a direct comment to the reader in the last paragraph.

This is one nasty story that Kris loved. So knowing she loved it and I had no sense of the story, even looking back at it, the best choice when doing a blurb in my situation is extreme caution and surface first-page stuff.

So that's what I did. Extreme caution.

And the best way to do that is use the first sentence or so in the blurb. Two out of three in this chapter did just that.

So watch for those first-hook sentences when writing blurbs. Might save you time.

Author Problem Check

Did I get into any author problems on any of these three stories? All were difficult because of author problems. But I think I stayed out of them once again.

Were there any passive verbs in any of the three blurbs? Nope, none that I can see.

Did I once go "and then this happens" with the plot I did reveal? Nope.

I don't think they have any author problems. But all three wanted to have more plot in them. These three in this chapter were very, very difficult to do.

5

In the first chapter of this book, I touched on what I call "The Author Problem" and gave a basic formula that I sometimes use to give blurbs a structure.

And in chapter two I laid out another formula for writing blurbs.

In the third chapter I talked about a method Lee Allred uses.

In the fourth chapter I talked about the idea that sometimes using first lines can help.

So now on to more blurbs, and in this chapter I want to talk about how to use setting and focus on one detail as a way around tough sales-copy issues.

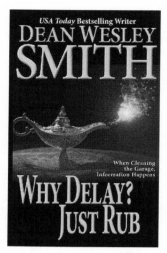

Why Delay? Just Rub: A Bryant Street Story

Weird things happen on Bryant Street. Even when cleaning a double-car garage.

Late spring, very little sports on television, weather threatening to rain so no golf for Jack. Time to clean out the garage.

Also time to find the old lamp in a pile of garbage. Of course, Jack rubs the lamp to try to clean it.

And on Bryant Street, that means the entire chore of cleaning out a garage snaps into strangeness.

A twisted tale of a man, a wife, and a dirty garage as only can be told on Bryant Street.

Another short Bryant Street story that would be ruined if I gave too much away. With the cover I told the plot point of finding an old lamp with a Genie in it, so I could work around that.

Bryant Street, as I said earlier, is a series I have been writing for over forty years. My first writing corporation was named Bryant Street.

Bryant Street is a subdivision street where Rod Serling would be one of the normal residents. I just go from house to house in the subdivision telling strange stories.

So for this blurb, since giving anything away would kill this story, I opened with setting. Cleaning out a garage on Bryant Street.

Paragraph two is a character name with more setting. Just establishing Jack with a couple brush strokes as a simple, normal guy.

Third is a plot point obvious from the cover plus more setting.

Last paragraph functions as a hook with even more about the setting. Then a tag-setting line as a fifth paragraph.

Notice that the entire focus of this blurb is setting. All setting with a hint of plot and a one-name character. Nothing more.

A focus on the setting that is all in the first two pages is a great way to avoid giving away a plot point in a story that needs to be protected.

Setting. All setting.

Yet another method of writing sales copy for a story.

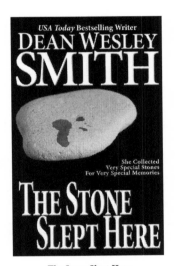

The Stone Slept Here

Jennifer Bends collects stones.

Special stones.

She puts her stones, both of them, on a shelf. No one asks her about the stones because the stones look plain, heavy, pointless.

But the stones contain memories.

Special memories.

And the stones contain a promise that only Jennifer and the stones know.

By far the hardest little story I have ever had to blurb. So I did the only thing I could do.

I blurbed the stones.

I put a woman's name in the first paragraph and said she collects stones. Special stones. Standalone to pound home the specialness.

Third paragraph I twist the collection to mean only two stones and that the stones are not normal stones that others would collect, but just plain. The hope is that readers would be puzzled enough to read the story at this point.

Staying focused on the stones, I gave a slight theme point away about the memories in paragraph three. Then repeat the "special" part again.

Then pounded the readers with the focus on the stones again in the last paragraph, bringing back in the character.

Again, only focus on the stones. And since the cover showed the stone with a drop of blood (perfect art for this story) I figured the cover art and the cover blurb and the blurb itself would be a full enough picture without giving anything at all away.

This one was hard, but by focusing only on one element, it allowed the sales copy to not give away anything yet make the story sound interesting on a human level.

So a slightly different way of focusing on only setting to help a blurb. This is focusing on only one element in the setting.

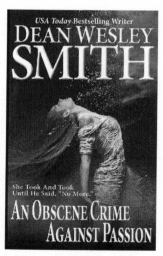

An Obscene Crime Against Passion: A Bryant Street Story

James Ward no longer cares what his wife does in her spare time. He no longer cares about anything, actually.

Deborah took his passion over years. Drained him until he could give no more.

But on Bryant Street, sick relationships often reveal hidden secrets.

Passion functions as a food for some, energy for others. But who knows what role passion plays on Bryant Street.

The lesson for this chapter is focus. This story is very, very twisted from the second page going onward. (And again the art for this story is flat perfect.) But I wanted to give none of the twists away.

So I had to focus on the theme of the story that was in the title: Passion. And the fact that a simple theme such as passion can be really twisted on Bryant Street.

So, first paragraph introduces character, a passionless man.

Second paragraph introduces the wife, the person who stole his passion. Both are identifiable standard characters living in a subdivision.

Then I nail home the Bryant Street aspect in paragraph three as well as the fact that this is a relationship story.

Then in paragraph four I go back to the theme of passion twisted with a Bryant Street reference. And actually, that paragraph gives away some plot, but it is not clear in any fashion, but a reader, after reading the story will understand the double and triple meaning in that last paragraph.

I also purposely put in the "passion play" reference.

I was tempted to call this an urban fantasy story. But decided that actually was too much and that the fantasy elements later in the story weren't that important compared to the Bryant Street and relationship aspects of this.

Choices. The fun of writing sales copy.

Author Problem Check

Did I get into any author problems on any of these three stories? All were difficult because of author problems and because they were all so short. But I think I stayed out of the author problems once again.

Were there any passive verbs in any of the three blurbs? Nope, none that I can see.

Did I once go "and then this happens" with the plot I did reveal? Nope. I basically revealed no real plot on any of these.

I don't think any had author problems this chapter. But as with the three in the last chapter, all three wanted to have more plot in the blurb. These three this chapter were very, very difficult to do.

But by focusing on a setting or a detail or a feeling, the blurbs stayed in sales and out of plot.

So remember that as a way to deal with writing sales. Focus down. Often that is more than enough.

6

In the first chapter of this book, I touched on what I call "The Author Problem" and gave a basic formula that I sometimes use to give blurbs a structure.

And in Chapter Two I laid out another formula for writing blurbs.

In the third chapter I talked about a method Lee Allred uses.

In the fourth chapter I talked about the idea that sometimes using first lines can help.

In the fifth chapter I talked about focus and using setting to get through problems with blurbs.

So now on to more blurbs, and in this chapter the new approach is to focus on character only. No or little plot.

Just character in the blurb.

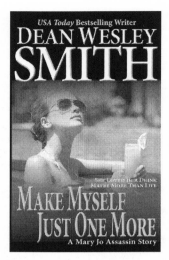

Make Myself Just One More: A Mary Jo Assassin Story

Mary Jo kills people for money. After a thousand years, she knows patience and skill and how to cover her tracks.

Mary Jo loves her job. She makes a lot of money as a hired assassin.

She also loves vodka and orange juice. Passionately, but not in a dangerous way. After a job well done, she rewards herself with the drink.

Mary Jo might be the coldest killer in all of fiction. Or at least the only really cold killer who loves vodka and orange juice.

This is the very first ever Mary Jo Assassin story.

I had no intention of starting a brand new series when I started this. But as she cleaned up the blood from her last kill and worked to cover her tracks, I realized I might have something here.

The problem came in doing the blurb. This again is one of those stories that even telling about the first murder she commits would give away the story. So this needed to have a different approach.

So first I thought about setting, but the setting is a standard suburban home and actually doesn't play much into the story. So I figured I would just focus the blurb on her.

A complete character blurb.

And her love for screwdrivers. And her love of her job.

I tossed in the fact that she has been doing this for over a thousand years as a reader hook (does not play into the story, but is there a couple times.)

36

So all four paragraphs in this blurb are about her. No plot at all. Nada. Zip.

I couldn't even call out a genre on this because it clearly is a crime story. Sort of. I made that clear. But a crime story by an ancient assassin in a modern subdivision. Well, not a normal crime story.

So I skipped calling out a genre and just assumed that those who wanted to read about a very different hired assassin might buy this story.

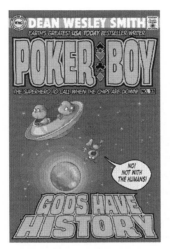

Gods Have History: A Poker Boy Story

Poker Boy often solves problems and saves the world with his mutant talent of asking stupid questions.

Sometimes really stupid questions.

So when he asks the seemingly simple question over lunch one day about how the gods originated, he stirs up more than even Poker Boy bargains for.

So how did the gods originate way back before Atlantis? Might be better to just not ask. Too late for Poker Boy. He asked.

Since I have written over fifty Poker Boy stories now, they've become really hard to blurb.

So for this blurb I went back to the topic from last chapter. I focused the blurb on one element. And it is an element of the character as well, so it sort of fits in this chapter.

Focus on one element of the character.

First two paragraphs are focusing on Poker Boy's method of solving major problems.

Then I brought in the one plot element from the first page, the question he asked.

Then in general terms, I hinted at the results of the questions in hopes to draw readers into the story.

Last paragraph was a summary of the entire question thing, and shows a little of the Poker Boy attitude as well.

For those of you who are Poker Boy fans, no worry after you read this story. Poker Boy is not going in that direction. This was just a history story.

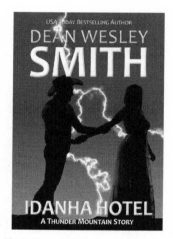

Idanha Hotel: A Thunder Mountain Story

May: 1902. Megan Taber bakes in the fancy new Idanha Hotel in downtown Boise. Her rolls and pastries and pies bring in patrons from all around the area.

Widowed from her husband five years before, her entire life focuses on her baking. And she loves it. She considers baking her art.

Joe Vaughn, a scholar, eats breakfast every day at the Idanha Hotel dining room because of Megan Taber's baking.

A story of two people, tossed together by events and great food.

This the second Thunder Mountain story in this group of stories from July. And this one needed a different approach as well since the story stands alone just fine, but also can be expanded out into a pretty good novel with a few additions.

So the blurb had to be clear and clean. So once again, I went to the focus on the character all the way through the blurb.

First two paragraphs are also focused on one element of her character as well. Baking.

Third paragraph is the introduction of hero, but again focused on her baking.

Last paragraph tells readers this is a relationship story, with a focus once again on the food element.

Interesting that writing stories in series can sometimes be easy, but writing blurbs for series stories most certainly has problems.

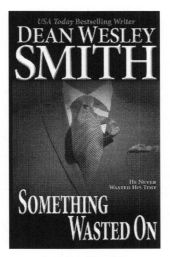

Something Wasted On

Professor Johnson Hubbs, professor of psychology, knew exactly when he came up with the idea of his new study of human nature and patterns.

In his new study, he wants to know how many times people say, "I wasted my time on (blank)."

He overhears a woman say that to another woman about her husband and then expand in great detail while Hubbs attempts to eat a wonderful chopped beef smothered in marinara sauce. Ruins his lunch, but gets him a new study.

A story of simple professor asking a simple question.

This blurb could only be done with a complete focus on character. Even the cover I did focuses on character.

Why? This is a character story, completely.

In fact, not at all sure that most people would think this even had a plot in hindsight.

So the only plot element I put in was the question, which is in the first line. I thought of using the entire first sentence in the blurb, but the sentence was too loose, so I didn't.

So this is the prime example of not blurbing a plot but blurbing a character only. Even down to a meal he was eating.

Focusing only on character also has the side benefit that readers read for character. And if you can make the character interesting enough in the blurb, then readers will read for that character through the plot events of the story.

I always have character in blurbs, but I often follow the patterns I set in the first two chapters or so unless the story just won't allow it. Then I turn to either all setting like last chapter's topic, or all character.

There are many, many ways to approach writing sales copy for a story. Keeping awareness of readers will help you make the choice.

Author Problem Check

Did I get into any author problems on any of these four stories? All were difficult because of author problems and because they were all moderately short, meaning under 4,000 words for all of them. But I think I stayed out of the author problems once again.

Were there any passive verbs in any of the three blurbs? Nope, none that I can see.

Did I once go "and then this happens" with the plot I did reveal? Nope. I basically revealed no real plot on any of these.

I don't think any had author problems this chapter. But as with the three in the last chapter, all four wanted to have more plot in the blurb.

But the focus on character kept me out of that problem, for the most part.

So remember focus on character as yet another way to deal with writing sales. Focus down into the character, one aspect of the character.

Often that is more than enough.

7

In the first chapter of this book, I touched on what I call "The Author Problem" and gave a basic formula that I sometimes use to give blurbs a structure.

And in Chapter Two I laid out another formula for writing blurbs.

In the third chapter I talked about a method Lee Allred uses.

In the fourth chapter I talked about the idea that sometimes using first lines can help.

In the fifth chapter I talked about focus and using setting to get through problems with blurbs.

In the sixth chapter I mostly used a focus on character only. No or little plot. Just character in the blurb.

Now in this chapter I will focus on using genre devices and tropes to blurb a story without giving any plot away. Readers know genres and what they love, so by using a genre structure in a blurb, you can bring them into a story.

Nobody Slept Here: A Ghost of a Chance Story

How can a ghost make love to a live superhero?

Ghost of a Chance Agent Eve Bryson really, really wants to figure that out.

Superhero Deputy Cascade wonders the same thing.

A ghost and a superhero in love. They share everything except sex. What to do?

This is the third story in this series with these two characters in the July stories.

So I needed to be careful again on the plot of this. So I went to the first page and used the first line of the story. Tough to ruin a story when only using a first line.

Then I focused on what kind of story this is. It is a romance, clear and simple. So from that same first few paragraphs of the story, I used more details about the relationship.

Notice, I introduced her, then him, then flat said they are in love but have a problem. That is classic romance structure. So I played off the structure.

And the last line is the key to all romances. They meet, they have troubles, what to do to get to happily ever after, in this case, sex.

Pure romance structure to relay a story.

Leaking Away a Life: A Poker Boy Story

Poker Boy works as a superhero in the gambling side of the world. And he reports to Stan, the God of Poker.

Very bothered, Stan comes to Poker Boy with a problem. Very personal and unusual.

Another superhero working for Stan faces monster problems, and not the kind of problems that come from rescuing others.

This other superhero needs to be rescued from himself.

Sadly, we often all face our worst enemy every morning in the mirror, an enemy sometimes impossible to beat, even for a superhero.

Over the fifty or sixty Poker Boy stories I have written, he sometimes tackles trying to help someone with personal issues. And he has mostly failed.

This is a story of addiction, but how to get that across without saying that and chasing off most of the readers?

The title, for anyone who knows professional poker, spells out the story completely.

A "leak" in professional poker is a poker player who also gambles. Poker is a sport where skill wins, but often poker players win all their money playing poker, but will have an addiction to a form of gambling. They leak away all their money on their addiction.

All major sports have this problem as well. Baseball players like Pete Rose. The list is endless.

So to write this blurb, I couldn't just describe all that I just described. So I had to drop back to a character focus for the first two lines. Then a plot point in the third and fourth lines.

Then the last line I came out to general "we" to try to give the idea without blurting it out that this was an addiction story.

So in this one, I used the addiction story tropes to clue in readers. "...rescued from himself." Prime example. Second example is "facing ourselves."

Anyone familiar with addiction knows all that. But most people might not think "Oh, an addiction story" when they read the blurb, but it is all there in the blurb.

Sales is the key here. What will give the readers a way into the story and yet when they finish, they will know the blurb fit the story perfectly and won't feel misled.

This addiction area of stories, a sub-genre of a number of major genres, actually, is one of the hardest to blurb and still have readers want to read the story. Caution is required.

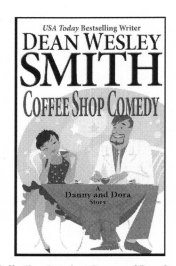

Coffee Shop Comedy: A Danny and Dora Story

Danny needs a voice.

Dora needs a way to deliver her jokes besides selling them to other comics.

Both write and love comedy. Both love coffee. Their attraction catches them both by surprise. Can they solve each other's problems?

The origin story of the famous crime-solving comedy team, Danny and Dora.

This the meet cute of a romance to start with. So I followed the standard romance structure in the blurb.

A guy and a girl meet. They are attracted, they have problems.

However, that said, this won't be a romance series when I start writing the books from this. So I wanted to add in that kicker for future readers who might find this story out there and wonder what the hell was going on.

There is no crime in this story. This is just a meet cute romance start. It will only be in the future when this Burns and Allen team start to travel with their comedy act and solve crimes along the way.

This is going to be a really fun series to write.

So in summary, I did a complete romance structure blurb, then added in the future kicker line for the mysteries down the road.

And notice the cartoon look of the cover. That relays comedy but also was used for a time on some fantasy and comedy romances. So readers are familiar with the comedy covers for romances.

Author Problem Check

Did I get into any author problems on any of these three stories? All were difficult because of author problems and because they were all moderately short, meaning under 4,000 words for all of them. But I think I stayed out of the author problems once again.

Were there any passive verbs in any of the three blurbs? Nope, none that I can see.

Did I once go "and then this happens" with the plot I did reveal? Nope. I basically revealed no real plot on any of these. Just some character issues.

I don't think any had author problems this chapter.

Plot Structure Method

The focus on plot structure really made these three blurbs easier to write for me.

So remember focus on plot structure as yet another way to deal with writing sales.

I realize the problem with this suggestion is the assumption that those reading this know plot structure. All new writers do not, and most early professionals are just starting to learn this area of writing.

So if you do not know plot structure for what you are writing, learn genre plot structures. Plot structures are reader-focused learning.

What do readers expect in various genres?

Learn the answer to that question. And then in the blurbs to your stories or novels, you can play into those reader wants with your blurbs.

And help yourself sell more copies.

8

In the first chapter of this book, I touched on what I call "The Author Problem" and gave a basic formula that I sometimes use to give blurbs a structure.

And in Chapter Two I laid out another formula for writing blurbs.

In the third chapter I talked about a method Lee Allred uses.

In the fourth chapter I talked about the idea that sometimes using first lines can help.

In the fifth chapter I talked about focus and using setting to get through problems with blurbs.

In the sixth chapter I mostly used a focus on character only. No or little plot. Just character in the blurb.

In the seventh chapter I focused on using genre devices and tropes to blurb a story without giving any plot away. Readers know genres and what they love, so by using a genre structure in a blurb, you can bring them into a story.

Another good way to blurb stories is by author reputation. Or pull quotes to help a blurb get the reader into the story. But not doing that in this book since my purpose for writing these is to be in their own book. I might add some of that in for blurbs on Amazon and Kobo and such. So keep that in mind as well.

So now I have ten blurbs left to write. Instead of focusing on different techniques, I'm just going to write these blurbs over the next two chapters and talk about what I used for each blurb and why. But do keep in mind the seven major techniques used to build a sales blurb.

The Cavern: A Thunder Mountain Story

Stout used to own the Garden Lounge where the time-traveling jukebox sat. He sold the Garden to live with his love, Jenny.

Now Jenny's cancer diagnosis gives her only five months to live.

Bonnie and Duster, the original owners of the jukebox, will not stand for that diagnosis.

A Thunder Mountain story of love and death and living?

I have written numbers of Thunder Mountain stories and five or six novels now set in the world of Bonnie and Duster Kendal. This story was the hardest of them all to blurb.

I started to talk theme, decided that made no sense, backed up and went to a standard form of first paragraph setting the scene and characters.

Second paragraph give the main problem.

Third paragraph brings in Bonnie and Duster for Thunder Mountain fans to let them know the two are in the story.

The fourth paragraph I told the readers what the story was about.

So back to the structure of the first few chapters of this book with this blurb.

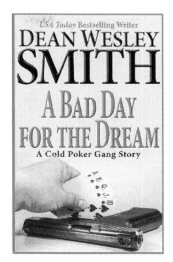

A Bad Day for the Dream: A Cold Poker Gang Story

Thirty years ago in Las Vegas, Becky Penn said goodnight to her mother to go out with friends and vanished without a trace.

Retired Detectives Bayard Lott and Julia Rogers, members of the Cold Poker Gang, take on Becky Penn's cold case.

They love working with other retired detectives and playing a little poker once a week, all to solve cold cases.

A puzzle mystery unraveled carefully by the retired detectives who make up the Cold Poker Gang.

Puzzle mysteries are really tough in short-story form. And I have made the Cold Poker Gang novels very, very twisted.

And this is a start of one of those really twisted novels. However, in the short story, I wrapped it down and seemingly ended it.

So how not to give any plot away, which is really, really tempting in a mystery because that's the cool stuff.

So I opened the blurb with the set-up in the story. Then I introduced two of the main characters in the second paragraph.

Then I go to more set up of the Cold Poker Gang.

Then in the fourth paragraph I tell the readers what the story is about. So once again I went back to the first few chapters of this book to use that standard way of writing blurbs.

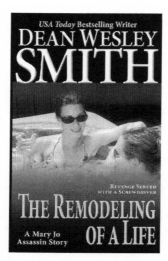

The Remodeling of a Life: A Mary Jo Assassin Story

Mary Jo's last client tried to have her killed and then shorted her on her money.

Mary Jo needs to remodel the client's life. And get her money.

In the process, she also remodels her own life while enjoying the occasional vodka and orange juice.

A cold, calculating modern assassin story of revenge served with a screwdriver.

The title of this story works at many levels here. And the story follows perfectly the first Mary Jo story in the book. The two both stand alone, but link.

So first paragraph I put in the hook.

Then in the next two paragraphs, I put in her motivation and also what happens after her last case was finished and how she moves on. Plus a reminder of the vodka and orange juice drink.

Then in the last paragraph I told the readers what the story was about.

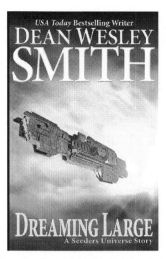

Dreaming Large: A Seeders Universe Story

The Dreaming Large, *a Seeders mother ship vanishes without a trace while approaching the edge of a galaxy.*

Chairman West and his crew on the Rescue One *must find out what happened to the huge mother ship. And the over half-million lives on it.*

But as they approach the galaxy's edge, the last known position of the big moon-sized mother ship, what they find surprises them all.

They find nothing. Absolutely nothing.

A galaxy-spanning science fiction story of the unknowns in space.

This time I needed to focus on the plot of the first page. And nothing more.

So the first paragraph sets the problem.

Second, third, and fourth paragraphs all relay what is on the first page, plus setting the main character and the mission and the problem he faces.

So I set the overall problem, set the mission, set the main character, set his problem.

Last paragraph tells the reader exactly what the story is about just in case anyone missed that it was a science fiction epic in space.

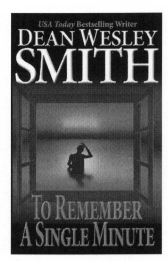

To Remember a Single Minute

Remember Incorporated. A company that promises that once the disease took Mike Hanley's mind, he would remember one single minute of his life in stark clarity.

Any minute.

He just needs to pick the minute.

But of all the wonderful minutes in his entire life, which one can he pick?

A science fiction story with a haunting question.

This is an idea story. And it packs a punch and is on a tough topic, one we all either face or deal with.

So I needed to make the plot clear, the part on the top of the first page of the story.

So for four paragraphs, I relayed the opening of the story. And the main character's problem.

Then in the last paragraph I flat told the reader what the story was about.

Author Problem Check

Did I get into any author problems on any of these five stories?

I think I stayed out of the author problems once again, looking back.

Notice, this review is a pattern every chapter that when you write sales copy, you also should do.

Were there any passive verbs in any of the three blurbs? Nope, none that I can see.

Did I once go "and then this happens" with the plot I did reveal? Nope. I basically revealed no real plot on any of these except what happened on the first page of the story.

I don't think any had author problems this chapter.

9

In the first chapter of this book, I touched on what I call "The Author Problem" and gave a basic formula that I sometimes use to give blurbs a structure.

And in Chapter Two I laid out another formula for writing blurbs.

In the third chapter I talked about a method Lee Allred uses.

In the fourth chapter I talked about the idea that sometimes using first lines can help.

In the fifth chapter I talked about focus and using setting to get through problems with blurbs.

In the sixth chapter I mostly used a focus on character only. No or little plot. Just character in the blurb.

In the seventh chapter I focused on using genre devices and tropes to blurb a story without giving any plot away. Readers know genres and what they love, so by using a genre structure in a blurb, you can bring them into a story.

Another good way to blurb stories is by author reputation. Or pull quotes to help a blurb get the reader into the story. But not doing that in this book since my purpose for writing these is to be in their own book. I might add some of that in for blurbs on Amazon and Kobo and on the back of the paper editions. So keep that in mind as well.

So now I have five blurbs left to write. Instead of focusing on different techniques, I'm just going to write these blurbs and talk about what I used for each blurb and why.

But do keep in mind the seven major techniques used to build a sales blurb.

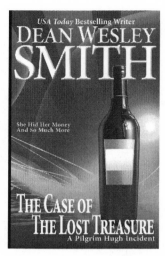

The Case of the Lost Treasure: A Pilgrim Hugh Incident

Hired by heirs to find two million in treasure hidden in a completely empty house, Pilgrim Hugh finds himself stuck.

The house sparkles and no stick of furniture remains.

Original house plans show clearly that no room hid behind any walls. And millions of dollars in cash takes up a bunch of room. But where?

A puzzle mystery that stumps for a short time even the great Pilgrim Hugh.

I returned to the focus on plot and genre structure on this blurb.

I set the problem in the first paragraph and introduced the viewpoint character.

I set the scene in the second paragraph.

I banged on the problem again in the third paragraph, all of which is on the first page or so of the short story.

Last paragraph not only sets the genre clearly, but gives a hint to Pilgrim Hugh fans that this is a different story because Pilgrim Hugh seldom gets stumped by anything.

A Study of an Accident: A Bryant Street Story

Dan remembers clearly the time before the accident.

He remembers his wonderful wife and daughter. Impossible to forget. He refuses to eat or work or even move most days.

He made a mistake, they died. He lives. He blames himself for their deaths.

Someone knocks on his home door. And the truth flips as only it can on Bryant Street.

Very difficult story to blurb as many Bryant Street stories are. Any hint at the plot on this one will toss the entire value of the story away.

I went with everything from the first page. Background, his wife, his state of mind, all in the first two paragraphs.

Then I say he made a mistake and blames himself for their deaths without going into how he blames himself in any fashion.

The one plot element I put in was in the last paragraph. Someone knocks on his door. That is a plot element, but it spoils nothing and gives nothing away. Then I wrapped it back to Bryant Street with the last line.

I hope the puzzle will get readers to join a character feeling sorry for himself long enough for the plot to kick into gear. Tough to do in a blurb. Really tough.

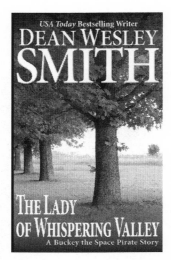

The Lady of Whispering Valley: A Buckey the Space Pirate Story

Buckey's best friend loves to recite limericks and can travel in time. Not bad for an oak tree named Fred.

But Fred must help Buckey and the love of his life find a way to live together. Not an easy problem considering Mary lives a hundred years in the past.

But an oak tree that recites limericks knows tricks of time.

Can true love be blocked by the simple passing of time?

And can Fred come up with a limerick that fits the situation in time?

Yes, Buckey the Space Pirate stores are as strange as they sound. Maybe even more so.

The first Buckey story I ever sold was back in the early 1980s. It was called "The Sexual Voyage of the Starship Shirley" and from there Buckey got really strange. And then he met Fred, the talking and time-traveling oak tree.

So how to blurb a story that has a ton of history, much relayed in the first two pages?

I just focused on the characters, which should be interesting to most anyone.

Then a quick point of the problem of the story, then more on the characters.

The goal was to show the strangeness of these stories.

The Rude Improbable Presumptive: A Poker Boy Story

He calls himself The Presumptive.

Poker Boy thinks that might be the most stupid nickname he ever heard at a poker table.

So Poker Boy calls him Idiot Boy (but not to his face) because of the name and the guy's bad play.

But in Poker Boy's world, nothing ever turns out the way they look. Even for Idiot Boy.

All first-page introduction stuff in this blurb. I make it clear that Poker Boy is at a poker table in this story, which happens about one in ten stories.

Then I put in the first line, only with the tense changed. So used that technique.

Then I just did quick character introduction of Poker Boy and his opinion of the other guy.

Last line I twisted it into a warning that Poker Boy stories are never what they seem. Good for new readers and fans of Poker Boy.

Start with a Coffin: A Captain Brian Saber Story

Brian Saber awakes with a start in his nursing home room.

On missions, Captain Brian Saber defends the Earth Protection League in his warship The Bad Business. *Tonight, he will be asked to do a very special mission without fighting.*

But he loves any chance to be young again and help the league in deep space on the very edges of League space.

Swashbuckling space battles in deep space, fought as only those in the last days of their lives can fight. No alien finds safety around Captain Brian Saber.

This last story in the book might have been the hardest to write sales copy of them all.

I call this my old-people-in-space stories. Because of an issue with the connection with space and time and matter, a person regresses in age when in faster-than-light travel.

So for a century, since the days of Atlantis when the Earth Protection League was founded, old people from Earth were recruited to defend the frontier. Saber would be in his eighties and stroke-ridden on Earth, in his twenties near the border.

And, of course, there's more, far more than ever could be put a story blurb.

So I started the blurb with the first line of the story, altered slightly.

Second paragraph I put in the summary of the plot first page. Plus a little more about his ship.

Third paragraph is back on character opinion of Brian Saber.

Fourth paragraph I flat just tell the readers what the story is about, then bring in Brian one more time.

Author Problem Check

Did I get into any author problems on any of these five stories?

I think I stayed out of the author problems once again, looking back.

Notice, this review is a pattern every chapter that when you write sales copy, you also should do.

Were there any passive verbs in any of the three blurbs? Nope, none that I can see.

Did I once go "and then this happens" with the plot I did reveal? Nope. I basically revealed no real plot on any of these except what happened on the first page of the story.

I don't think any blurb had author problems this chapter.

SUMMARY

In this book I outlined seven different approaches to writing sales copy for stories. Seven different structures.

And in the last two chapters I showed how you can mix and match the different forms as a story demands.

Remember, in writing sales copy, you must stay out of plot and keep every verb active. That is much, much harder than it sounds for an author who wrote the story.

So do the review as I did every chapter.

Stay on the plot from the first page and restructure every sentence to make it active.

Then, and even more importantly, think what readers will want.

- Will the blurb be interesting to some readers?
- How will they feel reading the blurb and looking at your cover?
- Does your blurb tell the reader they don't want to read your story. Too graphic, too sexual, things like that.
- And if the reader thinks they know the entire story from your blurb, they have no reason to buy it.

So always think about readers on the other sides of your words when writing sales copy.

One Last Word

These blurbs were designed for a single book. If they were going to be on back covers or in Amazon, I would add something about the author.

But my name is on this book and the blurb of this book and the author bio talks about me, so I didn't add that part into each blurb.

But when these go into standalone form, I will add the author pitch part of each blurb, sometimes at the start, sometimes at the end. But it will be there.

So don't forget that element, even if all you can says is "Author of the (blank) series, (author) brings you another..."

Sales.

It's a hard word for writers to get their minds around. But it can be done.

So in writing story blurbs, there are structures. If in doubt, just use a structure, stay out of too much plot, and keep all verbs active.

Have fun.

NEW YORK TIMES BESTSELLING AUTHOR

KRISTINE KATHRYN RUSCH

CREATING YOUR AUTHOR BRAND

A WMG WRITER'S GUIDE

INTRODUCTION

Every Thursday, I publish a blog on writing or the business of writing. I initially started the blog in 2009, and except for a six-month hiatus in 2014, I have written a post without fail every week. In the spring of 2017, I got the bright idea to write a short blog post on branding.

As I wrote the blog, I realized I had a larger topic than a single blog, but it wasn't until I started getting comments on that blog that I understood how large the topic actually was. Readers asked very good questions about things I mentioned in passing. I realized, as I read the comments, that what I thought was obvious, was not. Most people had thought branding was about book covers, and very little else. They had no idea how big branding actually is. Business and advertising majors lose entire semesters to branding classes. Branding experts get paid big bucks to "re-envision" an entire business, from the bottom up, just so that business can be marketed.

I wrote blog after blog, encouraging questions, because somehow, in my years in broadcasting and advertising, I had absorbed most of this stuff into my marketing DNA. I didn't know what other people didn't know. And in order to write about this to non-marketers, I had to figure out what people —and writers in particular—needed to learn before they could understand some of the major concepts.

If I wanted to make these posts useful, I needed feedback.

And I got it. You might want to go to the posts, which are still on my website kriswrites.com, and read the comments. I answered a lot of questions directly, and not all of those answers made it into this volume. In subsequent blog posts, I answered the major topics, but not the minor ones. (I have a life; I would have been writing about branding and marketing for the rest of my known days.)

I have put this book together from those blog posts. I'm keeping them in the order in which I posted them, and I'm keeping the colloquial real-time language. Please remember, as I cite "current" examples, they were current in 2017.

I wrote these blogs for writers. If you're looking for a great overall book on branding, one that will help you brand your automotive store or your online quilting business, this book will help you understand the concepts of branding in simple language, but there might be a more specific and on-point book for your niche.

Writers, publishers, both indie and traditional, will benefit from this book much more. It is, I believe, the only book on branding written with the publishing industry in mind.

A word on terminology: when I mention *traditional* publishing, I mean the industry that grew up in the early 20th century in places like New York and London, and publishes thousands of books per year. Those businesses include international conglomerates and large publishers that have existed since the 1980s at least

When I mention *indie* publishing, I mean the industry many call "the shadow industry," which has arisen since Amazon's Kindle entered the marketplace in 2007. *Indie* writers include writers who self-publish, and those who publish through very small publishers (sometimes started by the writers themselves, but which are a separate entity from the writer).

Most of what I write is geared toward indies. There are more and more indie writers every day, some of whom make hundreds of thousands of dollars per year without doing a lot of branding or marketing. Early on in the post-Kindle world, it was relatively easy for a self-published writer (who wrote good books) to make a small fortune at their writing with a minimum of marketing effort. Now, however, it has become harder to get discovered. (I wrote a book on that as well, called *Discoverability*.) One relatively easy way for readers to find a writer's work, however, is through branding.

Branding is the simplest way to gain reader recognition. Gaining that recognition is not as easy as putting an ebook up on the 2009 Kindle platform, but using branding to gain that recognition is easier than all those marketing tips from so-called gurus who appear for a year or so and then vanish when their way of gaming the system ceases to work.

This book will help you understand branding. The book will also help you figure out what to do for *your business*. If you're looking for a book that will give the Five Steps to Proper Branding—a kind of plug-and-play sort of book that gives you the Secrets to Quick Branding—this ain't it.

What this book will teach you are the basic concepts of branding. It will also open your mind to the possibilities of branding, of the various things you can do for your business. I hope the book will give you ideas, and make you want to dive deeper into the possibilities of marketing your work in a way that's as unique as the books you write.

In order to brand like that, however, you need to understand how branding works, how readers (and other consumers) respond to it, and what you can and cannot do to attract their attention.

This book is designed to give you that basic understanding and to help you convert that understanding into useful action that's right *for you*.

Ready? Here goes…

"I've just been spiffing up my image a bit."

IN THE BEGINNING...

I feel like I've been on a particularly grueling business trip, and am slowly recalibrating back into my office. I worked very hard in the front part of April as I prepared for the science fiction writing workshop I ran on the Oregon Coast.[1] Then the workshop happened. Lots of great discussions, great questions, great stories, and dedicated work later, we finished...and I got the Mother of All Colds.

I've been staggering my way through the past week, trying to rest and trying to do a few non-brainy things. The thing is, my brain, which is weird on a good day, is really weird when I'm sick. It takes all of the stuff that I've been thinking about, mixes it all together, and then comes up with connections that my healthy brain would never consider.

I value those connections, because they sometimes help me see things I missed—or missed writing about. In this case, I came up with a list for the Business Musings blog.

Before the workshop, I had been blogging about newsletters, so marketing was on my mind.

At the workshop, I talked to writers about the importance of telling a good story as opposed to writing lovely sentences. And yet we focused on craft, too, the importance of the right sort of detail to make stories come alive.

And I'm still negotiating several TV/movie projects, which has been annoyingly distracting, considering 80 percent of them won't come to anything. At least two of the deals are for entire series, which got me and Dean to discuss the possibility of trademarking those series, and whether it's worth our time.

Then, in the middle of the workshop, two books arrived in the mail: *Fallout* by Sara Paretsky, and *The Burial Hour* by Jeffery Deaver. I was reading manuscripts at the time, and so put the books near my reading table as a reward for finishing the workshop. Paretsky has already made my Recommended Reading List on my website and, as I write this, I'm still enjoying the Deaver.

The thing is: I had forgotten I ordered the books. I certainly didn't know they would arrive during the workshop. That arrival was a very nice surprise.

And yes, this all factored into the soup of thoughts that whirled through my brain that last week.

I have read Paretsky since the 1980s and Deaver since the 1990s. I don't like all of the books Deaver and Paretsky write equally, but I like the authors enough to preorder, sometimes with only a title attached. It's never a gamble to order books from either of those writers. Both of them write fascinating stories that take me away from whatever I'm doing, even if the stories don't always work.

I have maybe a dozen books on preorder at any one time. When I finish a book by one of my favorite authors, I look on Amazon to see if the next book is available to preorder. If it is, I preorder it then so I don't have to think about it.

If I'm truly anticipating a book, I'll check that preorder occasionally to make sure I actually paid for the upcoming release because I really, really, really want that book. Generally, though, books just show up in my mailbox. Those books either wait for a moment or a mood—this winter, I couldn't read anything but Regency romance as friends, family, and cats kept dying around me—or, in some special cases, I read the book immediately upon receipt.

I am a customer—a loyal customer—of those writers whose books are on preorder. Or, in a few cases, I'm a loyal customer of a particular book series, but I don't care about other things that the author writes.

Amazon, bless them, sends me reminders when an author whose work I've ordered a lot writes a new book. I don't even sign up for the alerts. They arrive. I read them.

I do get a newsletter from a few of my favorites who have gone indie. That helps finding their books. But I've unsubscribed from more indie newsletters than I currently subscribe to. Getting an email a day (yes, one indie did that) was truly annoying.

I try not to send too many newsletters, although I sent a newsletter per month to two separate lists in the first six months of 2015 as my Retrieval Artist released. That was my big flurry, and it was tiring. It took some writing time.

I try to do newsletters when I'm brain-fogged, which means I wrote a couple this past week. I have promised on that list not to spam these folks, so I only email when I have actual news.

The first newsletter was for the fans of my Diving series to let them know that the newest book is included, in its entirety, in *Asimov's Science Fiction Magazine.* That newsletter copy is pretty short, but it is conversational. It gives the readers two pieces of information: *The Runabout* is available now in a magazine should you want to buy now. Or if you prefer to wait, then the book will be out in three standalone formats in October.[2]

The Diving list is pretty tight. It's been several days since I sent the newsletter. My open rate (for the emails that can be tracked by the silly algorithms) is steady, and no one has unsubscribed. A lot of folks clicked through the email links (which always surprises me, because I never click an email link. I just open a new window, go to whatever website, and find the page myself). The Diving newsletter had a good result.

Then I wrote my overall newsletter. [3] This newsletter is considerably longer than the Diving newsletter, even though it has some of the same information. I had a lot more to inform readers about than just the release of *The Runabout.* I also am in a writing Storybundle, along with nine other writers. I have even more to say than that, but I felt that if I dealt with much more, I'd be inundating people. Better to save some firepower for May's newsletter—whenever I get around to it. (If I get around to it. May looks busy on the writing side.)

Again, colloquial language, but more of it. And a weird design, because I have to keep myself amused somehow. Again, good click-throughs. A few more unsubscribes than usual—but that was because I told people to unsubscribe.

What? you ask. Why would anyone tell people to unsubscribe?

Because I want the readers of a particular series, who don't want all the noise, to sign up for the newsletters for those series. That way I don't spam the readers. So I reminded everyone they could subscribe to a series/pen name newsletter, and then they could unsubscribe from this one.

According to the unsubscribe comments I got, about eight people took me up on that—and promptly subscribed to the other newsletters.

Yeah, yeah, I know. The newsletter gurus for writers say don't scatter your newsletter subscribers to more than one list. Because then your readers won't be focused on you and will have less chance to buy something else from you.

I figure my readers are both smart and know what they want. If they want to try something else I've written, they will. If they want a newsletter that tells them all of the publications, then they can subscribe to the big newsletter. And if they don't want to subscribe to a newsletter at all, they can see what I post on my website when I do a news post.

Which leads to the third thing I wrote in that cold-fogged week. I wrote a news post that appeared on Saturday. The post dealt with *The Runabout*, the bundle, and three short story publications I'd neglected to mention in the past two months. The post was even longer than the newsletters.

The responses have been great, and mostly in email or on social media. I've received questions about the Diving series from the fans, including some very thoughtful long letters filled with guesses about the future of the series. I've gotten some questions about other series (which always happens when I send out the big newsletter with only one series mentioned). I also got some great comments about the news post, including a question or two about the short story anthologies.

I love the interactions with the fans, but I also like the way they're engaging with the series. That means a lot to me personally, since my days are mostly spent sitting alone in a room and making things up. Those things matter to me, but it's nice to know that they matter to others as well.

I should have known that, because I am a reader and a consumer of stories, and I love series. Last week, I also spent way too much time worrying about the consequences for Our Heroes in the last storyline of the season for *Marvel's Agents of S.H.I.E.L.D.* So, yeah. Fans get invested. Readers do, too.

All of this thinking got folded into some other reading I was doing. Courtesy of Randy and J.T. Ellison, I received a copy of Targoz Strategic Marketing's Reading Pulse survey.[4] They wanted some comments on it before it went live, and I did a quick dive into the survey before the workshop.

As I read it, I realized I needed to spend a lot of time with this thing, because it's actual research on reading that's useful, not wish fulfillment. Here's how the press release describes it:[5]

Based on six years of survey research, the syndicated study provides book publishers, agents, and sellers with an accurate picture of readers, and delivers actionable data on what readers want and how to influence them to buy.

It does deliver "actionable data." I got very excited by what I read. I got permission to share bits of this with you, but I can't share all of it, because the survey isn't public. It's designed for larger companies with the resources to buy surveys like this. (That's how they get funded.) Randy says there will be a different version for indies that won't be as expensive. But that won't appear until after the big push for the survey to traditional publishers in the next few weeks or more.

This survey can be tailored to a particular company. If I were running one of the Big Five? Four? Three? Two? (who the hell knows) major publishers, I'd be plunking down the money for a customized version of this thing. Because there's a lot of information here that could change traditional publishing forever.

It won't, however. Even if traditional publishers buy this survey, they won't act on the suggestions inside. The corporate headwinds are too strong. A lot of what's in here would cost department heads their jobs, and devastate the sales departments. Of course, a lot of what's here would result in new hires as well, for new jobs that would have a completely different focus.

That kind of sea change is almost impossible in large companies. But in small ones, it's definitely possible.

I had avoided thinking about much of what's in the survey until after the workshop, when I thought I would have the brainpower to do a deep dive into the numbers. I have only had brainpower for a day or two. The deep dive is coming this week.

So what's been rolling around in my head isn't the proprietary numbers that I can't tell you or the changes I'm thinking about for my own business based on these facts. Instead, it's a section at the end of the survey that essentially has actionable information for Writer Me.

The section at the end talks about Brand Name authors. There's a long list of writers by genre that readers identify by name. And the survey found something that I was aware of, but not that I had really thought about.

Almost all of the Brand Name authors that readers are familiar with are traditionally published. And most of those Brand Name authors are baby boomers. Not just baby boomers, but on the upper end of the baby boomer scale. One genre didn't have a single person in the top ten brand names under the age of sixty.

I would normally dismiss that kind of finding as irrelevant. Writing is a career that many people start late. It's not at all unusual for "new" writers to be in their fifties, so by the time their name is established, they'd be in their sixties.

But I looked at the names more closely, and saw a completely different problem. The survey broke into four rather broad genre categories: Mystery, Thriller & Crime; Romance & Paranormal Romance; Literature & Literary Fiction; and Science Fiction & Fantasy. Then the survey noted the top ten most recognized names in each of those categories, chosen by readers.

Of the forty names on those lists, only three got their start in this century. Those three included two whose books were made into major movies, and one author who (as far as I can tell) jumped on the coattails of one of those two. (That's not something to be ashamed of in any way: John Grisham jumped on the coattails of Scott Turow, and eventually surpassed Turow in numbers of books published and recognizability and a whole bunch of other things.)

The remaining thirty-seven brand names were nurtured in a completely different publishing climate. One I'm not going to count because he's an actor, not an author, and I have no idea how he got on the list. So that brings us to thirty-six. Two got their start before 1960. Five got their start in the 1960s. Six got their start in the 1970s. The bulk got their start in the 1980s, with only two getting their starts in the 1990s.

(I'm doing this off the top of my head, so I might be wrong on the exact start dates for the previous century. But I do know for a fact that not a one of those thirty-six names got started in this century.)

That pre-2000 publishing climate allowed series writers to build. It also allowed writers who only wrote standalone titles (and there are several on these lists) to have lower book sales on one title but still buy the next.

In the 1990s, a publisher could let a series author go, and another publisher would pick up that author—and buy the series out from the old publisher, keeping all of the books in print.

From the late 1990s onward, traditional publishing stopped nurturing careers. It stopped trying to grow a brand name, and instead tried to create one. It's still doing that. As this survey noted, many of the authors on the Brand Name list now write books with co-authors, trying to boost the "younger" writer's career. (The survey did not count those books in this part of the total.)

Writing with a brand name does not grow a writer's career the way that nurturing a series does. It increases that writer's sales, but only for a book or two. If the publisher does not continue to help that writer by sticking with them through a number of books, that writer will disappear like everyone before them.

I studied those lists of names for much too long. I also studied the list of up-and-coming writers, noting that many of them are also over fifty. Many of those writers have had long careers, too, but they somehow managed to survive the purges and are now being recognized by readers.

Then I went to my Amazon order screen and looked at my preorders. I currently have sixteen books on preorder. Three are from the same author, a romance writer who is doing a series I love. Two are from the same thriller writer. One is an anthology I've been looking forward to.

So...twelve authors on that unscientific list. Four got their start in this century. One started indie, but is doing a trad pub series now. All four of the authors who started in this century are romance authors.

All of them.

I read new writers all the time. I read a lot of anthologies and indie books. The preorder field only represents trad pub because I prefer to read in paper, and it's almost impossible to preorder indies in paper. So my preorder list is 100 percent trad pub—and very representative of the findings that the survey had.

I have been reading the eight authors since they got their starts way back when. And they've held me throughout some ups and downs. I'm a lot more forgiving than traditional publishing is, although I have been known to dump long-time authors after about five books. Two of the brand names on the survey list are writers I no longer read, so I miss them like you'd miss an old lover. I really want them to write books I love again. But those writers aren't writing what I love anymore. They both are repeating themselves, and I find their work dull now. Sadly.

So, the conclusion my cold-fogged brain served up to me was twofold. First, traditional fiction publishing in at least two genres is in a great deal of trouble. They haven't nurtured their new voices.

Second, because there's trouble ahead, there's going to be a lot of room for indie bestsellers to become brand names as these brand names die off or stop producing. Readers will be looking for something similar.

Not something manufactured. As I mentioned above, Grisham rose on

Turow's coattails, but not because Grisham was trying to be Turow, but because Grisham—a lawyer—already wrote fiction, and Turow was a slow writer. Grisham filled the hole.

That's how brands used to start. At a bookstore, I would say, give me something like...Scott Turow, and I'd get hand-sold a John Grisham novel. This is happening in some bookstores with fantasy novels that are "like" Game of Thrones, because George R. R. Martin is so slow.

But there's more to it than being in the right place at the right time with the right book. It's *how* to be in the right place at the right time. And that has nothing to do with names on a newsletter list. It has to do with producing a lot of product.

The two-book writer on my preorder list? That's John Grisham. He's been producing two and three books a year for thirty years now. He's got a lot of backlist. And most of it (all of it?) is still in print.

That's something indies can do. We can keep our books in print.

But we need to brand them.

And that cold-fogged brain of mine realized that I have never dealt in depth with branding. Because branding is not just making a name big on the cover of a book or making sure all of the books in a series look the same. There's so much more to branding than that.

This is the introductory post, then, to a longer series on branding. It became clear to me after reading this survey that I needed a refresher. I also needed to give a lot of thought to branding, not just my names, but my series.

The Hollywood negotiations and trademark discussions brought that home, as well as the fan reaction to the newsletters. I gots me a lot of thinkin' to do, and I do that thinking best by writing.

So why not a series of blogs?

Which is exactly what I'm going to do.

"Sven, you are diluting the Viking brand."

TYPES OF BRANDS

I've been talking to myself lately. Actually, I've been talking back to podcasts, vlogs, and emails. Ever since I said I would be doing a series on branding, I've gotten links to great branding tips. (Please, keep them coming.)

Every single link I received that dealt with branding from a writer's perspective talked about cover branding. Lots of great information in each and every one of those blogs or podcasts or discussions, but every time the writers mentioned branding in reference to a cover, I would mutter, *There's more to branding than covers.*

A whole ton more. In fact, when I mentioned at the regular Sunday professional writers' lunch that I would be doing this series on branding, one of the wags across the room from me asked, *Without an entire semester? How can you do that?*

Very generally. Because as my fellow writers who also have MBAs know, branding isn't a one-off topic. Business schools have entire courses and majors in branding.

Branding, at its best, is an art and a science.

As I got ready to do this series, I went over to my favorite default, *Adweek*, only to discover that they only have five subtopics listed on the header of their website, and one of those is "brand marketing."

Okay. I promise. No entire semester. No gigantic course. But lots of information geared at making you think outside of the box that writing and publishing has put you in.

First, I'll start, as I always do, with a definition.[6]

According to Brick Marketing, which had the best pithy definition I could find:

> *A brand is the idea or image of a specific product or service that consumers connect with, by identifying the name, logo, slogan, or design of the company who owns the idea or image.*

Sounds simple, right? But it's not. My usual go-to source for definitions, Investopia.com, has a long and complicated definition of "brand" that goes into some of the topics we'll discuss in future blogs (but not today). When Investopedia gets into the nitty gritty of the definition of a brand, it makes this very important assessment:[7]

A brand is seen as one of its company's most valuable assets.

I bet you never thought of your brand as an important asset in your business. I'll bet that, aside from "branding" your name on the cover of your indie-published book, you've never thought of branding at all.

The first thing all of these sites discuss in examining brands is "brand identity." As Investopia says, "A company's brand identity is how that business wants to be perceived by consumers."[8]

Investopedia hastens to point out that brand identity is different from brand image. Your brand identity is *how you want* customers to perceive your brand. Your brand image is *how customers actually* perceive your brand.

Yeah, yeah. Already too much detail.

Some writer blogs are savvy enough to know that the writer can be the brand. The publishers rarely are the brand. Harlequin was a brand once upon a time, although it has pretty much blown that by diluting its brand identity. Baen Books has a brand identity that's pretty consistent with its brand image—that of providing science fiction and fantasy to sf/f fans in the know.

Over the years, publishers have had brand identity that coincided with brand image, but as more and more mergers occurred, publisher brands got swallowed up or disappeared entirely. What does Penguin Random House stand for now? Who knows? Not even they know.

Branding is marketing on an advanced level. Some of it does concern names on the cover. Some of it concerns the way a writer gets perceived. Some of it concerns a whole bunch of other things.

Back in the days when traditional publishing reigned supreme (and dinosaurs roamed the Earth), writers left branding up to their publishers. The people who interacted with the writer—editors—didn't know anything about branding. The sales force generally took charge of the marketing, and wouldn't even consider branding an author until the author had already had some success.

At that point, the sales force would tell the editor that the writer should probably stick to a particular type of book (say, books about tiny robots), because that was the writer's perceived brand. But aside from that kind of malarkey, and decisions made in the art department about the size of the name on the cover, traditional publishers rarely, if ever, thought about branding.

Which is just plain stupid, considering that writers partner with their publishers so that their publishers will handle the marketing.

But I digress.

So as indie publishing grew, and the writers who had the most experience with marketing turned out to be the hybrid writers, they talked about what they knew: names on the cover, making sure the stories remained the kind of stories readers wanted from that writer, and so on and so forth.

Leaving, as my poker player husband would say, tons and tons of opportunities on the table.

Realize, before I go any farther, that this series of blogs isn't for you. It's for me and for the people who work with me on my books. Because I know all this stuff and I've been too damn busy to apply it to my own work outside of a throw-spaghetti-against-the-wall-and-see-if-it-sticks kinda way. Some of that is because I spent the last eight years clawing back the rights on my traditionally published books. Some of that is because I've been simultaneously building five different businesses at the same time.

And some of it was because I didn't feel ready yet to do this kind of marketing push.

But now's the time.

I have to admit, though, that it took Randy Ellison and his Targoz Strategic Marketing's Reading Pulse survey[9] to kick me over the top. There's a lot of good information in that survey, things that I need to implement in my business. I was planning to do this, with some extra research under my belt, in the next year or so, but the survey kicked me forward. I will discuss some of its conclusions when I get to that point in this series. However, if you want to see some of the conclusions, go to The Hot Sheet, sign up for their 30-day free trial, and click on the May 3, 2017 links[10]. (By the way, they have some great material as well, almost every week.)

Randy's work made me realize how haphazard our work has been on my publications, as well as on Dean's, and the publishing company I co-own, WMG Publishing. We moved toward branding and marketing a few years ago, but dropped that as we reorganized the business. We're ready to do so again, with people who are invested in learning about this aspect of publishing.

But marketing isn't as simple as some of the writing blogs make it sound. As I said in *Discoverability*, you need to know what your target audience is. You also need to know exactly what it is you're marketing. And that's where branding starts.

According to one business website, there are eighteen different kinds (types) of brands. I went over there and yeah, they're right, there are a ton of different kinds of brands. But most aren't relevant to what we're discussing here.

Some business courses cite ten different kinds, but the consensus seems to be that there are somewhere around five, six, or seven different types of brands.

For our purposes here, we'll go with six different types of brands. They are:

- **Service**
- **Personality**
- **Product**
- **Organization**
- **Event**
- **Geography**

Let's start with the two I'm going to dismiss as irrelevant to writers. (Most of the time. All of this is most of the time.) Geography refers to places that need to brand themselves. "What Happens in Vegas, Stays in Vegas" is one way that Las Vegas branded itself. New York has billed itself in a variety of ways, from the city that never sleeps to "I [heart] New York." Virginia, on the other hand, declares that "Virginia is For Lovers," and New Mexico is "The Land of Enchantment."

That's branding on a **geographical** scale. Sometimes that's relevant to writers because some writers (like Linda Fairstein) become inextricably tied to a particular setting or place, but it's rarer than you'd think.

Event refers to big repeating events, like Burning Man or South by Southwest. These things become brands, and they're centered around some kind of experience that people will have jointly. The Chicago Blues Festival is an event brand.

Some writers do event branding—particularly if they're doing something special with a book tour. A few years ago, Gallery Books put ten of its romance authors on a bus and made the bus tour into an event. The bus had a special logo, just like the tour did. Called "Belles on Wheels," the bus tour became an event, and the promotions began months before, including drawings, big reveals of tour dates, and of the bus itself.[11]

Had Gallery Books done this Belles on Wheels tour every year, it would have become an event worth branding, the kind that readers would have looked forward to. It might have become something that the press noticed, something that communities planned for, and something that actually benefitted the authors who were on tour.

It did not. It was a one-time event, not an ongoing event, so it became less of a big deal than it could have been.

Other writers did some of this branded event touring on their own dime. For the life of me, I can't track down the marketing on these things with my handy-dandy Google. (A brand, by the way.)

Mostly, though, the brands that will matter to us as we go through this series are:

- **Organization**
- **Service**
- **Product**
- **Personality**

Most of the marketing advice concerning branding that you hear for writers is about **personality** branding. (Some places, like the Dummies site[12] [also a brand] differentiate Person brands from Personality branding. Yeah, yeah. I'm not going to get as technical as I can, okay? If you want that, follow the links yourself, and dive into that rabbit hole headfirst, like I did.)

Personality branding is pretty straightforward. The person brand is focused on a famous person, while the branding is all about the personality. This works for groups as well as individuals (think Kardashians). The biggest personality brands belong to people like Oprah or Martha Stewart or Emeril Lagasse.

Sometimes a person becomes so famous they become a brand whether they want to or not. (Cher, Prince, or any one of a dozen celebrities at any time in history.) But generally speaking, the personality brand was nurtured by the personality herself.

The biggest personality brand that I know of in romance is Debbie Macomber. Everything she does, from her books to her speaking tours, reflect who Debbie is—or at least, how she presents herself to the world. For a while, James Patterson had a personality brand. He's in the process of diluting it by writing with co-authors and doing a bunch of other things that we'll discuss later.

Stephen King, on the other hand, has a personality brand that he doesn't pay much attention to. If he did, he would only write horror fiction. Yet, his name is recognizable and his brand is the diverse fiction (within certain limits) that he writes under that name.

Organization brands are just that: branding done for organizations. The Red Cross is a brand. A lot of organization brands are tied to personality—a charity started by a famous person, for example, might become an organizational brand in and of itself.

Publishers are organization brands. Your indie publishing house could become a brand. Baen Books is a brand that sells itself as a brand. So does Tor Books. So did Harlequin, but since Harlequin was bought out, it doesn't do so any longer. Eventually that organizational brand will simply go away.

Service brands are based on the experience, on what the consumer gets —the service, if you will. If you're run a housecleaning business, you're providing a service. If you do it well, then you will eventually get recommendations based on the name of your company.

A service brand is based on trust. The consumer has to believe that the service they will get from the brand will be good—or at least good enough.

Uber is a service brand: in theory, you can trust that app will bring you a car that will get you from one place to another safely. Considering many of the problems that Uber has had, it still hasn't entirely mastered the trust part of a service brand.

Writers aren't just a personality brand. They're also a service brand. Writers who become Big Names provide a guaranteed service—the reader will get an enjoyable escape from their reality for a few hours. Even if the book isn't up to the Big Name's highest standard, the book will still be good enough that the reader won't regret the purchase.

Product. Certain products have brand awareness. 7 Up is a brand and also a product. If you buy 7 Up in Dallas, and then buy another can of 7 Up three months later in Detroit, you expect the exact same taste experience.

A product brand can be an individual item like a can of soda or it can be a series of items, like Ford trucks, all built to the same standard, and all with the same expectation of quality. I'm not saying the product is good; that depends on your taste. But the quality of the product(s) should be the same across the board. One brand-new Ford truck shouldn't be impossible to drive off the lot while the other model of brand-new Ford truck drives like a dream.

Writers can have product brands, which I will get to shortly. If a writer writes a successful series, that series becomes a product brand.

Businesses can have different layers of brands. The business can be (and often is) its own brand. The business might also have a personality brand. For example, Virgin Atlantic has Richard Branson, who is a personality in his own right.

For those of us in Oregon, we deal with the personality of Phil Knight, the co-founder of Nike. In Oregon, Phil Knight and the Knight family are both a regional brand (yes, another kind of brand) and a personality brand. Outside of the state (and outside of American sports), most people have not heard of Phil Knight, although they have heard of Nike.

Nike is an organization brand, a business brand, and if you shop in their stores, a service brand. Their products, though, have their own branding, which gets very esoteric.

Sometimes the products share branding. When Michael Jordan was the face of basketball in the 1980s, he got an endorsement deal with Nike to produce a branded shoe—the Air Jordan. Those shoes were so popular that they are still being produced today, even though Jordan himself has not played professional basketball since 2003.

Highly successful writers often end up with three different kinds of brands, whether they know it or not. Those writers are personality brands. They also are service brands (for providing a specific kind of read). And, if they're known for a series, they end up with product brands as well.

Sometimes this happens accidentally. George R. R. Martin was very well known in science fiction when he sold his fantasy series to HBO, but he became a three-way brand once the show hit the airwaves. George did a lot of media (and he's funny), so he became a personality brand. The series books ended up being product brand, even though George has written a bunch of other books outside of the series. And for better or worse, he has become a service brand, although at the moment, that part of the brand is mostly known for not finishing books on time, which isn't really helping the brand much at all.

Most writers who either still exist in traditional publishing or started there end up with their brands accidentally. They lost control of the brand creation early on, so what they end up with is their brand image, without ever giving thought to brand identity.

Some writers focus on branding from the beginning.

Lee Child is very clear about the fact that he chose his pen name with an eye toward branding. In an article titled "Lee Child" written by Oline H. Cogdill in the Holiday 2016 issue of *Mystery Scene*,[13] Child called his name change a "show business thing." But he thought about that "C" last name and chose it for a marketing reason.

"When I started," he said, "there were a huge number of authors whose last names began with a C. I wanted readers to see my books as quickly as possible."

In the interview, he intertwines service with product, and discusses both of those brands (without using the word) in a single paragraph. He said, "I sort of have an emotional contract with the reader. They want Reacher, and I think it would be upsetting and weird if I put out a book without Reacher. And even if it was the greatest book, I don't think readers would accept it."

Other writers write more than one series. A number of brand name writers, Stephen King and Dean Koontz among them, write books in more than one genre. But they don't really think about intertwining branding and bringing the consumer into the art.

Child does.

It's all a choice about the kind of writer you want to be, and the kind of work you want to do.

I believe that a writer should write what she wants (even if it is the same series with the same character) and then worry about marketing that material. Because of the haphazard nature of my own career for the past twenty years, I have too much varied material, and I need to separate it out so that readers can find what they want and what they're looking for.

"Kristine Kathryn Rusch" can be a personality brand for some consumers, but I'm better off marketing my Rusch books as both service and product brands. Readers will get a promise from me for the Diving series, that it will never be set in 2017 here on Earth. They get a different promise from me for the Retrieval Artist. And so on and so forth for all the series I write under Rusch.

I have an easier time with Kris Nelscott, one of my pen names. I'm not ever taking Nelscott out of gritty historical mystery that deals with issues of race and gender. There, my work will resemble Child's—I know that Nelscott readers want a particular kind of story and that's what they'll get.

The same with Kristine Grayson. That brand is goofy paranormal romance. If Grayson were to write a gritty 1960s detective novel, she would be breaking faith with her readers.

Rusch doesn't have those constraints, but that creates its own problems, as I mentioned above. Although I do give branding some thought with the name.

One reason I changed the name of this blog from the Business Rusch to Business Musings is that I didn't want my last name constantly associated with the word "business." Of course, I didn't think of that when I founded the business blog in 2009, so the name change was a course correction.

The Business Rusch is much more memorable than Business Musings, but I don't want memorable on the title of this blog. I just want it to be a side thing that I do.

The first thing we writers have to do as we figure out branding is what kind of brands we provide. Are we personality brands? Service brands? Product brands? All or none of the above?

Because that will matter on how we market things, and how we use our brands to good effect.

So during the week, figure out what kind of brands you already have. If you don't write a book series, but you have a large readership, you probably have service and personality brands. If you write a series, add in product brand. If you have more than one series, you probably have more than one product brand. And if you have pen names, then you might have more personality brands.

You need to know who you are and what you have before you can leverage any of that.

The other homework I'm giving you this week is to pay attention to the brands around you. Not just the brands from writers, but from companies. As I wrote this blog this afternoon, I was hyper brand aware. I noted the brand on my TV, the brand in my tablet, the brand of tea that I drink, the brand advertised on my T-shirt, and the brand of the laundry detergent I was using.

Brands are everywhere now, and we pick the brands we use for a variety of reasons. Keep track of your reasons, because your consumer choices will influence how you market your own products. Make a list of what you like and don't like.

Because you need some brand awareness as we go deeper into this series, and doing those simple things will help you with that awareness.

Until then...

"And you say we paid the agency how much
for this slogan?"

HOW TO BUILD A BRAND: THE EARLY STAGES

When I do marketing posts, they tend to freak my loyal readers out. Sometimes, the posts freak me out, too. What writers want from marketing blogs are simple suggestions that boil down to this:

Do x, y, and z, and you'll get these fantastic results!

Only it doesn't work that way. Or rather, it doesn't work that way for everyone. I'm writing this on Sunday, after our weekly professional writers lunch. We have writers of different levels at the lunch, including writers who've worked for decades, and writers who are on their third or fourth year as full-time professionals.

We discussed Amazon ads, which we all jumped into at roughly the same time, using the same or similar methods. We all have had stunningly different results. Those of us who've been in the business longer haven't seen the uptick that the newer authors are seeing—which makes sense, since the ads are about information and discoverability, and we're better known.

Besides, the hot new thing in indie publishing marketing is only the hot new thing for a few weeks or a few months. Then everyone jumps on the bandwagon and the hot new thing becomes tepid. The innovators move on to other things, hoping some of those things will become hot, and everyone else waits for the xyz instruction on what to do next.

Sorry, folks, you won't find the hot new thing here. This book doesn't provide a list of prescribed steps requiring exact action to guarantee success.

I don't guarantee nothing.

I am going to add one very important caveat, which will be in each and every chapter: if you bring any of this marketing stuff into your writing—your storytelling, your creative process—you are screwing up big time. You'll ruin the very thing your readers love about you.

Your readers love your ability to surprise them. Your readers love the fact that you take them on a journey that seems both familiar and unusual. If you do what you believe your readers want, you'll retain the familiar and jettison the unusual. You will never be able to surprise them again.

You will ruin your art.

Marketing is not about your writing art. Marketing is a separate art, one that will take study and diligence—and, most of all, patience.

I know, I know. You all want something that will bring results immediately. So do I. But building a brand is not about going fast or cutting corners. It is about continuity, reliability, and establishing your place in the market.

So please, please, as you read this book, do not bring the marketing ideas into the place where you actually write and create the stories that are uniquely yours. Once you've finished those stories, then you can figure out how to market and brand them.

In the previous chapter, I discussed the types of brands. If you haven't read that yet, I suggest you do so.

Writers who have been in the industry a long time or who have more than one series or use more than one name might have many, many brands.

I will deal with that down the road. The information in this post will apply to *all* of your brands. I'll be giving you a lot to think about, though, and if you have a lot of branded items, you might get overwhelmed. That's a warning.

After I posted the previous chapter as a blog, a few of you asked (in the comments and in private) when is the right time for a writer to start branding her work. Well, here's the thing. The moment you publish your first piece, you've begun branding. Branding happens whether you do anything or not. (Traditional publishing has relied on that aspect of branding for decades now, letting brands develop by themselves and then jumping on them once they're already established.)

Brand image—the way that customers perceive your brand—begins the moment a customer (reader) reads something of yours. That customer will get an impression of what you do, and that impression can be reinforced with other work.

If you're the kind of writer who writes one character or one series, then your branding will focus on that singular thing. However, if you're the kind of writer that I am, the kind who writes in multiple genres and in many styles, then you will have a brand image that focuses on variety and, perhaps, surprise. The readers, however, will define the specifics of your brand for you.

Think of it this way: you might describe someone's work by saying, "He writes all over the map, but his stories always have happy endings" or "Her stories are always filled with great characters, no matter what genre she writes in."

You can help brand image along by creating a brand identity. If, for example, you write fantasy and mystery, your fantasy books might have one look and marketing scheme, while your mysteries have another.

Those of you who are just starting out will have both an easier time of this and a harder time. Easier because you have less material to work with, and can shape the handful of things you've already done into a marketing campaign. Those of us with a lot of material and a history in traditional publishing will have a great deal of work that was mismarketed or allowed to die a horrible death or doesn't reflect what we're working on now.

For the sake of this chapter, though, let's pretend we all only have one brand. Just one.

We now need to build that brand—not with what we write, but how we bring what we write to market.

To build the brand, we have to do some things that are simple to say and very hard to do. I'll give you the list, and then I'll explain.

1. **Define Your Business**
2. **Define Your Target Audience**
3. **Research Similar Businesses**
4. **Figure Out What Makes Your Brand Unique**
5. **Figure Out What Your Brand Is Not**
6. **Create A Brand Mission Statement/Tagline**
7. **Be Consistent**
8. **Be Patient**

There are a million other things involved in building a brand, and we will revisit this part of the topic as the time comes. That's why this chapter is subtitled "The Early Stages."

So, let's go through the list from a writerly perspective.

1. Define Your Business.

The definition here is not "I am a writer." You must be more specific than that. Start globally and work your way to the specific. And you must think about this from the outside in, not the inside out.

Rather than "I am a writer," you could say, "I write the multi-volume Made-up World Fantasy Novel series." Or "I write award-winning short science fiction." Or "I write sexy contemporary romance novels set in Venice."

You might have an actual agenda, like some writers I know. Some write to give their readers an escape. Others try to improve the world around them. Still others present diverse characters in a modern setting, or characters who are differently abled and heroic or from some group underrepresented in fiction.

Some writers don't have an agenda, and simply write.

One way to figure out how to define your writing business is to ask people what they associate with your work. Is it a marvelous voice? Great characters? A unique milieu?

Your business definition is something you will continually refine over the years, so you're not completely stuck with it. If you want to understand how business definitions evolve, read *Shoe Dog* by Phil Knight, the founder of Nike. In many ways, that book is about the evolution of a brand. Nike went from selling other people's shoes to creating shoes to selling apparel and other sports-related items, all the while maintaining the uniqueness of the Swoosh (the brand symbol).

Your business definition will evolve over time, just like your business will evolve over time.

2. Define Your Target Audience.

When you're starting out, you won't have an audience. You'll only have a target audience. Those are the people you want to sell to. If you define your target audience as "all readers," you won't sell to any readers.

When I got the rights back to my Kris Nelscott novels featuring African-American detective Smokey Dalton, I knew immediately that my target audience was African-American readers. I know that's strange to say, given that the series was traditionally published, and those readers should have been high on the priority list for my traditional publishing company.

But that company had no idea how to market books with an African-American protagonist and, I believe, had no idea that there were African-American book clubs, magazines, and bookstores. (Seriously.) So the moment I reprinted those books myself, I made sure that they were advertised in various African-American outlets. That has led to a steady growth for the series and the Nelscott name (which, I admit, are two separate brands, but the instruction applies).

Your target audience might be people who loved the *Guardians of the Galaxy* movies. Or people who love World of Warcraft. Or people who collect Disney comics.

In the spring of 2017, KFC published a romance novel in which Colonel Sanders is the romantic hero. (I am not joking.) I'm assuming the target audience is romance readers who eat KFC. I also have a hunch that this was a great marketing ploy someone came up with, because I saw news about this novel in everything from *Adweek* to *The Washington Post* to romance blogs. And here I am, giving the book free advertising as well.

The marketing ploy worked. Will it work for Taco Bell? Maybe. But if Taco Bell does it, and MacDonald's does it, and Arby's does it, eventually readers will stop paying attention and will move onto the next big thing.

So define your target audience. And go as narrow as you possibly can. You want to be specific here, not general. The more specific you can be, the easier it will be to build your brand.

3. Research Similar Businesses.

By similar businesses, I do not mean similar writers. You work in the entertainment industry, folks. So look at what others in the entertainment industry are doing. What you're writing might be closer to the Sandman graphic novels than anything anyone else is doing in prose fiction. Or maybe you're writing books that are like *Sherlock*, the BBC's modern take on Sherlock Holmes.

It will be better for you and the brand you're building if you can pull ideas from outside of the publishing industry, or even from outside of the entertainment industry. Perhaps, like romance writer Sarina Bowen, you're writing books about hockey. Maybe your marketing should bring in elements of NHL marketing and elements of romance marketing. How do you brand that? Research and find out.

4. Figure Out What Makes Your Brand Unique.

Chances are you started writing to fill a niche that no one else was filling. You loved 1970s Gothic romances, and they went out of print. Now you're writing Gothic romances for the new century, with strong heroines and brooding heroes. Or Gothic romances for the LGBTQ community. (Oh, that sounds good.)

When I talked to George R. R. Martin as he was developing the fantasy novel series that became Game of Thrones, he talked about writing historically accurate epic fantasy. If the world was built on a medieval society, then it needed to have medieval values and medieval cleanliness, and medieval violence. (I think he achieved that.) Those ideas were revolutionary in the genre back in 1993-1994. The made-up fantasy worlds back then had more in common with wish-fulfillment than they did with the historical past.

Again, drill down. Figure out what makes your work unique. If you aren't writing in a series, figure out what it is about your writing that makes it yours.

Writers trained in traditional publishing have a tough time with this, because they're trained to say what their work is similar to, not what makes it unique. Forget the similar to part. Focus on what's different.

The more specific you get, the harder it will be for you to see what makes your work yours. So enlist the aid of others who love what you're doing. They'll tell you what makes your work special. Then you need to believe them, and run with that.

5. Figure Out What Your Brand Is Not.

You have probably said it, and have probably said it forcefully. "My novels are about a Cold War spy, but he's not George Smiley." "I write novels about crime scene investigation, but I write about the real crime scene investigators, not that magic stuff they did on CSI." "I write novels set in space, with an Empire and people fighting the Empire, but I try to keep the series based in science, unlike Star Wars, which is more fantasy."

And so on and so forth.

In this category, I often think about the comic *Get Fuzzy*, which is about a single guy living at home with his nasty cat and his very nice dog. Sounds just like Garfield, right? Only Garfield is gentle, and Bucky, the cat in *Get Fuzzy*, is a tiny little psychopath who rains terror on everyone near him. (I'm sure there are many other differences, but I haven't read Garfield in years. I prefer the Buckster.)

6. Create A Brand Mission Statement/Tagline.

The brand mission statement really helps, particularly if you can do it in a paragraph or a single line. It depends on what part of your business you're trying to brand. Debbie Macomber, for example, has been called "the official storyteller of Christmas," but that's only for one series of books. (They've been made into Christmas movies for the Hallmark Channel.)

My own pen name, Kristine Grayson, has a tagline which I did not think up myself (dammit). That tagline was one of the few good things to come out of my final Grayson traditional publisher. The tagline is "It's not easy to get a fairy-tale ending."

Yeah, that needs tweaking. (I hear Dean bitching about the passive voice as I type this.) But the idea is right, since the books are fractured fairy-tale romances.

Come up with something like that, something that can be as identified with your brand as "Just Do It" is with Nike's, and you'll really have a winner.

7. Be Consistent.

Most writers completely misunderstand this one. They think it means write the same book over and over again.

Instead, it means write the best book you can. Be consistent in your commitment to quality, whatever quality means to you.

If your books need to have a happy ending to satisfy you, then make sure they all have a happy ending. If you're writing historically accurate Westerns, make sure that you don't commit horse opera under that name. Or if you do, make sure you're clear: Cowboy Dan, known for his historical accuracy, throws caution to the wind and writes a dime novel filled with exaggeration. He hopes you have as much fun reading it as he had writing it.

With that, Cowboy Dan is acknowledging that the consistency in his brand might not be the historical accuracy, but the Western time period.

Once your business is defined, once your audience is defined, and once you know what is unique about your work, then you know how to make sure your audience senses the consistency—even as you change things up.

Consistency also applies to marketing. Make sure that if you decide on a logo or a typeface for your book covers that you use that same logo everywhere, and keep the typeface consistent. Your series books should be visually related to each other. And if you do visual ads for those books, those ads should resemble the books in some way even if the ads don't use the same art.

If your books are upbeat, make sure your marketing is upbeat. If you're writing humor, make sure the marketing is funny. If your books are dark and brooding, make sure the marketing is dark and brooding.

If you're consistent throughout your marketing, you'll reinforce the brand itself.

8. Be Patient.

You can't build a brand overnight. You can't even modify an existing brand overnight.

You can start branding, and you can make headway, but brands take years to develop.

I love how Raoul Davis expresses this in his article, "7 Keys to Building a Successful Brand" on the BusinessCollective website.[14] He writes:

> Be patient with your brand. Take on every new outreach initiative with care. Think of it as your baby. Just as you wouldn't start feeding solid food to a 3-month-old, don't rush any of your outreach activities, whether they be PR, advertising, or marketing materials.

He's right. Some of the things I'll do for my long-established series would be completely wrong for your brand-new series. But it's even more complex than that.

Brands and businesses morph. So do writing series and writing careers. I know many a writer who started in one genre, burned out, and moved to another. Some writers found their voices later. Janet Evanovich started as a romance writer, but felt constrained by the genre. She wrote twelve romance novels before she invented Stephanie Plum, the character who made Evanovich's bestselling career.

In the previous chapter, I asked you to think about your brands. I also asked you to up your brand awareness, by examining the brands you use and the ones you ask for by name.

Your homework this time is to pick one of your writing brands (if you have more than one), and see if you can analyze it using the tools above.

Don't be surprised or upset if you can't find answers easily. That's normal. This is a whole new way to think.

Be patient with yourself. And think about this: the experts in marketing always talk about "building" or "growing" a brand. You don't build or grow anything overnight.

One step at a time, one idea at a time.

And whenever you're feeling overwhelmed, set the marketing aside, and do what you love. Go back to your writing office, forget this marketing stuff, and escape into one of your stories.

Because without those, this branding stuff means nothing at all.

"We've decided to market this product to disgruntled 25 to 54 y.o. women in bathrobes."

DEFINE YOUR TARGET AUDIENCE: THE EARLY STAGES

I love my blog. I love it because the readers make it so much better with your questions and comments.

When I posted the previous chapter as a blog, I got an unexpected result. In that post is something that seems pretty straightforward to me—the phrase "define your target audience." Some of you remarked in the email and the comments that you've been struggling with this one thing for a very long time.

Oh. What a revelation to me. When I write these blogs it becomes clear to me sometimes just how many things I do automatically.

I've worked in retail since I was sixteen years old. I owned my first retail store at the age of twenty-one. I currently am co-owner of three brick-and-mortar retail stores and um...three?...five?...online retail stores (it depends on how you count some of my businesses).

For me, finding a target audience is like putting on socks in the morning. The socks are in a drawer, I open the drawer, give the choice exactly three seconds of thought, grab the right pair, and go.

The rest of you don't see a single sock drawer. You see one of those sock collages where every sock that the photographer can fit in the scene is presented along the floor, in a beautiful and colorful pattern. Yeah, that takes tons of work. And no, that's not what I mean.

Thank you, thank you, thank you for bringing this step to my attention.

It is hard to define your target audience if you've never done it before. And I had forgotten that entirely.

Let's start as basic as we can.

What Is a Target Audience?

A target audience is a specific set of people to whom you want to market your book.

I know, I know. You want everyone to read your book. But if you step back and think about it, you know that you will not achieve that, no matter what you do. Not everyone reads, for one thing, and not everyone reads all genres or all the writers in a particular genre, for another.

You need to drill down into who you want to market your books to. Once you figure out who you want to market to, then you can figure out how to market to them.

Why Does Choosing a Target Audience Matter?

Choosing a target audience matters so that you can tailor your marketing campaign to that audience.

This weekend, I had dinner with a group of friends. We were talking about TV and movies, and one friend asked me if I had seen *Get Out* yet. She thought I would love it.

I said I don't find humor in the situation they were presenting.

She looked at me like I was nuts. Humor? she said. It's a horror movie.

I said all the marketing I saw called it a comedy. Then she really looked at me like I was crazy.

We discussed the movie (heh! Word of mouth) and I decided, yes indeedy do, I would love to see that film. Absolutely. Based on what she said, not on what I had heard from the marketing.

When I got home, I decided to double-check. Had I actually seen marketing that said this film was a comedy? Turns out, I had never seen the trailer, which looked like a generic bad horror movie trailer (which wouldn't have appealed to me either).

So I looked at the online and print press, and saw headlines like this: Jordan Peele on making a hit comedy-horror movie out of America's racial tensions, and an entertaining and clever satire that is equal parts funny and terrifying. On and on and on.

No one I spoke to that night mentioned that the film was funny. Not a single soul.

On that level, it was a marketing fail, probably done because Jordan Peele is best known as a comedian (or was, until this film did well). The trailer, though, which I just watched, does appeal to horror audiences.[15]

That's a proper target audience for the film.

You can have more than one target audience for your product, but I'll get to that in detail in a future post.

If you know who your target audience is, you can talk to them directly, in a language and a tone that would appeal to them.

You see examples of marketing directed to target audiences all the time. During the United States football season (fall) in 2014, the National Football League finally figured out that it had a demographic it had never targeted before—women. Ad after ad featured women watching the games (not serving food like they did in the past), buying gear, and dressed in clothing with a particular team's logo. Some of this was because of the scandals that had engulfed pro-football (and the NFL wanted women on its side), but a lot of it had to do with studies that had shown that 46 percent of all NFL fans were women. And until those studies, the NFL had ignored that particular (large) portion of its audience.[16]

The NFL made a significant change, with some pink merchandise that supported breast cancer awareness, and a variety of female apparel from maternity jerseys with team logos to form-fitting T-shirts to leggings to just about anything else you could imagine. Fantasy football advertising showed women beside men choosing teams (or women in groups cheering on their teams). The change has worked and continues to work, growing the audience, despite the controversies still engulfing the sport.

That's just one example of targeted marketing. There are a million others. You target audiences all the time without thinking about it. It's as natural as breathing for you.

How? Well, my friends targeted an audience in that discussion. They believed that I would love *Get Out*. I needed to see it, and they hard-sold it to me.

In that same conversation, discussing some TV shows, the speaker apologized to another person in the room, knowing that person wouldn't be as interested in the topic as everyone else was.

We know our friends. We know which friend to share the gory novel with, which friend can only tolerate sweet romances, and which friend reads nothing but nonfiction. You wouldn't foist a sweet and unbelievable romance on the nonfiction reader any more than you would give the sweet romance reader the gory novel.

Find Your Target Audience Without Research

Later, we'll discuss how to refine your target audience or even expand it through research.

But right now, most of you have no idea who your target audience is and you're flailing about trying to find your target audience.

You're looking outside your writing room, seeing no one lined up to read your work, and wondering how to find your audience when you have no audience at all.

You're doing it backwards.

You've finished your novel. Now, take that novel from your creative office into your marketing office. (I'm using a novel here because it's a finite thing. We'll discuss career branding and marketing later.)

Figure out what that novel is. Fantasy? Science fiction? Urban fantasy? Steampunk? Drill down, figure out your subgenres.

Then, figure out what the book focuses on. Are the characters Chinese-American? Native American? Is the book set in Chicago? Does the book have all female characters?

Any one of those factors might focus your marketing. Two of them focuses it even more. Three of them helps tremendously.

So…your novel is steampunk set in Chicago featuring Chinese-American characters. Your target audience might be readers of Amy Tan or Ken Liu. You might look for book clubs that focus on books with Chinese-American characters or themes.

Or you could focus on the history of Chicago, and market to the Chicago media in one way or another. Would Chicagoans like seeing a steampunk version of their city? I think they might. Or would they like to see how the Chinese were treated when they settled in Chicago over a hundred years ago? Perhaps.

Try it. You can drill down your marketing that specifically.

Pick just one target audience to start. And then…

Tailor your marketing message to that audience.

How do you do that? You put yourself in that audience's shoes. What will appeal to them? When the NFL targeted its female fans, it didn't show them hosting hen parties while the men scarfed snacks in the living room. That would have talked down to women. Instead, it created products specifically for women and then marketed those items to women. Some of the ads for the Super Bowl featured women, cheering as vociferously as the men usually did.

In a really good (albeit a bit too advanced for our purposes) article on defining a target audience, the authors Neil Patel and Aaron Agius interviewed Yaro Starak of Entreprenuers-Journey.com.[17] They asked him how to build an online presence. He immediately focused on targeted marketing, and started with this:[18]

> *I'd first focus on establishing a crystal-clear empathy with the audience I was planning to serve, so I know what their problem is, how they feel about it and what they currently do to try and solve it.*

Empathy. You're writers. Find out what the readers you've targeted like and then put yourself in their shoes. Figure out what would appeal to them as well as what would turn them away from your product.

Talking down to those women the NFL wanted to target would have destroyed the effort the NFL made. Someone, somewhere, spent some time figuring out what parts of the NFL appealed to women, and then pointed the marketing in that direction.

Yes, sometimes that takes research, and we'll deal with that in a future chapter. But just as often, all it takes is a bit of thought and a whole lot of empathy.

Traditional Publishing Marketing

The thing that started me on this branding series was the Targoz Strategic Marketing reader survey, because in it, the data Randy Ellison compiled showed over and over again that most of the stuff traditional publishing does as marketing doesn't work at all. It's clueless marketing, based on ancient assumptions.

If you're following the traditional publishing path, you're probably doing marketing wrong. If you're doing what every other indie writer is doing, you're probably doing marketing wrong.

You have a unique product and you have (or will have) a unique brand. You have to make that work for you.

It sounds so easy, and it's not. It's a hard thing to do.

Which means…

You will get the marketing wrong.

More often than not, you might target an audience only to find they really don't give a damn. Or while you're targeting one audience, a different audience for your work has developed.

I was surprised when I went to book signings ten years ago that a major audience for my Smokey Dalton books was expatriate Southern white women raised in the 1960s who, as children, were not allowed to walk into African-American neighborhoods.

Time and time again, I talked to these women, who loved the books.

Later I figured out what had happened. St. Martins Press, terrified that a white woman had written a novel about an African-American detective, had tossed the first novel into the sink-or-swim mystery marketing channel. Had I been African-American, they would have marketed the book to African-American audiences only.

Instead, St. Martins hid the book from African-American audiences. Which meant that the readers who picked up the book were often white. And the white women who found it probably would not have gone to the African-American section of the bookstore, so to those women, this book was unusual.

The African-Americans who found the books loved them, too. But that audience grew slowly, which surprised me at the time.

While I worried that African-Americans weren't reading the book, a whole different audience was growing that I hadn't seen until I went to some signings and gave a few talks at mystery gatherings.

This is what happened with the NFL. They marketed 100 percent to men, and only gradually realized that half their audience was female. Whoops.

What do you do when you discover an unexpected audience?

You can do several things. You can retool your entire marketing strategy for a different target audience. Or you can do what the NFL did, and add in a completely different marketing campaign tailored to the audience you just discovered that you had.

It's Okay To Miss

Your target audiences will shift over time. Some of that will happen naturally given what you're writing. Some of it will happen because of world circumstances. For example, in an article about the development and marketing of *Get Out*, there's this little tidbit:[19]

Conceived in the Obama era, Get Out *hits theaters with even greater resonance now...*

"This movie was intended to call out racism in what many people were calling a post-racial era," Peele said. "People didn't want to talk about race. Now, it's an undeniable part of the discussion again."

Target audiences change. Or grow. If steampunk suddenly becomes as hot as apocalyptic fiction did a few years ago, then you would tailor your Chinese-American Chicago steampunk marketing to include the new target audience who had just discovered steampunk.

Specific, specific, specific.

The more specific you are in defining your audience, the better chance you have at building readership. Readership grows outward from one reader to two, two to three, three to four, and so on. At some point, the readers will end up doing the work for you, like my friends did for Jordan Peele. My friends targeted me as the audience; your readers will do the same for you.

So, as you search for your target audience, don't focus on the audience you do or don't have at the moment. (We'll deal with that aspect of this down the road.)

Focus on the audience you want. The audience you believe is perfect for the book you wrote. The audience who would appreciate it more than anyone else will.

Talk to those people in language that respects them—and language that interests them.

Yes, this will require some thought on your part.

And since I've been assigning homework, let me assign something here.

Instead of fast-forwarding through ads on your favorite TV shows, watch those ads. See if you can guess what target audience those ads are going for. You can test your responses by looking at the demographics for that particular show after you've done your guesswork. You'll see how well that show is doing in an age group and income category.

But I'll wager you'll see that in the ads without even looking at the demographic information.

And let me give you a mighty big clue: listen to the background music. Usually it's a hit song from a particular time period. If you know the time period (say the 1990s), you know that the ad is appealing to customers who are in their late thirties and early forties. The theory is that familiar music will make the viewer more receptive to the product.

(In my case, the hit song from my era often pisses me off at the product and makes me yell *I'm not that old!* at the TV, which is the indoor equivalent of *Get off my lawn!*)

I hope I answered those of you who asked about finding your target audience. Subsequent chapters will have more on this. But, please, do this work first.

BRAND IDENTITY

After the previous chapter went live as a blog, a lot of people had questions. Most of them appeared in the comments of that post. I answered most of those comments on that post, which you can still find on the website.

However, I chose to answer one in the body of the next post, which is this chapter on brand identity.

One thing I will say is that most of you seem to think of your audience as a thing, not as a person. As I said in the previous chapter, you start with one reader, then get another, and another, and another, to build an audience. In that sense, musicians have it better than writers.

A musician plays to empty bars. A musician watches as patrons come in, talking and laughing, and pay attention to their friends. Eventually, someone looks up and watches the musician. Then that someone elbows his buddy or shushes a friend to hear the end of a song. The friend starts listening. Then someone else notices that the two of them are listening. And soon the entire table is listening.

That's how an audience builds. Some of those people might return to hear that musician the following week. And the musician, remembering that moment, might play the same song or something similar before going on with her set list.

Your audience is not a thing. It's people. (Every time I type that sentence, I think of *Soylent Green*. That's not what I mean, though.)

As you find your audience, imagine people or a person or a table in a crowded restaurant, all of whom are slowly starting to pay attention to you. Make your audience real *to you*.

My inclination as a completist is to write all of the target audience posts at once, but that won't help you, because you can't understand some of the upper-level marketing stuff without understanding other basic branding concepts.

Also, I can tell from the questions I'm getting, both on the site and in my email, that many of you have not read *Discoverability* or the previous chapters. There's an attitude that you need to have in your marketing that most of you are missing.

Most of you want instructions. Do X and you'll get this result. Do Y and you'll get that result. I'm sorry, folks. Once we're past marketing basics—and branding is upper level, not basic—then that kind of talk is just silly.

Almost everyone who is selling a marketing system for writers is selling what worked for them at a very basic level. (Probably getting them from zero sales to a hundred sales or something small like that.) Once those people start talking about their success and boiling it down into a system, they become marketers only, and not writers. Those folks are selling a system that is as worthless to you (outside of a few stealable tricks) as any system promoted on late-night infomercials, with just as much hype and disappointment as those systems usually provide. Those systems are a get-rich-quick scheme—for their creator. Not for you. You're the one handing over the money.

I've said before, and I'll say it again: you will not get a system here in this book. You will get a way to approach branding and a way to think about it. The mindset is the important thing, because trends change. But marketing is something that has been around since the birth of capitalism. Marketing is flexible. You have to be, too.

Once you learn the mindset, then you have to do the hard work of applying it to your writing.

If you have trouble even conceiving of that, I'm afraid I can't help you beyond this: ask yourself why you have put up mental barriers on this particular topic. Why don't you want to learn how to do it right? Why don't you want to learn the mindset that will enable you to be flexible as trends change? What, exactly, are you resisting?

In order to do the upcoming posts on targeting your audience, I need to continue getting into the nitty-gritty of thinking about brands. You need some basics before you can move to how to use some of this to target audiences effectively.

Remember, the overall topic of the series is how to build a brand. In order to do that, you'll need to understand some basic concepts.

I must confess I didn't know some of the actual terminology before I started writing this as a series of blogs. I did know the concepts, but that was because we had to use them in my varied jobs. I didn't go to business school nor did I work for an ad agency or any large corporation that was organized around terminology. (When I formally worked on advertising, I was in radio, and we were shorthanded, so everyone did everything.)

So, in this chapter, we hit one of those terms that is completely obvious, but I hadn't ever used before in conversation.

Brand Identity

Brand identity is how you want customers to perceive your brand. You define the identity, although the customers may not accept that definition. (The customer's perception of the brand will appear in a different chapter.)

Right now, remember, we're dealing with building the brand. (If you haven't read the chapter "How To Build A Brand," go read it now.)

So you get to think about how you want that brand to be perceived. You need to imagine your target audience as you develop your brand identity. What do you want your target audience to think about your brand?

Remember, you're *building* a brand. You probably don't even have an audience yet. But you have a target audience—people you hope will buy your product. Those are the people (yes, people) you imagine as you decide how you want them to perceive your brand.

Let's start wide with the overall steps to building a brand identity, and then I'll refine for writers below. (Please don't skip ahead.)

Overall Steps to Building Brand Identity

Sounds so simple. Elementary steps that are (ahem) very similar to figuring out your brand.

But...let's have Investopedia really freak you out. Here's what they say about building a brand identity:[20]

> *Building a brand identity is a multi-disciplinary, strategic effort; every element needs to support the overall message and business goals. It can include a company's name, logo, design; its style and the tone of its copy; the look and composition of its products; and, of course, its social media presence.*

That freaks me out just reading it. Do I really have to do all of that?

Yep.

Over time, though. Not right away.

And remember, you don't have to get it right the first time. You can modify, change, reconsider, and redevelop your brand at any point in your business's history. Remember how I told you in some previous posts that I've been dealing this year with a lot of Hollywood types who are interested in my science fiction? Turns out one reason why is that Syfy is "refreshing" its brand.

Apparently, some genius at Syfy believed (years ago) that reality TV was the way to go. Now, Syfy is jumping on the scripted series bandwagon because of the streaming afterlife. Syfy mostly missed that boat and now needs scripted content immediately. Hence people are contacting me to see if my sf book series are available for option. (Everyone wants science fiction right now, not just Syfy, but Syfy's rebranding efforts are relevant to us here.)

Here's what Syfy is saying:

> The network's reboot, which rolls out on June 19 (and globally later in the year) will include a new logo and typeface, but is much more than just surface level. "This is a wholesale change, top to bottom," says Alexandra Shapiro, evp, marketing and digital, entertainment networks, for NBCUniversal Cable Entertainment.

Go to the article from the link in the endnotes,[21] and enable video so you can see what they're doing with their logos—and yes, I mean logos plural.

Syfy is also returning to its roots. The "re"brand is actually a return to the original brand, in many many ways. (I remember when the channel started, because a friend of mine was influential in putting the channel together, using the vision Syfy is coming back to now.)

So...don't worry as you start into branding. Everyone rebrands eventually, especially when the branding isn't working the way you want it to.The key is to start setting up your brand identity, and work forward from there.

If you go to that *Adweek* article on the Syfy channel, you'll also see how the channel is taking its overall brand and breaking it down for each subset —the TV audience, the internet audience, the social media audience. You'll also see how Syfy is using the new branding on the TV shows themselves.

Remember, each TV show has its own brand, brand identity, and marketing strategy. Marvel's *Agents of S.H.I.E.L.D.* took its branding one step farther in the 2017-2018 season, and divided the season into three story arcs, each with its own brand.

You can do all of that with your writing. It just depends on how creative you are.

So let me boil brand identity down for writers, as much as I can without getting too specific. (Remember, you can do this your own way. You don't have to use mine.)

I'm going to go from the small to the large, because it's simpler to write about—and probably because that's how writers will create their own brands.

Brand Identity For Writers

A Book:

Most writers just brand their books. Writers don't think about their entire business. So let's start with branding a single book.

Note: I'll be doing all of the following on the fly, as you should when you start spitballing your branding ideas.

I'm going to use my standalone first novel, *The White Mists of Power,* as the example. We haven't really done much overall marketing with this book in recent years. It was heavily marketed by one of the last master marketers at a major publishing house when the novel first appeared in the early 1990s.

Definition

The White Mists of Power is what used to be called a high fantasy novel. The labels are more fluid now. For our purposes, the book is set in a made-up world with kings and queens and peasants and magic, but no magical creatures. It shares certain elements with George R. R. Martin's Game of Thrones series, but it lacks elements as well. *The White Mists of Power* is not a series book. It's not as dark as George's books (although my book is not light), and my novel doesn't have dragons.

The White Mists of Power is adventure fantasy fiction with appealing characters in a made-up world, with a lot of magic and a lot of politics.

Target Audience

Off the top of my head, the target audience is: people who liked George's books/TV series; people who like Ursula K. Le Guin's Earthsea; people who like Jacqueline Carey and Victoria Aveyard.

And as I type those names, I realize that in addition to the usual fantasy readers as my target audience, *The White Mists of Power* could be marketed as New Adult. That's an audience that wasn't even defined twenty-five years ago, and it would be new to this novel.

Personality/Voice

The novel's voice is pretty straightforward. The novel's not humorous or light in any way, although it does have music running as a subtheme. The voice is pretty close to my normal voice, so if I were marketing the book, I would use my usual speaking voice.

Brand Message/Tagline

Tougher to do here, off the top of my head. But I'd do something involving politics and growing up. The original tagline, appropriate to 1991, was "An Epic Fantasy About A Bard's Quest For His Stolen Inheritance."

Basic Branding

All of the marketing here will follow the look of the book itself.

Possible Out-of-the-Box Marketing

In addition to the usual stuff—cover branding, blurbs, using key words that would reflect the books I cited above—I might do a Spotify playlist involving music similar to what I would think that Byron the Bard would play. The Spotify playlist would have a thumbnail icon that would either be similar to, or be a small image of, the cover of the book. I would do a few other things that might bring in readers 18-30, who wouldn't even know that the novel exists.

A Series:

Let's go with something very different here. When I first planned this post, I was going to use one of my sf series, but I think my Kris Nelscott Smokey Dalton series is a better teaching tool.

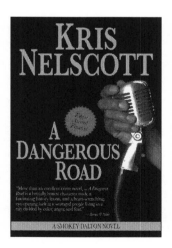

Definition

The Smokey Dalton novels are crime novels, set in the late 1960s/early 1970s with an African-American detective. They are straight private eye fiction, but set in a world rarely seen in modern mystery fiction (even now). The books are historically accurate and veer into noir.

When the books first appeared, the only similar series was by Walter Mosley. His Easy Rawlins series spans decades, though, and is set in a different part of the country. (L.A. for him, and Memphis/Chicago for me.)

Both series are very political, and use historical events as pivots for the mysteries. The Smokey Dalton series is critically acclaimed and award-winning, and has received attention, not just from the mystery press, but the mainstream press as well.

Target Audience

Mosley's readers, of course. Readers of George Pelecanos, because he also uses historically accurate backdrops and African-American characters. James Sallis's readers.

More than those readers, though. African-American readers, not just those who read mystery, but those who read historical fiction and historical novels. Readers of political fiction (and nonfiction) set in the 1960s.

Teachers, librarians, and an audience I've wanted to build—museum bookshop curators. I could easily see these books in the gift shop at the National Civil Rights Museum in Memphis, for example. I suggested this to my traditional publisher, who laughed. WMG will eventually try for this, but hasn't yet.

Personality/Voice

Very serious. Very political. Very focused on equality. Very focused on history as it relates to 2017. If Kris Nelscott/Smokey Dalton was all I was doing, I would be tweeting (more than I do) and writing blogs about Black Lives Matter and Voting Rights and Chicago Southside politics.

Brand Message/Tagline

Again, tough to do off the top of my head, and unlike *The White Mists of Power*, this was something my traditional publisher failed at. I think the tagline would probably be something about Smokey himself—a man who takes justice into his own hands. It would take some refining to get to exactly what I want here.

Basic Marketing

All the Smokey Dalton books have a similar cover design, with different (but similar) art, the same font, the same interior, and a similar pattern to their back covers/interiors. If you look at the books separately, they should appeal to a reader all by themselves. And if you look at the books together, you would see that they are part of a series.

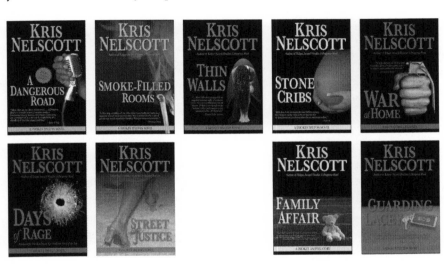

Possible Out-of-the-Box Marketing

I already mentioned the museum shops as possible outside-of-the-box marketing. There are a lot of book festivals that target African-American readers, and I would see if I could get the books on their recommended lists. I would also do articles/advertising/blogs in publications/websites that focus on Civil Rights, the past, and the future.

The Writer Herself:

Initially I was going to use me (Kristine Kathryn Rusch) here, but I'm going to use Kristine Grayson because she's a much more typical writer than Kristine Kathryn Rusch is. Grayson moves outside her genre a little, but not all that far. (Unlike Rusch who goes from nonfiction to noir to goofy fantasy romance to hard sf to damn near anything else that strikes her fancy.)

Definition

Kristine Grayson writes goofy paranormal romance and occasionally goofy fantasy short stories. She writes some YA novels, which are straight fantasy only, about the characters in her romances, and one Middle-Grade short that should have a few more added in. She also has a tongue-in-cheek Western series featuring a married couple that only exists in short fiction right now, but will probably be a novel series at some point. I'm also hoping to write goofy fantasy mystery novels with a romantic element using some of the characters from the Charming series of books.

Grayson has overlapping novel series—the Charming series, the Fates series, and the Santa series. They're unified by the weird use of magic and the irreverent tone. They're also all romances.

Grayson is non-traditional paranormal romance, without shifters and raw sex. Her romances are sweet romances (with some sex, mostly fade-to-black), her mysteries are soft-boiled rather than hard, the YAs don't tackle social issues (hard, anyway), and the books are all tied together by an off-kilter fantasy world in which fairy tales are real.

Target Audience

Readers who want to relax, smile, and not think about the problems of the world. Even with the upcoming mysteries, and in the YA novels, a happy-ever-after ending is guaranteed. Readers can come to Grayson to escape a bad day or a bad year.

Back when I was traditionally published as Grayson, I asked my trad publisher to target the audience of *Once Upon A Time* and other fractured fairy-tale kind of TV shows (there were a lot at that point). The publisher didn't, of course, going only down the romance trade channels, which kinda sorta worked...badly.

Personality/Voice

Goofy, strange, weird. The voice is very strong (and often contradicts itself—or goes off on tangents [Grayson loves tangents] and silly side angles), filled with puns and lots of uncomfortable punctuation (rather like this sentence).

If I were only writing as Grayson, my social media presence would be a lot like the paragraph above. I would also be sharing fun, goofy things—nothing political, nothing dark, and nothing that does anything more than help the readers escape a bad day.

Brand Message/Tagline

Brand message: Everyone needs a happy ending.
Tagline (needs refining): It's not easy to get a fairy-tale ending.

Basic Marketing

All of the Grayson books should have a similar look, but each series should be branded to each other. Maybe the Grayson books would share a font with the author name. Or maybe the similarities would be in layout. (Name always at the bottom, or something.) The books should be recognizably Grayson, though, even if the series are different from each other.

Possible Out-of-the-Box Marketing

Marketing to fantasy readers, especially those who like fairy tales. Maybe even a somewhat different edition that appeals to readers of a different genre.

Genre/Subgenre

If you write a lot of standalone books in a particular genre or subgenre, you can do the kind of marketing I mentioned above for those books, making them a brand by genre/subgenre, even though they stand alone. Think of the Syfy channel here, and how it will be marketing its sf shows.

Or the CW channel, which has a superhero brand going—deliberately—and they cross market (with crossover episodes and everything) deliberately.

That's thinking outside the box.

A Business:

If you have a separate publishing business that publishes your writing, you will need to have different branding and logos for that business. That business will need all of the other stuff—the mission statement, the look, the taglines, and yes, even its own voice.

Thinking about Brand Identity for Writers

I used the examples above just to show you how you should be thinking about your own brand identity. Sometimes you can do all of the above—different brands, different attitudes. Sometimes you can roll the brand identity into one entity, often the writer herself. But that can trap you into one product or one genre.

That's what happened to the Syfy channel. They went too deep into one kind of product, and ultimately it hurt them and lost their core audience. They're rebuilding to recapture that audience.

If you think of yourself as a TV channel, like Syfy or the CW, then you can figure out how to craft your brand identity. Some TV channels have a lot of different programming with different tones (think ABC or the BBC). Some focus on only one thing, like some of the family channels.

Each programming item has its own brand identity as well, but that identity has to mesh with the channel's identity on some level. And then there are the standalone shows—the movies, the specials. Figure out how they fit into the channel as well.

There must be a vision behind your brand identity. Isolating and articulating that vision is 90 percent of branding. Then you can move forward with all of your other ideas.

Since I've been giving you homework, here's some:

Figure out what possible brands you could have. You don't have to do the write-ups that I did above. Just select what kind of brands you're interested in from your own work, and give some general thought about how you would begin your brand identity work.

Good luck!

"Now give us your spontaneous response."

BRAND IMAGE

The publishing industry has been shifting since 2009. Indie publishing has become a force since 2011 or so. At first, we writers were excited simply to make all of our work available. Then we started to do a bit more. However, things that worked six years ago don't work now.

The problem is that the marketing gurus for writers are just other writers with an okay idea. As I've said all along, we writers must accept that we're small business owners and start acting like it.

One way we need to act like business owners is to accept the responsibility for the presentation of our products. I've been writing about that for a few years now, but I've also known that I haven't done everything I could.

It took a few other things to push me forward on branding—not just cover branding (which I dealt with in *Discoverability*) but also with branding the way other businesses do it.

I've been idly noodling on all of this branding stuff off and on for weeks. Some of it comes from planning this series, but most of it comes from where my careers stand at the moment.

Branding is a new area for writers, particularly on the level that we've been discussing throughout this series.

It's something we all need to learn how to control and understand. We're in this same boat together. We're now in the position where we can apply general business practices to our writing.

When it came to branding, writers couldn't do any of this work before. Here's why:

Until the indie revolution, writers ceded all of their promotional efforts to traditional publishing. Fifty years ago, the branding that traditional publishing did was for their own publishing companies. I'm currently reading Robert Gottlieb's book *Avid Reader*. The first section on his career at Knopf is particularly fascinating—and particularly applicable to this series.

Gottlieb worked at Knopf after Knopf's brand had become synonymous with quality literature. The attitude the readers, critics, and booksellers took toward Knopf was that whatever they published was excellent. (I remember this: I grew up in a snobby literary household. A lot of the books we bought were Knopf books—and they were good.) Previously Gottlieb had worked at Simon & Schuster, which had a different reputation.

He writes about the perceptions of the two different companies (and the impact on the work he did) this way.[22]

... I had come to realize that I was not the only one for whom the Knopf name had always held great resonance. Once the house began to show renewed energy, there was no difficulty attracting writers to the home of the Borzoi. The quality of our design and production was a further attraction. Perversely, at first I found this phenomenon unsettling—even a little irritating. Nina [Bourne] and Tony [Schulte] and I had spent so much energy trying to convince the publishing world that Simon and Schuster was a place of distinction—"Please pay attention to A Legacy! Please try Catch-22!"—that we weren't sure how to behave in a situation where everything we published was presumed to carry distinction because we were...Knopf. It was particularly unsettling when books of ours that definitely lacked distinction nevertheless received the benefit of what was something of a free pass. We got used to it, however, the way one always gets used to being spoiled.

What he is writing about here, very clearly, is brand image. Brand image is the way that the customers *perceive* the brand, not the way that the business *markets* the brand. (I'll have a more extensive definition below.)

Back when Gottlieb was at the height of his editorial powers—the early 1960s through the mid-1980s—the publishing companies had distinctive voices and personalities. I remember reading an essay from Stephen King back in the 1980s, when he discussed how much he wanted to be published by a particular company because it was a prestige company (not something that published schlocky genre fiction). I remember feeling both happy that he confirmed my opinion about the company, and concern that he would change his own personal writing style to get into that particular company. (I worried needlessly. He did get the literary acceptance—in this century—for the work he was doing, not the work he thought he should do.)

Traditional publishing companies no longer have the kind of brand recognition that they enjoyed fifty years ago. All of that is due to mergers. The imprints have vanished, the brands are gone. In looking up that Stephen King quote—which I did not find—I saw that he is published these days by Scribner, which was F. Scott Fitzgerald's publisher ninety years ago, and still run by the Scribner family. (The company was founded in 1846.)

In 1978, Scribner merged with Athenaeum. Athenaeum merged with Macmillan in 1984. In 1994, Macmillan merged with Simon & Schuster—yes, the very company that Gottlieb once worked for, and which was once trying to convince the world that it published quality work.

Scribner still tries to hold onto its literary reputation, but it doesn't have one—not in the way it did in the mid-20th century. Its identity has been horribly diluted by all of this merging and messing with the brand.

The same with Knopf. It went through two different mergers in the past twenty years, and while the publisher is still identified by its Borzoi colophon, it doesn't really have the cachet it once had.

Why is this important to what we're talking about here?

Because the attitudes formed in the period of time when publishers had distinct identities still inform writers today. Writers still believe that a publisher will help them promote a book—and one way the publisher used to help promote was with the publisher's own brand.

You knew what kind of book you would get from Harlequin, from Knopf, from Scribner, from Pocket Books. With a handful of exceptions, that is no longer the case.

Buried in that Gottlieb quote was another thing that writers still expect, but which hasn't happened for most writers since the 1990s:

The quality of our design and production was a further attraction.

Part of that design and production was coming up with a brand identity for each writer published by Knopf. Each writer's books had a distinctive look, which also fit into Knopf's brand identity. (Please look at the chapter on brand identity so you can see how this works.)

In those days, when a writer got picked up by another publishing house, the new publisher usually purchased the entire backlist from the previous publisher, and rebranded.

In short, the branding was done by the publisher.

By the time I came into the business as a novelist, in 1991, this trend was slowly dying. So whenever a writer switched publishers, her brand identity ceased to exist.

Some publishers tried to create an illusory brand identity—such as pretend that all of the previous books still mired at other publishing houses did not exist—but readers rarely fell for that.

Writers who got their start in traditional publishing after 1990 or so have no consistent brand identity. None. Only a handful remain lucky enough to have stayed with the same publisher during that time, and those writers might have a consistent brand identity.

I say might because the publishers kept merging, and new editors and new managers came on board, and often the old designs—the old branding —got tossed as newer people took over the publishing house (often to get laid off four or five years later).

Traditional publishing houses no longer have identities. Neither do their writers.

When indie came about, most self-published writers copied what traditional publishers were doing to promote books. And if the traditional publisher was not doing something, writers failed to do it, too.

Some writers had a vague sense that they needed to control their brand identity, and those writers did consistent work on their book covers or their series.

This is where that myth comes from—the one that says the only way to be successful is to write in a series. Everyone knows that a series should have consistent branding, and so series are instantly recognizable. They're easier to market, because they're easier to identify.

If you're a writer like me, though, or like Stephen King or Joyce Carol Oates or any one of a dozen other writers, you don't like playing in the same sandbox each and every day. Your published works are all over the map.

Most writers act like traditional publishers in that instance, and throw up their hands (after eating them first—okay, I hate that phrase, but it's appropriate here). Publishers believe it's impossible to market a writer who writes in multiple genres, with multiple voices, and multiple tones. And because publishers believe it, writers believe it, too.

But it's not impossible to market a multi-genre writer. Fifty and sixty years ago, publishers used to market writers who wrote all kinds of things.

It's all about branding—both identity and image.
So let's talk about brand image now.

Brand Image

The definition of Brand Image from BusinessDictionary.com:[23]

> *The impression in the consumers' mind of a brand's total personality (real and imaginary qualities and shortcomings). Brand image is developed over time through advertising campaigns with a consistent theme, and is authenticated through the consumers' direct experience.*

Okay. There's a lot to unpack in those two short sentences. We'll leave the most fascinating phrase, "a brand's total personality," until last.

But I know some of you read the definition and immediately panicked. *Advertising campaigns?* you thought. *I can't afford an advertising campaign.*

Ignore the word "campaign," and go back to the chapter I did titled, "How To Build A Brand." In it, I explained how branding is advertising, and how you can build a brand slowly. (If you need more ideas, pick up my book *Discoverability* or look at the free [but out of order] posts online.)

The key word in the front part of that sentence isn't "advertising." It's "consistent." Remember, we discussed consistency. In short, write the best books you can (of any genre), and then be consistent in your presentation. Everything from your logo to your typeface to your actual paid advertising (if you have any), even if that advertising is just Facebook ads, make sure you're presenting the same message in similar ways.

Consistency is primarily about quality, though. And the quality is defined by you, whatever you do best. We'll have more on that in future posts, and if this isn't clear, then pick up a copy of *Discoverability*.

The other important phrase in that sentence? "Developed over time." You can't do this fast. No matter how much you want to.

We can't ignore the fact that your brand image is "authenticated through the consumers' direct experience." How many times have you purchased a product only to discover it wasn't as advertised? Sometimes it's better than advertised. And sometimes, it's not as good at all. I can't eat dairy any more. I was happy to discover some vegan cheese that's amazingly good, but so far, I've not been able to replicate pizza, no matter what all the advertising says. (And I'm sorry, chewy and sweet is not what I think of when I think of pizza.)

So you can tell your customers—readers, in our case—that you're giving them the best book they've ever read, but all they'll do is compare your book to all the other books they've read, and you'll probably come up lacking.

Readers make up their own minds about good and bad. What they like about your work might not be what you think at all. So, if you advertise your romantic suspense novel with a bit of humor as chick lit, the chick lit fans will probably hate the book—because your branding, once authenticated by the customer's direct experience, came up lacking.

So, what was brand image for writers before the indie revolution?

It was entirely predicated on the writer's name. J. K. Rowling was quite aware of this when she wanted to write downbeat mysteries. She knew her name was associated with a certain wizard and a certain tone. Her mysteries are nothing like that. So, she tried a secret pen name. Even once she was outed as Robert Galbraith, she kept the name, because that's a signal to readers that the Galbraith books are significantly different than the Harry Potter books.

It's good news for writers that our brand is tied to our names—even now. Because that way, readers will know what they're getting, just by seeing your byline.

Sometimes that expectation is fairly narrow (Harry Potter for J. K. Rowling), and sometimes it's quite wide (all kinds of mystery/suspense/horror/literary genres and subgenres for Stephen King). The consistency isn't necessarily in the genre of the book or even in its characters. It's in the way the writer writes—the way the writer thinks. (More on that in later chapters.)

So...if you've been publishing for quite a while, like most of us who started in traditional publishing, you have a brand image. It might be small, known only to a handful of readers, but their experience with your work gives them an opinion about what you do.

Please note that sometimes the experience they have with your work is like my experience with *The Walking Dead*. I know the TV show exists. I know lots of people love it. I also know I will never, ever, ever watch it, no matter how many times someone implores me to do so.

That brand image is both a positive and a negative thing. I have judged *The Walking Dead* and determined it's not for me, based on reviews, advertising, clips, and the conversations of my friends. I won't sample it any further. My perception of the show (true or not) is that it is not Kris-worthy, so I'm avoiding it.

Those of you who are just starting out have no brand image. None. You haven't published anything yet. Or maybe you haven't published enough. One novel does not a brand make.

So let's finally get to that phrase "brand personality."

A brand is an entity, something that exists by itself.

Gottlieb discusses that in the paragraph from *Avid Reader*. There was a perception of Knopf that was separate from everyone who worked there, separate from the building and the actual list. It was a perception that anything with the Borzoi colophon on it was a quality book—whether that was true or not.

Here's the ironic part: even if a reader didn't believe a book published by Knopf was a quality read, the reader didn't blame Knopf. The reader either blamed himself for not understanding what made the book quality or the reader would say something like, "Well, that wasn't up to Knopf's usual standards."

Not that the book itself was bad or unworthy of being published.

Back in the 1960s and 1970s, it would have taken a whole mess of really bad books to convince readers that Knopf was not a high-quality publisher. It would have to take a lot of evidence to show that Knopf was in decline. The house published Nobel and Pulitzer winners in higher numbers than other publishing houses. It also won a lot more of the literary awards other than the bigs. The decline would have had to have been across the board—in reviews, in awards, and in the loss of the really big "quality" writer names before people stopped associating Knopf with quality.

You'll note that this has happened in the past twenty years. Most of you have never heard of Knopf.

The word "personality" should be heartening to you. Because if the writer is her own brand, then the writer's personality becomes an essential part of the brand.

A writer personality is just like a human personality. Wait! It is a human's personality. With all of its quirks and foibles, with its sense of humor and its vitriolic anger. Readers who like a writer (as opposed to a series) expect to see different sides of that writer, just like you expect to see different sides to your friends.

Determining Your Brand Image

Sometimes it's pretty obvious. Newbies have no brand image at all. None. Zero, zip, zilch. No one has heard of you, so you can build from scratch.

If you're a famous writer, you'll see your brand image reflected back to you in the media coverage, reviews, and—if you're traditionally published—in the way your publisher blurbs your books.

If you're a midlist writer or if you're indie or hybrid, you probably have no idea what your brand image is. Amazon reviews aren't helpful, and you won't have media coverage.

At this point, early on in your branding adventures, I would say that you should ignore your brand image. In other words, follow your parents' advice: stop worrying about what everyone thinks of you.

Just do your own thing.

Part of your own thing, though, is developing your brand identity, which we talked about earlier. If you follow the steps in the chapter on brand identity, and if you are consistent about it, you'll be able to control some aspects of your brand image.

Big Business and Brand Image

Big businesses (not publishing) often hire polling companies to determine what a product's brand image is. The polling company does double-blind tests, comparing one product with the business's product, to determine what the consumer thinks.

Unless you're a truly rich writer, you can't afford to do this kind of work, nor should you.

Polling your newsletter subscribers won't help you here. They're a self-selected group of people who like your work. Your brand image includes people who like your work, people who avoid your work, and people who hate your work. Ironically, the same attributes probably govern all three responses.

The only time that brand image should matter to you at this early stage of building your brand is when your brand image goes seriously awry. By seriously awry, I mean things like Chipotle's E-coli problem a few years ago. They were known for fresh ingredients without preservatives, and some of the coverage of the E-coli incidents said that the lack of preservatives caused the E-coli problem.

Chipotle has been doing serious damage control ever since, working very hard to rebuild and repair its brand. Coke did the same kind of rebuild more than thirty years ago now. Some genius came into Coke headquarters and decided to get rid of the signature product, replacing it with another product. That lasted less than a year, and Coke spent nearly a decade rebuilding its brand image. (That's where the phrase Coke Classic came in. Once upon a time, that was what Coke was, and nothing more.)

Writers rarely need that kind of damage control. When they do, it's for something truly serious.

Janet Dailey plagiarized Nora Roberts. (Dailey was having issues in her personal life, and couldn't meet her deadlines, so she tried stealing instead.) Dailey kept her career, thanks to the intervention of one editor who had championed her from the beginning, but Dailey's brand is tarnished even now.

George R. R. Martin is on the cusp of something serious as well. Every year that goes by without a new book in his fantasy series tarnishes his reputation even more. Much of the large fan base he was building has peeled off in disgust. Will they return when (if) he publishes the next book? Probably not all of them.

Is this a serious enough problem for him to worry about? I don't know. I would be worried about it. But I'm a different kind of writer, with a different personality. The same kind of pressures (the whole world is waiting breathlessly for your next work) nearly sank J. K. Rowling, but she managed to get through it. Whether George does remains to be seen.

If you are lucky enough to know aspects of your brand image, you can play to that image in marketing. Use the positive—and the negative—to attract readers. Sometimes going straight into the face of the negative gets the attention you want for marketing.

As an example, let me use my antipathy to *The Walking Dead*. If I were designing an ad campaign for the TV series, I'd do a lot of what the series is doing now—all the positive reviews, all the great comments, all the surprises. But I'd also have one series of ads that would say something like this:

Think The Walking Dead *is all about the zombie apocalypse? Zombies, zombies, zombies all the time? Then you're missing one of the best shows on television about hope, forgiveness, sacrifice, and what it really means to be human. Zombies—they're just a metaphor. Except when they devour your brain...*

That might bring in a few viewers who didn't realize the show has depth.

The Important Difference Between Brand Image and Brand Identity

Brand image is all about the past. Brand image is what people have experienced with your brand. Past tense. You hear it all the time when folks discuss Stephen King. They think he's a horror writer. That's still his brand image to some people. But he's much more than that.

They have no idea what he has written in the last twenty years.

Brand image looks backward.

Brand identity looks forward. Brand identity is all about the future. You build a brand identity. You can change it, too. Slowly, of course. You can rebuild your brand identity—and if you do it right, you'll eventually change your brand image to something that comes closer to what you want it to.

The biggest difference between brand identity and brand image, though, is control. You control your brand identity. You'll never completely control your brand image.

I find those concepts freeing. I would rather be working toward the future than struggling to control the past.

That's why I tell you to write the next book.

When you try to figure out what your fans "want," or what they expect, you're looking backwards. You're saying, What did I do right and how do I do it again? rather than remembering the passion that brought you to writing in the first place.

What you did right, back then, was write without thought to your "fan base" at all. Write the next book, finish it, market it while you're writing the next book, and stop obsessing about what other people think.

Your brand image will take care of itself, particularly as you learn how to market your current projects.

Worry only about your brand image if something goes seriously, horribly wrong. And let me reassure you here—most writers never have a Janet Dailey level problem in their career. The chances of you suffering through a horrible, serious wrong are pretty slim. You're not going to have fiction contaminated with E-coli.

If you're savvy enough to understand your brand image, use that. If you're not able to see what your brand image is, ignore it.

The real key? Stop worrying about it.

Write the next book. Be consistent in your branding. Market as best you can.

Any time you get stuck in the past, you're making a mistake.

Writing is all about the future.

Keep looking ahead, and you'll be just fine.

"Speaking of consumers, I would like to introduce our new VP of Loyalty."

BRAND LOYALTY

I started this series on branding because of this phrase: brand loyalty. I have been getting frustrated with the advice coming from this year's round of marketing gurus, all of them bent on harassing readers into buying a book.

It took me a while to put my arms around what was bothering me about that, besides the personal. I hate getting nagged. I'm sure you do as well.

I own many different businesses, and three of them are brick-and-mortar retail stores. We built the first of those very slowly, with an eye to repeat customers.

Repeat customers are more than just the people who like what we're doing. Repeat customers are the bread-and-butter of any retail business.

Much as I hate to tell you this, folks, as indie writers, you're in retail. You're selling your books directly to the customer. You might use platforms like Amazon, Kobo, and D2D rather than sell off your website, but you're still providing a product to a customer, just like the book and collectibles stores that Dean and I own are doing.

According to the global management consulting firm, Bain & Company, repeat customers typically spend 67 percent more than first-time customers.[24]

Dean and I have owned retail businesses in the past, before we knew each other and after, and we both learned the value of repeat customers, one satisfied customer at a time. I vividly remember one couple who came to the frame shop and art gallery that I owned in the 1980s. They had my then-husband frame a small but delicate piece of art for them. (My ex was an artist when it came to framing; unfortunately, he left that business.) The couple liked the work so much that they decided to have us frame all of their art. They spent about $3,000 per month, 1980s dollars, until their collection was framed. And whenever they bought new art (which was often), they framed it with us.

No one else spent as much, although others came close. After that couple's first test piece. After they decided they liked us.

When Dean started Pop Culture Collectables, his goal was to get repeat customers. (Mine was to get rid of the collectibles that we no longer wanted.) We live in a tourist town. A lot of people come here and destination-shop once a year at their favorite stores. I'm proud to say that Dean's hard work paid off. A large number of folks make stopping at Pop Culture Collectables (both stores) one of the goals of their trip. (They can get items online, but it's not the same.)

Writers build brand loyalty as well, but until just recently, they had no idea they were doing so. As we discussed in both the brand image and brand identity chapters, writers in the past let the traditional publishers build the writer's brand, and those publishers did a piss-poor job of it.

Publishers tried to make book buying all about them, and what they curated, forgetting—or never really realizing—that in publishing, customer loyalty is brand loyalty...to a particular writer.

I envisioned this particular blog series after I read Targoz Strategic Marketing's Reading Pulse survey (courtesy of Randy Ellison). Targoz surveyed almost 3,000 people—readers and non-readers alike—about their reading and book buying habits. (Most studies target readers or heavy readers only.) A lot of the information in the survey confirmed what I already assumed, but I hadn't seen any statistics that backed up my assumptions.[25]

The survey also found some data that was just the same as every survey of book buyers: the number one reason people buy a book is because the book was written by one of their favorite authors. When book buyers purchase a book, 60 percent of those buyers do so because the book was written by "a favorite author or an author [they] had read before."

Study after study backs up that particular piece of data. I've cited other studies that have shown something similar in the past. One of those studies came from a now-outdated Romance Writers of America survey commissioned in 2014. (Outdated because much of the survey had to do with format and where books get purchased.) At that point, romance readers told

Nielsen (who conducted the survey) that the most important factor in deciding which romance to buy was the story (at #1) and the author (at #2).[26]

A Codex Group survey, conducted about the same time, found that "consumers are willing to pay a 66 percent premium for a book by a favorite author over an unknown author."[27]

Doesn't that 66 percent look familiar? It's almost the same as the Bain & Company percentage referring to repeat customers. Huh. Weird. I wonder why (she types with great sarcasm).

It makes perfect sense, because what those readers are doing is acting like a rational consumer. Consumers all have loyalty to certain brands. We all have loyalties to certain brands. Coke or Pepsi? Ford or Toyota? Apple or Microsoft? Amazon or Everybody Else?

Brand loyalty is the holy grail of marketing. Marketers believe that once a customer becomes loyal to a brand, that customer is hooked for life.

Not entirely true, of course. If the brand messes with its main product, then the customer gets peeved. I no longer buy "clean and pure" Ivory soap, because a decade or so ago, some idiot at the company had to justify their phony-baloney job by adding scent to every bar of Ivory. I had used the soap because I'm allergic to scent. I don't use the soap any more, and like any loyal customer who had to go elsewhere, I'm still peeved about it.

I'm sure you have similar stories about things you loved until someone "improved" them.

Brand loyalty exists partly because the brand provides something important that the consumer is looking for. The other reason that customers become brand loyal is that it makes their decision-making easy.

Behavioral psychologists and behavioral economists disagree ever so slightly on whether or not something called "choice overload" causes consumer fatigue/depression/anxiety, but the one thing they do agree on is this: when faced with a lot of choices, consumers often default to the choice that they're familiar with.[28]

We've all done it: we have five minutes in a bookstore at an airport or the book section of a grocery store, and we need a book right now. We start by looking for a writer/series we love. If we don't find that, we search for a writer we like. If we can't find that, then we try someone new. If you're anything like me in that scenario, you're silently cursing, because you don't have time to find the right book. I often walk out when my five minutes is up with no new purchase at all—and I suspect I'm not alone in that.

Brand loyalty—name loyalty—is something that we writers desire, but it's not something that we can simply will into being. And it certainly doesn't come about by bribing your reader.

Customer loyalty can be bought. In fact, customer loyalty is all about "What have you done for me lately"? According to the Retention Science Blog:[29]

> *Customer loyalty can be encouraged and improved by maintaining overall low prices and offering regular loyalty discounts, special offers or multi-buy deals. This will convince your regular customers that you are still the cheapest merchant on the market. In this way it will prevent them from purchasing their products elsewhere.*

Customers are loyal to the price or the deals. Yes, they like the product or the store or the atmosphere, but they can live without all of that if the price is wrong for them.

Brand loyalty is earned. From the same blog:

> *Consumers who are loyal to a brand remain customers because they believe you offer a better service and higher quality than anyone else. This happens regardless of pricing or other financial reasons.*

In fact, the blog points out, that brand-loyal consumers will often try other products marketed under the same brand—even if those products are more expensive than the average product on the market.

Think Apple. Apple's most brand-loyal customers will buy all Apple products, even though they're often the most expensive on the market. Why? It's not just the products, although if the products went downhill, the loyal customers would eventually leave.

It's what CNBC calls "the ecosystem."

Apple integrates its goods and services, and its innovation into a well-designed mesh of stores, apps, and products that make it easy for the customer to move from one service to another. According to CNBC,[30] the "ever-growing, sprawling ecosystem of software and services that allow you to do more with the products if you continue to invest in that ecosystem."

Apple's competitors, for the most part, don't provide a comfortable ecosystem. They're trying to reverse engineer an ecosystem, while Apple had it from the start.

Think about this: the most popular companies in today's business world tend to provide more than a good product at a great price. They provide service, ease of use, adventure, and a way to interact with that system.

That's why Amazon is so successful right now. They, too, have an ecosystem.

What has that to do with writers? We don't provide an ecosystem.

Or do we?

People come to us for stories, entertainment, a certain point of view. What they end up liking is our voice and the way we tell our stories. If we entertain them, they come back. If we provide their favorite entertainment, they wait for our next project, whatever that may be. At this stage, they might become an evangelist for our work, letting others know we exist. This is an organic thing, not something you can force, no matter how much you beg.

Then there are hardcore loyalists, who will buy everything we do. Or they might like one aspect of what we do so much they want all of that thing, whatever it is.

Sometimes, they might perceive your work as unique, even when it falls solidly within a genre or a series of archetypes.

I was listening to Joanna Penn's podcast, The Creative Penn, on a break from this blog, and I came across this snippet from Dan Blank on episode 325 that perfectly illustrates what I mean.[31] He said:

> *I don't really like fantasy books, I don't really like the whole magic and wizard thing, but I love Harry Potter. I'm reading Harry Potter to my six-year-old right now. Again, because Harry Potter to me is not about wizards. It's about friendship, and loyalty, and how you use power, and choices you make in life and all that.*

To him, the Harry Potter books are not fantasy novels. They're something other, something greater than fantasy, which is not something he normally reads. (The entire podcast episode is worth your time, especially if you are focused on building your business.)

He is not a consumer of fantasy novels. He is a reader of Harry Potter. And Harry Potter speaks to him.

Which brings us to one other aspect of brand loyalty for writers. Some writers, like me, write in multiple series, formats, and genres. We also write standalones. My most loyal readers like everything I do. Most of my readers segregate my work either by genre or series or length. (Some don't read short fiction, for example; others don't like horror; and some only prefer one of my series.)

There are layers of loyalty to my brand enmeshed in this. I can't guarantee that "my" readers will buy everything I produce. But I know that some will buy everything in the Retrieval Artist series or my Kris Nelscott Smokey Dalton books or my Kristine Grayson novels. So I have separate newsletters for those to inform the readers of those what I'm doing.

The accepted wisdom is that if you write in only one series, then you will be more successful. And to some extent, that is absolutely true. If you hit on the right series, and if that series has certain factors that make it a recognizable brand.

Harry Potter himself is a recognizable brand. J. K. Rowling has also written mysteries that aren't doing as well as the Potter books but which are still wildly successful by most measures.

However, according to that 2014 Codex survey,[32] the author with the strongest brand loyalty is Lee Child. While his books do not sell as well as J. K. Rowling's Harry Potter series or even as well as John Grisham's books, a stunning 70 percent of Child's fans buy his next book. Compare that with Grisham's fans, 41 percent of whom will buy his next book.

There's a significant difference between Child's books and Grisham's books. Grisham writes many different kinds of books. He writes YA as well as legal thrillers. He writes standalones that are sometimes thrillers, and sometimes straight literary novels. He publishes short story collections. He's written nonfiction at book length.

Lee Child has only written books in the same series about the same character. There's a wide variation in the techniques that Child uses to tell these stories—some are first person; some are third. Some are multi-viewpoint; some are single viewpoint. Some are set in the present; some are set in the past. But they all focus on Reacher, and his response to whatever problem comes his way.

In other words, fans know what they're going to get. They don't have to study the book jacket or read the opening to find out if the book is in a genre that they like. Child minimizes the risk for the buyer by producing very similar products.

It's very smart, and something he did by design. His nearly twenty years of experience in British television taught him how to market a product. It's not fair to say he assembled Jack Reacher, but Child did give thought to building brand loyalty. As someone who worked in television, he knew how to build an audience, which is the first step toward building loyalty.

In a Forbes article by David Vinjamuri titled "The Strongest Brand in Publishing Is...,"[33] Child explains how he thought about getting brand loyalty for his series. I'm not going to quote all of that here because I'd quote a large chunk of the article. So I'm only going to share what I consider to be the most important part of Child's thinking.

He said that the main factor in building brand loyalty is consistency. (He's right, as we discussed in some of the earlier branding chapters.) Here's how he applied that concept to his own writing plans:

> *A series is better than a sequence of [unrelated] books in terms of building brand loyalty. There are two components of loyalty: one is the author and the second is the subject. If you like the author but you're uncertain of the content of the next book, that's an obstacle. It runs counter to the literary view of writing that values originality and growth. Jack Reacher is the same person in every book.*

Child is right about subject matter being an obstacle to a fast purchase. I adore Stephen King, and would count him as one of my favorite writers, but I am not interested in the Dark Tower series. Yet King routinely outsells Child, based on the strength of his imagination and voice.

There's also a danger to consistency as Child applies it here. I was a Jack Reacher fan for about twelve books, but after a while, I grew tired of the very thing that Child calls a virtue here—the fact that Reacher does not change from book to book. I have gone from preordering the next book to not reading the series any longer, because, quite frankly, as a reader, I have become bored.

Do I consider myself a standard reader? Not by any stretch. But I am a fairly standard consumer. I have brands that I like and that I don't want to change (I'm looking at you, Ivory) and brands whose adventuresome spirit I love. I am an Apple user and I love their ecosystem. If they focused on only one product, I'd have moved on by now.

The same with Amazon. Because I live at the ass-end of nowhere, I'm excited to see if the Whole Foods purchase makes it easier for me to get certain kinds of groceries that are simply unavailable here. I trust the Amazon brand to deliver food to me unspoiled, no matter the distance, at a price that I can afford. If Amazon had stuck with books only, like it did twenty years ago, I would not spend as much money with them as I do.

Go back to the earlier chapters. If you are the kind of writer who can write the same thing over and over again and not get bored, then you might be able to develop the kind of brand loyalty that Child is talking about.

I can't. I don't want to repeat myself. So even though I know what he did is very smart, it's not something I can or will replicate. I have to plan my own brand work around that decision.

That said, I am much more interested in building brand loyalty than I am in building customer loyalty. I didn't have the words for this until I started this series.

I don't want people to buy my books because they're discounted or because I keep offering better and better variations of a good deal. I want people to buy my books because they enjoy my books.

My slow-growing newsletter, which is double the size it was last year, gets almost no promotion from me. I want readers to sign up because they're interested, not because I ran some promotion on Twitter.

I'm also aware that a large number of my readers will never sign up for a newsletter, never visit this website, never follow me on Twitter. But they will buy the next book in either a favorite series or in general.

These are the people I'm cultivating. And until 2017, I would have called them fans of my work. I think it's more accurate to say they're brand-loyal customers.

I appreciate them all. My motto is one reader at a time. And do my best to get them to come back to buy more.

How do I do that?

I write the best damn books I can. Everyone's time is precious, including that of readers. They will stop reading an author who no longer entertains them. They will never read an author out of obligation (once they've left school, that is). They all have To Be Read piles that are very high. You want your novels to be one of the books that's actually read, not on the TBR pile.

Remember, folks, writers are the brand here. Your byline is the brand. Not your publisher, not your cover. The name you write under is the brand you are building.

That's important to what comes next.

According to the American Marketing Association, brand loyalty is about the experience a customer has with a brand, not the price the customer pays or what they save.[34]

Remember the ecosystem comments about Apple. Apple provides an all-around experience for its customers. It doesn't just provide a product.

This is a place where writers can excel. More on that below.

Brand Loyalty in General

Let's continue with general brand loyalty for a moment. Here are the things that show up on almost every list of how to get customer loyalty. They are, in no particular order:

1. **Focus on What You Do Best**
2. **Provide Value/Quality**
3. **Be Authentic**
4. **Be Unique**
5. **Make Sure Your Brand is Consistent**
6. **Focus on Customer Service/Make the Consumer Experience Pleasant**
7. **Engage with Your Customers**
8. **Segment and Reward Loyalty Levels**

Or, let's look at it in a different way: brand loyalty is about trust. The consumer trusts the brand to fulfill some need, some promise. One marketer, James Kane, believes that brand loyalty comes about with a "yes" answer to these three questions:[35]

1. *Do you make my life safer?*
2. *Do you make my life easier?*
3. *Do you make my life better?*

Overwhelming and confusing, I know. It's worse if you look at all the websites. A lot of them confuse customer loyalty with brand loyalty, brand image with brand identity, product with company.

I'm going to try to clarify all of this stuff for writers, now.

For the sake of this next section, we're going to consider the writer herself as the brand, not the writer's series. Just the byline.

Brand Loyalty for Writers

Let's start with those three questions, and the word "trust."

To have brand loyalty, the reader needs to trust the writer will provide a great experience. But does that experience make a person's life safer, easier, and better?

Some nonfiction does, automatically. But in this book (and on my blog), we deal with fiction. Does fiction make a reader's life safer, easier, and better?

Absolutely. Fiction gives a reader time to relax, to go elsewhere, to think about other things. In doing so, fiction makes a reader's life easier, and often, by giving just a bit of entertainment, it makes a reader's life better.

Does fiction make a reader's life safer?

Of course. Fiction teaches empathy, for one thing, opens new worlds and new ideas to a reader, and most importantly, makes a reader feel like he's not alone. All of those things—and many more—can make a reader feel safer.

A great author can provide all three to the reader without thinking about it. The writer has no idea how she connects with her readers. The only way she can do so is...

1. Be the Best Writer Possible.

Write at the top of your game with every project. Continue to learn and grow. Try new things. Constantly improve. Become the best storyteller you can. Only write things you're passionate about, and that will make you the best writer you can possibly be.

2. Provide Value/Quality.

Don't put out a half-assed project. Make sure your books are copyedited, your covers are good, and your stories as important to you as possible. Don't write something because someone told you it will sell. Write something because you love it and you want to write about it.

If you write what you love, readers will respond.

3. Be Authentic.

Write what's important to you, not to anyone else. Write from the heart. Even if your writing is in some way flawed, anything that comes from your heart will be one hundred times better than writing that comes from some intellectual "I should write like this because someone told me to" place.

4. Be Unique.

Lee Child dealt with this in the Forbes article I listed above. He said this about the way he created Jack Reacher:[36]

I ignored all the other series. If you start with a laundry list of things then the book won't be organic.

If you want to write something that has been done to death because you love that idea, then write it, but make it yours. If you want to write something that no one else is writing, and you have no idea how to market it (or what it even is), write it, and then figure out how to communicate it to your readers.

5. Be Consistent.

This can mean that you write the same series, genre, or character, if that is what you want to do. But it doesn't mean you have to.

You need to be consistent in the above four points. Your work should always be the best it can be. Make your product branding recognizable—something that screams this is a book by you. (If you'll note, on my novels, the last name Rusch is usually a focal point.)

If you are continually writing what you love, then you will write from a part of you that is uniquely you. That alone will keep your work consistent. Your perspective is yours alone, and impossible to replicate in any way.

Trust the writing process. Trust your work. And trust your readers. They will find what's consistent about your work, even if you can't see it.

. . .

6. Make It Easy for Your Readers to Find Your Work.

We writers don't do normal customer service things. We don't have retail stores (or most of us don't, anyway). We market through other retailers. We are introverts, and we don't like spending hours interacting with people. Many writers don't even like social media or blogging online.

So how do writers provide a good customer experience and/or customer service?

Simple. This is actually what we excel at. The good customer experience happens inside the stories we tell, the worlds we create, the entertainment we provide.

Customer service, though, is a different thing. Make it easy for your readers to find another book of yours. Make sure that you have the opening chapter to another novel at the end of your current novel. If you have a newsletter that you use to update your readers on the next project, put that in your books as well.

Have a static website with easily accessible information on the books/series. (This is where I fail, because I built mine wrong—at least under Rusch. For Nelscott and Grayson, and for my Diving and Retrieval Artist series, I do just fine.)

Figure out what questions your readers usually ask, and set up a FAQ so that those questions get answered easily.

And think about this: if you want something from a writer as a reader, chances are your readers want that from you. Provide it, whatever "it" might be.

7. Engage with Your Readers.

This does not mean you have to spend hours on social media or send out weekly newsletters. Nor does it mean you need to answer every question on Wattpad or do an online Q&A.

Figure out how you want to interact with your readers. I give my readers free stuff, but not in the obvious way. I don't put my books on a retail site for free.

Instead, I run a free piece of fiction—in its entirety—every Monday, and have done so every week since 2011. I post a blog for free every Thursday and have done so, except for a six-month hiatus while I finished a big book project, every week since 2009.

I also do a monthly recommended reading list, based on what I read each month. I had stopped doing that for lack of time, but my readers asked me to bring it back. I had thought that no one was reading it, but the moment I stopped, I got letter after letter after letter asking for its return. I now make the recommended reading list one of my major priorities.

Am I constantly writing, talking to, dealing with my readers one-on-one in a public or social media setting? No. But I do give them ways to interact with my work, which is what I care about. I love sharing my stories, my reading choices, and my thoughts on the industry, and people seem to love reading those things.

This is how I chose to engage with my readers, and they seem to enjoy it, if my email and comments are any indication.

You can find a similar way to engage your readers as well. It might be different from mine, but that doesn't matter. What matters is what works best for you.

8. Segment and Reward Loyalty Levels.

I am leaving that language from brand loyalty posts by other people here, because I don't know how to say it better. What the above phrase means is that you reward readers based on their level of engagement.

I provide a lot of free material on this website because, quite frankly, I was really, really, really poor once. I know how important it is for a reader with no money to have access to something good to read. Sometimes those readers end up in better circumstances and will eventually pay to read my work. Most often, though, they won't. But they will be the biggest cheerleaders of my work. They will point out to others that my work is available for free; they will spread word of mouth about the quality of the product, because they're reading it each and every week.

I learned long ago, though, that some people will pay a great deal for something they value. In addition to the free end of the spectrum, it's important to provide the limited edition/expensive end of the spectrum. There are people who love having an exclusive or one-of-a-kind item, and if you can provide it as a writer, do so.

I did a lot more of that years ago, and am coming back to it. The nice thing about that product is that it makes a great giveaway to a loyal reader who cannot afford something that expensive.

Patreon and other platforms provide a different way to segment engagement—people pay for what they want or pay to support whatever they are interested in. Kickstarter has shown that a handful of hardcore fans can fund up everything from movies to music to novels.

You shouldn't just focus on the people who can afford your work. Nor should you focus solely on those who need low, low prices because they're bargain hunters.

Make sure you provide something for everyone. And give those somethings some thought.

9. Develop an Ecosystem.

J. K. Rowling is doing that very well with the Pottermore website. Pottermore is more than a beautiful website. It's a place to interact with other J. K. Rowling fans, to enter the "wizarding world," to find things to buy, to talk about the books, characters, and ideas in her work. It is an interactive place that brings fans together.

She doesn't run the site personally, but she does oversee it, and it was her idea.

You can do something similar, if you so choose, or you can figure out other ways to create an ecosystem. Sometimes simply releasing story bibles or ephemera or cut scenes will fill this same gap.

The Biggest Key to Brand Loyalty

Acknowledge that you are a brand. Build it one reader at a time. Know that your readers are people, not numbers on your newsletter.

And remember this lovely statistic, courtesy of the Kellogg School of Management at Northwestern University:[37]

Up to 15% of a business's most loyal customers account for 55-70% of its total sales.

It's not how many people buy your books that's important. What's important is how many of those people read and like your books. What's even more important than that is how many of those readers return to your next book, and your next, and your next.

Stop chasing big numbers of downloads or newsletter sign-ups. Start thinking about providing value to your readers.

Then you need to value each reader—even if you only have ten of them. Someday, those ten readers will become twenty, those twenty readers will become 100, those 100 readers will become 1,000.

To put it in retail terms, you want repeat customers. You want to be a destination writer, just like our retail stores in a tiny tourist town are destination stops for people on their annual vacation.

If you think of your readers as people, if you remain grateful for their willingness to spend their hard-earned time and dollars on you, you're on the road to building a brand that will inspire loyalty.

Just remember: one reader at a time.

"After a few false starts I have finally finished
my business marketing plan."

DEFINE YOUR TARGET AUDIENCE: THE INTERMEDIATE STAGES

In the past eight or so years since indie publishing took off, writers found that the commodity they lack the most is time. Time to write. Time to research. Time to read. Time to market.

We get inundated daily with shoulds and have-tos. Someone is always so much more successful than we are, and they're successful at something we've wanted for a long time.

Then there are the overnight sensations, the folks who claim to make $50,000 to $100,000 per month on their writing, even though they have only published five or fewer books. They have some kind of marketing system, and 100,000 people on their newsletter list. They have figured out how to game Amazon's algorithms or they're the first people to use that brand-new marketing tool (cough: Facebook ads) that some gigantic corporation has come up with. Or the first to use it effectively.

They promise: if you only follow these five steps, you, too, can make $50,000 to $100,000 per month on your writing as well.

Only it never works that way. First of all, there's no way to know if the folks who claim to have a working system actually do have a working system. There's also no way to know if that $50,000 to $100,000 they earned in one month was for just one month or if they consistently earn at that level.

Have they done it for four months? A year? Five years?

Because, I don't know about you, but what I care about in this business is staying in it for the rest of my life. That means building a business, not being an overnight sensation. (Or, becoming, as the music industry so aptly calls it, a "one-hit wonder.")

This book and my blog are geared toward the career writer, not the person who is in it for a fast buck and will leave when the going gets rough. (As many of my readers have noted in my comments and emails, the gurus of 2011 and 2012 have mostly disappeared. Even their websites are down. The ones who have survived have transitioned to career writers and generally don't use gimmicks any more.)

Sure, it would be great to have $100,000 month. You can bet that if I have that kind of spike on five books, I'll be banking the money for a rainy day. I will hope that the money will continue. I will bet that it won't.

Because I have earned that much money in a month off and on throughout my career, and I've learned that what goes up does come down.

The nice thing is, though, if you build your writing career properly, what comes down doesn't come down as far as it had before.

Here's what a proper income spike should look like:

In other words, you have a sales spike, and while you will lose many of those readers, you will keep quite a few of them. You'll end up with more regular readers than you started with. Provided you have a good product that inspires brand loyalty—which is something we dealt with in the previous chapter. Brand loyalty, for writers, is generally to the writer's byline, not to the publishing house or genre or anything else. Sometimes brand loyalty is to a series or a series character. But for the sake of our purposes in this series, think of your author name as the brand, and everything else will fall into place.

When I wrote the initial target audience chapter, I assumed that you either had no idea who your audience actually was or were so new that you had no audience. Today's chapter assumes you have an audience, but you have no idea who they are.

Now, a lot of what I write in these branding chapters takes into account the fact that none of us have any time. Most of us lack the big bucks that major corporations have as well. So doing some of the market research things that marketing and advertising blogs tell you to do to figure out who your audience is are things that we either don't have time to do or the funds to pay someone else to do it.

Besides, how many of you want to send out newsletters or updates to readers, asking them to take marketing surveys? Think about it from a brand perspective. How annoyed would you be if your favorite author wanted all of your personal data so that she could sell to you and people like you better than she already is?

If my favorite author was a nonfiction writer who was a marketing guru and her topics were only about marketing, I probably wouldn't be annoyed. But if my favorite author was a Regency romance writer who had never contacted me before…well, at best, I'd ignore the email. At worst, I'd make a little mental note of my annoyance and do a small compare/contrast: is it still worthwhile to me to buy her books after she annoyed me? Probably yes. But if the annoyance continued…

So how do you find out about the audience you already have? And how do you find out about the audience you might be able to build?

The answer is both simple and hard. You take the information you already have available to you, extrapolate from it, and continue to pay attention to the world around you to gain even more information.

Sounds straightforward. But what does all that mean? What information do you have already? You probably had no idea you have information, except—if you're lucky—emails from readers who liked your work. And please, don't email them back asking them for personal details. Just thank them for taking the time out of their day to make your day a bit brighter.

So, let's find out about your audience by using my audience. (Remember, I'm doing this branding series for myself, to apply the marketing knowledge I have from other businesses to my fiction business. So, I'm multitasking—using what I know to help explain the concepts I'm dealing with here, and educating myself in my own branding at the same time.)

I write two different science fiction series. Right now, I'm deep in my Diving Universe series, a space opera set far from Earth. The stories have a strong female protagonist, a bit of time travel, and lots of action, but also quite a bit of hard sf as well.

How do I find out who my existing audience is?

I look at the also-boughts on Amazon. As I wrote this chapter, I looked in real time at two different books—the first novel in the series, *Diving into the Wreck*, and the third book in the series, *Boneyards*.

The first thing I look at to do audience research is the also-boughts on Amazon and the other e-retailer sites that have also-boughts. Several apps will do this for you. But in the beginning, do it yourself. It helps with your understanding of marketing.

In addition to my own books in the also-boughts (Yay! That means people who liked this book bought other books of mine), I want to know who I share my readers with.

On *Diving into the Wreck*, I find Linda Nagata's brand-new novel (yikes! I need to pick that up), Ann Leckie's newest novel, a writer I've never heard of named Laurence Dahners, John Scalzi, Tanya Huff, Lindsay Buroker, C. J. Cherryh, Sharon Lee, Lois McMaster Bujold, and on and on for another hundred novels or so.

What do these names tell me? They tell me a lot, actually. Here's what I can see just from the names listed.

•I have hardcore sf fans among my readership. They know some classic authors like C. J. Cherryh and Lois McMaster Bujold. They're also up-to-date on the new classic writers, like Ann Leckie.

•My readers buy military sf. Linda Nagata's book is military sf, and farther along in the list, some Mike Shepherd books appear. They're also military sf.

•My readers love space opera. Lois's books are both military sf and space opera, but they lean more toward space opera (in my opinion). C. J.'s are also split between military and space opera, leaning more toward space opera. Ann Leckie's Ancillary Justice series is modern space opera (which is space opera with a touch more hard sf). If you scan through the list, you'll find a lot of space opera in the also-boughts.

•My readers like books with strong female protagonists. The Tanya Huff book covers feature a woman with some kind of futuristic gun (remove the gun, and the covers could work for some of my Diving books).

•My readers like sf with crime in it, as witnessed by the John Scalzi novel on the list.

•My readers like series books. In addition to reading everything in the Diving series, the also-boughts show a lot of repeat names, as readers work their way through other series.

•My readers are adventurous. These also-boughts are all over the sf (and fantasy) map. The books include *New York Times* bestsellers, award-winners, and brand-new indie writers launching their very first series.

I could go on, but I'm not going to.

With the first book in the series, I can see the also-boughts of the people who decided to try the series. But what about the people who are sticking with it? After all, they are my actual audience.

By *Boneyards*, there are a lot more Rusch books in the also-boughts, which pleases me. Linda Nagata reappears right away, as does Lindsay Buroker, Mike Shepherd, Sharon Lee, Tanya Huff, and Lois McMaster Bujold. But some other writers have bumped their way up the list, like Robert J. Sawyer, Yoon Ha Lee, and Elizabeth Moon. Again, lots of books in series, lots of military sf and space opera, less fantasy, and some very hard sf, more than with the first book.

Not a surprise to me, because the Diving series is written in a very challenging fashion—mixing first and third person, past and present tense, time periods all over the map, and a complex backstory.

I'm able to refine, just from that short glance alone, what the Diving readers are looking for. I can't go wrong in assuming that the readers of the Diving series want space opera, a little bit of military sf, and some hard sf as well. They're not afraid to read some challenging works. There's a lot fewer fantasy novels on the list (except for some of mine) as we get to *Boneyards*, so this is a purely sf series.

Let's compare that with my Retrieval Artist series. That's a more mature series—fifteen books long as opposed to six—with a genre mix (detective plus science fiction). I glanced at the first book in the series, *The Disappeared*, and a middle book, *Anniversary Day*.

Some differences between Diving and Retrieval Artist show up almost immediately. Two and a half screens of also-boughts on *The Disappeared* before another name besides mine shows up. Most of those also-boughts are the rest of the Retrieval Artist series. (That happened with Diving, too, but there are fewer books in that series.) Then the Diving series shows up with one book, some fantasy books of mine, and finally...Andy Weir, William Gibson, Elizabeth Moon, that John Scalzi novel again, and a few pages down, Lois yet again.

No military sf at all. Very little space opera. No obviously strong female protagonists. Fewer female sf writers. Harder sf and sf that combines detectives and mystery stories. Some challenging writers who appeal to the hardcore sf reader. A similar audience with crossover, but not the same audience at all.

By *Anniversary Day*, the middle of the series, Andy Weir is nowhere to be seen. A lot more John Scalzi, some Walter Jon Williams, and even Connie Willis has joined the list. Ann Leckie is back as is Linda Nagata. Nathan Lowell is on the list along with James S. A. Corey and David Drake.

A bit of military sf, then, but not much. Space opera, some award-winning writers, even more challenging hard sf works, and a lot of cross-genre mystery works. Fantasy combined with mystery, sf combined with mystery. So the mystery is an attraction but the worldbuilding is as well, since there are no contemporary or historical mysteries in the also-boughts.

That surprises me. I would have thought that mystery readers would have crossed over. But they haven't. Fantasy readers have (also surprising to me) but not mystery readers.

One cannot assume, in doing this work.

Different platforms have different information. I went from Amazon to Kobo to see if they ran also-boughts. They don't call the books listed with mine as also-boughts. They're called "related titles" and they feature an entirely different group of authors and series. (I'm suspecting they are also-boughts, since not all are on-point with genre.)

The names here also give me a lot of information about how Kobo, at least, perceives my audience for these works. If the books listed below are, in fact, also-boughts, then I see how different the international audience is from the U.S. audience.

I could do this all night, and so could you, but suffice to say there's enough information in the also-boughts and related titles surrounding your work to give you the glimmerings of an understanding about your current audience.

But the title of this chapter is your target audience. You want to grow your readership, right? Then you target the readers of the writers on your also-bought list. In the bad old days, you would have had to buy a list or market blatantly (Readers Who Love Lois McMaster Bujold Will Love Kristine Kathryn Rusch!)

You don't have to do that now. If you do paid ads on Amazon, you can target readers who buy books by authors on your also-bought list in your ad buy. You can do the same with Facebook ads and all kinds of other paid advertising that relies on algorithms.

That's just the tip of the iceberg. There are many other things you can do. If you're new or if you're rebranding your series or if you're writing a new series, you can make your covers similar to the covers of the books in your also-bought list. That's why Tanya Huff's book covers could work (with slight modification) for my Diving series—especially the Diving covers done by the original traditional publishing house a long time ago.

Looking at also-boughts is just one technique among a thousand to help you figure out your current audience.

If you know your genre and subgenre, you might be lucky enough to find marketing surveys that list the "average" reader of that genre. The Targoz Reading Pulse survey that started me down this branding road has an entire section on the "average" reader. I got Randy Ellison's permission to share some of that with you throughout this series.

For example, almost all reading and book buying surveys find that women buy more books than men. Some surveys find that women also read more books than men. I'm not sure if that's accurate. The buying more books than men makes sense, because all marketing surveys find that women generally do the purchasing if they're in a committed relationship. That goes for everything from groceries to tools.

There are a million simplistic articles online as to why, including some stupid articles that say women like shiny objects which is why they spend more money. (Seriously!)

But the real reason is more utilitarian. From a 2013 article in Forbes by Bridget Brennan, an expert who spends her entire career studying shopping patterns:[38]

> *In virtually every society in the world, women have primary care-giving responsibilities for both children and the elderly (and often, just about everybody else in-between). In this primary caregiving role, women find themselves buying on behalf of everyone else in their lives.... If you're in a consumer business, it means that women are multiple markets in one. They are the gateway to everybody else.*

Since I know that more women buy more books than men, and I also know that the readers of my Diving series buy a lot of books by women and with women on the cover, I would assume that the majority of my readers are women.

But I don't know that for a fact, and the Reading Pulse survey makes me reconsider my assumption with this little tidbit:[39]

> *Science Fiction & Fantasy (SFF) is one of the few genre subsets that has a majority male readership (68% male). The average SFF reader is a married 30-year-old (55%), college educated (52%) male who is a moderately active reader (38% read 12 or more books a year, and 35% read 5–11 books a year), buys a moderate number of books to*

match (20% buy 12 or more books a year, and 32% buy 5–11 books a year), and cares about convenience above all else.

A quick mental double-check of the fan mail I've received, a scan of my Twitter followers, and my other social media interactions makes me realize that I have a lot of readers who fall into the demographic listed by the survey.

The survey goes on to show that these readers read a lot of series and tend to buy a lot of ebooks for the convenience. Which leads me to think about the fact that my also-boughts are filled with other books from the same series, and then books from other writers' series, again, backing up some of the information in the survey.

How do I use this? We'll deal with that more in some of the following chapters, but the first way to use it is to leave my assumptions at the door. I'm not just marketing to women when I market sf books. I'm marketing to a largely male audience, who loves books in series.

Does that mean I should stop marketing to women? Heavens, no. But it does mean I should expand my own thinking about marketing my work to include the male readers, maybe more than I already have been.

There are other ways to use this information as well. If and when I plan to rebrand the covers of these series, I might consider a bit more military sf covers for Diving and some more noirish covers for Retrieval Artist. Or see what the current crop of covers for other books are at the time.

I might end up gearing my Diving promotions more toward the space opera crowd, and my Retrieval Artist promotions more toward the mixed mystery and fantastical world crowd. I have choices, now that I understand what the readers like about the series.

I've only used a few pieces of information here to show you about target audience. There's a lot more information out there—such as the marketing studies for movies in the same genre or for similar TV shows (*Star Trek, Stargate,* and *The Expanse,* anyone?) All of that becomes useful in dealing with the midrange target audience—the existing audience.

As I said above, we're all pressed for time, and simply using some of these simple tricks will refine your marketing to reflect your target audience. And to grow your audience by appealing to the readers who like similar works.

What you want to do is get those readers to sample your work, but you don't want to give that work away. You want the readers to value your work enough to buy the next book, not wait for another freebie.

How do you do that? There are a million marketing tricks. For example, the first book in the Retrieval Artist series is cheaper than the other books by a significant amount (but still expensive enough that I can occasionally discount the book for a Book Bub or some other promotion).

I have introductory bundles for Diving and the Retrieval Artist so that readers can buy the first three books in both series for less than buying the books individually.

And I often participate in promotions like a Storybundle, which unites writers of similar works. The hope is that readers who are fans of one of us will buy the bundle to get ten books for $15 (and support a charity), and read my book, decide they like my work, and buy more of it.

That's another way to do cross promotion with other authors. It works, too. I noted that on one of my Retrieval Artist books, there was a sprinkling of Rebecca Cantrell's work. That makes sense—she has a series that mixes crime with the fantastic, and that's the work that appeared on the also-bought list.

Good marketing really is a science, but we're writers. We only have time to do so much.

Fortunately, a lot of folks are making data collection easier and easier for us, so that with just a bit of knowledge, we can use newly created tools to our own advantage.

You just have to be willing to spend an afternoon delving into your own readership—without bothering the readers themselves. Their purchasing habits have provided you with enough clues to move forward on your branding and your marketing—without losing too much writing time to all this advertising work.

Don't be intimidated by this. Remember, you can get your marketing wrong—and probably will. But the key isn't to do perfect marketing. The key is to try, maybe fail, try again, maybe succeed, and then keep trying all kinds of things.

However, keep in mind that your most important job is to write the next book. You want to see those also-boughts filled up with your own work, like mine are. Because that means that readers liked what they read and went on to buy the other books you've written. The more books you have for them to find, the more they'll buy. The more they buy, the more likely they are to become regular readers.

And, as I mentioned in the brand loyalty chapter, the regular readers are the ones who become brand loyal. Returning customers are more than 60 percent of every single retail business.

They should be part of yours as well.

Don't forget them in your search for new readers. Remember to acknowledge your faithful readers, because they are the ones who put the food on your table. They're the folks who already form your audience, and they're the ones who deserve your loyalty in return.

How? Well, that's a topic for another chapter.

But do say thank you every now and then. Because you wouldn't be where you are without them.

He had reduced his business strategy
panic attacks to under three hours.

HOW TO BUILD A BRAND: THE INTERMEDIATE STAGES

I'll be honest with you: I struggle with these branding posts. Not because I am unfamiliar with what I'm writing about. I know this topic inside out, upside down and backwards. I've built two publishing companies. I've built retail companies. I've worked in advertising. I've worked for places that were so aware of their brand…that they knew when a topic or a product deviated from that brand in a harmful way.

Unfortunately, the way that traditional publishing was—and is—structured, writers who work in that part of the industry have no control over their brand at all. (I can think of 1.5 exceptions—James Patterson took over his marketing right from the start, so he always controlled his branding; Lee Child also gave branding a lot of thought, but left the actual marketing to the publisher. He's the .5 in the equation here.)

So as I wrote these posts, I felt a deep frustration. Because my brand, in almost all of its forms, is extremely messy. Kristine Kathryn Rusch writes all over the map, but was never marketed as a writer whose focus is diversity (in content as well as in genre). Kris Nelscott's traditional publisher was so frightened of my skin color and my topic that they never ever came up with a consistent cover brand, let alone a marketing plan. Kristine Grayson's two traditional publishers had diametrically opposed marketing plans for the books. (The first one worked; the second one…didn't.)

I'm frustrated because I'm trying to fix something that is badly broken in my own career. Many other writers—once traditional and now hybrid or indie—have the same problem. And God forbid if we have tried different genres or had series abandoned in the middle. Traditional publishing was, in its way, antithetical to any kind of consistent branding, at least for the midlist writer, at least in the past twenty years.

These posts, as I said from the beginning, are for me, writing to myself about all the various things I can do to improve my branding or, in most instances, take control of it.

The simplest way for me to take control of my branding would be to pare down everything I do under Rusch to one series, one subgenre. That's what Lee Child does. If I had his Jack Reacher series, I could easily rebrand it, take over the advertising, take over the brand idea and brand identity, and create something unique.

Believe me, I've thought of that. Not for Rusch, but for Grayson, and for Nelscott. I'm refining those latter two brands a bit.

But I have a hummingbird brain. I alight on different things at different times. I read that way, too. I'm not the person who can do the same thing day after day, year after year for the rest of my life.

If I were in the lucky position that most of you indies are in, I could define my Rusch brand from the beginning as something that spans genres, that uses a multitude of styles, that promises quality of a certain type, but never compromises on some things.

I would make my hummingbird brain—my tendency to mix up genres and styles and moods—a huge part of the branding.

I'll be doing that going forward, of course, but that feels a bit to me like closing the barn door after the horses got out—decades ago. (Hell, in this metaphor, that barn might not even have a door any more. It's toppling, needs paint, and maybe needs to be torn down so we can build a brand-new barn. {sigh}.)

I find the topic overwhelming, never more so than in this particular chapter: How to Build a Brand: The Intermediate Stages. The intermediate stages are, technically, where I am, on everything.

Only the foundation I'm building on—in the marketing side—is wobbly. The foundation—on the writing side—is so solid that you could take a jackhammer to it and you wouldn't even chip the concrete.

This is the point where I remind you that everything we discuss in this book is about marketing, which you should never, ever, ever take into your writing office.

If you write what authentically interests you, you will develop an audience. If you decide that you're going to write Jack Reacher-light because it worked for Lee Child, and that's the only reason you're going to write it (a marketing reason, by the way), then you will fail at developing any kind of audience.

And as we've seen in previous chapters, what you want is a loyal audience, one that returns over and over to your work because they love it, not because your work is cheap or because they're waiting for the next Reacher novel and yours will do in the interim.

So…remember. Everything I'm discussing here is about marketing, not writing.

In the first how to build a brand chapter, I explained a lot of the ideas and terms I'll be using in this chapter. If you haven't read the previous chapter, you should do so now.

In that chapter, I assumed you were building your brand from scratch. Maybe you had a few books or a series or a couple of series, but you had done no marketing, really, and hadn't done anything more than considered branding your covers.

For this chapter, I'm going to assume you've been at the writing game for a while. You did the work from the previous chapter on identifying your existing audience, and now you're going to try to make use of that information somehow.

To review, here are the steps to building a brand, no matter what stage we're discussing:

1. **Define Your Business**
2. **Define Your Target Audience**
3. **Research Similar Businesses**
4. **Figure Out What Makes Your Brand Unique**
5. **Figure Out What Your Brand Is Not**
6. **Create a Brand Mission Statement/Tagline**
7. **Be Consistent**
8. **Be Patient**

Because of what we've been working on, I'm going to assume you've defined your business. I'm also going to assume that you now know who reads your books. (As well as you can know it, without doing expensive market research.)

So, let's move forward, shall we? We're going to use my work as the basis of brand building here, and we're going to do it on my two series that I mentioned in the previous chapters.

Before we get there, though, let me be clear: what I'll be doing on branding the Rusch business incorporates all of my Rusch books and all of my various Rusch series. In 2010 or so, I gave serious consideration to pruning my existing series and work down to one or two items.

I decided against it, not just because of my hummingbird brain, but because of my existing audience. I have readers who read everything I do. I have readers who only read the mystery short stories, readers who only read the fantasy books, readers who only read the time travel stuff—and readers who only read the nonfiction.

If I pared down to my two big science fiction series, I would be losing readers rather than gaining them.

That said, my series themselves are brands, with loyal readers who eagerly anticipate the next book. I'm not going to look at Rusch as the brand here, but at the series as the brand.

Unlike the previous chapter, where I looked at the series separately, here I'll look at them together.

Research Similar Businesses

As I mentioned in the original "How To Build A Brand" post, it's almost impossible to research other writers. We're still in the early stages of writers accepting that they are a business, let alone branding themselves as one.

However, I'm going to assume I did the due diligence on wider business brands—TV, gaming, movies—of a similar type.

Now, we'll deal with similar businesses that my existing readers liked. That means looking at the other series and authors listed in the also-boughts on my books (listed in the previous chapter).

Look at the covers, look at the way those series (or authors) are being branded, see if there are any similarities with your work, and then see if there's anything those other writers/series are doing on marketing that you can do as well.

Mostly, you'll be looking at covers, blurbs, where these writers got reviewed, whether or not they advertise on websites or do Facebook marketing, that sort of thing. Is the first book in the series lower priced? Is there a hook that seems similar?

A lot of that research factored into the previous chapter. I learned about the readers and what they're interested in from the also-boughts, and showed you how to do the same. (There are other ways to go about it as well—market surveys, surveys that the film and TV studios do, demographic information in *Ad Week* and other places that will also help you research, if you're so inclined. There are many online tools that will help you as well. Because those tools change daily [it seems], I'm not going to list them here.)

Figure Out What Makes Your Brand Unique

In your research (above), you're looking for similarities. But while you use those similarities for things like keywords and Amazon ads, you also need to know how to separate your work from the works in the also-boughts.

What makes your series/work different from those others?

In the case of my Diving series, a lot of the also-boughts are space opera or military sf (or both), but very few of them have time travel, and even fewer have the rather literary writing style that (for some reason) my brain keeps insisting belongs in this series. Also, the Diving series continues to win readers awards and also exists in shorter formats (short stories, novellas). While most of the series that are in the also-boughts started as shorter works, almost none of them have produced shorter works in the series once the series started.

How I'd use that, besides helping with the newsletter or Free Fiction Monday, I have no idea. But I'm sure I can come up with something.

As for the Retrieval Artist, most of the sf detective series follow the same-old, same-old plotline—detective encounters something weird, detective explores the something weird, detective solves the something weird.

The Retrieval Artist series, from the start, has been modeled on Ed McBain's 87th Precinct series, as well as Elizabeth George's Inspector Lynley series (which is incorrectly named). Both series feature multiple characters and often focus on one of the side characters without exploring the main character.

Unlike those two mystery series, though, I decided (for some reason) to try every subgenre of mystery in the Retrieval Artist series—from cozy to police procedural to locked room to thriller. The *Anniversary Day* saga was supposed to be one standalone thriller novel. Hah! Fooled me. Because I was dealing with sf, I couldn't use shorthand to explain anything, so the single book became three, then became six. And that's worth marketing all on its own.

There are a lot of similarities to the other series/works on those also-boughts, but there are a lot of differences as well.

When you go through yours, make two lists—one of similarities and one of differences. You'll be surprised at the things you'll dig up.

Figure Out What Your Brand Is Not

In doing the work of discovering similarities and differences, you'll figure out what your brand is not. You'll actually see it pretty clearly.

The also-boughts confirmed what I already knew about the Retrieval Artist series. It's not military sf by any stretch. Sometimes it's not space opera either. Even though it doesn't have the literary stylistic tricks that Diving has, the Retrieval Artist series falls into the very center of the sf genre, which is why writers as diverse as Robert J. Sawyer and Connie Willis are on the also-bought list.

Even though I think of Diving as hard sf, the readers don't. The hard sf writers/series in my also-boughts are writers like Linda Nagata, who writes hard sf, but with a military slant. Mentioning the core of the sf field is probably a lot less important to the Diving readership than it is for Retrieval Artist.

Some of the things that the books are not seem obvious to me, but wouldn't to readers. While Diving is adventure fiction, it is more Christopher Nolan than *Pirates of the Caribbean*.

The Retrieval Artist books are more mystery than sf, even though they wouldn't exist without their sf setting. The Retrieval Artist books always do what mystery novels do—they put order on chaos. Whatever the major problem is in those books, that problem gets resolved by the end.

But, because mystery readers are loathe to cross to sf, marketing to pure mystery readers is not what I should do in the intermediate stage here. Because, as the also-boughts show, pure mystery readers aren't crossing over.

However, readers who like mystery in their sf and fantasy are crossing over, so more of the marketing should focus on them.

Create a Brand Mission Statement/Tagline

I resist doing that for each series because of who I am. It limits me creatively as a writer.

But as a writer brand—Rusch—the mission statement/tagline is something like "All genres all the time." Or "expect something different." Or something along those lines.

Of course, I haven't been able to develop that organically from the beginning of my writing career (like so many of you indies can), so I'm reverse engineering this part.

As I was researching this part of the chapter, I did find two cool mission statements for existing brands. I had forgotten all about Apple's mission statement, which also served as its tagline for years: *Think different.* Which continues to define what they do. They're not just a tech company. They're constantly trying to change how we live our lives. Trying to be different.

The other cool mission statement that I found comes from Nike. Their advertising tagline is *Just Do It*, which, quite honestly, I love. I find it inspirational in a good way.

But that's not their mission statement. Their mission statement is this: *To bring inspiration and innovation to every athlete in the world.*

You see it in their products. Their product lines run from the person who walks to work and doesn't put out much effort to the elite athletes who sign endorsement deals with them.

That statement informs everything they do.

Which is why I'm really clear about Rusch. My mission statement for Rusch is my mission statement for life. I need to challenge myself constantly, trying new things, experimenting and growing. That's who I am as a person and as an artist.

The mission statement for Grayson is easier: *It's Not Easy To Have A Fairy Tale Ending.* Grayson will always be goofy paranormal with a touch of romance, usually focusing on myths and fairy tales.

And for Kris Nelscott—realistic hard-boiled fiction from the not-so-distant past. That's not a great mission statement because I haven't refined it. But the Nelscott books deal with the search for justice in a world filled with injustice. I'm so certain of that brand that even though I set some stories in the 1960s and 1970s, I can tell you if they're a Rusch story or a Nelscott story from the theme.

Nelscott is not quite noir because my protagonists get justice in every book. They don't necessarily do so legally, however. But they do "win," and they do their best to be heroes, even in a world that doesn't accept them as such.

Have fun figuring out your mission statement. And realize that it might change down the road as your view of your own art changes.

Be Consistent

I pretty much said what I needed to in the first chapter about Building a Brand. Just because you now know who is reading your books doesn't mean you should change anything. In fact, you're building just fine with what you're already doing. Just keep doing it.

If you want to see consistency on a smaller level—the cover level—look at Allyson Longueira's blog on WMG Publishing's website. She examines how she, as an award-winning graphic designer, thinks when she establishes the cover branding for a series of books. She uses art and examples. Take a look.[40]

Be Patient

You're still learning and growing as a business person. You may not get a lot of result from your branding…yet. What you're trying to build is brand loyalty, and that takes years.

Inc.'s website has a good short article from 2013 about building a brand.[41] The article emphasizes that it's not the external features of the brand that are important, but how the brand makes the consumer feel. Does the brand give the consumer a positive feeling (as in *Oh! I love the last book. I want this new one*)? That's the ideal.

What I love about this article, though, is this analogy:

> *Your brand is like a bank account. When you delight customers, it adds value to the brand. If you have a string of great products, customers will forget the occasional flop. Apple is a case in point. Few people remember that they've had some real stinkers.*
>
> *Similarly, when you irritate customers, it extracts value from the brand, and eventually you end up overdrawn and even if you change your ways and come out with some great products, it may take years, if ever, for customers to forget the taint.*

Building a brand happens slowly, one product at a time, one interaction at a time, one customer at a time. You can't force a quick reaction. In fact, if you try, you'll probably make a bad impression.

Think of all the complaints that readers are making about that sharing of newsletter lists among writers. That's making a bad impression, just like constantly haranguing your readers to buy, buy, buy your same five products is also making a bad impression. The brand then becomes associated with something bad, not something good.

Character Matters

There's still a lot of marketing psychobabble here, stuff that makes most writers run and hide. I found the perfect way to think about a brand for writers, though, in an article called "How To Build A Brand From Scratch" by Seattle marketing firm Audience Bloom.[42]

The post's author Jayson DeMers has this lovely analogy right smack in the middle of the article:

Instead of thinking of your brand in the colorless term of a "corporate identity," instead, think of your brand as a human being—a fictional character. What would this person be like in real life? How would they talk? What would they look like? How would they dress, walk, and act in different situations? Can you see this person making a good impression with your target demographics? Why or why not? Make adjustments accordingly, and sculpt your character as you would for a character in film or literature.

He then points out that, for years, Apple used this very concept in its Apple versus PC ads featuring Justin Long and John Hodgman. Those ads were memorable and spot-on in the way both brands were perceived at the time.

You folks do character sketches all the time. This is in your wheelhouse. So give that little exercise a try.

Finally...

In this intermediate stage, you're still refining your brand. You haven't finished building yet. (You'll never finish building, but you will be able to slow down on construction at some point.)

Give it time. You don't have to do all of this at once.

Remember, the best thing you can do is produce the best product ever. Write the next book. And the next book. And the next book.

Yes, marketing is important. But you're a writer, not a marketer. You will be building a brand just by publishing more than one book.

Go slow, be patient, and remember that you're in this business for the long haul.

The most important things you can do? Write and publish. Devote 90 percent of your time to those things. Then focus on the marketing for the remaining 10 percent. As you do, think about building a brand. Think about adding to that brand bank account.

Do one or two things, then go back to writing.

And have fun!

HOW TO EXPAND YOUR TARGET
AUDIENCE: CHOICES

The next three chapters about target audience came about because my blog readers asked how to define your target audience. In the first How to Build a Brand chapter, I listed eight steps to building a brand. Step 2 was Define Your Target Audience. I then explained what I meant by that in 400 words —and thought that was sufficient.

Defining, building, and expanding a target audience is as natural as breathing for me. But not for most writers. Most don't have business experience, and apparently most have not worked in companies that jealously guard their brand and their image. So most writers have not learned how to operate in a business world that includes an audience.

And by that, I mean, consumers.

I'm not saying readers, because not everyone reads. But most people buy books—even if those people don't read. That's why I found the Targoz Reading Pulse survey that started this entire branding series so valuable. Targoz talked to readers and non-readers about their book buying habits.

Why are non-readers buying books? Because they have friends, family, and loved ones who read. A lot. So if the non-reader wants to give the reader a special gift, the non-reader buys a book.

Everyone buys a book at one point or another. Most people buy at least one book in a year.

But that doesn't mean that people buy just any book. And that also doesn't mean that when you start thinking about expanding your target audience, you will be able to expand that audience to include all book buyers.

Yet this is where writers start. When they think they need to define their target audience, writers immediately jump to "How do I get everyone to buy my book?" More savvy writers jump to "How do I get all fantasy readers to buy my fantasy novel?"

Neither of those approaches is very helpful, and most turn away more readers than they appeal to.

The reason I initially divided the target audience posts into three was because there really are three steps toward building an audience.

1. **You must acquire an audience.**
2. **You must recognize that you have an audience—a very specific audience.**
3. **You might decide to expand that audience.**

Please read the previous two chapters on this subject before you read this one. I want to make sure we're on the same page here.

For the sake of this chapter, I'm going to assume you have done the homework from the second target audience chapter. You now have an idea as to who reads your work. (The enterprising among you might actually have more than an idea. You might have actual numbers.)

Most writers—most businesses, in fact—believe that the next step is to actively grow that audience. And that belief is a mistake.

In your writing business, as in all business, there is no one-size-fits-all model. That goes to everything from building a business to building a brand. Even if you're in the same field as someone else, your business is different. What you do with that business is based entirely on your goals for that business.

Um, what? you might ask.

Yep, expanding an audience fits into your business goals, not just into branding. Change happens all the time in business, but growth happens only when a business actively pursues that growth.

You'd think that businesses would want to grow, but rapid growth can be harmful to a business. When Dean and I started Pulphouse Publishing, we had planned for slow growth only, and instead, we had exponential growth. It caught us flat-footed. We had not planned in any way for exponential growth—not in staff, or production, or expenses. We started behind, and never really caught up.

Writers who experience rapid growth, especially early in their careers, rarely make it past the first five novels. The writer expects the next books to do as well as the first. Sometimes the sophomore effort does better, but rarely. And by the fifth book, the writer is so deep in their head that they're no longer having fun with the writing itself.

I'm watching that with dozens of successful indies, who are always chasing the same numbers they had on previous books or in previous months, instead of banking the money and going back to having fun with the writing. The fact that the writer had fun with the writing is why the first book (or books) did so well in the first place.

This is why, throughout the entire book, I'm telling you that the things I'm discussing apply only after the writing is over. Never take these principles into your writing office.

The writers who do take these principles into their writing office often end up writing a genre they hate or forcing themselves to write the same type of book over and over again, even if it bores them.

And the marketing-heavy writers, the ones who became successful because they had some marketing gimmick, realize within a year or so that the gimmick no longer works for them. Either the writer must come up with a new gimmick or they need to plant butt in chair and start writing again.

Most writers, though, are not heavy marketers. Most want to ignore marketing altogether. While that's no longer possible in today's indie world, writers can plan a marketing day each week or a marketing weekend every few weeks to focus on what they want.

Once the writer has figured out who their readers actually are, then the writer needs to figure out if they want to grow their audience.

Or, let me rephrase that, the writer must choose whether to focus on growing their audience slowly or aggressively. Or ignore the idea of growing the audience at all.

Strategy One: Ignoring Growth

From the beginning of the modern publishing era, writers left growing the audience to their traditional publishers. That left most writers hard-wired to ignore growing an audience. Writers figure that the audience will take care of itself.

If you do the elementary things we talked about earlier in this series, branding to series, good covers, good blurbs, and (most importantly) writing great and compelling books, then some growth will happen, even without any action on the writer's part.

Eventually, however, that growth will stop. The writer's audience will actually decline. The decline comes from attrition or from inattention or both. Readers die, have life events that make them stop reading for a while, or they actually forget the name of the writer and miss the next book.

Or the genre moves, or gets glutted, or changes labels. Urban fantasy was once part of contemporary fantasy. Then urban fantasy became its own subgenre. And then urban fantasy outgrew contemporary fantasy, and became a genre in and of itself.

If an indie writer ignored those developments, leaving the covers and blurbs (and key words) the way they were for the contemporary fantasy market, the audience would no longer find the books. The audience would fade away, because the writer had stopped doing basic marketing—had stopped paying attention.

However, the ignoring-growth strategy will work for years at a time. Think of it as plateaus. A writer focuses on growing her audience for a year, then manages to grow the audience. She turns her attention to writing a group of books, has a marketing plan for them, and puts them out, without looking at growing the audience at all.

Three years later, she realizes her audience has plateaued, so she focuses on growing the audience again. She's successful: the audience grows. She then lets the audience plateau while she focuses on the writing again.

And so on and so forth.

The strategy is pretty simple:

1. **Focus on your core business.**
2. **Grow your reach.**
3. **Focus on your core business again.**
4. **Grow your reach again.**

And so on, as long as you would like to do that.

It's a strategy that includes ignoring the growth for a while, and believe me it works. I do it for a different series all the time. I focus on them, then I move to a different series, and focus on it for a while.

However, you need to choose to do this. You can't just close your eyes and walk through this modern marketing world. If you're going to ignore audience growth for a while, plan it, and then come back to it. Otherwise, your audience will decrease rather than increase.

Ignoring growth is a short-term strategy. It does not work in the long term. For the health of your business over years, you must grow your audience and your reach.

For example, if your subgenre gets glutted, and you haven't grown beyond your core audience, some of that audience will peel away because they're tired of the same-old same-old. If you have slowly grown your audience over years, you can afford to lose some of those people.

You won't make as much money, and your sales will go down.

Don't panic. Start figuring out how to grow your audience again.

And no, I don't mean write in a different subgenre (unless that interests you). Figure out how to market to the readers who've gotten tired of the same old branding, the same old blurbs, the same old sexy vampires (okay, that's just what I'm tired of. Nothing to see here. Move along).

Refresh your brand—or find people who haven't yet entered this market, and get them to read your book. You can do it.

Savvy companies refresh brands all the time, bringing in people who would once vow they never want to read about another sexy vampire again.

Strategy Two: Slow Growth

Most writers chose to slow-grow their audiences. Most publishers who actually know business and marketing do the same. Growing an audience slowly makes sense in the way the industry works now.

Due to a lack of shelf space decades ago, publishers worried about growing a writer's audience only when a new book came out—and only for a few weeks at that. Readers had to be aware of that book in those few weeks and buy that book then, or the book would vanish.

Now, though, there's no reason to buy a book until the reader is ready to actually read that book. Rather than subjecting readers to a fire hose of Buy! Buy! Buy!, the writer can make readers aware of the writer's works bit by bit.

Slow growth means doing a promotion for Book #1 one week, doing something to bring attention to the writer himself a few weeks later, doing a promotion for Book #5 a month after that. The attempts to grow the audience reach out to different groups with a different product at different times.

Rather than acquiring thousands of potential readers in a six-week period of time, the writer gains new readers by the handful—ten here, a hundred there, five later on, fifty in a month or so. Over time, those handfuls add up.

The audience doesn't grow by leaps and bounds. Instead, the audience accrues, going from an anthill to an actual hill so slowly that the writer might not even notice the growth until she looks back a few years and realizes that her book sales were one-fifth what they are today.

This strategy is a bit more complex than Strategy One. For Strategy Two, the writer actually needs a marketing plan, with ideas on ways to grow the audience bit by bit.

Strategy Three: Aggressive Growth

Most of the strategies for writers to grow their readership that come from so-called marketing gurus are actually aggressive-growth plans that these gurus stumbled upon. Aggressive-growth strategies rarely work for the long-term.

Businesses that attempt aggressive growth usually have a reason for doing so—and that reason is not getting their product in the hands of millions rather than thousands.

There's usually a business reason for doing it quick and dirty, because quick and dirty can hurt the brand if done incorrectly.

Aggressive growth strategies require a huge investment—usually of time or money or, most often, both. Done correctly, an aggressive-growth strategy can increase a brand's audience by five to ten percent, but rarely more than that.

Aggressive-growth strategies also require constant nurturing. Businesses can't do the same thing over and over again. There will be diminishing returns. So any business attempting aggressive growth needs a rotating plan of ways to promote to a variety of different markets in a variety of different ways with a set purpose in mind.

The most effective aggressive-growth strategies have a large data focus. They require the company to try something huge and expensive (in time or money). While that huge and expensive something is ongoing, the company rakes in data, judging whether or not the huge and expensive something is actually worthwhile.

If the huge and expensive something doesn't move the growth needle at all, then that particular huge and expensive something gets abandoned.

The company then moves to the next thing on the list. Yes, that thing too is huge and expensive, but it's completely different. The company tries that second huge and expensive something, doing the same data analysis, until the company succeeds at getting what it wants from its aggressive-growth campaign—or until the company runs out of time and/or money to run an aggressive-growth campaign.

If a slow growth strategy is complicated, an aggressive-growth strategy is complicated on steroids.

Personally, I would love to see a writer-business do a proper aggressive-growth strategy, pulling in big marketing firms and big data. I'd love to know what works or doesn't work.

But we're talking about a sustained three- to six-month campaign in which the company invests hundreds of thousands of dollars and thousands of hours of work time. To my knowledge, no traditional U.S. publishing company has done this in the 21st century. I know of a few that did this kind of marketing work in the early 1960s, essentially inventing book marketing as traditional publishers do it now, by finding what works and what doesn't work.

For your indie business, an aggressive campaign to grow your audience would require you to do the opposite of Strategy One. Rather than focusing on writing, you would focus on marketing 24/7, and write only when necessary to add to the product base.

All of you have heard of writer-marketing gurus who do that. They go on blogs and talk about their marketing strategies, then mention that they need to take a month "off" to write the next book.

Strategy Four: The Combination

The combination strategy combines ignoring your growth with aggressive growth. You write for a few years, then market aggressively for a year or so, then go back to writing. Or compress the timeline—write for six months, aggressively market when the new book is done, then ignore marketing for another six months and write the next book.

It sounds good, but you'd have to be a good marketer and a good writer to pull this off. Most writers are good at writing, but not at marketing. And most marketers are good at marketing, but not all that great at writing.

It's rare to find both in the same individual. Of course, if the writer has a lot of money, then she might want to consider partnering with someone who has a lot of marketing expertise to figure out a new, aggressive, marketing plan that will get that writer's work in front of thousands of people—without doing the same thing that traditional publishers have done for years.

Details, Please!

By now, you've noticed that I went vague on you with Strategies Two through Four. I did that on purpose.

I realized as I started into this topic, that I could write 400 words on each strategy and get tons of letters from you asking for more explanation, or I could actually devote the kind of time that the topics need.

So the next two chapters will explore growing your audience slowly and growing your audience aggressively. You can figure out on your own how to combine marketing strategies.

Things to remember as we move into the next two chapters—slow growth rarely interferes with building a brand. Most people aren't going to notice if you promote to one group or another, or try to find a new audience and fail.

Aggressive growth risks alienating everyone. Done incorrectly, it can piss off existing customers and drive away new customers. Marketing that focuses on aggressive growth will often result in consumers forming an opinion about the brand without trying the brand, which is antithetical to what you're trying to do.

Your goal is *brand loyalty*—getting readers to return every time you put out a new book. If they form an opinion about you without reading your work, they won't pick up the next book or the next. They might be curious about your work, but they won't be loyal to the brand.

And if that happens, then you'll have to rebuild the trust in your brand—with people who have never even tried it. That requires a whole new marketing strategy, and often one that's subtle and sensitive and the exact opposite of aggressive.

So, your assignment this time is to think of how many brands you have opinions of because they did a massive marketing campaign that bothered you or made you feel like the brand was not for you. Maybe look around your community and see if someone is doing aggressive marketing right now.

Notice who hooked you with a hardcore marketing campaign or figure out if any anyone ever caught your attention with that kind of campaign.

These campaigns and brands should not be books or writers. Everything else is fair game. But remember, the book business has been unbelievably crappy at both branding and at growing an audience, so taking lessons from the book industry is like taking lessons on skydiving from someone who has never gotten into an airplane.

Have fun with this, and I'll see you in the next chapter...when you're ready.

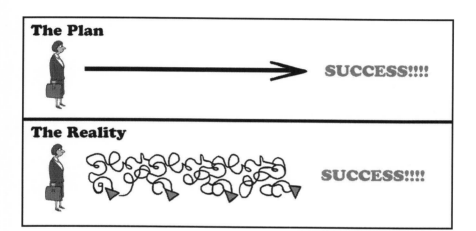

HOW TO EXPAND YOUR TARGET AUDIENCE: SLOW GROWTH

Writers always believe that they can become a bestseller if they only goose their sales properly. I actually had a brand-new writer scream at me once about this very thing. Back in the early days of Amazon's Kindle, she had "sold" 50,000 copies of her only novel by giving it away for free.

"I'll take my fifty-thousand sales over your sales any day," she shouted at me.

I said, calmly, "Talk to me in five years," and walked away.

Four years later, she's nowhere to be seen. She managed to write one more book under that name, tried the same technique with a brand-new name, wrote one or two more books, and when she realized she hadn't made more than pocket change on all of it, quit writing altogether. I have no idea what she's doing now.

Years ago, when I encountered writers like her, I'd feel bad when they quit. They were usually good writers who claimed they dreamed of writing since childhood. Yet when they realized that writing and selling books isn't as easy as reading and buying books, these writers quit.

I have learned that it's better to let these writers go and try other things. Writing was one stop on their journey, not the journey itself.

Why am I telling you this? Because so many of the gurus that have come along since the advent of the Kindle have also vanished. Or, like the marketing guru that I heard recently on a podcast, they've revamped their business to focus on production, not on marketing.

In nonbusiness terms, focusing on production means writing the next book. And the next. And the next.

However, writers do need to do some minimal marketing these days. I cover that in my book *Discoverability*, and I cover some of it earlier in this book.

I also discussed it in the previous chapter on how to expand your audience. Please go read that chapter now.

Before I started writing this chapter, I Googled the topic, just to see if I could find some current research. Instead, I found dozens of articles that offer generic business advice, and they all start with the same thing I mentioned in the previous chapter: make sure you're ready to expand your reach.

That woman who screamed at me? She wasn't ready to give her book away to anyone, let alone 50,000 potential readers. Because she didn't have a follow-up book. Even if those readers had read her novel, they couldn't buy her next, because she didn't have a next.

I tell writers to have at least ten books before they start into the free route. If the writers are writing in a series, then they need to have at least four books before giving the first away free. And never do permafree on any of your books at an ebook retailing site (like Amazon or Kobo). That limits the promotions that you can do with the book. If you want readers to get your book for free, make them come to your website and download the book there. A link to BookFunnel will make the download easy and will also enable you to capture the email addresses of the people who downloaded, so you can send a specific newsletter to them when the next book comes out.

Make it clear on your website that downloading the book means these people are volunteering their names and email addresses for a newsletter. If you don't, the newsletter services will mark you as spam.

There. I've just given you one tip on how to expand your audience. But rather than dispense tips, I'm going to show you a game plan on how to design your own marketing for slow growth.

First, let's talk terminology. When I'm discussing marketing in this chapter and the next, I mean actual marketing. Promotion, advertising, newsletters, videos, that sort of thing. I do not mean blurbs on the back of your book or designing a cover. I assume you'll do those things as a matter of course.

Marketing, for the purposes of these next two chapters, is unusual, active behavior, behavior that other businesses would hire, say, an advertising agency to do or a marketing person in a publishing house.

Also, for the sake of these two chapters, I'm going to assume a few things. I'm going to assume that you have written and published more than one book. I'm going to assume you did the work I assigned you in the second target audience chapter and actually figured out who your current audience is. I'm going to assume that you want to keep the newcomers and that you want them to become loyal to your brand.

I'm also going to assume that you've evaluated your business and determined that you're ready to grow the audience.

As marketer Tracey Wallace wrote several years ago when she was still blogging for Mashable, "...you need to be secure in your own market before expanding to a new one. The trick to expanding is to never take too much focus off what drew customers to you in the first place. Otherwise, you risk losing them (and thereafter, your business)."[43]

The Mashable article—in fact, all of the articles I found about expanding an audience assume that the business needs to develop new products or move into a new neighborhood to expand the business's reach. That's true of most retail business, but not necessarily true of writers.

Books are—and have been—so poorly marketed that most existing books never reach an audience that would enjoy them. Because book marketing was always based on velocity—selling a book to a lot of people fast, and then assuming the book was "over" a few months after release— most books (including most bestsellers) never reached full market penetration.

Ah, hell, let's be honest here. Most books were never targeted at a market at all. Books received a genre label (and remember, genre is a sales tool, not a definition), a genre cover, a few marketing dollars, and a general push to the genre's readers and that was it. Traditional publishers still do that.

Indies do it, too, only they use key words and copy each other's covers and branding ideas. Indies believe that if they want to expand their reach, they need to write in a whole new genre. (Well, I've heard some writers say, urban fantasy didn't work for me. All the shifter types have been taken. So I'm going to write billionaire erotica! Sigh.)

Your game plan shouldn't be trying an entirely new type of product (unless writing in a new genre interests you). Your marketing game plan should be to slowly expand your audience with your existing books.

How do you do it?

Here's where I could do what the marketing gurus do and tell you fifteen tricks that are guaranteed to work right now.

The problem is that there's really no guarantee except this one: the tricks probably won't work six months from now. They'll be useless to you, because there will be a newer, bigger, hotter marketing trick by then.

I'll touch on hot marketing tricks in this chapter, and I'll teach you how to use those tricks as they are designed in the next chapter.

But first…

The Game Plan

1. Figure out how much time you're going to invest in your marketing.

This is weekly or monthly time. Are you going to have a marketing hour every day? A marketing day every week? A marketing weekend every month? A marketing week every quarter? Figure it out, and hold to that. Don't do any marketing at any other point. You're heading for slow-growth, not rapid growth. You need to plan things that will fit into your timeline and still give you hours and hours to write and publish.

Your schedule is under your control. Pick the least disruptive option for the way that you do business.

2. Decide what you want from your marketing.

Yes, yes, I know. You want to grow your audience. But what segment of your audience do you want to grow? I mentioned in a previous chapter that my traditional publisher didn't market my African-American detective novels to African-Americans, so when I got my rights back, I focused strongly on marketing to that demographic, particularly readers.

You probably know where there are gaps in your market. Maybe you want older readers for your acclaimed YA series. Or maybe you want to widen your readership in Australia.

Once you have figured out who you're targeting, then you set up a plan. That plan will be unique to whatever group you want to expand. It's not going to be a one-size-fits-all plan.

In my case, I targeted African-American book clubs, so that readers could discuss the series, the writer, and the choices. Cush City provided a great book club list for just that purpose. I also bought BookBubs (and BookBub lights) for the first book in the series and placed the book not in the mystery category, but in the African-American category.

I did other promotions as well, but these were the ones I started with.

You're now the Director of Marketing for your publishing company. So direct your marketing.

3. Pick one book or one series to focus on at a time.

If you're like me, you'll have a dozen different projects going at any given moment. I rotate my own marketing to fit whatever book/project is coming out this month or this year. I have a marketing game plan for that project, and I do my best to hit that plan.

I don't worry about the other projects during that time.

It's a little disingenuous to say I only focus on one. I don't. I have many projects premiering in a year, so some of my marketing plans overlap.

Sometimes, that's serendipity. When I initially wrote this chapter as a blog post, I was doing some minor marketing on my Diving series. In September, a new book, *The Runabout*, appeared. That book went up for preorder about the time I wrote that post, and I let the Diving newsletter know about it. I also posted a blog about the preorder on Tuesday.

I've posted about *The Runabout* before, because early this year it became the first full novel ever published in its entirety in *Asimov's*. That publication was great—I got reviews, some new fans, and...many many many pages of advertising in that magazine. The best kind of advertising, the kind where people actually read my work and decide if they like it.

So I've done small marketing on *The Runabout* before the book officially appeared. I did a fuller press in September. WMG sent out review copies. Audible is promoting the audiobook because it was produced by Audible Studios. So there's a lot of marketing already going on.

And...something else came up. About a year ago, I noted that writers were doing starter kit bundles for their book series. You want to get into a long series? Buy the first three books as a bundle.

I suggested to WMG that we do that with all of our series. Allyson Longueira, WMG's publisher, decided that she could allot only so much staff time to the project, so the bundles have appeared slowly—one, two, or three a month.

That, plus a "bundle" of the Uncollected Anthology that I'm a part of, and seeing some gorgeous short story bundles that friends were putting together made me think of curating a bundle of bundles for Storybundle. That went live at the same time as the original blog post for this chapter. I had a lot of choices for which one of my own starter kits to include, but I decided on Diving because…you know…*The Runabout.* So, I figured, let's get some new readers on board before the book came out.

I'm in a lot of Storybundles in 2017 because of WMG. Dean or Allyson or someone (I can't remember) came up with the idea of organizing Story-bundles around *Fiction River* volumes (Dean and I are the series editors and masterminds behind *Fiction River*).

Limited time bundles, like Storybundle, enable writers to band together to promote each other's work. We end up sharing readers. The readers decide if they want to continue with the new-to-them authors' work.

The sharing doesn't happen quickly. Readers take their own sweet time to sample works by writers unfamiliar to them. About a third of bundle purchasers get to everything within the month. The rest take a year or more —or never get to the purchase.

How do I know this? Not just because readers write to me and tell me when (if) they plan to buy the bundle. (The morning I wrote the original post, someone emailed to say she had to read the previous bundles before buying a new one.)

That's anecdotal stuff. I have actual data. This spring, WMG included an online lecture through Teachable [44] [link] in one of the bundles I curated. That lecture had a specific download code, good for a long time. The bundle ended, we know how many bundles were sold, and how many of those people have used the code.

I've seen similar things with first books in a series that appeared in a bundle, but spread across multiple platforms. The bundles, like anything that involves reading or actually consuming the product, take a lot more time than free downloads do, but they produce better results.

Remember, our goal in growing our audience isn't just to get names on a list. Our goal is to make readers who will return whenever you produce another book. That's why I prefer things that encourage newcomers to read my books and stories, as opposed to things that simply get me a bunch of names.

You'll note, though, that I cited data above. I've alluded to other data as well. Data are very important when you're doing actual marketing and here's why.

. . .

4. Test, evaluate, decide.

Once you figure out what you want to do, you'll try all kinds of marketing strategies. Because your time is limited, you'll only do one or two at a time.

Consider your first foray into a certain marketing strategy a test. Figure out how you can evaluate that test, using data that our internet world so freely makes available.

Once the test is completed, decide if the marketing method is something you want to repeat, modify, or discard. Again, that's something only you can decide.

In March of 2017, Ron Vitale wrote a marvelous blog about precisely this process.[45] He had decided to use Instafreebie six months earlier after hearing great things about it, and how well it worked. He had set goals for the Instafreebie experiment, goals that the experiment hit only partially.

Then he had to evaluate whether he would be better off spending that time and money on Instafreebie or on some other marketing strategy. I'll keep you in suspense about his decision because I want you to read his blog. I want you to see how this kind of marketing experiment works, and what kind of thinking you should put into it.

5. Keep your ear to the ground.

Marketing is often about trying something different, not about following the crowd. That said, the crowd sometimes has great ideas.

In my weekly blog, I complain a lot about the "current gurus" but partly because I'm constantly listening to them. Most of these people have only written a handful of books (if that). Their success comes from extreme marketing. If I only had one or two books, I could really focus down on marketing as well. (And I'd be the most miserable person on Planet Earth. I love writing. I like marketing—sometimes. At every full moon on every fifth month. Maybe.)

Sometimes, though, those extreme marketing gambits contain the nugget of a good idea. After listening to the Amazon ad gurus, I urged WMG to try Amazon ads. We're doing ads slowly (a few per month) and leaving them up. We're finding a sweet spot, but we've only put up twenty-one of our books so far (out of 600) because life's too short.

I also put together something as I listened to the folks who kept saying the ads worked. They were nonfiction writers who had one or two novels. So, I wondered, was it their nonfiction that sold through the ads?

We put up some nonfiction books after that little realization, and voila! the sales off the ads for those books were much higher than the fiction sales. But we're using Amazon ads for something other than direct sales. We're using them as advertising, and advertising (as those of you who've read *Discoverability* know) is all about eyeballs and impressions and being out there, not about one-to-one direct sales.

Because of the internet, you can find out about the latest hottest trend the week it becomes the latest, hottest. You can try old things as well. You can find all kinds of ways to promote. BookBub's blog often lists some of the current hot things [46], and many are worth experimenting over. For example, BookBub's blog included fascinating ideas after Book Expo, some of which I want to try.[47] They do this sort of blog often, and it's worth investigating.

6. Keep an eye on the culture.

Every fall, a new TV show takes over the culture. That show might dovetail with a book you wrote. I tried to get my old traditional publisher to market my fairy tale books to the *Once Upon A Time* crowd when that series started, but noooo. Specificity would have been too hard for my traditional publisher.

By the time I got the rights, *Once Upon A Time* wasn't as hot, and there were other things to focus on.

Zombies were hot for a while. If you had a zombie book, then promoting it to *The Walking Dead* fans was a good idea. Or runners who used the Zombies, Run! app. (And if you want to learn more about marketing and business read this Lifehacker piece about the app.[48]) Advertising your book on an app or partnering with the app (in the case of Zombies, Run!) by offering the book as a contest reward, would be a great marketing strategy.

TV, movies, games, apps—popular culture is always obsessing about something, and if your work ties into that something, then promote it in the moment.

Be creative. Be fearless. Have fun.

7. Be the first writer to try this.

I read *Adweek* a lot, always scouring the ways that other businesses in the entertainment industry are doing their marketing. *Adweek* has many free newsletters, and I swear I get an idea a week from at least one of them. Some of those ideas cost too much money to execute (right now) and some would cost too much time. But some spark low-cost ideas for me or have a nugget based in the middle that I hadn't considered before.

I also learn things that are broader than how to market my books, like the importance of branding throughout a company. As I mentioned earlier in this book, Syfy changed its branding and its programming—and I discovered this through *Adweek*.

A lot of writers have made a name for themselves as marketers because they were the first—the first to do bookmarks (Debbie Macomber), the first to do TV ads (James Patterson). You know you've hit something when you get a good result. Then it's up to you whether or not to share it.

8. Realize that good results might not be replicable.

Sometimes surprise is the most important thing. Or, sometimes promotions work for one book and won't work for another. You can do great things with the first book in a series that you can't do with later books. That's why I tell you not to make that first book permafree. There are a million marketing opportunities—advertising opportunities—that go by the wayside when you have that book forever free. Bundles are one. A BOGO sale is another. There are many, many more.

Some promotions work well in one genre and don't work at all for another one. And some worked great in 2012 and don't work at all now, like Kindle's free bestseller list. Five years ago, readers read the free books and then moved to the author's other works. Not so much any more.

Some promotions really are a function of the time and place. (See #6 above)

9. Realize you can't do everything.

After you start exercising your promotion muscle, you'll start getting more ideas than you can possibly execute. Do the ones that fit into your schedule and your budget. Then use the data to figure out if you're investing your time wisely.

. . .

10. Some (most) promotions will fail.

Especially if you haven't defined your goal for that promotion. If your goal is to grow your audience, then keep that as your focus always. If the promotion doesn't actually grow your readership, which you can measure by increased book sales, then dump the promotion, no matter how many names it adds to your newsletter or how many free downloads people have taken.

11. Measure your overall success in months and years, not in days and weeks.

Your goal is to increase your readership over time. So, if you do successful promotions, your sales should be greater (on those projects) than they were at the same time the year before (barring unforeseens in the culture like nasty elections or major terror attacks, things that make people watch the tube instead of read). Greater than might be a hundred sales greater than or several thousand greater than.

Your growth pattern will not be a straight line. It'll be a series of waves, with plateaus and downturns. But you should, overall, end up with more readers than you started with.

Slow growth means exactly that. You're growing your business—your customer base, your loyal reader base—a little bit at a time.

The business world has another term for slow growth. You'll often hear the word "sustainable" in connection with expanding a business. Rapid growth isn't sustainable, and can often hurt an unprepared business. Even slow growth can be hard to maintain at times.

But slow growth is sustainable. It's not predictable, but it is something that you can maintain over months and even years.

The coolest thing about slow growth is that moment when you realize that you have way more readers than you ever thought you did. You weren't tracking them day to day or obsessing about them. You just noticed on the way to doing something else.

Keep your focus on growing your audience, manage your time wisely, and write the next book. If you do those things over the space of years, you'll still be writing and publishing five years from now. If you don't control your time and you forget to write, you'll be doing something else— like that woman who screamed at me.

She failed. Not as a promoter, but as a writer. And she didn't fail because she made mistakes marketing.

She failed because she quit writing. She quit trying.
That's the only way to fail in this business.
So experiment with marketing. Have fun with it.
Just like you have fun with your writing.

"Our marketing expansion seems a little haphazard."

HOW TO EXPAND YOUR TARGET AUDIENCE: AGGRESSIVE GROWTH

Here's the surprising chapter. Many people who read my blog regularly probably think that I'm opposed to major marketing campaigns. I'm not. I'm opposed to them when they're done incorrectly.

What's incorrectly?

Pretty much everything you see from traditional publishing to most indies. You have to look outside of publishing to see how to do a smart, aggressive growth campaign designed to grow an audience.

Why do I say traditional publishing and most writers do it wrong? Because…(wait for it)…an aggressive campaign to grow your target audience is part of a long-term strategy.

Publishing has turned aggressive growth campaigns into a short-term strategy, one that has no real upside.

Here's what I mean.

Traditional publishing in modern times is based on the velocity model—selling a lot of books fast, then ignoring the product, and moving to another product.

Standard business growth is the exact opposite. You develop your company, develop your brand, cultivate your consumers, and then, once your business is large enough, consider making that business bigger.

When you decide the time is right to aggressively grow your audience, you should pull out every trick in the book and design a few of your own. You will work very hard on getting people to sample your wares. Most of the people who try your books will not continue reading them. Most people —because they didn't like the book they sampled or they have only so much time or other favorite authors—will not return to your other work right away. And that's okay, because your efforts here should have netted you 5 to 10 percent of the readers you targeted.

In other words, a properly done aggressive growth campaign will get you more readers. If you're inexperienced with growing your readership, you'll be disappointed. Not by the results on this book, but on the next one.

Writers never think of comparing the sales of the book before the growth-campaign to the sales of the book published after the campaign ends. But those are the important numbers.

Let me make up some numbers to show you what I mean.

Let's say you've published a series of books. Each book in the series stands alone, like books in mystery or romance series do. You decide to do an aggressive growth campaign for book six. You've had steady readership growth with books one through five.

Book five's sales were about 10,000 copies (over the first three months after release). Please note that I picked 10,000 copies because the math is easy, not because I know something about average series sales.

You do your variation of an aggressive growth campaign. Your goal is to get book six in front of hundreds of thousand of potential readers. You hope that 100,000 will actually buy the book, over and above your 10,000 loyal readers—and you're successful.

In the first three months of release, you sell 110,000 copies of book six.

Fast forward to book seven, which comes out a year later. (Why a year? Because you spent so damn much time marketing. Ideal strategy would be six months later, but we'll ignore that for the moment.)

In the first three months of its release, book seven sells 20,000 copies. Double what book five sold before your massive marketing push. Yet most writers would be horribly disappointed. Most traditional publishers would cancel the series right then and there, declaring it a failure.

But you're an indie writer, not someone in traditional publishing. Books one through five are still in print.

Readers are not predictable folk. So, of the 100,000 new readers who bought the book, 50,000 actually read it in a timely fashion (meaning the first three months). Twenty-five-thousand read it eventually, and 25,000 more might get to it one day.

Already your "readership" is down to 75,000, and one-third of them might not have read the book they own by the time the new book comes out. Generally speaking, the release of a new book reminds slow readers that they already own one of your books, and they should read it now.

Of the 50,000 who've read book six by the time book seven comes out, 10,000 were unimpressed and will not buy your next. Another 10,000 liked it, but not enough to run right out and get another book with your byline. The remaining 30,000 split in a variety of directions.

Some read the series from the beginning. Some go back to book five. Some buy book seven and forget all about books one through five.

You can measure some of this. After a huge marketing push on book six, you will see a lump of readers work their way through the entire series. Even if the series is compelling, the lump will spread out over time. Why? Because some readers don't like binging. So they'll read one of your books, then five books by other writers, then another of your books, then ten books by other writers—and so on.

You can't predict how all readers will read. What you can do is make sure you have a lot of books available, so that the readers who discovered you in the big marketing push have a lot of product to choose from after they've finished the initial book.

And that's where traditional publishing falls down. They don't brand anything in a series, and stupidly, they take books out of print or make the books hard to find or keep the high ebook prices on backlist, so readers will find less expensive reads elsewhere.

If some of a traditionally published writer's books are with a different traditional publisher, the publisher who does the huge push tries hard not to mention the writer's other works. Which is stupid, but it's modern business.

It hurts not only the new publisher, but the writer as well.

So...indies...you want to run an aggressive marketing campaign. You want to spend a lot of time promoting your latest novel, and you want to grow your readership fast.

Here's what you need first:

You need a lot of product

An aggressive growth campaign is not something a new writer should do. By a lot, I'd say you need at least five books in your ongoing series.

Or, if you're doing trilogies, you need two completed trilogies before designing an aggressive growth campaign for the first book in your newest trilogy.

If you're writing standalone books, then you need at least ten (hopefully in the same genre), so that readers have a lot of choice to buy more books of yours once they've finished the book you've put all your marketing dollars behind.

You need a realistic goal

Are you running an aggressive growth campaign because "everyone does it" or because someone told you that you needed to get a lot of readers fast or because you're emulating traditional publishing? If so, abandon this idea now.

Your goal needs to be concrete for your business. I can think of two great reasons to run an aggressive growth campaign.

Reason One: You want readers to learn that you (or your series or your book) exist. This is an informational campaign, targeting at making potential readers notice you when they haven't noticed you in the past. You'll get new readers here, but generally speaking, you won't get a one-to-one growth. By that I mean, you will not get one reader for each dollar spent. You may not see how the money you've spent translates into readers for months. This is how traditional publishing used to market books in the 1960s, when traditional publishing did marketing better than they do now. This is how books like *Catch-22*, which only sold 7,500 copies in that all important first month, became long-term bestsellers.

Because the publishers back then invested in aggressive marketing techniques on the books they believed in for months after publication—if not years.

Your goal, when you do an informational campaign, is long-term. You want people to notice you, keep noticing you, and finally cave in and buy the book they've "been hearing so much about."

Reason Two: You want to actively put the book in the hands of readers, get reviews, get word-of-mouth going, and essentially give the book away. This can be a double-edged sword, because the readers and the reviewers and anyone who gets the book might end up hating it.

However, you do not give the book away for free...except to targeted power readers (like the owners of bookstores [yes, there still are bookstores]). You reduce the price of the book and do major promotional campaigns like BookBubs and other short-term strategies that I'll mention briefly below.

The goal of this strategy is to get a reader to sample one novel of yours from beginning to end. You have to trust your skills enough to believe that once the reader finishes the book, they will want another one of your books. And when they finish that book, they will want another and another.

The readership numbers I mentioned at the beginning of this post? That's what usually happens with this kind of aggressive growth campaign.

Back to the things you need before you start executing the campaign.

You need a budget

Yes, budget first before your game plan. And the budget has to be a two-fold budget.

Budget 1: You need a financial budget for your campaign. Are you going to spend $5,000 growing your audience? $10,000? $20,000? $100,000?

You need to realistically set this budget, and you need to stick to it.

You will not be able to do everything you want to do—no one has an unlimited advertising budget, not even movie studios. You work within the budget you have, and make the best choices you can based on that budget.

Budget 2: You need a time budget for your campaign. If you're running the campaign—and most indies will be doing this alone—then you need to set aside a certain number of hours per day or per week to work on this campaign. You will be spending a lot of time on marketing, and to do this right, you will probably be losing writing time.

Losing writing time will cost you money in the long term. You have to factor that financial loss into your business's annual budget. (Not in the advertising budget.) You will not make up this financial loss even if you gain new readers—not that fast, anyway. Over time you might.

But better to be prepared than to be upset at the lost writing time.

You need a timeline

This aggressive growth campaign will last for a finite period of time. You can pick anything from one to six months. But do not go past six months. People will get heartily sick of you flogging this book if you're doing it longer than six months.

In fact, I initially wanted to tell you to do no more than three months, but that's not realistic. Some of the strategies for this kind of campaign take months of prep time. You want to place a banner ad on NPR? They only have so much space and a lot of competition for that space. Plus they have rules about the specs for the ad and you might not hit that the first time.

(Note that I am not talking about the Google ads you see on the websites you go to if you don't have your ad blocker on, but the ads you see even with the ad blocker, the ones built into the site itself.)

There is a sweet spot between getting people's attention and annoying the heck out of them. It depends on the product and what you're going to do with the ad.

Here's how I would develop a timeline on a major aggressive growth campaign:

Pre-Timeline: Research all the methods of promotion you're interested in. Try a few in your slow-growth plan to see if those methods are all hype or if they actually work. If you are partnering with others—running ads or publishing bundled stories—figure out their deadlines and specifications.

Month One: Mail Advance Reading Copies, get your preorder(s) up if you plan to do that, prepare your ads, get your partners lined up (whoever they might be).

Month Two: Get readers to begin word of mouth, do some prepublication work (if you're doing this before publication), maybe give some related fiction away free on your website, use older works to beef up your newsletter—maybe even start a new newsletter and do a special promotion to get those thousands of names that some people taunt. Learn Google, Facebook, and Amazon ads if you haven't already done that, make sure your website is spiffy, your Facebook Page ready, and so on.

Month Three: Launch the book and the campaign, do all the special things you've planned, maybe cycle through BookBub and BookBub light, buy TV ads, radio ads, or whatever big expenditures you're going to do.

Month Four: The second half of your campaign here, whatever that might be. Make sure you've included something unique to you and your project, something memorable that no one else has done.

Month Five: Slow back down to your normal slow-growth advertising, gather your analytics.

Month Six: Review the campaign, write it up internally so that you have notes on how it went for future campaigns. List what worked and what didn't. Plan to revisit the analytics three months from now to see if there are surprises.

Note in my timeline there's only two intense months of visible promotion. In this case, I scheduled them around the publication of the book. But you can do this same kind of promotion around an existing book. You don't have to do it on release. For example, if you published a Christmas book in 2015 in a series that you're still continuing, you might want to center a major aggressive growth campaign around that Christmas book, and make sure the visible part of your marketing happens in November and early December.

Your only limit here is your imagination (and your time and your budget).

You need to be traditional

Figure out what kind of book marketing works for you as a reader, then replicate it. Try the things you've heard about. Do what you always wanted a traditional publisher to do, but you couldn't get them to do it. Do review copies for established review publications that handle your genre. If you're writing literary fiction, send ARCs to the *New York Times* or work with the American Booksellers Association's Red Box program to get the attention of bookstores. If you're writing genre fiction, then get your review copies to the leading bloggers and review magazines, even if you think there's no hope of a review.

You're going for attention here, and you're spending some money. Do the thing readers expect. Some regular readers will find you. I find books bimonthly from *Mystery Scene Magazine*—their print edition. I know others do, too. Figure that out for yourself.

You need to be creative

I've been saying throughout this book that traditional publishers have no idea how to market any more. I've said that for years, but the impetus of this series came from the Targoz Reading Pulse survey. What inspired me the most in that survey was a category called "Media Reach by Genre."[49] The Survey, remember, interviewed readers and nonreaders alike and found out what their interests were—outside of book publishing.

Why is this important? Because it helps you be creative.

For example, the survey found that romance readers watch more television than the average person, but their viewing habits are pretty specific. They do watch network television, but they don't watch Fox. They don't watch much cable TV—except for Lifetime. Almost half of romance readers watch Lifetime once a week.

Other notable things in this section about romance readers include the fact that they read the print version of *People* magazine. One in three romance readers read *People* every week—and actually read it. They don't just buy it.

And then there's this lovely statistic: 64 percent of romance readers read their local print newspaper every week and 47 percent read the online version.

In fact, this section notes that almost all readers read their local newspaper, either online or in print. (Depends on the readers' preferred genre as to where or how much they read in their local paper.)

I read those statistics and did a literal head slap. I've worked in local media off and on my whole life. WMG's publisher, Allyson Longueira, used to run the local newspaper. Local papers—particularly those in smaller communities—are always searching for good hooks for articles. What better than a local author who has a new book release—particularly if that local author is going to buy a print ad to go along with that story?

Cable stations like Lifetime have slots for local advertising. They also have places on their websites for local promotions. Target your audience, and develop an ad.

Or, if you're writing a cozy mystery filled with recipes, hold a party at a local hotel in which local chefs do a cook-off from your recipes. Give away copies of your book, and invite all of the local media to attend from the TV stations to the radio stations. Get friends to live-tweet the event, and run the event live in Google Events or on Facebook.

As I said above, you're limited only by your imagination. (And your time and your budget.)

You need to be unique

Go outside the norm and do something really unusual. The chef idea above is one of those, but there are a million ways to do this.

In the book, *Avid Reader*, publisher Robert Gottlieb—who was one of those megamarketers who invented most of modern book marketing—talked about the marketing campaign for *Catch-22*. In the early 1960s, they put postage-paid comment cards inside the hardcover copy of the books, asking readers to fill out the card with their opinions of the book and send the cards back. Gottlieb then did an entire six-month marketing campaign filled with reader comments.

That's so much easier today. Develop a hashtag for your book and at the end of the book, ask for reader comments along with that hashtag. Or do a group reading of the book (everyone read at the same time) and then live tweet as they go along (this is not for the faint of heart; you will see stuff you don't want to see).

Memorable campaigns will stick in the reader's mind. I went back to the Gottlieb book because he mentioned that one of the big supporters of *Catch-22* was NBC News anchor John Chancellor. On his own dime, Chancellor created thousands of "Yossarian Lives" stickers, which college students then used to deface buildings and tables and books. I remember going to universities years later and finding "Yossarian Lives" stickers on library carrels or inside bathroom stalls. That campaign went on forever— and created a life of its own.

On the day I wrote this chapter, I logged onto Twitter for my usual 140-character dose of culture (or not), and discovered a unique marketing campaign for *Guardians of The Galaxy Vol. 2.* Just in time for the streaming release (August 8, 2017) and the Blu-ray version (later this month), the team that brought you the movie did a three-minute cheesy music video.

The video is in keeping with the offbeat tone of the movies. Since the music in both movies is deliberately 1970s (for a plot reason), this video harks back to those 1970s dance shows that most of you are too young to remember.

This is pure marketing, designed to go viral, and to give the fans something fun and interesting. Now I will help the video go viral by sharing it in the endnotes.[50]

Why did I share it? Because this is what I mean by unique. Sure, sure, other movie promotions will do something similar as soon as this fall because this worked. But they won't be as fun or interesting, and probably won't be as memorable either.

This is what I mean by "be unique."

And have fun.

You need to brand your marketing campaign

And this is where the happy music comes to a screeching halt.

Wha…Wha…What? You ask.

Haven't you ever noticed that all major marketing campaigns have a theme? A look? A brand?

If you're doing this to increase the readership of your series, then you can brand the campaign to reflect the series. But you can only do that once.

You'll need to come up with a whole new brand the next time you do a major marketing campaign.

All of the stuff we talked about with branding itself, way back at the beginning of this book—all of that applies to an aggressive growth campaign. *All* of it. From the look to the target audience to the taglines to marketing to the right places, your campaign has to be a thing just like your book is a thing.

And they should really be separate—in that, a good campaign should reflect your book or your style, but be a creative endeavor all its own.

You need to end your campaign

It has to have a limited shelf life, never to be repeated. Not just because of your timeline, but because the moment marketing becomes repetitive, people tune it out.

Besides, you need to end your campaign because you have a life and you have books to write.

You need to use data to determine your campaign's success

Everything you did might meet the goals you set for the campaign. Or, just as likely, everything you did might fail.

That's called a learning curve, folks.

And the reason I mention the learning curve is because...

You need to learn from this effort

You might learn that aggressive growth campaigns aren't for you. You might learn that you love aggressive growth campaigns more than you like writing. You might learn that aggressive growth campaigns work for you.

You might learn that you had a semi-successful campaign and you want to change a few things should you do it all over again.

If you are successful, realize not all of that success will be replicable. Some of it will work because you're the first to do it (Guardians Inferno) and some of it will work because you're using tried-and-true methods and some of it will work because people were bored in August of 2017 and your campaign was able to cut through the noise.

Make notes about the things that you think will work in the future, and chalk the rest of it up to learning.

You need to take a long break

If you're going to incorporate aggressive growth campaigns into building your target audience and ultimately your brand, realize that this is a tool you should unleash rarely.

If you do a big aggressive growth campaign every time you release a book, people will expect it of you and at some point, you won't be able to deliver.

Better to do an aggressive growth campaign every few years, once it has become clear that your previous campaign has plateaued. The data will not accurately reflect a plateau for at least a year, maybe more. So continue with your slow-growth campaign, write a lot of books, and come back to this when there are new tricks and techniques that other people have pioneered that you want to try.

Or when you have time to burn, or $10,000 to burn.

Or, maybe you'll want to hire a staff to do a campaign for you. I tried this several years ago, and it was an unmitigated disaster. That was primarily my fault because I hired the wrong people to do the work (a distinct possibility whenever you hire someone). I've done smaller things since with a much newer, much better team, and that seems to be working out.

One secret

You can do a half-assed aggressive growth campaign. You target a few things that you've always wanted to do, and throw some time and money at them.

WMG Publishing did a small aggressive growth campaign this fall for my latest Nelscott novel, *Protectors*. The book is the beginning of a new series, but it's related to the Smokey Dalton series, so fans should find it interesting.

But we needed to inform a slightly different audience about the book, so our entire campaign is about getting out the word that the book exists. Oh, and that it's unlike anything anyone has done before. And that it is related to the previous Kris Nelscott books in setting and with one familiar character.

I'll report on the marketing of all of this about a year from now, once we see what's happened. The book just went up for pre-order (as I initially wrote this chapter). I got a proof of the paper Advance Reading Copy today (the ebook ARC went out weeks ago), and we're having a meeting next week to tweak our strategy.

This is not a major tens of thousands of dollars campaign because we don't have the time, but it is a six-month awareness campaign that will take more time and more dollars than any campaign we did before.

It's not quite what I'm talking about in this blog, but it's close.

Aggressive growth campaigns are not for the faint of heart or the weak of wallet. These campaigns take time, money, and a lot of creativity to pull off well.

If you're going to do one, make sure you have a lot of marketing under your belt. Also make sure you know what you want from the campaign. Be prepared to throw thousands of dollars into the mix without seeing any results at all.

Also be prepared to have a lot of success. Because that can happen with aggressive growth campaigns. Make sure you can handle the growth.

With writers, that's relatively easy—if you've done what I listed first. You need a lot of product, so that the readers who joined up in this campaign have other reading material of yours while they wait for the next book of yours.

Remember all those lists in brick-and-mortar stores in the early days of Harry Potter? If you liked Harry Potter, you'll like this fantasy series by this other author? Those existed because by book three, it became clear that these voracious Harry Potter readers needed something to tide them over to the next Harry Potter book a year away.

You want people to use your backlist to tide them over until the next book in your series. You can do that now, thanks to the fact that books can remain in print permanently these days.

Use that to your advantage.

So, essentially, if you want to do some major aggressive growth campaign, your timeline should start years ahead of the campaign. Make sure you've written the books. Then do the campaign.

Write many more books and do another campaign.

Rinse. Repeat.

And most importantly, save your firepower until you're ready. If you're going to spend money and time on a campaign like this, do it right. Don't do it the way traditional publishers do it in 2017. Do it the way they did it in 1963.

Because, oh, did I tell you? By the six-month anniversary of the publication of *Catch-22*, when the publisher took out several full-page ads in major newspapers all over the country to promote the book's word of mouth success, the book itself had only sold 35,000 copies.

It would eventually sell millions and millions. It's never gone out of print. But in 1963, the publisher was patient, using their creativity and their campaign to slowly build the book.

That's what you'll do with any kind of growth campaign—even an aggressive one. You're building your brand slowly. One reader at a time—even when you go after a big bunch of them at once.

You have to keep them.

And remember, keeping your readers isn't about tweeting all the time or haranguing them to buy.

It's about writing good books, telling great stories, and making the readers fall in love with your work.

It's about the writing.

It always has been, and it always will be.

Enjoy.

"I know transformation isn't easy.
I pulled a muscle once."

READY, SET, GO!

And now you know everything there is to know about branding for writers, right?

Um, no. We have just scratched the surface here. What I wrote in these chapters in 2017 works in 2018 and will work in 2019. But there are a lot of techniques, new apps, and incredible opportunities that exist now for writers that didn't exist when I wrote the initial blog posts. That's why I didn't get greatly specific on techniques.

Branding is the most important marketing thing you can do for your work. It also takes a lot of time to get the right brand.

Be willing to experiment. Be willing to change. Be willing to try new things.

But most of all, have fun. Branding—and marketing—are, in their own way, as creative as writing. They're just different. And something you can noodle at as you do other things.

Keep your eyes open and look at how others do it. As I write this, I'm sitting in a café. The napkins are branded with the logo. The woman behind the counter wears a branded T-shirt that is different from the branded T-shirt another employee wears. Every sign has the logo. The wall has an artistic rendering of the name of the place. The totally delicious brownie I'm savoring (and eating here) came in a plastic wrap that has the café's logo. The only thing not branded is the cup for my iced tea. If I was in Starbucks, that cup would be branded but the brownie package wouldn't.

Each place is different. Each business is different. Each writer is different.

Learn how to be your own best marketer, something original just for what you need to do and for your work.

Surface from your writing every now and then, look around at the marketing that's everywhere in our culture, and then see what you can steal. Or what's changed since you went deep into your book.

Once you figure that out, see what you can actually do.

And after you do it…

Write more. Because that's the basis for everything.

Thanks for picking up the book! I hope it helped you switch your mindset on branding.

And good luck with your writing and marketing projects!

ENDNOTES

CHAPTER 1 - IN THE BEGINNING

1. www.deanwesleysmith.com/workshops/
2. mailchi.mp/kristinekathrynrusch/boss-returns
3. mailchi.mp/kristinekathrynrusch/cool-writing-news-boss-returns-and-a-bit-of-gratitude
4. www.readingpulse.com/
5. www.targoz.com/market-matters-blog/2017/4/21/voice-of-the-reader-survey-finds-rising-book-prices-are-driving-buyers-to-delay-purchases-buy-used-books-or-use-subscription-services

CHAPTER 2 - TYPES OF BRANDS

6. www.brickmarketing.com/define-branding.htm
7. www.investopedia.com/terms/b/brand.asp
8. www.investopedia.com/terms/b/brand-identity.asp
9. www.readingpulse.com
10. hotsheetpub.com
11. xoxoafterdark.com/2014/02/20/2014-belles-wheels-bus-tour
12. www.dummies.com/business/marketing/branding/the-types-of-brands
13. www.mysteryscenemag.com/store/product.php?productid=17688

CHAPTER 3 - HOW TO BUILD A BRAND: THE EARLY STAGES

14. businesscollective.com/7-keys-to-building-a-successful-brand

CHAPTER 4 - DEFINE YOUR TARGET AUDIENCE: THE EARLY STAGES

15. www.indiewire.com/2017/02/get-out-jordan-peele-interview-1201785271
16. www.adweek.com/digital/nfl-scores-touchdown-female-fans-159674
17. www.entrepreneurs-journey.com/
18. www.quicksprout.com/the-complete-guide-to-building-your-personal-brand-chapter-2

19. www.indiewire.com/2017/02/get-out-jordan-peele-interview-1201785271

CHAPTER 5: BRAND IDENTITY

20. www.investopedia.com/terms/b/brand-identity.asp
21. www.adweek.com/tv-video/in-brand-reboot-syfy-doubles-its-scripted-series-and-broadens-scope-to-include-superhero-programming

CHAPTER 6 - BRAND IMAGE

22. Gottlieb, Robert, *Avid Reader: A Life*, Farrar, Strauss, and Giroux, 2016, hardcover edition, p. 147
23. www.businessdictionary.com/definition/brand-image.html

CHAPTER 7 - BRAND LOYALTY

24. www.factory360.com/brand-loyalty-5-interesting-statistics
25. www.readingpulse.com
26. www.rwa.org/p/cm/ld/fid=582
27. www.forbes.com/sites/davidvinjamuri/2014/03/04/the-strongest-brand-in-publishing-is/#378ba5d5ebfa
28. www.behavioraleconomics.com/mini-encyclopedia-of-be/choice-overload
29. www.retentionscience.com/customer-loyalty-vs-brand-loyalty
30. www.cnbc.com/2017/05/01/why-people-keep-buying-apple-products.html
31. www.thecreativepenn.com/2017/06/12/publishing-industry-launching-non-fiction-dan-blank
32. www.forbes.com/sites/davidvinjamuri/2014/03/04/the-strongest-brand-in-publishing-is/#289bcd1eebfa
33. www.forbes.com/sites/davidvinjamuri/2014/03/04/the-strongest-brand-in-publishing-is/2/#6edc62624be6
34. www.ama.org/events-training/Conferences/Pages/secret-loyal-customers.aspx
35. www.ama.org/events-training/Conferences/Pages/secret-loyal-customers.aspx
36. www.forbes.com/sites/davidvinjamuri/2014/03/04/the-strongest-brand-in-publishing-is/2/#46e425884be6

37. factory360.com/brand-loyalty-5-interesting-statistics

CHAPTER 8 - DEFINE YOUR TARGET AUDIENCE: THE INTERMEDIATE STAGES

38. www.forbes.com/sites/bridgetbrennan/2013/03/06/the-real-reason-women-shop-more-than-men/#2d3a43e674b9
39. www.readingpulse.com

CHAPTER 9 - HOW TO BUILD A BRAND: THE INTERMEDIATE STAGES

40. www.wmgpublishinginc.com/2017/07/10/publishers-note-using-tools-for-series-branding
41. www.inc.com/geoffrey-james/how-to-build-a-strong-brand.html
42. www.audiencebloom.com/how-to-build-a-brand-from-scratch

CHAPTER 11 - HOW TO EXPAND YOUR TARGET AUDIENCE: SLOW GROWTH

43. mashable.com/2013/12/27/opening-new-market/#_6OwceMkIaqg
44. wmg-publishing-workshops-and-lectures.teachable.com
45. www.ronvitale.com/blog/2017/3/29/is-instafreebie-still-an-effective-marketing-technique
46. insights.bookbub.com/category/book-marketing-ideas
47. insights.bookbub.com/top-book-marketing-takeaways-bookexpo-2017
48. lifehacker.com/behind-the-app-the-story-of-zombies-run-1632445358

CHAPTER 12 - HOW TO EXPAND YOUR TARGET AUDIENCE: AGGRESSIVE GROWTH

49. www.readingpulse.com
50. youtu.be/3MMMe1drnZY

USA TODAY BESTSELLING AUTHOR

KRISTINE KATHRYN RUSCH

DISCOVERABILITY

HELP READERS FIND YOU
IN TODAY'S WORLD OF PUBLISHING

A WMG WRITER'S GUIDE

INTRODUCTION

THE REASON FOR THIS BOOK

Everyone—including self-published authors—is worried about the "mountain of crap" that self-publishing will (has?) brought into the industry.

Everyone ignores two important facts: one person's crap is another person's beloved book, and publishing has always produced books in great volume. The recently merged Penguin Random House (or Randy Penguin as one of my favorite PRH authors calls it) will publish 15,000 new titles in 2014, not counting everything in its backlist.

I hate to say this, but a lot of those 15,000 titles will be crap—at least to someone.

The number of books published in the United States has always been extremely high. If you add up the number of books published worldwide, you'll realize that, with so many choices, it's amazing anyone reads the same book at all.

Traditional publishers tell writers two contradictory things:

1. Only traditional publishers can help books find an audience.

2. Writers must promote their traditional published books in order to find an audience.

Um, well, no.

If traditional publishers actually knew how to find an audience, then writers wouldn't have to promote their traditionally published books. It's really that simple.

Traditional publishers don't know—and have never known—how to get books in the hands of readers. And writers generally mispromote their books.

Yet readers find books anyway.

Among writers, the promotion discussion has gone on as long as I've been in the business. And it's always startled me, because I have a background in business outside of publishing. I've also been very active inside traditional publishing, and the one thing I learned early is that traditional publishing has no idea how to market anything well.

First, let me share some terms with you.

By "traditional publishing," I mean publishers who work in the old model that existed before the changes in the industry.

That model works like this:

Writers provide content (product) to **Publishers.**
Publishers distribute that content to **Distributors.**
Distributors distribute books to **Bookstores.**
Bookstores distribute that content to **Readers**.

The *new* model, which has evolved in this century (and has become prevalent in the years since 2009) works like this:

Writers provide content (product) to **Bookstores.**
Bookstores distribute that content to **Readers**.

Most people call this model *self-publishing*, but I call it *indie publishing*, because, if you're going to do it right, you will need a team to help you. At minimum, you'll need cover designer, a copy editor, a line editor, a content editor, and an accountant.

You can learn how to do covers yourself and how to handle your own accounting. But you'll always need a second eye (a copy editor) on your team. And once you have a team, you're no longer a *self*-publisher. You're an *independent* publisher.

I've worked in traditional publishing in every single job except as an agent (and you'll note that I don't include agents in either model above. In this modern world, they're not necessary). I have started two separate successful traditional publishing companies, and advised the owners of several other traditional publishing companies.

I've edited, worked in bookstores, and helped distributors. I've even worked in libraries.

I know publishing. And since ebooks and print-on-demand disrupted the staid old publishing business, I've also become what's known as a *hybrid writer*, someone who indie-publishes *and* traditionally publishes her work.

Because I can never do just one thing, I've owned successful retail businesses. I'm in the process of buying another—or, to be more accurate, buying *back* the business my husband and I sold seven years ago.

I've owned at least ten businesses. (I always forget one or two, which is why I'm not being exact here. I'm too lazy to go back and figure it out accurately.)

I still own five. One of those five is my writing business. Another is a publishing company. The rest exist outside the realm of publishing entirely.

I'd like to say that most of my writing has been in fiction, but that's not true. I've written nonfiction professionally since I was sixteen years old. For more than a decade, my primary writing income came from my work as a business writer for major magazines. I interviewed the owners of countless start-ups and long-term success stories. I wrote business cover stories on everything from Hollywood production companies to game companies to investment firms.

I also worked as a broadcast journalist and spent a few years as the news director of a non-profit radio station, where I learned how different non-profits are from for-profit businesses.

I have written ad copy for radio, newspapers, and television. In the modern era, I've written ad copy for Kickstarter projects and other online ventures. I've done marketing for almost every business I've been involved in, and I noticed, well before one of my blog readers mentioned in the comments, that "Publishing is the only business in which marketing is an entry level position."

Yeah, and it shouldn't be. The fact that it is shows how unconcerned traditional publishers are with marketing.

This book will not tell you how other writers market their books. Instead, I'll look at the way other *businesses* market their *product*.

Once you finish writing, your book must go from being your baby to being a widget. If you cannot make that shift, then close this book and set it back on the shelf (or delete this free sample from your ereader). Until you can honestly call your writing a *product*, you will not be able to do the things listed inside this volume.

I have written this book with a specific target audience in mind. That target audience is composed of *established* writers. Beginners can read this volume for information for their future, but until you've published several titles, the content of this volume is not for you.

I initially wrote this book in 3,000-word chunks that I posted on my weekly business blog. The original posts are still online, along with the comments from all of the readers. You can find them on my website, kristinekathrynrusch.com. Some of the comments are very useful. Some are...well, you'll see.

I did write the blog posts out of order, so some of the context that you get in this book is missing. Also, some of the information is dated already, even though I put up the first post less than a year ago. That dated information is still available on the website, but I have updated that information for the book.

Because I initially wrote these chapters for my blog, I had to put up a set of assumptions. I wanted all of the readers to know where I'm coming from —and I still do.

Here are the assumptions I'm making for this volume:

Assumption #1: You will read this book in order. Usually people who buy self-help books read only the chapters that interest them. If you read this book out of order or skip chapters, you will miss a lot of important information. This book will only help you if you read it in its entirety.

Assumption #2: With only a few exceptions, we will be talking about *fiction* here. There are promotion techniques that work for nonfiction— even on the first book—that do *not* work for fiction. I don't want to muddy the waters here. We're discussing *fiction* in this book.

Assumption #3: You have learned your craft well enough to intrigue readers. You know how to tell a good story; you have grammar, spelling, and punctuation under control; you create interesting characters; and you write what you love.

Assumption #4: If you have indie-published your work, then your work has a good blurb, a great cover, and a well-designed interior. Your work is available in ebook and trade paper formats. (I also hope you have audio books, but for our purposes here, I'm not going to assume it.)

Assumption #5: If you have indie-published your work, your ebooks are available in every ebook venue you can find. Your paper novels are in extended distribution on Createspace or through some other print-on-demand company. In other words, if a bookseller whom you don't know and never will know wants to order your paper book, that bookseller can call up a catalogue from a major distributor (Baker & Taylor, Ingrams) and order your book at the proper bookseller's discount.

Assumption #6: If you are traditionally published, your books are with a company that makes the books available in ebook and paper formats, and *your books are still in print*. (If they aren't, ask for those rights back and then publish the books yourself.)

Assumption #7: You have at least a minimal web presence. You have a website that readers can easily find. You have a list of your published books somewhere, also findable. You have some passive marketing in place. (A mailing list, a social media presence, or a contact button on your website. *Something*.)

Assumption #8: You have published more than one book. Most of what I tell you won't work on one novel. You'll need several—or at least a novel and some short stories. If you're haven't published much, make sure you've done 2–7, and *write the next book*.

Those are the assumptions.

Now, I have one big WARNING:

Everything I say here, everything, MUST take place *after* you've finished *writing* your story/book/novel. Do NOT take ANY of this advice into your writing office. *None* of it. Be an artist: write what you love. When you're done, *then* worry about marketing it. This new world of publishing allows us to write whatever we want and *publish* it. Please take advantage of that. When you *write*, be an artist, be a great story-teller, not a marketer or a salesperson.

I know, I know. Lots of warnings and assumptions. But I had to be clear, because these points are *extremely* important.

Because if you don't fit into the target audience for this book, then much of what you find here will not apply to your work. It's as simple as that.

A lot of the information you'll read here will challenge your cherished preconceptions of the way books should be marketed. If you've been around publishing—both traditional and indie—you've absorbed the conventional wisdom about book marketing.

The main tenet of that convention wisdom is this: publishing is a special business, and traditional rules of marketing do not apply to it. That tenet has been around since the 1940s, and it's just plain silly.

Traditional publishers have never reached the majority of readers because traditional publishers haven't tried. Most of the indie publishing marketing gurus are making the exact same mistake, focusing on the discount marketplace at the exclusion of the average customer.

This book will give you ideas on the best way to reach readers, show you solid marketing techniques, and help you evaluate the success of your publicity campaigns.

The book will also help you decide the most important part about marketing your own work: when you should let your work speak for itself.

Ultimately, this book should help you figure out what's best for you when it comes to marketing your work. What's best for you might not be best for me. Every writer is different.

My goal in writing this book is to help you make an *informed* decision about marketing for your writing business. Once you're informed, you can do anything you want—follow conventional wisdom, follow traditional marketing, or subvert everything.

If you're informed, you'll have a reason for doing whatever it is you're doing—rather than following the crowd.

And that's the most I can hope for.

All writers believe they need to market to rise above that tsunami of crap. Mostly, what you need to do to rise above is pretty simple and straightforward.

Write well. Do your passive marketing correctly. Write a lot.

Very simple to say.

Very hard to do.

But I have faith in you. You picked up an unconventional marketing book. That's an important first step.

When you close this book, you'll know enough to make the right choices for your business.

Remember, marketing is always *your* choice. Not a requirement. And not something someone else can dictate.

Good luck with your writing—and your marketing. And remember to enjoy it all.

—Kristine Kathryn Rusch
Lincoln City, Oregon
August 8, 2014

THE BASICS

1

WHAT IS DISCOVERABILITY?

…besides a modern buzzword?

Discoverability is, in its purest form, marketing. The problem is that in modern American culture, salespeople and marketers have become the butt of a thousand jokes. Dumb, loud, clueless, the salespeople and marketers have become the people that the rest of us laugh at.

Until we need them.

Then, the savvy among us realize that sales and marketing done right isn't just a cookie-cutter process: it's an art. And the best practitioners of that art are often invisible.

Their artistry is also invisible.

We live in a consumer culture, surrounded by mostly invisible marketing that influences us in subtle ways. Most of what we notice and call marketing are the loudest forms of marketing.

Let me give you two examples:

1. The Call-to-Action:

A call-to-action is exactly what it sounds like. You address an audience or group and give them an instruction that includes an immediate response. *Buy Now! Hurry, Before This Sale Ends! Tell Your Friends!*

Those late-night infomercials? The ones that put up a phone number and say, "Call in the next fifteen minutes, and we'll throw in a kitchen sink"? *Those* are call-to-action commercials.

You'll note that until the FCC changed the rules here in the United

States, call-to-action commercials were often louder than other commercials.

There's a reason for that. The reason is to get your attention so that you will take the action (whatever it is) immediately.

2. Push Marketing:

In marketing, there's something called a "push-pull strategy." Most of us only notice the "push" part, and don't realize when we've been subjected to the "pull" part.

Most television commercials are push marketing. The advertiser *pushes* the product to the consumer, loudly and often. The point of push marketing is to push the consumer toward the product and force the consumer to buy.

Clearly, push marketing works only in certain cases. Movie studios use push marketing in the week before a major release, advertising a movie trailer over and over again until most of us can recite the contents of that trailer. Once opening weekend starts, the push marketing usually ends.

Pull marketing is the opposite of push marketing, in that the advertiser *doesn't* advertise the product. Instead, the advertiser uses a variety of subtle techniques to *pull* the consumer into the store.

Consumers *pull* products. They pull the products off the shelves (virtual and otherwise). And sometimes, companies let consumers do all the work—the pulling.

The bulk of the marketing you see and don't realize you've seen falls into the pull-category. Book covers pull the eye to the book. The scent of baking bread pulls you into a bakery.

The problem is that a consumer must already be onsite before pull marketing usually works. In this day and age, pull marketing often happens on the Internet, so you're already online. You are pulled without even knowing it has happened.

Most companies use a combination of push-pull. They push until you're familiar (overly familiar) with the product, then let the product pull you to buy it. Movie marketing has evolved into push-pull. The trailer pushes the movie, and then once the movie's released, the consumer gets pulled in—and, if the movie is good, pulls in friends as well, through word of mouth.

Marketing is a very complicated subject. Universities offer majors in business and marketing. Entire schools are dedicated to the subject. I urge you to visit the marketing listing on Wikipedia. If you hit the link that takes you to types of marketing, you'll find seventy-five different types of marketing listed, and I know that's not an inclusive list.[1]

Think you know everything about marketing? People who teach

marketing don't know everything about marketing. People who have been in the marketing business for thirty years don't even know everything about marketing.

You don't either.

Because the biggest key with marketing is that it evolves.

Someone somewhere will come up with a whole new strategy that will do the job, and then others will jump on the marketing bandwagon. They'll refine that strategy for different industries, and after time, that strategy will become old and stale.

Then someone else will revive an ancient strategy and make it new.

Conventional wisdom is not marketing.

Marketing is always new, always fresh, and always exciting.

That's why advertising execs burn out. Because to be fresh, exciting, and new takes energy, and at some point, even the most savvy exec must take a break. Renew, rethink, and revive.

Because we associate marketing with its loudest and most obnoxious forms, we think it's easy. After all, we know how to demand that people buy our work. We've seen it done millions of times. Literally millions.

Actually, though, the best marketing isn't easy. It's hard to do well, and it's almost invisible. The best marketing makes you think that buying the product at that moment in time was *your* idea, not the idea of the company that made the product.

And yet, chances are the reason you bought that particular product wasn't because you needed it, but because someone had marketed it to you.

Since we're doing definitions here, let's deal with marketing.

I love how Wikipedia defines marketing:[2]

> *Marketing is the process of communicating the value of a product or service to customers, for the purpose of selling that product or service.*

I love that definition because that's primarily how I'll be dealing with marketing in this book. Marketing, in this definition, is *discoverability* (with the hope of selling the book after it's "discovered").

But honestly, in business, marketing has a larger meaning. The fact that it has a larger meaning confuses the issue, particularly when writers read blogs written by true business marketers. The writers don't understand that there are parts of the business marketing definition that writers should ignore—because we are dealing with an *art* product, not a *manufactured* product.

The Business Dictionary defines marketing like this:[3]

The management process through which goods and services move from concept to the customer.

The Business Dictionary then goes on to define the process, using another marketing phrase—the 4 Ps of Marketing (and no, I'm not making that up).[4] The 4 Ps of Marketing are items that businesses believe to be in their control.

Remember: there's a lot about business that is *outside* of your control. Worrying about those things gets you nowhere.

So, in business theory, the four things you can control (the 4 Ps of Marketing) are

Product, Price, Place (Distribution), and **Promotion**

We will discuss all 4 Ps in this book, although not quite in that way.

In a regular business—such as a manufacturing business (where you make cars, for instance)—you can refine the **product** to appeal to the most buyers. Most writers believe refining the product means writing to market —i.e. if vampires are currently selling well in novels, then the writers should write a vampire book.

That belief is wrong.

Writers create art, and art is best when it's *not* manufactured. You write what you write, and *then* you market it.

This is why I said in the introduction that if you can't think of your **finished** book as a product, you aren't ready for the material in this book.

You commit art first. Then you declare it finished.

Then you look at that art, wave your magic wand, and transform that art into a *product*. Once you have a *product,* you must figure out how to *package* that product to appeal to the *correct* readers.

So in our 4 Ps of Marketing, we're not going to have **Product.** We'll have **Package.**

Please remember that.

We'll spend a lengthy section on **Price,** and revisit that often. Because price isn't something arbitrary or something that your friends had success with. It's a *strategy* that you have to understand before you set the price for your product.

Mostly, I don't deal with **Place** or distribution in this book, except to tell you how to maximize your distribution efforts. In the assumptions from the

Introduction, I assume you have already distributed your book to every available ebook and paper retail venue that you can reach.

The more places your book is available, the better chance you have at selling a lot of copies of that book. It seems logical, but traditional publishers have *never* followed that model.

Finally, **P**romotion will be the other pillar of marketing that we'll discuss in this book.

Writers who have no business background think all marketing *is* promotion. That's only one small part of marketing and/or discoverability. I will spend a lot of time on **P**ackage strategies and **P**romotion strategies.

By the end of this book, you should see how things as subtle as the correct image on your cover will help with your discoverability efforts.

You don't have to be loud to get your book discovered. You don't need to price your book in the discount section of the bookstore to do it, either.

What you need is a great story, proper packaging, and just a little thought about how you want to present your product when you take it to the market.

My goal with this book is to help you market your novels in the most effective way possible. That effectiveness will be about time as well as money. In fact, as I say throughout, time is more important than money.

The more time you save, the more you can write.

The more you write, the better *all* of your books will sell.

We'll discuss that in several chapters here in The Basics.

So let's get started.

2

WHO ARE YOU?

Generally speaking, a good publicity campaign starts by defining the campaign's target audience.

Here, however, instead of figuring out your campaign's audience, we're going to figure out who you are. Because until you know your strengths and limitations, you can't do any planning well.

What I know about you is that you're a writer. I hope that you're an established fiction writer, because established fiction writers are *this* book's target audience.

I also know that you want as many readers as possible to find your books. In a perfect world, the readers would find your work without anyone doing anything.

But the world's not perfect, and to get attention for your book, you'll have to do a few things. I've outlined a lot of those things in the chapters of this book.

Some of those things are passive marketing, which I define as a one-and-done type of marketing. (Many of the tricks of passive marketing form the invisible marketing that I mentioned in Chapter One.)

Another thing that I'll discuss in future chapters is active marketing, which means that you'll have to do something on a regular basis.

As I wrote about *all* of these things on my website, I heard from my regular readers. They were frightened or upset, worried that they couldn't do anything I suggested for a variety of reasons.

Some writers lacked the funds.

Many writers lacked the time.

But mostly, the writers lacked the will.

Believe me, I understand.

I'm very good at marketing. But that doesn't mean I like all of it. In fact, I hate some of it. I know how to do it, and I would rather have someone else help me than do it myself.

However, I also know there are some things that will take me five minutes and take someone else hours. I do those things, and maybe, someday, I'll train the other person.

Part of my attitude toward marketing comes from the fact that I have done it since I was a teenager. I learned to write ad copy in junior high (yes, in the days before those years were called "middle school"). I learned to write *good* ad copy in college. I did a lot of PR and marketing for various companies in my twenties.

And, for my sins, I did countless on-air pledge drives for the non-profit radio station I worked at. When you do on-air pledging, you know immediately when your pitch is working and when it isn't. The phones ring in the studio if you're doing well, and they're silent if you're not doing well.

(By the way, on-air pledge drives are all call-to-action [see Chapter One]. Literally. And just as annoying as any other call-to-action.)

I have trained myself to do most of my marketing as a matter of course.

I don't even notice most of the passive marketing that I do. But throw me into active marketing, and I'll do it very well.

I'll also bitch about it to my friends.

Before I do any active marketing these days, I also weigh its importance compared against the time I spend writing.

Award-winning writer Scott William Carter has actually come up with an acronym for this weighing. He calls it the WIBBOW test. The acronym stands for this:

Would I Be Better Off Writing?

Usually, the answer is yes.

As I say throughout this book, the most important commodity you have is time. And the best thing you can do with that time, my writerly friends, is to write.

Finish the next book and the next book and the next.

The more product you have on the market, the greater the chance that readers will find you. It's the simplest way to market your work and the one most suited to writers.

But we're all different.

Which is a real bummer. Because what most writers look for is one-size-fits-all marketing.

If the marketing strategy used by Writer John put his first novel on the bestseller list, then clearly that marketing strategy will work for every writer. Right?

Wrong.

Marketing follows a standard statistical model. The outliers are complete opposites. The successful outliers are the handful of people who invented the strategy. The complete failure outliers are the handful of people who are the very last people ever to try that strategy.

The packed middle is filled with all the writer-lemmings who follow the one-size-fits-all marketing crowd. They have some success, but mostly, the strategy gives them just enough traction to disappoint them—because those writers didn't make millions like the successful outliers.

Writers get the idea for one-size-fits-all marketing from a couple of places.

First, the writers want easy marketing strategies because most writers would rather write than market their work. I get that. So would I. You have to do minimal marketing (most of it passive), but there are marketing models that allow more time for writing and less time for active marketing.

We'll discuss those in this book.

Second, as we'll see in Chapters Eight through Eleven, traditional publishers have used one-size-fits-all marketing for nearly eighty years.

The idea that each book is the exact same product, the way that each jar of peanut butter is the same product, is hard-wired into the conventional publishing wisdom.

As readers, we know that's wrong. What *Huckleberry Finn* has in common with *The Goldfinch* is that they're both novels. But they are not the same book or even the same kind of book.

They appeal to different readers.

Sure, you could do a Venn diagram of the readers for each book, and find a overlapping subset of readers who like both books (that subset includes me), but most of the readers only like (or have read or want to read) one of those two books.

The books are dramatically different. The way that peanut butter and hummus are different. Peanut butter and hummus are both food. They're (usually) both brown. They can both be spreads for bread or crackers. But peanut butter and hummus don't provide the same eating experience.

They're not even close.

Just like *Huckleberry Finn* and *The Goldfinch* aren't even close.

So why market those two books the same way?

We'll talk about how to market different titles in different ways later. I'll give you lots to think about on that topic.

But right now, we're discussing you, and your writerly expectations. You expect—indeed you probably *hope*—that you can just do what other writers have done when it comes to marketing, and your books will automatically sell.

Hell, I hope for that each and every day, but in my nearly forty years in publishing, I have never seen any plug-and-play marketing that actually works.

(And right now, I'm feeling a bit stunned that I've been in the business forty years, and must remind myself that I started publishing professionally at *sixteen*. [Breathe, Kris. Breathe. Before your ancient lungs explode...])

Writers tend to form communities, and in those communities, you meet all types.

We know the "writers" who talk a great game but have never committed a word to the page. We know the writers who write a lot, but can't publish or mail anything. They put every word in a drawer and never let their writing see the light of day.

We know the writers who produce a lot; writers who never talk about what they write *ever*; writers who publish more than anyone else combined; writers who made a million dollars with their very first book; and writers who promote every single thing they write so heavily that you avoid them so you don't have to buy their latest because you feel forced into it.

Sometimes one person embodies several of those types.

There are the sales-enthusiast writers who hit *The New York Times* bestseller list, they say, because they flogged the hell out of their latest book. They're intimidating.

(They combine the promotion writers with the production writers.)

And then the writers who seem like lottery winners. They also hit *The New York Times* bestseller lists, but they rarely leave their house, and they hate to talk on the phone, and they really don't want to go into public *ever*.

(Those writers are usually a combination of the writes-a-lot writer and the never-talks-about-it writer.)

We define the lottery-winner writers as "lucky," and the sales-enthusiast writers as "hacks."

We say that the stars aligned for the "lucky" writers. They hit the cultural zeitgeist with the right book.

We say that the "hacks" conned the unwashed masses into buying a subpar book because the unwashed masses wouldn't know quality if they saw it.

We're wrong about both types of writers.

Both are excellent *storytellers* whose books caught the national attention. Each part of that sentence is important. The books wouldn't have sold at all if their *stories* were bad. And they wouldn't have sold well if the books hadn't (somehow) caught the national attention.

(Please note that I didn't say the books were well-written. We're not *writers*, folks. We're *storytellers*. I explain the difference in my blog posts, which you can see for free, and also in a book called *The Pursuit of Perfection.*)

The thing you must remember throughout this book is that we're talking about marketing. We're not talking craft, except that we assume you (the established writer) know your craft so well that readers enjoy your books.

When we discuss marketing, you need to remember that all we're talking about is *informing* the consumer that a book (or an author or a series of books) exists, so that the consumer can purchase that book.

Bestsellers share something in common besides a well-told story. They share the fact that somehow a mass of consumers *discovered* the book at the same time.

Bestsellers in America (and most countries I'm familiar with) are based on velocity—a lot of copies have sold *in a short period of time*. A bestseller will hit a list by selling thousands of copies in a week. If that book stops selling the next week, the book still gets the bestseller label.

If a book sells *tens* of thousands of copies over the space of a year, but never more than 600 or 700 copies per week, that book will *never* hit a bestseller list—yet it'll sell more copies than a bestselling book.

We'll discuss this more in the section titled "The Old Ways," but I will repeat it a lot, because it's important. Traditional publishing is not set up to handle the slow-selling book that will eventually outsell the bestseller.

But as an indie publisher, you can nurture those books and let them form the basis for your entire business.

I'm telling you all this here, because marketing, particularly in entertainment (books, games, movies, comics) is *velocity*-based, geared toward the sales that spike and then trail off.

The books that hit bestseller lists have had great informational marketing—the active kind, the kind we *all* notice.

The books that sell tens of thousands of copies, but at a much slower rate? They often have little more than passive marketing. They're word-of-mouth books. The *readers* end up promoting those books more than the writer ever does.

We discuss that in the section marked "Passive Marketing" and in Chapter Twenty: Word of Mouth.

Most writers would rather have the slow-selling book than the velocity book, not because of the numbers, but because most writers would rather be writing.

For my promotion of most of my books, I would rather let those books speak for themselves, and let the readers determine which books sell well and which ones poke along.

However, every once in a while, I finish a book that I want to have shouted to the rooftops. I want active marketing and a lot of it. I'll spend the funds to buy ads and I'll go out in public to flog that book, if I believe the flogging necessary.

Everything I mention in this book is something I have done.

I just don't do those things for every book. And some of the things I mention I'll never do again.

But that's me.

I've learned over *decades* what works for me the writer-person and what doesn't.

Now, you need to start figuring out what works for you.

How do you do that?

Writers are great at imagining themselves in other people's shoes. That's what we do for a living. So imagine what it would be like to be the Hottest Literary Figure in the World. Do you want J.K. Rowling kind of attention? Do you want to be on every TV book show, attend conventions every weekend, speak at libraries?

How would that impact your writing?

Think about it before choosing it.

Writers are lucky. We form communities, and we share information. Some of those communities are online, and some are in person. They're all subject to horrid infighting (I think writers love to fight more than they like to write), but they can also be very supportive as well.

Observant writers will see most writerly types in their communities. We all seem to "grow up" with the same types. And by "grow up," I mean that new writers will find communities of other new writers and befriend those writers. You might be different ages, but your careers will start at the same time.

The careers will never go in the same direction. Some writers will fade, others will rise. Some writers will quit, some writers will seem unstoppable.

But we'll all encounter the intimidating go-getter writer. That writer is a promotions maven. If there's a trick to promoting a book, that writer will do it. In fact, that writer will do it *while* producing a lot of good work.

When I was in high school, I was the intimidating go-getter writer. Then, in college, I met Kevin J. Anderson, and realized I was an amateur when it came to going-and-getting. Kev is a marketing and promotions maven and he manages to write as many (or more!) words than I do per month.

I don't have that kind of energy. I never have.

As my community of writers broadened, I realized that there are writers in the world who make Kevin's go-getter nature seem like he's standing still.

These writers rocket into the consciousness of a genre or of the entire literary world. Some of these writers rocket into the cultural consciousness in the United States. Others (a handful every year) rocket into the international consciousness.

Sometimes the rest of us think we have to be just like the go-getter writer to succeed. And we don't.

I tried to be like Kevin for a few years, before I met Dean and he helped me figure out how to use my own talents to promote (or not promote) my work. I relaxed when I realized I didn't have to follow Kevin's model to writerly success.

What I didn't know for years was that Kevin worried he had to follow *my* model to writerly success. I intimidated him just like he intimidated me. We both knew that the other person was better at some things, and not as good at others. And we wanted it all.

Stephen King was the big hot international writer when I was getting my start, so imagine my surprise when I found out that King hadn't achieved his vision of writerly success. His was based on his English major roots—good reviews in *The New York Times Book Review*, awards, and recognition as a *good* writer, not a hack.

He got that in the last fifteen years, as the "hack" label moved to other good writers like J.K. Rowling (because of her phenomenal sales).

We all watch, learn, and envy a little. And we're always feeling like we should do more.

We need to understand how different we all are.

We have different work habits. We write in different genres. And we have a different level of tolerance for promoting ourselves and our work.

For example, I'm an introvert, although I present as an extrovert.

The different between introverts and extroverts is that introverts get exhausted by their interactions with others, and extroverts draw energy from being around others.

Introverts don't hate other people. I love watching and listening to others. I like people a lot. They just tire me out.

Conversely, extroverts might not love other people. Extroverts just draw energy from others. I've known a few extroverts who are true misanthropes.

Extroverts aren't necessarily the best at promoting their work. Extroverts often forget that other people in the room have valuable opinions. But extroverts often know how to work a crowd.

There are extroverted writers. I know several of them, some with a lot of success, some with none.

The danger for the successful extroverted writer is that the in-person promotion becomes an addiction. Getting the rock star treatment is wonderful—the massive hotel rooms, the fantastic meals in fantastic restaurants, every move profiled (positively) by the entertainment media.

The problem with that isn't what you think I'm going to say—that the media will turn on the rock-star writer. (It will, but writers are smart; they're aware of that.)

The problem is that the extroverted writer will stop writing. You'll often see comments about celebrity writers (sometimes in their obituaries) that their best work came early. That's because most celebrity writers stop writing and become celebrities instead.

Introverts have the opposite initial problem, but the danger is the same: the introvert also stops writing.

Traditional publishing forces all its bestselling writers to go on book tours to promote their work. Those writers often get minor celebrity treatment (and sometimes get rock-star treatment)—the same lovely hotel rooms, the same fantastic meals, the same media coverage.

Only all of that *drains* the introverted writer, and brings a crowd into her workspace. I don't know for certain if Harper Lee stopped publishing because she stopped writing; I do know that she was an introvert who became a celebrity writer, and she hated it. Just like J.D. Salinger.

Both of those writers withdrew from the public.

And because their only choice fifty years ago was to publish traditionally, they had only one way to withdraw. They stopped publishing.

Indie writers can *choose* what kind of marketing campaign we use for our work. We can be very public in our promotion or we can be very quiet about it.

We can hire people to do a lot of the targeted marketing for us, or we can save the money and do it ourselves. By hiring people, I am *not* talking about hiring a publicist. Publicists charge and arm and a leg and most of them do—you guessed it—one-size-fits-all marketing. See Chapter Five for more information.

We can write a lot or write a little.

We can choose.

And so, now, can traditional writers. The introverts can say no to the book tours and the big press coverage. If their publishers don't like it, then the introverts can move to another publisher or they can indie publish their own work.

They don't have to do what their publisher demands, if that doesn't work for them.

Choice is the watchword for the modern era of publishing.

Or, to be more specific, we have a watch-phrase: Writers Can Choose.

As you read this book, think about what you want from your marketing efforts on your own titles. Then think about the assets you have.

Those assets are

1. **How much time you can devote to marketing.**
2. **How much money you can devote to marketing.**
3. **How creative you can be about marketing—without taking away from your writing creativity.**

Then figure out what your limitations are.
The limitations are similar to the assets:

1. **How much time you have for marketing.**
2. **How much money you have for marketing.**
3. **How much creativity you can spare for marketing.**

Most importantly, you need to figure out what you want from that marketing. (See Chapter Four: How to Measure Success)

Then you marshal your assets and your limitations, and figure out the plan that's best *for you*.

Your plan will not be right for me.

Nor will it be right for other people in your writing community.

This is your plan—and it might vary from book to book.

Realize that one-size-fits-all marketing is the worst way to market. Put some thought into marketing, and then do it your way.

If that way doesn't succeed, try again.

But always keep your eye on that WIBBOW test—and write the next book.

3

HOW TO THINK ABOUT YOUR WORK

(WHEN MARKETING IT)

We all know that our industry—publishing—is going through a massive disruption caused by new technology. The disruption is in two areas—the production system and the distribution system.

It's easy and cheap to produce a book these days. Understand that I'm not talking about writing one. I'm talking about the things that happen after the book is finished. Please be clear on that, because if you misunderstand that point, you'll miss the point of the entire chapter.

In the past, it took tens of thousands of dollars to produce an actual physical book. Then you'd end up with a warehouse (or a garage) full of books, and no way to get them to a customer.

In the early part of the 20th century, a lot of writers self-published and ponied up large amounts of money produce the book. But by the middle of the century, writers couldn't get the books to market, even if the writers produced the books.

Traditional publishers created a lock on the distribution system that was pretty extreme. Books went from the publisher's warehouse to hundreds of distributors all over the country, who sent the books to bookstores, grocery stores, truck stops, and drugstores. Anyplace that wanted books could get them.

That system was already breaking down when Amazon started up in the mid-1990s. The main part of the distribution system had collapsed by the end of the century, murdered by large stores that wanted centralized ordering. The day of the local distributor who knew what his customers wanted disappeared.

Books got delivered to bookstores and a few non-bookstore chains, like grocery stores. But the small non-bookstores that used to get a spinner rack of books? Those stores couldn't order books if they tried.

The markets that got books to readers contracted.

Traditional publishers responded to this contraction by getting rid of the bulk of their sales reps, leaving a small sales force that mostly sold to a handful of buyers. Traditional publishers changed editorial strategy to meet the new reality, trying to find books that would appeal to a mass audience, just as the mass audience in all other parts of entertainment was breaking into pieces.

If traditional publishers want to know why Amazon was successful, it was because Amazon distributed books to the people who wanted them. Amazon didn't try to dictate who should get what book. (Nor did it chastise its customers for shopping elsewhere, something a lot of independent bookstores still do.) The shopping experience on Amazon wasn't pleasant at first; it isn't always pleasant now. But it is useful, and more importantly, easy.

Thanks to Amazon and other online retailers, books went from the publisher to the online site to the customer. Note that this procedure cut out at least one middleman.

Combine the changes in distribution with the ease of production, and suddenly, midlist writers and wannabe writers didn't have to go to traditional publishers to get books to readers. If the only change in the system had been the rise of low-cost self-published books and there had been no ebooks, writers *still* would be going direct in much larger numbers than ever before.

As the outlets for books shrank, traditional publishers did nothing to compensate. Nothing.

Here's what a physical book rack is. It's advertising. Even if a shopper does not buy a book off that rack, she sees the books, notes them, and maybe decides to buy them from her favorite store or get the book from the library. People discover books by browsing. I don't care how good Amazon's analytics are, they simply do not compare to that moment of discovery—that moment when a weird-looking book catches your eye, you pick it up, and realize that it's heavier than expected and the deckle edge makes the book prettier than you originally thought.

Holding a book is a sensual experience, one that book lovers adore. You might decide to buy the ebook instead, but you might never have seen that book if you hadn't been standing in that store at the moment the book was on the shelf, and you happened to see an intriguing cover (or title or something).

Traditional publishers panicked about the changes in distribution, but did nothing to combat it. They didn't increase their sales force so that sales reps could market books directly to independent bookstores. Traditional publishers didn't woo regional grocery chains (as opposed to national ones). Traditional publishers didn't talk to museums or truck stops or department stores, any other place that used to take books.

Traditional publishers gave up without a fight.

Worse, they maintained their marketing strategy, as if the old 20th-century system was still in place.

Remember this when you read Chapter Ten: The Old Ways. Please understand that those old ways were built for a completely different world. And they were built for a different type of business.

The different type of business is where the paradigm shift comes in. To deal with the shift, let me explore some basics.

The first basic is this: Writers do not sell books.

Repeat after me: *Writers do not sell books.*

Writers license copyright. In my blog, I always follow that statement with this one: if you don't understand what I mean, then buy *The Copyright Handbook* from Nolo Press and *read* it. I tell writers that all the time, and I can always tell by their later questions and their actions whether or not they have read and *understood* the book. Too many writers simply have not a clue what copyright even is.

Let me tell you.

Copyright is *property*.

And an even nicer thing about copyright is that it's intellectual property. Unlike a physical object, which can be sold and you'll never see it again, intellectual property exists in many forms. My husband, Dean Wesley Smith, believes those forms may be infinite. He limits them to a writer's imagination. On his writing blog at deanwesleysmith.com in a post called "Killing The Sacred Cows of Publishing: You Can't Make a Living with Your Fiction," he likens intellectual property to a bakery—a magic bakery—which sells only pies.

I'll let Dean explain:

Think of us (every writer) as a huge bakery and all we make are pies. Magic pies, that seem to just reform after we sell off (license) pieces of the pie to customers.

And each pie can be divided into thousands of pieces if we want. The Magic Pie secret ingredient is called "Copyright."

Every story we write, every novel we write, is a magic pie full of copyright.

We can sell (license) parts of it to one publisher, other parts to another publisher, some parts to overseas markets, other parts to audio, or eBooks, or game companies, or Hollywood, or web publishers, and on and on and on. One professional writer I knew licensed over 100 different gaming rights to different places on one novel. He had a very sharp knife cutting that small section of his magic pie.

You really need to read the article in which he discusses the magic bakery. It has a different focus than I have here. But I'm going to add just one more thing from Dean's post:

You create the inventory, the pie, just once, but can license it for your entire life, having pieces you licensed keep coming back to the pie over and over, and your estate can keep taking and licensing parts of that pie for seventy years past your death. Nifty, huh?

Are you all starting to see why Kris and I are harping all the time about bad traditional publishing contracts? If you give too many rights to work away for too long, it never returns to your bakery to make you money. (Maybe in 35 years...again, study copyright.)

Magic pies are a great thing. They'd be even better if they had magic calories that stuck to you if you needed them, and dropped off if you didn't. But that would be another story.

Here's a different way to think about your book, copyright, and intellectual property. Think of it as *property*. Let me be more specific. Think of it as a house that you built. You already have a home, so you're not building the house for personal shelter.

You put time and effort into that newly built house, not counting the costs of construction (which, in the case of writing, would be the care and feeding of the writer, the overhead [which is the computer time and the electricity], and on and on). So you have an investment in that house right from the very beginning.

When the house is finished, you could sell it. You would probably make quite a bit of money up front if, of course, you built the house right and you had the ingredients that people wanted, in a neighborhood they wanted. If you were good at house-building, you'd recoup your investment in that house, plus a percentage.

That percentage is your profit. It might be a few thousand. It might be tens of thousands. It might be hundreds of thousands. But that's all you will ever get from the house, because the house is no longer yours.

Pretty simple, huh?

Now, if you rent the house, you won't recoup your investment right away. It'll take time to make the initial investment back and even longer to make a profit. Once you pass that profit threshold, however, the earning continues. Yes, you might have to do some maintenance here and there, and you'll have to pay attention to the overall marketplace, particularly when it looks like the current tenant is about to leave. But the house will continue to earn for you as long as you own it and as long as you keep it on the rental market.

The analogy breaks down a bit here, because copyright is not like a house. At some point, the copyright on that property will fall into the public domain (unless you're really smart and know how to manipulate copyright legally to maintain copyright on some bits of the property—and no, I'm not going into that here). But stick with real estate for a moment.

Those of you who have read my blog or my books on the business of writing are familiar with the property argument for contract purposes. But we're talking about discoverability in this book, not contracts.

What's the difference?

Marketing.

When you put that house up for sale, you have *one* chance to recoup your investment. Just one. So you get the word out everywhere. You want velocity. You want that house to sell as fast as possible, so you can make your money back as fast as possible.

Then, if you rehab or build a lot of houses, you'll pour that money into another project and do it all over again. Build, sell, profit. Build, sell, profit.

By the end of the year (if this isn't a year like 2008–2010), you'll make a tidy sum of money. Not enough to retire on, but enough to get you through the next year and the next.

The problem is that you're working your butt off. You're working on the sell/velocity model. The faster you build, the faster you sell. The faster you sell, the faster you make a profit.

All of your marketing efforts focus on that first moment when your property goes up for sale.

But...

What happens if, two years after you sold that property, the neighborhood it is in gets gentrified? That neighborhood becomes the cool neighborhood, the one Everyone Who Is Anyone wants to live in. Those upwardly mobile folks pay ridiculous prices to buy a house there.

Will you get a piece of that ridiculous price?

Hell, no. You sold the house two years ago. All of it. Every last bit of it. You'll never see another dime from that house. You're done.

What if you kept the house and currently rent it out? Well, let me speak as a former rental agent (which I am): When a neighborhood becomes gentrified, the rents go up along with the housing prices. The cool people who can't buy (or can't afford to buy) will rent, and at inflated prices.

If you still own the house and rent it out, you'll be making more money per month than you made when the house was finished years before.

You might invest some money into marketing when the neighborhood becomes hot. One of the property owners I used to work for advertised his upscale rentals *even when they weren't available*. He was creating buzz, he was making them desirable, and when those rentals became available, they stayed available for *hours*, not days, not weeks, not months.

The man was a savvy marketer. He always advertised his upscale housing.

But he also owned student housing in a college town. He never advertised his student housing. Ever. He didn't need to. That's what I managed. The student properties. And they rented in about two weeks in March—for the beginning of the fall semester. By the end of the first week in March, all the good student housing was gone. Only the mediocre-to-crappy stuff remained. And that was gone by the second week of March.

So how did new students get rental housing? They didn't. They had to live in university housing—dorms or graduate apartments. New students didn't find out about off-campus housing until they'd lived in town for a while.

Discoverability.

Because there was a built-in (continually refreshing) market for student housing, and because there wasn't enough off-campus housing for everyone who wanted it, the student housing needed no boost from advertising dollars. In fact, that ad money would have been poorly spent.

But, the upscale housing needed the constant boost, because—to be honest with you—the neighborhood wasn't yet the best in the city. It aspired to be the best, but hadn't achieved it yet. Without the word-of-mouth, and the occasional buzz, those properties would not have remained full.

Was my old boss able to rent all of his properties? Hell, no. He had rentals that needed work and rentals in undesirable neighborhoods, which turned over every few months, instead every year. The complexes had a lot of vacancies. He also had new properties that had just been completed that no one had heard of yet, and were less than 20% full.

Was he panicked? Nope. That vacancy rate was built into the earnings projections. His marketing campaigns hadn't even started for the new prop-erties, and it wasn't cost-effective to market the old ones until they got spruced up.

I do want you to note something: The new properties didn't fill immedi-ately, and my old boss didn't panic. Because he wasn't working on the velocity model. He wasn't trying to sell something to recoup his money fast. He was handling earnings over time.

He was treating the properties as *investments*.

Here's another basic: The word "investments" as defined in the financial field (not in economics) is all about putting money into an asset with the hope of good return (in the form of appreciation, dividends, interest earn-ings, etc.). All investments involve risk.

The key to investing is to manage the risk in relation to the reward.

Before you make an investment, you need to calculate what sort of return you want from it. Again, let's go back to our house. If you need a quick return, you might sell the property. However, you might want to hold onto the property and make a small annual return in the hopes that the property will appreciate.

Before you do anything with the property, you decide what you want from it.

Now, let's return to writing. Most writers want to be published. Then they get published, and then they want their books to make money. Most writers hope to make millions, usually within the first year. Hardly anyone ever does that. Over time, perhaps, but never up front.

Writers rarely think about their time as an investment, and the writing they produce as an asset. These are tough concepts, because publishing changed twice in my lifetime, and the old thinking got engrained.

From about 1920 to about 1960, traditional publishers were smaller companies, generally owned by their founders. For example, I recently read *Hothouse*, the history of Farrar Straus Giroux. FSG's main owner from its founding in the 1930s to the early 1990s was a man named Roger Straus.

Straus tried to buy as many rights as possible from his writers, particularly in the early days, so that he could then apply the magic-bakery thinking to these assets he purchased from the know-nothing writers.

Straus kept the properties he bought in print, and he capitalized on waves that came through. That's why FSG made money when Isaac Bashevis Singer won the Nobel Prize in 1978. The company did not have to find Singer's backlist and reprint it. They had had Singer's backlist in print for years. They did have to do additional printings, but that's different, and less costly.

In other words, back in the old days, traditional publishers treated books as assets, not just in their accounting department, but in practice as well. If there was a bandwagon to jump on six years after a book was published, the traditional publisher had the in-house memory to know the book belonged on that bandwagon. Since the book was in print, the publisher could jump fairly nimbly onto that bandwagon with nothing more than a change of marketing.

The first wave of corporate mergers in publishing started around 1960, and got worse in the ensuing forty years. Traditional publishing kept books as assets in accounting department, but no longer treated books like assets in practice.

Instead, traditional publishing treated books like widgets and counted those widgets as inventory. Stock. Stuff that would grow stale and have no value—which was why writers could win awards a year after the book came out, and no reader could find the book, because the publisher had determined that the award-winning widget was already past its sell-by date, and didn't need to be reprinted.

Instead of making money off the bandwagon, traditional publishing let most parades march on by.

This thinking became so pervasive—forty-plus years of pervasive— that when Dean and I taught beginning writers, we told them that when they took their books to market, they had to think of the books as widgets.

We also told the writers to negotiate their contracts and keep as many rights as possible, treating the books as assets that needed to be protected.

Yes, back then, we were as crazy as the rest of publishing, and only recently have I realized just how deep the crazy went.

Because if you are marketing a widget that will spoil within a few months, then your marketing plan is based on getting the most out of that widget in the shortest amount of time. Not only that, but you'll need a different widget in the second month, and yet another widget in month three.

But, if you are accumulating assets, then you need to manage the asset. You might not choose to market the asset at all until you figure out exactly what you want from the asset.

The fascinating thing about assets, folks, is that their value isn't constant. The values are in flux. Sometimes an asset isn't worth what you paid for it, and sometimes the asset's value is outrageously inflated.

Here's the important basic about managing assets:

People who manage assets (investors) manage a lot of assets. How many investors do you know who only own one share of stock? No one. You can't make a living on one share of stock, even if you're lucky and bought at the bottom of the market.

No one who manages rental properties for a living only has one property. I know a lot of people with day jobs who also own one rental. Just like I know a lot of writers with one novel who also have day jobs.

So...

The paradigm shift is pretty simple to say, and difficult to comprehend.

Every item that you write is an asset. More than that, each asset can be divided à la the magic bakery into dozens, maybe hundreds, more assets. Then you need to decide how you want to spent on marketing each asset.

You need to evaluate each asset *before* you decide to market that asset. You need to figure out what you can expect from that asset *this year*, and how best to manage that asset *this year*. (You can also have a five- or ten-year plan. But that's more advanced.)

Not every asset needs a marketing plan. Not every asset needs careful tending. Most assets don't do well in the velocity method, although a handful do.

Because our assets exist in the entertainment field, we want customers to interact with the asset—whatever that means (play a game from it, see a movie based on it, read the short story that started it all). We want those customers to find each asset. We also want to make a small profit off of each asset, so that we can live off our investments.

When you start thinking of your writing as an asset that will appreciate in value over time, then you realize that applying marketing methods based on widgets that will spoil does your asset no good at all.

Your thinking has to change before we start talking about ways to market your asset. Or not market your asset. Or market some of your assets and leave the rest alone.

Think of my former boss, the man who marketed the assets that needed constant championing, maintained the assets that were doing well without any marketing at all, and didn't market the assets that still needed sprucing up. Each time he advertised something, he had a reason for doing so. That reason had to do with managing assets, not with becoming famous or making a financial killing using suspect methods because "that's how it's always been done."

As you move into the next year, practice thinking of your output—all of your output—as *individual* assets. If the magic bakery doesn't work for you *Star Trek* fans, then think of your work as tribbles hiding in a pile of grain. Each story can have a thousand lives, if you let it. Each life is an asset. And each asset might require marketing so that it can be discovered. Or it might simply need to be left alone to grow on its own.

It's a difficult shift to make, growing up as we all did in Widget World. But it's a shift we need to make.

It's time.

4

HOW TO MEASURE SUCCESS

How to measure success? Who is Rusch kidding? We're only on Chapter Four, and she hasn't even described how to market yet.

When I first wrote the blogs on Discoverability (which you can still find on my website), I placed this post last. As I wrote the post, I realized it should have been in the early sections.

Because most writers follow trends in marketing because they heard that those trends "work," but the writers never know what "work" actually means.

The difficulty with measuring success is that success differs from company to conglomerate, book to book, and person to person.

In this chapter, I'll discuss marketing "campaigns." I want you to think of marketing your book as part of a promotional strategy, not as a follow-the-crowd idea.

You need to plan, and one of the first things you must do is figure out what success means *for you*, for the project you're going to promote, and for the amount of time and money you'll put into it.

Throughout, I'll state some general suggestions and then show you a specific from my own career in 2013–2014.

Before I give you my list of ways to measure success, add one item to the list, something I've already figured out for my work years ago.

Figure out if you're going to do any kind of promotion or if you're going to let word of mouth happen and write the next book. As I said in the very first chapter, if your time is short, write the next book and forget all of this marketing stuff.

How do you measure the success of the write-the-next-book method? Slowly. Patience is the watchword for this method.

If you continue to write and publish the next book, followed by the same routine for the next book and the next, eventually—over a period of years (not months), you'll see a slow and steady increase in readership. Particularly if you have a website so that your readers know what order the series is in or what other books you have (which is especially important for stand-alone titles).

Let's assume you've used the write-the-next-book method for several books, but for your next book, you decide to do a bit of promotion.

Here's how you measure success of that promotion.

1. **Decide What You Want Out of Your Promotion Campaign**
2. **Figure Out How to Measure The Results (If You Can)**
3. **Measure the Results at Various Points During and Post Campaign**
4. **Determine if the Campaign is Worth Repeating**
5. **Make Notes About What You Learned—Good and Bad**

Note I do not say anywhere in here that success is increased sales or that it's in winning awards or anything that specific.

Success (or failure) is always based on your expectations of your campaign *and nothing more.* So let's start there.

1. Decide What You Want Out of Your Promotion Campaign

This sounds so simple and so obvious, yet no one in publishing ever does it, not even the Big Boys of Traditional Publishing. The Big Boys throw money at their bestsellers, but as I explain in later chapters, that money is spent in a wasteful and unconscious manner.

Recently, at the weekly professional writers' lunch that I attend, we were discussing the various campaigns that all of us had with our traditional publishers. We realized that the publishers had paid for those campaigns out of "advertising dollars."

In other words, the traditional publishers had a big pool of promotion and advertising dollars, and they bought group promotions with that money.

But the traditional publishers never allocated the money to each individual book title. So, for example, the promotions that Sourcebooks did on *A Spy To Die For* that I discuss in Chapter Nineteen: Publicity Campaigns most likely never had the cost of the Kindle promotion charged against actual book *Spy*. That cost just went into the overhead cost for the book.

You, however, are running your own business. So you must allocate your advertising dollars *per project*. That's how sensible businesses run anyway.

If you're going to plan your promotions per title, then you must also allocate the money you spend *per title*, and the results you want *per title*. You determine everything *per title*—or, in some cases, *per series*.

Never ever do you plan promotions as an overall expense that comes out of overhead. You should never have a general "advertising dollars" fund.

Even if you're promoting everything you've ever published, divide the cost and success (or failure) of that campaign per title. You should never promote "everything."

Here's why: If you've published only one or two things, you're wasting your time and money; if you've published ten or more things, then you're still wasting your time and money—unless all ten are in the same series (or maybe, just maybe, in the same genre).

Each promotion campaign needs a purpose beyond *I want people to buy my book*. (Or, the even less conscious *I want to sell millions of copies and die rich*. Don't we all?

Your promotion campaign needs a set purpose. You must be able to articulate that purpose. Here are some reasons to do a promotion campaign: You might want to increase your sales numbers. You might want to introduce your series to a new audience. You might want to enter a new market.

For example, here's how I decided to participate in a Storybundle with several other well-known fantasy authors. (For a limited time, Storybundle and other sites like it will "bundle" ebooks together, and donate some of the proceeds to charity. The buyers set their own price. They're usually getting six to nine books at a significant discount.)

Kevin J. Anderson asked me to take part in a major fantasy bundle with several other bestselling fantasy writers. I have published many fantasy novels, but if I was going to participate, I needed to include a book from a series.

My only fantasy series is one called The Fey.

I haven't paid a lot of attention to The Fey because I'm getting other books in newer series into print. I'll be getting to The Fey after I complete a few other projects.

So The Fey wasn't on my radar. I had a choice here: I could have said no, because participating in a bundle takes time, and time is definitely something to measure along with cost in every promotion.

This promotion wouldn't cost me any dollars, but I knew it would cost me hours. I decided the hours were only worthwhile if I got more than the income from the bundle out of it.

Being in a bundle with current big name fantasy writers after my fantasy career dropped off the reader radar is a great idea. So I decided to participate with the first book in The Fey series. I picked the first book for a reason: I wanted readers to move through the series.

I would get five things out of this promotion.

1. I would get the satisfaction of helping a charity I believed in. (In this case, it was the Challenger Center For Space Education.)

2. I would get exposure for my fantasy writings.

3. I would get some money from the bundle itself.

4. I would get a halo effect from the readers of the first book who would (if I had done my job as a storyteller) move to the next book and the next.

5. I would get a push from the increased attention that would force me to write The Fey: Place of Power trilogy sooner rather than later.

I saw all five things as a huge positive, definitely worth the hours and work it took to promote the bundle.

Did I achieve all five? When the bundle ended, I got paid (always nice), we made some money for the Challenger Center (even better), and within a week, I started to see a good halo effect on the other books. So I got three of the five, so far.

As for the other two, I don't know yet. ("Yet" being three months later, as I compile this book. The halo effect continues. The series is selling better than it was before the bundle.)

Did this bundle raise the profile of the series? Maybe. Time will tell. Will the fans nag me to get the next book done? (More than those who were doing so before the bundle?) I don't know, since most people haven't made it through all seven novels yet. Again, time will tell.

This is why I say you must measure the result at various points during and after the campaign. But before I could measure, I needed to...

· · ·

2. Figure Out How to Measure the Results (If You Can)

It's pretty easy to measure sales in indie publishing. You record the sales figures before the promotion, then look at those figures—on all pertinent sites—during and after the promotion. If you're doing it right, the promotion is the only change you've made to that title during that promotion.

In other words, don't run a BookBub ad campaign at the same time as a Storybundle. You can't measure the halo effect from the bundle at the same time as the halo effect from the ad campaign.

When I say measure in all the pertinent areas, I mean it. For Storybundle, which is DRM free and on its own site, I knew that I wouldn't see much of a halo for a couple of weeks. There were some very big names with ongoing fantasy series in that bundle and readers would read them first. Plus, the DRM-free aspect and independent site are important to my analysis as well.

Here's how:

A lot of less adventurous readers aren't going to try to download something from a site they've never used before. Even fewer readers will download something that isn't in their device's store. (Kindle people often don't upload a mobi file to their Kindle; they just buy from Amazon.)

In other words, the subset of readers who buy electronic books, are willing to buy something outside of their device's usual system, and are willing to buy from a site they've never used before, is pretty small.

In past bundles, I've seen the biggest halo effect in stores that have multiple ebook formats for sale. For example, after a bundle last summer with the first book in my Retrieval Artist series, the biggest halo I saw was on Smashwords, which allows readers to choose their format, just like the Storybundle does. Makes sense, right?

Fascinatingly, to me at least, the largest percentage increase in sales I'm seeing on this particular bundle right now is through Kobo, from Europe and Asia. This tells me that a wide swatch of the buyers of this bundle were from outside the US, and therefore outside of Amazon's ecosystem.

As I said, sales are easy to measure. The bundle itself had sales, and the halo effect is starting. But how do I measure the increased exposure? And how do I measure the increased demand?

I could only measure the increased exposure during the bundle by the promotion the other writers were doing. And, with the exception of one writer, everyone in this bundle stepped up and did *a lot* of promotion. That's all I can ask for as a participant. That meant that thousands of eyeballs that wouldn't have seen my Fey series have at least heard of it.

One thing about exposure—it's not measured in results. It can only be measured in repetition from various sources. So, of the ten authors who participated in the bundle, and all of the fans who promoted the bundle, other people *besides those who bought the bundle* did hear about my Fey series. I have a hunch—although I can't prove—that the handful of increased sales I received on *The Sacrifice* in March and most of the sales of the paper books came because of the exposure, from people who would never buy from the Storybundle site.

However, unlike the halo effect that's readily visible, I can't see this result and measure it. I can only guess or perhaps hope.

The same with Point E, increased nagging from fans. Most people who bought the bundle haven't read through the entire bundle yet. Of those people who bought the bundle, only a small subset will make it through all seven books of my Fey series.

I won't see any results from Point E for months. Which is why…

3. Measure The Results at Various Points During and Post Campaign

Some of my goals for that bundle won't happen for months after the bundle. I won't see the full halo effect for six months at least. So measuring it takes a long-term effort.

When you measure results over time, you can see how some promotions are not as successful as they initially seem.

For example, I just saw some figures from a heavily promoted *New York Times* bestselling writer. Her books were traditionally published. The writer's highly discounted first novel sold hundreds of thousands of copies. The writer's second and third novels sold only tens of thousands of copies. The writer's most recent novel, which hasn't been discounted at all, has sold less than 10,000 copies.

This tells me that the discounting worked—but not in the way the publisher wanted it to. Discounting encouraged people to try the first novel, but of those who downloaded the book, most either didn't read it or didn't like it. (I vote for didn't read it—yet.) One third returned for the next novels, probably when those novels were discounted.

We will discuss why some of the readers only came back in Chapter Seven: Types of Readers. Because, as you'll learn in this book, not all readers buy books for the same reason.

For example, when you promote only to discount buyers (those who buy according to price), you'll get return purchases—only when you have a discounted price.

You can see this in Amazon algorithms. Amazon has this nifty algorithm that shows up under this heading: *Customers Who Bought This Item Also Bought....* When you look at writers who sell a book or a bundle at $2 or less, you'll see under that heading more books at $2 or less. Often, you'll see a mix of authors in that list.

However, when you go to the pages for books of writers whose books *aren't* on permanent discount, you'll see that the *Customers Who Bought This Item Also Bought....* shows more of *that author's* work. Or if the author doesn't have a lot of books published yet, you'll see similar books in the same genre.

To me, and only to me, that kind of permanent discount is a failure as a promotion strategy. The writer is selling books, yes, but isn't building brand loyalty to her name (See Chapter Twelve: Branding). It's as if she's selling cheap cookies that might taste like Fig Newtons. When Fig Newtons are discounted, the buyers with less money buy the Fig Newtons. When Fig Newtons aren't discounted, the buyers with less money buy the cheap version of the Fig Newton.

Some writers will disagree with me. They might see those continual sales as a success. Other writers might be willing to take the risk that only one-third or one-tenth of their initial buyers will return to buy more books from that writer.

Be honest with yourself when you analyze the success or failure of your promotion. You might not get the result you wanted. You might get a better result, one you hadn't thought of.

Or you might be successful in the sales you received, but failed at what you really wanted which was, say, brand loyalty.

Only you can determine if those results are worthwhile *to you.* But look at all of the numbers and measures you can, and do so over time.

If you do a price promotion, and the sales figures don't increase when the price raises to its original point, then was the promotion a failure?

It depends on when you measured the promotion, and what your goals were.

Since my goals are always long-term, I look at it this way: If the lower-price promotion did not increase the *baseline of my sales* on similar titles, then I would consider that promotion to be a failure.

But in the short-term, some writers would believe the promotion to be a success.

Most indie writers panic when the sales numbers go back down, and feel that they need to constantly discount to goose sales which is, in my opinion, another mistake. Because you must...

4. Determine If the Campaign Is Worth Repeating

In my opinion, a campaign is only worth repeating if it brings *long-term* success, not short-term success. At some point, you won't have the time or money to goose sales. Or, as so many writers discovered in the past few years, what worked once doesn't work any longer.

Don't just repeat what other writers have done successfully, either. What works for them might not work for you. Be willing to try various things. Be willing to *fail* at various things.

But remember this: when you determine what's worth repeating, realize you shouldn't repeat it for every title. All of the tools in your marketing toolbox should be used sparingly.

Remember too, that a lot of data is a good thing. Shortly after the Storybundle, WMG Publishing discounted one of Dean's books, *Thunder Mountain,* to measure how well a new advertising site eBookSoda is doing on its promotions. WMG did an early promotion with eBookSoda a few months earlier, because we knew how well such a promotion had worked with other advertising sites. That first promotion was successful enough (for a small company) to warrant a new test, which WMG did not too long ago. Then, WMG tested a third book to see if eBookSoda remains on the go-to advertising list. *Thunder Mountain* is the beginning of a series of mixed genre romances (time travel and western and romance and science fiction) that Dean is writing right now, so it's a good book to use as a long-term test.

I ended up doing something similar with my novels, but because of serendipity. I was asked to be part of four book bundles in the first half of 2014, and fortunately all four are in different genres. I tried a standalone for one bundle (and it wasn't that successful). I did The Fey in another bundle. The first book in one of my Kristine Grayson romance series appeared in a third bundle. The fourth and last bundle included the first book in the Anniversary Day science fiction saga.

I get to measure the impact of the bundling by genre and by book type (series v. nonseries).

My attitude goes like this: I'm always looking to increase discoverability *over time*, so if something works in the short term, it better have more than a one-shot effect. Unless that one-shot is exactly what you're going for.

The Fey promotion in March 2014 is currently a one-off that came from the opportunity Kevin presented, rather than any real planned promotion of The Fey. It's not worth my time or my effort to do a big promotion on The Fey right now, since the new book is on the distant horizon.

However, that same month, WMG Publishing and I started a major promotion of the Smokey Dalton book series that I'm writing under the name Kris Nelscott.

The goal in the beginning of this promotion, which started as the Storybundle ended, was to inform readers that this series exists. Established readers needed to know that a new book was out, and new readers need to know the series is easy to get into.

For that reason, WMG and I decided to do a traditional promotion of the new book *Street Justice* (see Chapter Eleven: When The Old Ways Work). I finished writing *Street Justice* in spring 2013, and the book was ready to go (with edits and proofs and a lovely cover) by August of that year. Still, WMG did the ARCs and contacted reviewers, making sure the book went into the traditional system with the idea of letting the series' supporters—mystery bookstores and librarians—know that the new book exists.

Early numbers show that libraries are ordering this book more than they've ordered any other WMG title. Booksellers are picking up the book as well. Reviews have shown up in *Publishers Weekly* and *Library Journal*, among other places, and they're getting exactly the attention we want. The books are being ordered.

Right after the book appeared, WMG mailed a series of press releases to African-American news outlets, reviewers, and bloggers, letting them know the *series* exists. St. Martin's Press never notified this community that I was writing a series with an African-American detective. Time will tell if this promotion works, but it's only one prong in a year-long campaign.

Upcoming are promotions on *A Dangerous Road,* the first book in the series, as well as some book festival promotions, and more media work starting in the fall of 2014.

Already, the sales of the other books in the series are better than they were last year at this time. And by next year, they should be higher. When the next book comes out (in 2015, I hope, depending on my writing schedule), then there will be a halo effect from all of this promotion.

It's a studied campaign—a slow, old-fashioned one, with a focus on booksellers, librarians, and brand-new readers. The new readers are my favorite part of the promotion, because in the past, no one tried to grow the series.

This kind of campaign is hard to measure. It's tough to see a crossover between immediate sales and a campaign that's purely informational.

For example, St. Martin's advertised one of my Kris Nelscott books in *The New Yorker*. I saw no increase in sales that week through Amazon, which was, by the time the ad hit, one of the few places the book was still available. That book did not sell more copies than any other Kris Nelscott book.

What did happen after that ad appeared was that I heard from readers who couldn't buy the book.

Was I hearing from them because they saw *The New Yorker* ad? Or would they have looked for the book anyway?

I don't know. I *can't* know because I don't have enough data.

The key thing about informational ads and things done to tell readers something exists is repetition.

The more someone sees the name of a product (be it a book or a new brand of cookies) in the general course of a month, the more likely that someone is to pick up the item when they see it. Not *purchase* the item. Just pick it up and look at it.

Studies show that once an item is in a customer's hand, the customer is much more likely to purchase that item. So half the battle is won.

But success in an informational campaign is hard to measure.

And what is information advertising? Straight ads, signs, the book itself on shelves, blog discussions, reviews, newsletters, Facebook posts, and on and on and on. We'll discuss much of this in future chapters.

If you the writer post constantly about the things you've just published, people leave. But if people stumble upon mentions elsewhere—a magazine, a blog, an ad—they'll pay attention.

So, figuring out if you should repeat a campaign is important and so is one other thing…

5. Make Notes About What You Learned—Good and Bad

You need to keep track of what you've learned and what you assume from what you learned. What worked in 2011 in ebook publishing promotion didn't work in 2014, mostly because everyone jumped on the same bandwagon and the 2011 promotions weren't new and exciting any more.

We don't know what the hot new promotion will be two years from now, but we do know this: that promotion probably won't work as well five years from now.

Keep track of what works for you, what didn't work for you, how much money you spent, if you recouped that money, how much you might have earned, how much time it cost you to earn that, and—because you're a writer (and probably the sole employee of your business)—how many books/short stories you *lost* because you didn't have the time to finish them while doing your promotion.

All of that goes into your records.

Be willing to try something that failed in the past, because...what worked in 2011 doesn't work now, so conversely what works now might be what failed in 2011.

For example, WMG has just moved some of its promotional dollars away from the established reader-focused magazines to established book dealer venues. WMG has learned that the book dealer venues have had a direct financial impact on the books advertised there.

However, WMG wasn't in the position to advertise in those venues until 2013. The rules to get into those venues are pretty strict, and many small publishers never meet those rules. WMG, which didn't meet the rules three years ago, does now. So, the money shifts from one venue to another.

I'm sure the company will go through other changes in the next year.

I know that my promotional opinions are constantly evolving. But I pay attention to what's going on in the culture—not just for books, but for other entertainment products as well. I learn as much (or more) from the music and television industries as I do from what's going on inside book publishing.

The key to success in promotion is pretty simple.

Figure out if you want to do a campaign, what you want from that campaign, and then measure the results as they come in. Then assess, assess, assess.

Best case: the campaign achieved its goal and grew your business over time.

Next best: the campaign achieved its goal.

Shrug: the campaign did nothing at all (that you could tell).

Bad: the campaign cost time and money and did nothing at all.

Worst case: the campaign cost time, money, and alienated the very people you were trying to attract. (Whenever you think that's not possible, go on Twitter and watch some poor writer tweet every hour about his 99-cent novel.)

When you're ready to promote a novel of yours, go back through this series and see if anything jumps out at you. Plan what you're going to do. And then be honest about your results.

Good luck. Have fun.

And, most importantly, keep writing.

5

HIRING HELP

In Chapter Two: Who Are You?, I blithely say that if you have enough funds, you can hire help to promote your work.

And then I realized what a can of worms I opened.

Chapter Two is one of those chapters that I added *after* I finished the blog posts, so it wasn't tested by the blog readers. But I had done that blog for five years, and when I write nonfiction, those readers live in my brain.

And I have a hunch they all would have asked me how they could go about hiring a publicist.

It's a logical question, even though I never said that you should hire a publicist to handle the promotion for your work.

I said "hire help."

I often hire help. I don't do my own covers or line edits or copy edits. I did do my own promotion, but I'm handing a lot of those duties over to other people whom I've hired to help.

Not one of those people is a publicist.

Why am I so hard on publicists?

Because I've known dozens (maybe a hundred) traditionally published writers who've hired publicists in the past twenty years, and not once—not *once*—have those publicists done anything to earn their exorbitant rate of pay.

I've been watching indie writers make the same mistake in the past five years, and again, I've seen nothing that tells me the publicist is doing anything except writing press releases and occasionally making a phone call to media contacts. If those contacts say no, they don't want to use the author in question as a guest on their show—oh, well. What matters is the publicist *tried*.

Because I was a journalist, I've been down on publicists from the beginning. Most of them can't write a press release. Back when I ran a newsroom, hundreds of press releases arrived every day, and hundreds of press releases got thrown away. Rarely did we ever use the information in a press release for a news or entertainment story.

I've checked (repeatedly) with my colleagues still in the business, especially those who have moved to online publications, and they agree. One friend, the head of a major online publication, has a specific email address for press releases—an address he checks only once per week, usually to toss out the releases.

There are sites that use releases, usually trade publications or local news outlets that need content related to the region or the industry. But that's *nonfiction* stuff.

Entertainment press releases? Everyone does them, and no one reads them.

Publicists do more than write press releases. Publicists make phone calls and go to lunch with their contacts. They talk about a client and ask if the contact can use that client in an upcoming venue of some kind or another.

Some publicists actually run publicity campaigns—designing everything from ads to media appearances. But most publicists don't do those things. And if they do, they only do it for their very best (read: highest-paying) clients.

Publicists do have their place. They do good work for major corporations, usually on *one* assigned project. The publicist focuses on that project and gets results or never gets hired again.

Realize that most major corporations have a marketing team, including publicists (who usually have a different name inside the company). Those companies hire freelance publicists for very special projects, the kind that they want a full-court press on, and don't feel that the full-court press should come from an internal employee.

It's a strategy, like everything else in marketing and promotion.

The problem with publicists is that most are self-employed, so in those off months when they're not working on one project for a major corporation (or if they've failed and aren't getting hired this year), they hire out to whoever comes through the door.

That would be you.

Twenty years ago, high-level freelance publicists—the kind who did special jobs for major entertainment corporations or who were connected with book publishing—charged $20,000 per month (minimum three months) for standard services for any client.

Today, mid-level freelance publicists charge $20,000 per month, and those who can get away with it still ask for three months payment.

No publicist guarantees results. So you could be $60,000 out of pocket and get nothing. Two years ago, an indie writer I know hired a publicist and asked her for regular updates. He got regular invoices, but never saw any evidence that she had done anything but take his money.

Before I wrote this, I did a quick Google search to see if I could find current rates for publicists. I found that some publicists these days are charging $5000 for "the most basic services."

Meaning stuff you could do yourself.

Book publicists promise to get you onto major TV shows. One publicist site specializing in book marketing says that their book publicist was "famous" in book publishing circles and could get a writer on all the major talk show circuits. The site went on to explain why the client needs a publicist who is more famous than the client will ever be.

I got up, washed my hands, and cleaned the keyboard. I was afraid the slime had slipped through my monitor.

Once you read the section marked "The Old Ways," you'll see why you should never hire a *book* publicist who is famous in book publishing circles. As I mentioned in previous chapters (and will expand on in the upcoming sections), traditional publishing markets books incorrectly, so hiring someone who knows that world "intimately" is the perfect way to lose tens of thousands of dollars and get nothing in return.

If you have money to spend to help with promotion, then consider hiring an assistant. Someone who can make phone calls, mail your book galleys, answer questions, and contact local media if need be. You can write press releases if you need one or the first draft emails that go with review copies, and your assistant can sign them. Your assistant can help with your newsletters and maybe set up some social media sites.

If you don't have enough work to keep an assistant busy, hire a group of freelancers. One to help you design your website. One to help with a cover when you finish a new book. One to send out all the promotional materials for that book.

If you have money to burn on promotion, though, hiring someone might not be the way to go. You might want to spend that money on advertising or on giveaways or on whatever else you can think of for promotion.

Better yet, if you have money to burn on promotion, put the money in the bank until you write several more books. Then consider how you want to market all of those books.

But don't hire a publicist or some company that guarantees you'll get promoted. Certainly don't hire a company like Author Solutions to publish and market your book for you. Because companies like that are vanity presses. They take thousands of dollars, and produce shoddy projects that everyone in the business ignores.

My sister, a heavy reader who has nothing to do with the publishing industry, sent me an email she got because she's on a bunch of reader-only websites. The email was titled *Fantastic Summer Reads* and she added "really?????" in the subject line.

The email came from one of the new vanity presses associated with major publishers. The email was filled with typos, bad covers, and horrid advertising copy. Clearly the poor authors who had paid thousands to be included in this mailing had written the copy themselves.

If they hadn't written it themselves, then I can guarantee that they hadn't even seen the email before it went out.

Any company related to publishing that promises to take the work off you and guarantees a great result like getting on a bestseller list or being featured in a TV book club is a scam. Avoid anything that uses the word "guarantee" in its pitch to you.

Most publicists are savvy enough *not* to guarantee a result. They'll go out of their way to avoid the word "guarantee." What they will promise is *access*. They have contacts that will consider you for TV shows or slide your review copies past the entry-level position or get you a thousand radio interviews or maybe give you a chance to do a TED talk.

Maybe, consider, open doors.

No promises, but the hint of promises.

Stay away.

No publicist will let you dictate how she does her job. If you want the same kind of control over your work that you get when you publish your own books, then hire people who can help you with the campaign you designed.

Those of you with traditional publishers—remember that their publicists are fresh out of college, in a job that the publisher feels is unimportant. Those publicists work for your publisher, not you, and they're handling hundreds of books per month. You won't get any traction there, either.

And be careful. In the past five years, a lot of scams have arisen around indie publishing. From the vanity presses that the traditional publishers set up to agents with ebook arms (that take a percentage of copyright) to book "designers" who charge tens of thousands of dollars, scams have colonized this new industry.

Just recently, I've seen a lot of book marketing scams—ones that are targeted *outside* of traditional publishing. A publicist is an old-school way of doing things that doesn't work for individual writers. The book marketing scams guaranteeing a place on Amazon's bestseller lists are just a new way to take money from writers' pockets.

Avoid all that.

The best promotions, these days, are do-it-yourself.

When you hire help, hire help you can control. People who work *for you*, not for dozens of other people at the same time.

As with so many other industries, the Internet has made it easy for someone sitting in her basement to do better promotion than those connected publicists ever could.

I've watched go-getter author friends do innovative promotions that resulted in great visibility while rich author friends hired publicists whose contacts never came through.

Save your money.

If you want to hire help, finish this book. Design the kind of publicity campaign that's best for you or your work, and then figure out if you need some short-term assistance on that campaign.

Hire a team if you need it, an assistant if you need it. If you want a full-page *New York Times* ad for your book, then you can get that for $100,000—which would be a better use of your money than five months of hiring a publicist.

I don't recommend doing either of those things.

I suspect most of you reading this book *don't* have money to burn. You want inexpensive marketing that will get results. You want marketing that won't take a lot of time.

Here's the good news: the best, most innovative book marketing being done these days is being done by indie writers. Many of them are going far outside the conventional wisdom, and very few of them are spending a lot of money to do so.

Here's the bad news for those of you with a lot of money:

This is one area where throwing cash around won't make much difference at all. You'll just lose a lot of cash.

Hiring the wrong kind of help is a great way to lose a lot of money.

So think before you hand over your credit card—to anyone.

There are no shortcuts in publishing. Remember that, and you should be just fine.

6

THE MOST IMPORTANT THING

A WRITER CAN DO

Alert American music fans monitoring social media in the wee hours of Friday, December 13, 2013, became—for a few hours anyway—the most newsworthy fan base in the world.

Somewhere around midnight on either Thursday or Friday, depending on the time zone, Beyoncé—in the words of *Consequences of Sound*'s editor-in-chief Michael Roffman[1] —"simply uploaded her fifth, eponymous-titled album to iTunes, complete with 17 videos to accompany the album's 14 tracks, and then, you know, walked away."

She didn't exactly walk away. She actually accompanied the upload with an announcement on Instagram that you have to see just to understand its impact.[2]

Beyoncé said she wanted to go directly to the fans, and whoa, boy, did she. Within hours, the album, called *Beyoncé*, became the fastest-selling album on iTunes *ever*,[3] and became #1 in 104 countries.

When I drop a stealth novel and announce it on social media, do I get that kind of buzz? Of course not. And while I'll be talking about Beyoncé's unorthodox marketing strategy a lot in this book, I won't be doing so because I want you to emulate that strategy.

I want you to *understand* it.

Those are two very different things.

Beyoncé, Nine Inch Nails, Kanye West, and Radiohead have all pulled off a version of this kind of direct-to-fans release. First social media starts to talk about it, then regular media, and then the idiot pundits, who have no real idea what they're talking about. (It took me nearly an hour when I initially wrote this to find people who were writing actual articles, rather than folks who were opining about the way that Beyoncé had been born fully formed from the forehead of Zeus, and therefore could have done something like this as a babe in arms. [And yes, I can be even more snide, if I cared to.])

So why am I discussing Beyoncé's great media coup in a chapter geared toward writers in the middle of my discoverability book? Because Beyoncé understands that she has a career, and she also understands that her work is not produce—something that has to be hyped before it spoils—but something that she hopes (and her fans believe) will last a long time.

Her fans love her work so much that they went against modern music industry beliefs and downloaded a full album, rather than wait a week to get the individual singles (or the CD). When Target and Amazon decided not to carry the CD because the Internet release came first (which was very pouty of them, and quite hypocritical of Amazon), Beyoncé didn't whine or complain.

Instead, on December 20, the day of the CD's release, Beyoncé went to a Wal-Mart in Massachusetts[4] (where she was set to go on stage a few hours later), commandeered the intercom, wished everyone in the store Merry Christmas, and then told all those lucky Wal-Mart shoppers that the first $50 of their shopping spree was on Beyoncé. That act of generosity cost her $37,000, got her another round of media attention, and served as a giant fuck-you to Target and Amazon.

Can't find the CD on Amazon or in Target? No prob, fans. Wal-Mart has it.

Oh, my, that woman has style. And she trusts her fans. She has cultivated them for *years*.

Years.

Beyoncé came to national attention in 1997 when the group she was with, Destiny's Child, released its first album. But she'd been learning her craft since she was a little girl. You may not like her music. But there's no denying she's one of the top entertainers in the world—and she's worked her way into that position with almost twenty years of performance, craft, *work* behind her. And here's the thing most articles about the surprise album release fail to mention—just how much work it was to produce the damn thing. (Not to mention how hard it was to keep the gigantic secret under wraps.)

On the day of release, the only mention of how hard she actually worked appeared in the *Los Angeles Times*[5] (at least that I could find):

> *Beyoncé's sneak attack is the result of more than a year and a half of work. Recording began when the singer and her camp of writers and producers lived together in the Hamptons last summer. And the videos were lensed in places such as Houston, New York City, Rio de Janeiro, Sydney and Paris as she toured.*

That's what I want you *writers* to take from all of this coverage. Every bit of the hype, every bit of the shouting, started *after* the album was done. The album itself is one of at least twenty original albums she's produced, not counting other projects she's been involved in.

She's only 32 years old. Do you think this release will be the headline of her obit? Maybe if (God forbid) she dies within the year. But if she has a normal life span, this might or might not be the headline when she goes. I'm betting on not.

Yes, in some ways, the idiot pundits are right—only Beyoncé could have done this. But that's because Beyoncé stands on seventeen years of work, and seventeen years building a fan base, seventeen years of a *career* that, with luck, will extend into the future.

And she built the album *according to her vision*.

Not, as so many of you keep asking me on my website, on what she should have done or what someone else does. *Her* vision.

Because, in the arts, all we have is our individuality. The minute you try to do something the same way someone else did—from composing a story to choosing a genre to marketing your work—you've failed.

The first rule of being an artist is *to be an artist*.

What you're creating is unique, because it's yours. Your job as an artist is to always strive to tell your stories in your way. Who cares if fat fantasy novels are selling right now? Who cares if none of your friends read romance?

Write your books.

And always work to improve.

Improve your language? No, not unless you don't know grammar well—and that is the case for so many of you. You never got grammar, punctuation, and spelling in school. Learn it, for God's sake. Those are the tools of your trade.

Then learn how to make those tools dance to your tune. Not someone else's. Yours.

You cannot think about being discovered if you don't produce the work.

Every time we talk about discoverability, promotion, or sales, I always say that the best thing you can do to promote your writing is to write more.

How do people find your work? By having choices. Some people might like the cover on your very first novel, and buy it for that reason. Some people won't find you until your fifteenth novel. Some people like your short stories or, as some of you have pointed out on a recent blog of mine, some of people find your fiction through your nonfiction.

Write. Write a lot. Then write more.

Don't even bother to try to be "discovered" until you have a body of work. Not one novel. Not even two novels. Maybe not three or four or five. Worry about being discovered after you've *published* a good handful of novels or short stories or plays or nonfiction books. Enough to fill a computer screen when someone is scrolling, looking for something to read.

I am *not* telling you to wait to publish.

Got that?

I think you should publish the very first thing you finish. If you want to be traditionally published, send that very first thing to editors who might buy it. If you want to be a hybrid writer or an indie writer, then publish that thing after it's gone through a first reader and a copy editor. Get it out into the world.

You might not sell a single copy.

You might sell hundreds or thousands or tens of thousands.

The only way to know is to make the work available.

But first, you have to do the work.

That work is writing.

Write what you love. Tell the best story you can. Then, once you've finished that story, start a new story. Make it even better than the first.

None of the hype, none of the career stuff, none of the marketing works on just one book. Nor does it work well on only a few.

In fact, there's growing evidence that hype—traditional marketing—doesn't work at all.

Again, from *Consequence of Sound's* editor, Michael Roffman:[6]

> *Here's the problem, hype only works if the product's justified, and in today's cynical culture, where everyone has a voice and the haters have even louder one, hype hardly matches up even when the product* is *justified.*

Remember what we've been discussing these past few weeks. We've been discussing how to get the word out about your work. What used to work in the past applies to a completely different business model than the one that exists today. (If you don't understand that statement, please read Chapter Three: How to Think about Your Work.)

As I was going through the articles about Beyoncé, looking for the information I knew I had read but couldn't find quickly, I kept seeing one thing over and over again.

The only way to know if the album was worth the hype wasn't the 800,000 downloads in the first twelve hours, but whether or not people would still be buying the album in the second week and beyond. Because by then, word of mouth wouldn't just be that the album was out, but also about whether or not the album was good.

Well, the album was released in the middle of the chart-cycle (not on a Tuesday, like all good albums should release). In its second full week on the chart, the album still held the number-one position. *Billboard* called it "unstoppable," and added this:[7]

> *Thus, in its first 10 days of release, "Beyoncé" sold 991,000 and is (so far) the 12th biggest-selling album of 2013. There is one more tracking week left in the year—the week ending Dec. 29. It's likely that "Beyoncé" will finish 2013 among the top 10 sellers (all of which have sold at least 1 million this year).*

If the fans didn't like the album, sales would have peaked in the first week and dropped precipitously. This happened to many albums in 2013, just like it's been happening to books.

When an album or a book or a movie—let me start again. When *a piece of entertainment* enters the world, that piece of entertainment must then stand on its own. The hype can only carry it so far.

The best work gets carried by word of mouth. When you've cultivated millions of international fans, like Beyoncé, that word of mouth literally moves at the speed of the Internet. When you're me, that word of mouth takes months, sometimes years. When you're brand new, that word of mouth will definitely take years.

Does that mean you should study the market before you write anything, jump into the bestselling genre, and hope for the best?

God, no.

Write what you love. Constantly learn. Constantly improve.

In Chapter Four, I compared your writing to real estate. Your writing is an asset that will live for decades after you're gone (if you do it right). So following this year's trends is absolutely silly.

If you need to think about which neighborhood your rental houses are in, then here's how you do it:

Every writer starts in a neighborhood where the storytelling is okay. We've all lived in places like that. The house provides a roof, maybe a little charm, and needs a lot of work. But many of us still lived in those houses—and we enjoyed parts of them.

Your goal as a writer is to establish your rental units in better neighborhoods—neighborhoods where the stories are mostly good (although there are still a few clunkers). Someday, after *decades*, your storytelling skills will enable you to offer rentals in a neighborhood where the stories are very good.

And maybe, just maybe, you might actually work your way into the truly rarefied neighborhoods, the ones with great stories, stories that will appeal to millions of people.

Then, long after you're dead, your work might work its way into that neighborhood where Shakespeare dwells. The one where Jane Austen's lovely little houses still charm and delight. You won't live to see your work there, but your fans will.

The new fans, who have discovered you—

Because of your *writing*.

So...how do you get discovered? You write a lot. You constantly improve.

And you have patience.

Yes, I've said this before.

I'll say it again.

Some of the marketing I'll be discussing in this book will apply to people who have written enough to form a list of works. If you've only written one novel, you can stop reading for what to do next right now. Read for information only. Because...

You're not ready for the rest of this.

You haven't done enough work yet.

Write more. Study this book after you've finished *and published* more work.

The rest of you, we'll talk about the brave new world of publishing in future chapters—a world where a superstar totally avoids the hype machine and outsells all of her contemporaries who did traditional marketing.

Believe me, that gamble wouldn't have worked in 1985.

But we don't live in 1985.

We live in a constantly changing future, and this book will help you negotiate that—at least when it comes to marketing.

Write first.

Market second, if at all.

And that's the best advice I can give you. Period.

7

TYPES OF READERS

In the next few chapters after this one, I'm going to discuss various types of marketing. I'll also give a short history of marketing in traditional publishing. But before I do, I need to make sure that I'm clear about one last thing.

Readers are not a single entity. Nor are they monolithic.

Readers are different from one another.

Now you're peeved at me. You knew that.

But, as a writer, you didn't *know* it.

As writers, we have been "raised" in the business to believe that readers are one gigantic mass of creatures, all the same. Yet as readers, we know that's not true. Just because Gillian Flynn's book *Gone Girl* spent weeks on *The New York Times* bestseller list doesn't mean all of us will like the book. Some of us will love it and some of us will wonder what everyone else saw in it, even if we bought it. Some of us will look at it and wonder who the heck would buy it at all. Some of us will buy the book after the movie comes out in October 2014, because we hadn't heard of this major bestseller until New Regency Films started advertising the movie. (Because, y'know, traditional publishers don't spend money on TV advertising. That would be so... last century.)

We readers know that's how it works. We writers forget it.

And traditional publishers never think about it at all.

They treat all books by advance level. The amount of marketing dollars put into books varies according to the advance paid to the author, not how many fans the author has. In theory, advance and fans should correlate, but in reality, they don't.

Traditional publishers don't really pay attention to a fan base. Publishers sell books to distributors and bookstores, and so target their advertising to those companies. When the chain bookstores took over the business, traditional publishers only had to convince a handful of buyers for corporations to take tens of thousands of copies of certain books, based not on the author's sales record, but on what was "hot" or a "great cover" or a "new concept."

Independent booksellers bought what their customers wanted, but independent booksellers, who do not buy in bulk, have very little clout with traditional publishers.

So when you're thinking of marketing for books, realize the model you've seen for it (traditional publishing) isn't based on attracting *readers*. The model is based on attracting *book buyers* for major corporations, a hidden little industry that most of you have never ever seen. (I will explain how traditional publishing book marketing works in later chapters.)

As a result, no one has broken down the retail side of the business with the idea of targeting the advertising toward the actual final customer—the reader.

No one has except, of course, the romance writers.

A bit of history here.

The romance genre is a "young" one in terms of existing as a stand-alone genre. Yes, romances have been around since the dawn of time, but marketing books under the genre title "romance" has only happened since the 1970s. Before that, the books were broken into categories like "love stories" and "Gothic." Genre is a fashion, folks, not an absolute.

Because most of the romance genre is mostly written by women and sold mostly to women, the notoriously sexist publishing industry of the 1970s and 1980s did not believe those books sold. Remember, publishing would target booksellers, not actual readers, and many bookstore owners (mostly men) refused to carry "that stuff" in their stores. I bought my romances back in the day at drug stores and through Harlequin's subscription service.

It wasn't until 1982 or so that romance began to make an impact, and that was because the romance *writers* started banding together and *proved* to the industry that their books sold. Romance Writers of America was founded in 1980 with this kind of advocacy in mind.

And because bookstores refused to carry many romance novels, romance writers were the ones who developed all kinds of marketing techniques that many of you still believe you need to use now. Some of the techniques are absolutely valuable, and we'll be discussing them in later chapters. Some have seen their day, and we'll discuss those, too.

But what you need to know, what's important to know, is that the *writers* are the only ones who have ever done a reader survey for the point of marketing books. (Maybe I should say *female writers*, because Sisters in Crime also did a great reader survey, which I learned about when I posted this chapter on my blog.)

(Another sidebar here: it was an education for me to Google every term I could think of for reader statistics/reader surveys. Because I found a million of them. For ereading devices. For various magazines and online nonfiction publications. For schools and libraries, to see if kids are learning. But for book publishers????? Nada.)

The last RWA survey[1] that I found, which is on their website, comes from a couple of years ago. I'm going to cherry pick some of the information there over the next few chapters, because it's evergreen. Some of the information is probably dated, particularly the social media and ebook stuff. Still, I think you should look at it (the link is in the endnotes), especially if you're targeting readers.

The survey labels readers like this:

Avid readers who are always reading a romance novel.

Frequent readers who read quite a few romances.

Occasional readers who read romances on and off.

Remember, this study is *romance* focused only. And for romance, the statistics go like this (or at least they did three years ago):

Avid readers of romance: 31% of respondents

Frequent readers of romance: 44%

Occasional readers of romance: 25%

And here—my friends—is where it gets interesting. Looking just at me, Kris Rusch the Reader, I am a *frequent* reader, according to this survey.

However, if you look at my habits and bring in all books, all genres (including nonfiction), I am *an avid reader*. Right now, I'm reading four different *books*—two nonfiction (one history, one goofy) and two fiction (one mystery, one YA). I'm also in the middle of an *Entertainment Weekly*, a *New Yorker*, and an alumni magazine. Not counting the online reading I do or the two newspapers I read cover-to-cover daily. Or the manuscripts I read for *Fiction River* (the anthology series I edit), or when Dean finishes something.

I would call myself a voracious reader. I read all the time if I possibly can.

Readers are clearly not one big mass of similarity. As you can see from my example above, I'm a different kind of reader if you break the questions down by genre or by subgenre. Or by author. By whether or not I know the author or if I don't.

That RWA survey looks at reading *habits*.

But let's look at the *types of consumers* readers are.

True Fan

A lot has been written about the true fan in the past few years, but let me quote former *Wired* editor and (as John Scalzi calls him) Web Thinker, Kevin Kelly, who, so far as I can tell, started this meme[2] in 2008 or so:

> *A True Fan is defined as someone who will purchase anything and everything you produce. They will drive 200 miles to see you sing. They will buy the super deluxe re-issued hi-res box set of your stuff even though they have the low-res version. They have a Google Alert set for your name. They bookmark the eBay page where your out-of-print editions show up. They come to your openings. They have you sign their copies. They buy the t-shirt, and the mug, and the hat. They can't wait till you issue your next work. They are true fans.*

Long-Time Fan

This person has been reading your work for years and will buy your work when they're ready to. They are, in the words of the retail market, Brand-Loyal customers. You, the consumer, can choose between Skippy peanut butter or Jif peanut butter, but you're a choosy father, not a choosy mother, so you choose Skippy whenever you can. It's automatic. You need peanut butter, you buy Skippy. You need a book and the latest Neil Gaiman is out, so you buy Neil's book. But you don't go to signings, you don't buy the book immediately, and you don't stand in line to get the limited edition version of whatever, although you might be happy if your spouse got it for you for Christmas.

The key point: long-time fans have bought your work for *years*, sometimes for *decades*.

· · ·

Fan

These fans like a writer's work, but doesn't go out of their way to buy it immediately. Like the long-time fan, this fan is a brand-loyal customer. The only difference? They might not have been a fan for more than a few months, even if the writer has been published for decades. These fans would not call themselves long-time fans, but they will pick up the work when they're ready.

Sometimes Fan

The name says it all. This reader loves a certain aspect of a writer's work, but doesn't like other parts. I'm a sometimes-fan of Nora Roberts. I like her romantic suspense novels and will buy those when they appear. I occasionally like her contemporaries, and her paranormals I don't buy at all. (And I have a completely different take on her pen name J.D. Robb. See below.)

The sometimes fan knows her own taste. She might like Skippy peanut butter, but not *all* types of Skippy. Just creamy, not chunky. And not low-fat. Brand loyalty isn't here. It's *product* loyalty within the brand.

Genre/Subgenre Fan

The romance survey found these people, and called them avid readers of romance. When these readers have finished their most recent historical romance novel, they look for another one by a favorite author. When they can't find that, they go for something similar. Both surveys that RWA commissioned in 2011 and 2012 found this breakdown for purchasers of romance, and the genre/subgenre fans are at the top of the list.

Top overall decision factors when deciding on a romance:

- *The story*
- *The author*
- *It's part of a series*
- *Back cover copy*

Note that my preferences for Nora Roberts books, above, does not reflect my genre/subgenre fan preferences. I like paranormal romance more than I like contemporary romance. I just don't like Nora's paranormals. Your reader tastes are this nuanced. You know that. Think it through.

. . .

Reads Voraciously

These people buy books constantly or go to the library all the time. They always have a book and/or reading material close by, whether it's on their ereader, their computer, or their bookshelf. Voracious readers might not buy new. They might not be able to afford it. But they consider books as important as breathing.

Reads Occasionally

These people—who often have young families and full-time jobs—might have called themselves voracious readers at another point in their lives. But right now, they're too busy to read all the time. They read when they can.

Some readers have always been like this, though. Reading is just part of their entertainment diet. They might consider entertainment (TV, movies, games, music, books) as important as breathing, just not one type of entertainment.

Likes to Read

Even more than the Reads Occasionally people, the Likes to Read folks buy a book when the fancy strikes them. They're the people who claim to read one novel per year. Again, they probably slide into the Reads Occasionally category, depending on life circumstance, but they would never ever say reading books is as essential to them as breathing.

Non-Readers

Yes, they buy books. As gifts for friends. Of necessity, because they believe (rightly) that they should read to their children. But they're still not buying for themselves, and once the kids are grown, the book purchasing stops. Many of these folks never got into the reading-for-pleasure habit, and aren't interested in acquiring it.

Here's the important point about readers:

Readers embody **all** *of these traits.*

For example, I buy some authors as gifts for people. I will never read some of these writers I buy for other people *ever*. I don't like the subject matter or the point of view or something. I am a true fan for one or two authors, a longtime fan of many authors, and a genre/subgenre fan. I am a voracious reader for the most part, but if you break down my likes and dislikes, I am an occasional reader of some things (certain types of nonfiction) and a non-reader of others.

I'm sure you're the same way.

So…when you target your marketing, why do you treat all readers the same *even though you're not the same reader for every writer?*

Think it through.

This all-the-same marketing breaks down even further when you talk about *purchasing* books rather than just reading them.

Some readers cannot afford new books. They also can't afford ereaders, for the most part. These readers go to the library or, occasionally, the used bookstore. But they can't purchase books brand new, for whatever reason. They are a vast and influential part of the reading public. They influence what libraries put on their shelves, what used bookstores take into their stores.

But when we writers discuss *marketing* our books and *pricing* them, we can't target these people. They will see the marketing anyway, and do their own thing, but they won't hand money over *personally* to buy the books.

(I'm not trying to diminish the importance of these readers. I don't know what the statistic is—because, again, no one has done this study—but I think the underground community of readers who can't afford books is bigger than we think.)

Note: I'm not including the collectors, either (except as true fans), because I'm dealing with *readers*, and many collectors I know want the object and don't read the object at all. (Often, though, they'll buy a reading copy.)

So, the following categories are of people with cash in hand, people who *buy books*.

True Fans

Yep, they show up here again, because as Kelly says, they'll fork out tons of cash for whatever project their favorite writer does. These people might not be rich, but they spend a disproportionate amount of what money they do have on their favorite writers.

. . .

Always Buys New

These brand-loyal readers will buy a book from their favorite author when they see that book. *Not* when the book is released, but the moment the fan discovers it exists. They'll pay for the hardcover if the hardcover is out, the mass market if they missed the initial release. But they want a new copy for their shelves or their digital library.

Sometimes Buys New

The category title says it all. They'll buy new when they see the book, but they might consider the purchase before doing so. Or they'll buy the book at a used store as readily as they will from a new bookstore. Often, the readers buy these books to read and trade back in or give to friends.

My experience with Nora Roberts' J.D. Robb pen name fits in here. I buy those books new or used, I don't care. Usually I buy used. Why? Because I'm not a huge fan of them. I like them, and I know they'll provide a few hours of entertainment. I tend to read them on airplanes and then leave them behind when I'm finished.

I'm not sure if my J.D. Robb purchases will end now that I can read my ereader throughout the flight. I didn't read a J.D. Robb on a January 2014 trip to Vegas, and I would have in 2013.

I'm sure you have books/authors that you read the same way.

Always Buys Discounted Books

These readers never pay full price for anything, whether it's because of their own financial situation or their own financial preference. They'll find their books in the discount bin at bookstores or they'll watch Amazon for sales. They'll buy a lot of titles from used bookstore.

The key to these readers? They're usually voracious readers, but they're loyal to *price*.

In other words, they'll buy Skippy or Jif, depending on which peanut butter is cheapest or on sale that week. They like peanut butter, but they don't care what type they actually get.

They are probably more adventurous readers than the readers listed above, but they will rarely pay full price for anything. They will also bitch the loudest if prices that were traditionally low get raised.

. . .

Always Gets Free Books

These folks are the same as the discount buyers above. But for whatever reason, they don't buy books at all, choosing to get things only available for free.

Again, these readers are loyal to *price*—or lack thereof, actually—rather than writer, subgenre, etc.

That sounds harsh, I know, and honestly, the 100% free folks are rare.

But again, when we're talking purchasing strategies as reader/consumers, we each fit in all of the categories.

For example, I always buy Stephen King, Elizabeth George, Mary Balogh, and several of my other very favorite authors new. Always, always, always. I already told you about J.D. Robb, whom I sometimes buy new. There are many authors that I sometimes buy new—and a lot of them are new authors, if the books sound interesting enough and they fit into my genre/subgenre preferences.

I am a discount book shopper of nonfiction in particular, when I need research material. I will occasionally try something for free if—oddly—I'd already heard of the author or book. But I will rarely get to those books first.

Those are my reader preferences on price. I'm sure yours are different, according to your circumstance.

When I was a very poor newly divorced woman, I had $10 per week I could squeeze out of my budget for books (and I did this by eating less). I shopped at used stores and rarely bought new. I went to the library weekly. My circumstances were different and so were my buying habits, but not my *reading* habits.

The Whys and Wherefores

Why do I tell you all of this? Because, marketing one way to all readers—whether it's free or expensive, whether it's one type of book or another—ignores how complex readers as consumers really are.

When I talk about marketing *strategies*, I'm talking from this complex model, not the traditional publishing all-readers-are-the-same model.

I will refer to types of readers in future chapters. If you get confused, come back to this chapter for reference. As writers, we're cultivating readers, not appealing to buyers for major chains.

Always remember that.

THE OLD WAYS

8

ADVERTISING AND TRADITIONAL PUBLISHING

The new meme on the Internet writer boards goes something like this: *I'll write a book and sell it to traditional publishing. That'll build my audience. Then everything else I do will be indie.*

In other words, writers seem to believe the myth that traditional publishers are much, much better at helping a writer find an audience than the writer is herself.

That assumption was true, back in the olden days, y'know, about five years ago. Books got discovered through bookstores, and the only way to get a book in a bookstore was to go through a traditional publisher.

Then ereaders hit, along with the easy Amazon publishing platform, quickly mimicked by Barnes & Noble. Apple followed, and then Kobo, and now a book doesn't have to be in paper at all in order to find readers. Nor does that book need to be in a brick-and-mortar bookstore. Lots of writers are gaining a lot of readers without ever producing a paper book of their latest novel.

Still, a lot of writers, from old-timers to beginners, say the reason that they want to stay with traditional publishing is discoverability. Writer after writer tells me that a traditional publisher will promote their books.

For some writers, particularly huge bestsellers, this is absolutely true. For others, particularly midlist writers, it isn't true at all. And honestly, it's always been that way.

But for most writers in traditional publishing, their chances of any kind of promotion have *decreased* in the last few years rather than *increased*. Even as traditional publishers say that's one of the many services they provide.

In the last five years, traditional publishers started ebook-only imprints. I know a lot of writers who are taking those contracts, and expecting big-publishing promotion, without ever asking themselves how that promotion will occur.

In fact, even writers who take print-only deals believe that traditional publishers will do a lot of advertising for their work. And by that, most writers mean actual ads. In magazines. Online. In newspapers.

These writers believe firmly that they will benefit from an ad campaign *without a contractual guarantee to it*. They believe the ad campaign automatically comes with every book sale to a traditional publisher.

We all know why the only author whose books we see advertised on television these days is James Patterson. We all know that national television advertising is expensive. Writers don't expect television advertising for their books.

But they expect print advertising, and even that expectation is wrong.

Let's look at actual advertising for a moment before we get to the other ways that traditional publishers actually advertise books.

When I initially posted this chapter on my blog, I examined the November 2013 issue of *RT Book Reviews*. That issue was available online. It is no longer. But browse any issue of *RT*, in paper or online, and you'll see the trends I mention here.

RT Book Reviews is not an industry bible like *Publishers Weekly* is. *RT* is a magazine that's dedicated to readers. It got its start about thirty years ago as a mimeographed sheet put out for romance readers, back when romance was considered the lowest, most disreputable genre (besides actual porn novels). No reputable publication—from newspapers to magazines—would ever advertise, let alone review, a romance novel. Most romance writers used pen names, so that they wouldn't have to admit that they wrote "that crap."

RT was started to give romance *readers* a community, and it evolved into a glossy magazine with tens of thousands of subscribers, and a huge ad revenue stream. It exists to inform readers of entertaining reads in all genres. Not the latest literary novel or the novel most likely to impress your friends, but the novel most likely to help you while away a few hours on a particularly difficult day.

Publishers have figured out that the popularity of *RT* translates into book sales, so those publishers advertise, often with more than one ad in each issue.

(The publishers of *RT* aren't dumb. In the past year, another change in the magazine is that it stopped supporting indie publishing in its articles. Because almost all of *RT*'s revenue comes from traditional publishers, traditional publishing has become the magazine's focus. Indie writers and indie presses can buy ads, but usually won't get covered in the articles at all.)

A quick examination of the display ads in any issue of *RT* that show book covers by more than one author generally includes a phrase at the bottom of the ad that goes like this:

> *And Don't Forget Our Ebook Imprint* Really Cool Books
> *Featuring These Titles!*

A handful of book covers run along the bottom with very little to say what the book is about or why I should download it *today!* like the ad urges me to do.

Because so many authors I know are taking those ebook-only contracts, I started paying attention to the ebook-only promotion. And I discovered this: those ebooks are getting a weird kind of also-ran promotion.

It's almost like face-out windowing in a closed bookstore. You see the book in the window, but you can't touch the book or even look at the back cover. Because the shop door is locked.

Windowing—the practice of putting a book on a real brick-and-mortar bookshelf—works because the reader can pick up that copy, read the back cover, and decide to buy.

To buy these ebooks, advertised as also-rans in any issue of *RT*, the reader would have to haul out her ereader then and there, or remember the title of the book, or the author's name. If she did all those things then maybe, just maybe, she might buy the book.

But that seems like a lot of work for the potential reader to do, doesn't it? Would you do it? I don't think I ever have. If you want to see what I mean and you're a subscriber to *RT Book Reviews*, check out page 23 of the November 2013 issue.

There's usually an ad like this in every issue, always from a major publisher. In this particular ad from November 2013, the paper titles get a descriptive quote from their *RT* reviews, and the ebook titles are shown by the cover only.

I'm pointing this out, not because I think *RT* ads are bad—I don't. I think they help sales with the right project, when that project is available and done in the right way. Obviously traditional publishers believe *RT* ads help sales as well, because as I looked online for the ad that I was thinking of, I noted how many traditional publishers put money into *RT* every single issue.

Traditional publishers put advertising money into many magazines. From *Entertainment Weekly* to *Esquire* to *Vanity Fair*, publishers spend a small fortune on book ads. Those slick glossy magazines do not have an authors-only rate the way that *RT* does. (*RT* is author-friendly, and long before epublishing and indie publishing became a big deal, it offered ad rates for authors whose publishers refused to put any support behind a book at all.)

The other thing to note about *RT* traditional publisher ads, however, is that most of them focus on a single book. In that November issue, Kensington bought four ads for single titles, and ran them on separate pages. Harlequin had two single-author ads (ads that featured more than one book by the same author). Avon had one single-author ad, Penguin had three. The thing that marked a difference in the November issue was that it was one of the Christmas ad issues, so some of the publishers did group ads of Christmas-themed books.

Why is this important?

Because writers see these single-author and single-book ads and expect the publisher to buy ads like that for their books. Not every book by every writer gets an actual ad. In fact, most never get advertised in print or online publications.

However, writers who say that the traditional publisher will advertise their books are correct. The traditional publisher will do a few things that will raise a book's visibility—if and only if that book is published in *print* format.

Print books will appear in a seasonal catalogue that booksellers will look at. That's advertising, folks.

The print book might—and I stress *might*—get sent out for reviews. Reviews are advertising, folks.

The reviews probably won't get readers to pick up the books. But reviews aren't geared to readers. They're geared to booksellers. And booksellers, to a store, buy print books, not ebooks. (Which is why publishers only advertise print books in the industry bible, *Publishers Weekly*.)

A lucky few print books will get single-page display ads in magazines and newspapers. But I can guarantee this: unless you're an author who has already hit a major bestseller list and/or your book is the most important book being published by that traditional publishing house's imprint and/or you got paid an advance of $50,000 or more (in small genres like sf or westerns) or $100,000 or more (in larger genres like romance and mystery), your book will not get a single title ad. It won't happen.

In other words, from the moment the publisher offers you a book deal, you can have a pretty good guess as to what kind of advertising budget your book will receive. Most five-figure advances won't get any advertising, unless your book is the third book of a three-book contract, and the previous two books did waaaay better than expected.

Chances are, however, that even if that little miracle happened, you're still not going get your full-page ad.

Ad placement also matters. By that, I mean, where the book gets advertised.

For example, only the really big titles—the ones that will sell millions—get advertised in *Entertainment Weekly*. Why? Simple. A four-color full page *Entertainment Weekly* ad costs $197,000.[1] And that's for one ad that is in the magazine for only one week.

Think it through, folks. If your publisher buys your novel for a $5,000 advance, they're not going to spend nearly $200,000 to advertise your book. You'll note, if you read *EW* like I do, that very few books get the full-color one-page treatment. Most books get a one-third page full-color ad, which is still mind-bogglingly expensive at $88,800 for one placement. One placement.

Contrast that with a one-time full-page full-color ad in *RT*, and you'll find something a bit more affordable. A one-time full-page full-color ad there costs $3,800.[2] That $3,800 will keep the book in front of potential readers for one month instead of one week.

That's a considerable savings. But it's still almost the cost of that $5,000 advance, and not likely to happen for a mid-list book.

The *RT* ad is targeted to avid readers, but it also goes before significantly fewer eyeballs. The most recent listing for subscribers to RT that I could find with a quick web search showed 150,000 subscribers (2004).[3] I'm sure that number is larger now, with the magazine's web presence, but I can't imagine it being much more than 200,000.

By contrast, *Entertainment Weekly*'s subscription base was nearly 1.8 million as of 2012.[4] An *EW* ad will reach nine times the number of readers —also focused on entertainment, I might add—than an *RT* ad.

Even cheaper are the in-genre ads for a publication like *Locus Magazine* (for science fiction) whose most expensive ad is $1,050[5] for a one-time placement, in a magazine that comes out every month. *Locus* has fewer subscribers than *RT* by a long ways. It currently lists a 6,000 copy subscription base, and somehow takes that to mean 18,000 people read the magazine. The rule of thumb when I was editing for *The Magazine of Fantasy & Science Fiction* was that two people read each copy of the magazine, but *Locus* claims three. I sincerely doubt that.

Sure, a publisher might spend that $1,050 to advertise the latest book in a growing series, but that ad will be viewed by a few thousand readers instead of a couple million. (And the price of the ad is still one-fifth of that midlist advance.)

Suddenly, the print/online ads seem less likely for a traditional published book, don't they?

Here's something else to remember: It's not that hard for an indie author to reach 6,000 readers, through Amazon or Goodreads or a dozen other venues, which traditional publishers badmouth or ignore. (We'll discuss all of this in future chapters.)

Then there's the expectation side of advertising. Book publishers know that book ads are *informational* only. The ads do not increase sales at all.

The publishers buy the ads to inform the consumer that a new book is out. The consumer must see references to that new book several times before the book ever makes an impact on a consumer's consciousness.

Now, remember, there are a bunch of different ways for the consumer to see an ad for the book. The ad might be in multiple media (not just *EW*, but also *Vanity Fair*, for example, or *The New York Times*).

The book might get reviewed, and remember, that review is…drum roll…an ad. The consumer might see the book up front in a bookstore.

Or the consumer might see the book cover on the home page for Amazon or Barnes & Noble. Those spots are also paid advertising, by the way. Ain't no way an indie-published book would show up there without someone ponying up a great deal of cash.

After several sightings in various places from magazines to bookstore shelves, the consumer might (and I mean might) be convinced to buy a book she wouldn't normally buy. If she's a fan of the author, she'll buy the book as soon as she finds out about it, or put that book in her wish list or on her to-be-purchased pile. But convincing readers to buy a book through an ad just isn't possible. Readers must find other ways to connect with the book.

Usually that means picking the book up, holding it in their hands, and interacting with the book. Such interactions used to happen in bookstores. Now, often, they happen online. Which is why the "Look Inside This Book" feature is so very important to book sales.

Advertising specialists argue over how many ad views it takes to sell a product to a consumer. Specialists spend years and a mountain of money trying to figure out what the most effective advertising dollars are. The numbers vary, and they're hard to measure. As I did a quick search, I found statistics that ran from 2% of all ad viewers (for something with a coupon) as a good return rate, to a low of .01% of all ad viewers for repeat advertising. In other words, the experts don't have a clue either.

So think this through *as a reader*. Did you ever buy a book because you saw an ad that told you the book was out? Or did you buy it because you love the author's work, and the ad was just the first place to inform you that the book was out? And how in the hell can anyone measure that?

And why, if book ads are informational, are publishers spending tens of thousands of dollars to advertise their books, especially if there's no way to know how effective the ads are?

Because all advertising dollars in traditional publishing are spent to educate the consumer that a book exists. Publishers do a full-court press on their biggest titles in the week of release so that consumers go out and buy that book *immediately*. The more places that mention the book in its week of release, the more chances a consumer has to see the magic number of mentions and then act on the purchase of the new book.

This is exceedingly important to traditional publishers because they measure everything by sales velocity—how many copies the book sells quickly. Why? So that the book will hit a bestseller list—which then gives the book more advertising. (And that advertising is free.)

Traditional publishers can spend upwards of half a million dollars advertising one special title in one week of its release. Of course, the author of that special title got a minimum of a mid-six-figure advance.

Writers who got a four-figure advance will never ever ever get that kind of advertising. And writers who sold their book to a traditional publisher for a percentage of sales and no advance only to see the book come out in an ebook-only edition will be lucky to be displayed on the front page of the publisher's ebook website for a week.

If a writer is going to a traditional publisher for discoverability only, then the writer needs a few guarantees before signing her contract.

First, she'd better get a mid-five-figure advance or higher on that book. Any less, and she won't get the kind of discoverability she wants.

Second, her book had better come out in a print edition. Otherwise, she's better off publishing the book herself.

Third, (and least likely), she needs a guarantee of certain levels of promotion in that contract. Without it, the publisher could spend $50,000 on that book's advance, release the book in paper, and still not do the kind of basic promotion a book needs. No reviews, no catalogue copy, nothing.

Because no traditional publishing contract that I have ever seen for a writer who is not a bestseller guarantees that the publisher has to do anything except "publish" the book. And the definitions of what "publish" means are changing. In one contract that I saw recently, the definition of "publish" was that the publisher had to make certain the book was available for sale on the publisher's website and nowhere else.

In late 2013, *Digital Book World* published an interview with traditional publishing digital guru Mike Shatzkin.

In that article,[6] Shatzkin, who is a big defender and advocate for traditional publishing, said this:

> *As sales move online and concentrate at Amazon, a publisher can't really make a huge difference in Amazon compared to what an author can do on their own. So, the publisher has to make a difference in a diminishing part of the market, which is everything else.*

He wants traditional publishers to figure out how to have a presence in the market. Honestly, so do I. I'd love to see traditional publishers continue —with good author contracts and with an acknowledgement that they work in partnership with authors rather than believing that writers are necessary idiots.

In the article, Shatzkin admits how unimportant traditional publishers are becoming to the very thing that writers used to need them for—selling books to readers.

Traditional publishers have their place. Right now, that place is producing blockbuster novels and getting them out to readers in a coordinated way.

Writers need to see that place for what it is, not for what it was. Writers need to protect themselves going forward, making certain that if they partner with a traditional publisher, then the publisher will actually work for them, rather than put them in a mill that churns out books to make the publisher's bottom line possible.

Because traditional publishers had a stranglehold on the market, they used to have a lot of power in getting books discovered. As Shatzkin said, that world no longer exists.

But the myth does.

THE FIERCE URGENCY OF NOW

We're all familiar with the "fierce urgency of now." We have experienced it all of our lives. It's that feeling that we have to have something or have to do something *right now* or we'll lose the chance.

When it came to buying something, "the fierce urgency of now" once drove our purchasing life. Back in the days of brick-and-mortar stores only, back in the days of appointment-radio, appointment-television, and appointment-movie attendance, the fierce urgency of now was a very real thing.

If you didn't watch a TV show the night it aired, you might never get to see that show. If you didn't see a movie in the theater, you might never get to see that movie. If you didn't buy a book when you saw it on a store shelf, you might never see that book again.

The fierce urgency of now governed everything, because *space* was limited. Bookstores had only so much square footage, and that square footage was devoted to the latest books. The amount of time a new book remained on the shelf—known as "the turn"—went from nearly two months (for many years) to as short as two weeks (in the early 1990s).

Television sold advertising based on that fierce urgency. If television executives could convince viewers to stay home one night per week to watch shows, then advertisers flooded to those shows. Advertising rates went way up, and became the way that a show's success got measured—not just by how many people watched it, but by how expensive the ad buys were.

Movies were that way as well. If you read movie announcements in newspapers from the 1970s (which I do every time I write a Smokey Dalton novel), you'll see that the announcements often mentioned how many screens the movie was playing on nationwide.

The more screens, the more the studio bet on the movie's popularity. If a movie got a large audience, it stayed in a theater and the number of screens showing the movie increased. In the summer of 1973, *The Poseidon Adventure* stayed at the movie theater in my small Wisconsin hometown for at least a month. I memorized that damn movie (and contributed to its staying power by continually buying tickets) because there was no other film I could see within walking/biking distance. You'd often see "held over for an astonishing 6 weeks!" on movie marquees as if movies were theatrical performances filled with living players.

If the demand was high, then movie theater owners were loathe to trade out a popular show for one whose popularity hadn't been proven yet.

These habits slowly died as technology changed industries. For decades, charities made extra money sponsoring a movie night, spending the money to get a classic movie and charging admission so that people could see a film they'd only heard about. Some film societies—particularly those connected to universities—funded themselves by doing this.

Those societies died with the rise of videotape, cable, and DVD. Now, cable and DVDs are having trouble because of streaming. If I want to see an old movie, I find the streaming service that carries the film, and download it immediately.

The fierce urgency of now has a completely different meaning these days. Thirty years ago, it meant "See this or miss it forever!" Today, it means, "Bring it to me the instant I want it."

And that difference changed our entertainment culture from a limited top-down monolithic culture to a seemingly unlimited consumer culture. In the past, we had to choose from what the gatekeepers offered us. Now, we can choose not only from all of the things (or most of them) that were published, produced, filmed (you name it) in the past, but also from a wide variety of things that never got vetted at all.

Our entertainment culture has become dynamic, but it's also weirdly personal. When Dean and I started teaching professional writers twenty-some years ago, we would use certain movies as an example of good plotting because we knew that everyone attending our classes had seen those movies. Now, we can't make that assumption.

It's a good thing in many ways, because it forces us to give a reading list to each class, so that we all have the same background. But it limits the cultural conversation in ways that are unfamiliar to those of us raised in the monolithic everybody's-talking-about-the-same-things society.

Right now, the large multimedia companies are grappling with this change. Their businesses are still based on velocity, so they need consumers to buy a new product within weeks, sometimes days, of that product's release. In other words, the large multimedia companies still believe that the fierce urgency of now operates on the 20th-century model, and in book publishing at least, the traditional companies are very confused by the change.

They want you to buy now, so they're doing everything they can to get your attention (within the proper advertising budget, of course).

But the problem for them (and everyone else using the velocity model) is that the noise has become so loud that it's impossible to hear about one new product in a sea of stuff.

To make matters worse, consumer habits are changing. That change became evident to me over the 2013 Thanksgiving weekend in the United States. According to data compiled by IBM Digital Analytics Benchmark,[1] more people shopped online on Cyber Monday than ever before and—more importantly—more people shopped on Cyber Monday (as it's now called) than on Black Friday. The revenue for Cyber Monday was 31.5% higher than the revenue for Black Friday.

(For the non-American readers lucky enough to miss the advertising frenzy that the United States becomes at the end of November, "Black Friday" is the term Americans now use to describe the day after our Thanksgiving celebration. Black Friday marks the beginning of the holiday season—at least the shopping portion of it—and measuring the sales statistics has become a gloom-and-doom evergreen story in the press since the media started tracking Black Friday sales some time in the mid-1990s.)

The 2013 data came in from a variety of sources. One analysis showed that two days this shopping season (tracked from Halloween on) had over a billion dollars in online sales. The first billion-dollar online sale day was Black Friday, since so many retailers had the same bargains on their websites as they did in their brick-and-mortar stores. The second billion-dollar online sale day was Cyber Monday. Cyber Monday's sales were $200 million higher than Black Friday's sales.

The dominance of online sales is significant, because it shows that consumer habits are changing, just as we suspected all along. According to Brian Yarbrough, an analyst with Edward Jones, quoted in the same *Los Angeles Times* article that brought you all these other statistics:

> *You're seeing more and more consumers shopping online instead of going to bricks-and-mortar [sic] retailers. People are under the impression that the Internet has cheaper prices and is more convenient, allowing you to avoid the crowds.*

So you avoid the crowds and shop online. But you still need to be informed of the deals. Yes, there were literally a million sales that Monday. And the only way to know about many of them was to stumble upon them or to have them drummed into you ad nauseum.

For example, in the middle of November 2013, a car company that shall remain nameless started a nationwide television ad campaign promising two weeks of Black Friday. The reason the car company remains nameless is I simply can't remember which company it was. I was so irritated at the very idea of the commercial that I failed to register the name of the perpetrator.

That two weeks of Black Friday thing, weirdly memorable as it was, is something that will backfire. I have no idea how much money the car company made from its sale and promotion. I just know that next year, it'll try the same thing, and by then, we'll be sick of it. Such promotions will make a day like Black Friday insignificant.

Black Friday has already ceased to be a day and has become a "season." So has Cyber Monday. In fact, the week after Black Friday has been christened Cyber Week. The promotions continued.

I confess. Two companies got my business on that Cyber Monday. They were not companies doing heavy advertising. I stumbled upon their sales through my Monday reading, and bought products I normally buy in dribs and drabs throughout the year. The discounts were so deep, I bought those products in bulk.

That lead me to pause for a moment—not as a consumer, but as a business owner. Yes, consumer-me responded to the fierce urgency of now and whipped out my plastic, paying for those products immediately. But consumer-me would have bought those products at full price, spaced out between now and next December, a steady revenue—and more of it. Will these retailers even notice the loss of my money over the year? Probably not. But multiply that loss by thousands of customers, and yes, the retailers' revenue might well go down in the next six months or so.

That's the gamble of sales and deep discounts. If you dig into the articles about Black Friday sales and Cyber Monday promotions, you'll see comments from experts who follow trends, noting that 50% off is the new 25% off, and that the profit margins are being sliced even thinner to get customers in stores.

Some experts pointed out that many companies that used to participate in the Black Friday madness have pulled back, offering deals that barely compared to deals offered in the past. Instead those companies (mostly tech companies) now offer their deals in the off-season, when they can actually get press for those deals, changing the calculus of the fierce urgency of now to whatever they chose it to be.

You see this in book promotion. In 2013, a strange phenomenon happened in traditional American book publishing. Because of the Justice Department lawsuit alleging collusion among the Big Five publishers, the publishers stopped talking to each other. In the past, they would consult each other about timing of their bestsellers, particularly in the fall season.

One publisher would "own" the first week in October, because John Grisham's new book would come out that week. The next publisher would own the second week to make way for Scott Turow's new book, and so on.

When the publishers couldn't talk to each other, they had to guess. Book publishing would release its catalogs with the publication dates six to nine months in advance of the book's release, and by then, the release would be set in stone.

The publishers found that their biggest sellers were landing on the same weekend. Why is that a problem? Because only one book can hit the top of the bestseller lists. No sharing allowed.

The fallout hit as the fall season began. Many guaranteed *New York Times* bestsellers in previous years were not *New York Times* bestsellers with their 2013 books. Some former #1 bestsellers didn't even crack the top ten.

That velocity thing doesn't work when everyone plays the game. Or maybe it does work, and it shows which writers have succeeded in making their work a must-buy no matter what the season, and which writers failed.

Indie writers are seeing the problems with velocity also. A lot of writers are complaining that "free" doesn't work anymore or that they can't even get their titles into successful non-traditional advertising venues like Book-Bub, when they used to get their titles into those places in the past.

When you're the thousandth guy to jump on a bandwagon, then that bandwagon isn't going to be as big a deal as it was for the first hundred guys.

So, what makes people buy a product *now?*

All those marketing gurus have come up with three things. You'll find the same three things over and over again in marketing textbooks and on marketing blogs.

People buy *now* because:

1. They need the item.

Think about that. How often have you unhappily pulled into the gas station and spent the twenty dollars in your pocket just to get home? You didn't *want* gas at that moment, but you *needed* it.

"Need" has a variety of meanings, especially when it comes to entertainment. Some TV episode ends on a particularly good cliff-hanger. You *need* to see the next episode *right now*. If you're binge-watching, no problem. You're going to stream the next episode. If you're live-watching, you'll tune in as soon as that next episode airs.

The same goes for series books. The good ones get readers to return to each book in the series when the book's released.

There are problems with series, though, especially linked series. It's hard for a newcomer to start with book 10 or episode 50. That's why television producers back in the day mandated that serials belonged in daytime, and had lots of repetition so viewers could keep up. Now, when you hear about a particularly good serialized show, you can stream the first episode or season and see if you like it.

That's caused a change in television, and in the movies, truth be told. *The Hunger Games: Catching Fire* set a record over the 2013 Thanksgiving weekend by taking in more than $82 million in five days.[2] It's the second film in The Hunger Games series, and its take was greater than the Harry Potter film that had held the title previously.

However, you don't need series writing to get people to take in the entertainment right now. Sometimes you just need to intrigue the viewer/reader. For, along with The Hunger Games that weekend, a little stand-alone movie that could, *Frozen*, also took in more than Harry Potter.

For each rule of thumb, there is something that breaks that rule.

In other words, just because I say series are doing well in this environment, don't take that to mean write only series. Because word-of-mouth will elevate anything, stand-alone or a series.

Or word-of-mouth will tank something—even if it is in a series. As *Entertainment Weekly* pointed out in its "Summer Winners and Losers" column in September 2013,[3] the sequel book to *The Devil Wears Prada*, *Revenge Wears Prada*, didn't fare well after its first week. Why? It didn't meet reader expectation. The book hit the bestseller list, then quickly fell off as word got around.

Another reason people buy something right now? They find...

2. A great deal that is so fantastic the consumer impulse buys.

That's what got me on Monday. Choose: Spend $50 now or $100 over the next six months for the same item. I actually paused and checked my entertainment fund. Yep, I had the $50. So I bought, and saved myself $50 because I would have spent the money anyway.

But all of those videos you see every single Black Friday weekend of shoppers going insane and fighting each other for deeply discounted products?[4] Often those deals aren't really deals. Prices got inflated before the holiday so they could be "marked down." The items were going to be discontinued anyway. The list of deal scams goes on and on.[5]

What used to happen—what still happens—is the hype infects the consumer, and the consumer makes impulse buys. This happens mostly in brick-and-mortar stores, but it can happen online as well. The point of a sale is to bring someone into the store or the website. And most people, once they start shopping, buy more than they intend.

Hell, that happens to me every single time I walk into a grocery store *with a list.* I still buy more than I planned.

Even in the past, book publishing had trouble offering good deals or creating impulse purchases. The problem is even worse now. Let me try to explain.

No reader knows or cares who publishes a book. So traditional publishers, hoping to increase sales on all of their products, won't get readers into the "store" with brand loyalty, because the brand is the author name, or the series name, not the publisher.

Many readers don't know author names, either. Readers buy by genre or series or whatever has a pretty cover. They might buy a book because it's 99 cents, but that doesn't guarantee they'll buy another book by the same author because it was cheap.

People might buy a cheap book because it's cheap, but that doesn't mean they'll read the book. The first thing avid readers who set themselves up as book reviewers learn is that half the books they get for review, they wouldn't read in the first place. The same with free. It worked for a while. It rarely works now that everyone's doing it, because so many people rarely read what they get for free.

Plus, books have another problem with free. Readers know they can get free books at any time just by going to the library. It's not like getting a free watch. A free watch is pretty unusual. A free book resides in a building somewhere in town with a bunch of other free books—and that free book might be one you actually want to read.

The other reason people buy *now*?

3. A good deal with a time limit.

That was the second thing I bought on Cyber Monday. I bought something with a time limit.

I had a bunch of items in my online to-buy queue at a major online retailer, but I was planning to buy them when I was ready. I logged onto that site to check something else that day, and discovered a 30% off sale that would last another four hours. Those items, at 30% off, were a good deal. I had the money in my account. I bought ahead of when I normally would have.

I've seen indie writers use this scheme to good effect. Book bundling uses it well. Five books at a great price for two weeks? Most readers don't care if that bundle includes a book or two by someone they've never read. Readers like to discover new writers. Besides, they got three books they planned to read for less than they'd pay for each book individually.

It's the same with a reduced price sale, particularly on the first book of a series. So, a reader's heard about the series and wants to try it, but doesn't want to pony up full price. That limited sale—a week or so at a lower price—might convince them to buy now.

The key is *might*. The other key on these limited promotions is to have many other books that the reader can buy. Again, these promotions don't work for traditional publishers because traditional publishers are not a brand. (When was the last time you bought a book because it was published by Hachette? You might have bought a Hachette book, but you did so because of the genre, author, cover or some other reason.)

In the retail business, offering something for a lower price for a week is called a loss leader. A loss leader is a product sold at a *loss* that will *lead* the consumer to other products. You need the other products for the strategy to work—and those products must be recognizably yours.

If you've made it this far into this chapter, you've probably figured out that most of the standard fierce-urgency-of-now strategies don't work for book publishing. Not any more. In a culture where consumers control their own entertainment, they also control when they consume that entertainment.

That's where discoverability comes in. As I mentioned in Chapter Six, your job as a writer is to write the book, the very best book you can, and then write the next book. Your main marketing job is to let the consumer know that the book exists.

You tap into the fierce urgency of now when you do that.

But, if all of your marketing strategies mimic traditional publishing, you'll get a few sales when the book comes out and then the sales will die off.

So, here's what you do to change that:

1. Let your readers know when the book is published.

2. When you publish the next book in the series, make sure the first book is advertised in the back of that book (along with any other genre-related books you might do and a link to your website).

3. Jump on the right bandwagon. When *Downton Abbey* became successful, a handful of traditional publishers shocked the crap out of me by actually doing correct marketing. They brought back some titles set in the same milieu as *Downton Abbey*, with new covers. They targeted their marketing to a different crowd—the PBS crowd here in the US—and those books started to sell again.

4. Remember books don't age. Just like music doesn't. Just like movies don't.

Journey's song "Don't Stop Believin'" hit number 9 on the Billboard charts in 1981, the year of its release. Then the song became the 72nd most downloaded song in 2008, and the 84th most downloaded song in 2009. According to Wikipedia,[6] it is "the best-selling rock song in digital history with 6,065,000 digital units sold in the US as of February 2014 and the best digital song from a pre-digital-era."

What's old becomes new to each new generation. After Baz Luhrmann's surprising success with *The Great Gatsby* movie last summer, F. Scott Fitzgerald's 1925 novel hit—and remained—on the bestseller list, hitting number one right after the movie's release.[7]

In other words, just because your book isn't successful now doesn't mean it won't be in the future. Or, conversely, just because your book did well on its release, doesn't mean its selling days are over. It can be revived, if you time things right, with the idea of discoverability.

What do I mean by that? I mean that you have to let the book fade. You can't continually hype the same title. If you hype, you become the Howard Wolowitz of publishing. (The reference is to *The Big Bang Theory*. The endnote links to the video,[8] which explains this so much better than I could here.)

Instead, plan your moment. Wait months before reminding folks that the book has been released. Then wait a few years before starting promotion again—if the book isn't the first book in a series. Then you can promote that book each time a new series book comes out.

If you look at the Journey article on Wikipedia and examine the dates, you'll see that the song got a new boost as each generation discovered it. That's the sign of a great piece of entertainment—it can be enjoyed by people of different generations. I hope you're striving for that whenever you write. (I'm not saying write for people of all ages. I'm saying this: your book might be perfect for thirty-year-olds. When a new generation hits thirty, you want that generation to enjoy your book.)

5. Write the best book you can.

Remember that readers now determine the fierce urgency of now. You want them to pluck down their cold hard cash in the middle of the night because they need your next novel now. The only way for that to happen is to a) have published more than one novel and b) write great stories.

Readers will discover you. They just won't do it quickly or when you want them to.

That fierce-urgency-of-now thing? It's even more out of our control—everyone's control—than it has ever been. Right now, some person is finally discovering how great Shakespeare's plays are. I remember when I discovered it, by being dragged to a production in London's West End as a teenager. That guy's work has been around for hundreds of years, but he was new to me in 1977. He's new to others in 2015.

Write. Write more. Improve. Keep writing.

Have your work inspire that fierce urgency of now, because all the ads in the world won't make someone buy something they don't want.

Even on Black Friday.

10

THE OLD WAYS

Here's how writers decide to market their books:

They read blogs and articles, which tell them the best thing to do. Or, they mimic what they've seen other authors do. Or, they try to act like big traditional publishers, by funding their own book tours and doing signings.

I'd say that's no way to run a business, but honestly, that's how traditional publishers have run their businesses for a long time.

When I first posted this chapter on my website, I had to post in two parts for space reasons. After the first part ran, a long-time traditionally published bestseller (who happened to be a salesman before he became a writer) commented that publishing is the only profession he knew of in which marketing is an entry-level position.

I'll go one further than that. Publishing is the only profession I know of in which the people in charge of marketing are actively told *not* to familiarize themselves with the product.

Um, huh?

A lot of traditional publishing is based on "we always do it that way." That was one reason why, in 1993, a relatively unknown Edgar Award-winning author spent hundreds of thousands of dollars of his own money producing a television ad for his book. He did so because he had the money, and his publisher refused to do the kind of support the author believed would make the book sell.

This author wasn't a guy who simply believed in himself: He was one of the top ad executives in the nation. And he had worked his way into that position from the ground up. In other words, he knew his stuff.

That man? Not unknown any longer, and certainly not known only as an Edgar-winner. You know him as one of the bestselling authors in the world, James Patterson.

Am I recommending that you buy your own TV ads? No. I'm telling you to start thinking outside the box. Patterson did, twenty years ago before indie publishing was easy or cheap. He started using Little, Brown, his traditional publishing company, as if it were his own personal publishing company. Now, Michael Pietsch, the publisher of Little, Brown, says,[1] "Jim is at the very least co-publisher of his own books."

And it all started with that book, the one he advertised on his own. Here's the story from *The New York Times Magazine* in 2010:[2]

Publishing is an inherently conservative business. Patterson repeatedly challenged industry convention, sometimes over the objections of his own publisher. When Little, Brown was preparing to release "Along Came a Spider," Patterson tried to persuade his publisher that the best way to get the book onto best-seller lists was to advertise aggressively on television. Little, Brown initially balked. Bookstores typically base their stocking decisions on the sales of an author's previous books, and Patterson's had not done particularly well....What's more, large-scale TV advertising was rare in publishing, not only because of the prohibitive cost but also for cultural reasons. The thinking was that selling a book as if it were a lawn-care product could very well backfire by turning off potential readers.

Patterson wrote, produced and paid for a commercial himself. It opened with a spider dropping down the screen and closed with a voice-over: "You can stop waiting for the next 'Silence of the Lambs.'" Once Little, Brown saw the ad, it agreed to share the cost of rolling it out over the course of several weeks in three particularly strong thriller markets—New York, Chicago and Washington. "Along Came a Spider" made its debut at No. 9 on the New York Times hardcover best-seller list, ensuring it favorable placement near the entrance of bookstores, probably the single biggest driver of book sales. It rose to No. 2 in paperback and remains Patterson's most successful book, with more than five million copies in print.

Traditional publishing still doesn't allow much TV advertising on its books, preferring to use its ad money on things like magazine pages and book supplements (if anyone can find them). Why? Because that's how it was always done.

I mentioned *Hothouse*, a history of Farrar Straus Giroux, by Boris Kachka in a previous chapter. The book is fascinating if you're interested in the ways that some of these traditional publishing mistakes occurred. For example, Kachka mentions in passing[3] that founder Roger Straus's son—Young Rog, as he was called—worked with the Association of American Publishers in the 1970s to run some general book ads on television. Even though the ads showed positive results, the publishers were not interested in following up.

Young Rog wanted to grow the readership base, but the powers that be in traditional publishing held him back.

Traditional publishing often balks at bringing in new readers, claiming it doesn't want readers of that sort or that readers don't buy books that way. All the while, the publishers refuse to commission studies on how readers actually buy books, leaving that to government agencies or booksellers, most of whom don't have the money to commission studies either.

Traditional publishing's business model is based on velocity—that fierce urgency of now—and no long-term thinking at all. To traditional publishers, books spoil. Books leave the shelf within a few weeks or a few months and then become (smelly) backlist titles that are taking up warehouse space. It's tough for traditional publishers to realize that ebooks never spoil; it's hard for publishers to change their thinking.

Just like it's hard for writers. So many have dreamed of the "star" writer treatment.

What is that, exactly? A book tour, lots of interviews on local radio and with local newspapers (rarely local television, partly because local newscasts don't care about writers and partly because writers usually make for bad television). Long lines at book signings, adoring fans, and lots of public speaking engagements. A writer hand-selling her books at flagship stores because so many people have come to see her.

Ads in major markets. Books in every single brick-and-mortar store in the nation. Pallets of hardcovers littering the floor of airports and commuter train hubs all over the nation. Billboard ads of the book on the back of buses and on the escalators leading out of the subway (or, even more likely, the Underground). Reviews everywhere.

Everyone who reads, everyone who is worthwhile, talking about that one book. Your book.

I love that dream. I've achieved that dream on some of my titles overseas. It's been wonderful and discouraging at the same time.

You've all seen writers complain that such things are a burden or aren't what we expected. And generally, writers who haven't experienced it write off those complaints.

I'm going to ignore the complaints, because we're talking about discoverability here. All we need to focus on is this: Should we as writers, both indie and traditional, want the same things that every writer has had since the dawn of the bestselling novel in the late 1960s? And if so, why? If not, why not?

In Chapter Eight, I looked at ad buys and how you could tell if your traditionally published novel was going to get one. Let's now move to TV. It worked for Patterson—who spent his career as an ad executive, who wrote and produced television advertising for other companies.

In other words, he knew what he was doing, and it sold his book. The key here, though, is that *he knew what he was doing*.

There's no way to stress that enough. He knew what worked in the advertising market of 1993. He didn't take his publisher's suggestions. You know why? Because then, as now, traditional publishers did none of the sensible things that other big businesses do.

Traditional publishers don't measure the results of their ad buys. They don't look at the effectiveness of a sales campaign. All that stuff in Chapter Four? Traditional publishers do *none* of it.

For God's sake, traditional publishers don't even vary the type of ad campaign to reflect an individual product. Instead, they only vary their campaigns by a vague sense of whether or not a book will sell. Then they slot that book into a pre-established set of behaviors, which "worked for other books of the same type."

Um...no self-respecting ad agency would ever make a Nike shoe campaign look exactly like an Adidas shoe campaign, even though both campaigns advertise high-end athletic shoes. Of course, Nike and Adidas have different ad agencies. But assume they had the same agency. That agency would work very hard to make Nike's shoes look different from Adidas' shoes.

But one publisher of thriller bestsellers treats those novels exactly the same way that the competition treats its thriller bestsellers. Apparently, Clive Cussler writes the exact same book as Lee Child who writes the exact same book as Dan Brown. So that's why they get the exact same advertising treatment—even though all three of them have different publishers.

You know as well as I do those books are different from each other. You also know that with some writers, like John Grisham or Stephen King or

Dean Koontz, you can't predict from one novel to the next what type of book they'll write.

In other words, even within the author brand, the books are wildly different and should get different marketing.

But they don't. Because traditional publishers believe that marketing is something that is beneath them. When they do reach out and try to market something differently, they don't hire an ad agency to do it. They don't bring in outside experts. They don't market test. They guess.

Seriously.

And when that something different fails—and generally it will—it becomes part of publishing lore. *Oh, we tried that on a bestselling novel in 2002 and it failed miserably. Therefore, we know that doesn't work.*

Have you pulled your hair out yet? Because I do every time I think about this.

You shouldn't treat your books the way that traditional publishers treats theirs. Because they run the marketing side of their business poorly doesn't mean you should emulate them. Just because you've seen someone else do something doesn't mean you should do it too.

Before we look in-depth at traditional publishing marketing to see if it's something you want to do, I want to explain something that underlies everything I mention here, and in future chapters.

Award-winning hybrid writer Scott William Carter came up with an acronym to help him manage his time as he ventured into indie publishing. That acronym, WIBBOW, works on a variety of levels, but it especially applies to marketing.

The acronym stands for **Would I Be Better Off Writing?** Generally, the answer to that is yes. In this new world of publishing, where books remain in print, the best thing you can do to promote your previously published works is to write new works. I've said that in previous chapters, and I'll say it again throughout this book.

Okay. So now that you're thinking of time management, let's examine the thing every new writer wants and every bestselling writer wishes they never heard of:

The Book Tour

The book tour really is geared to "our sort of people." If you remember that traditional publishing came out of the East Coast elite in this country, that Ivy-League-good-money tradition of intellectual snobbery, a lot of traditional publishing's long-held attitudes make more sense:

Let's have our author go to bookstores, universities, and the occasional meeting hall, where like-minded people can discuss ideas without worrying about others getting in the way.

This tradition goes all the way back to the 19th century, when Charles Dickens did several speaking tours of American and made a small fortune. His books sold thousands of copies when he did that, but Dickens never saw a profit from the book sales. Why? Because at that point, the United States was the biggest thief of copyright in the world. Dickens' American tour made him money in appearance fees,[4] but no money at all from book sales.

But authors started going on tours after that, and their works sold after the appearances. The author tour became engrained in public life. Back in Dickens' day, a visiting author was sometimes the only entertainment for miles.

Audiences went way down with the advent of movies, radio, and television. As the crowds diminished, the audience became purified. "Our Sort" showed up faithfully and bought books. Those books, published in the US, put money in a publisher's hands. Publishers eventually realized that author appearances drove sales. The more sales that could be driven, the faster an author would rise on a bestseller list.

There is some belief among scholars that the last American tour Dickens did contributed to his early death. But his grueling tour was easier than the tours that traditional publishers put their writers on.

Most writers spend a month on the road, getting up early to do radio interviews, then doing stock signings at stores that aren't hosting an event, a morning signing, lunch on the fly usually before a local TV interview, an afternoon signing or more stock signings or an interview with some print media, then an evening event—a signing, a speech, a reading, something.

After that, the author either gets on a plane, and heads to the next venue or does so early the next morning. At the next venue, she does it all over again. Repeat for two weeks or until complete exhaustion sets in.

Such tours cost a small fortune to mount. The point of them, besides running the author ragged, is to increase a book's velocity.

One book signing in one city won't do it. A dozen book signings in two weeks in a dozen cities won't do it either. But combine two dozen signings along with several speeches, twenty to thirty media appearances (mostly radio, some local television), and the book will soon hit lists. Why?

Because the book's selling five copies at one signing, ten at another. A handful of people pick up the book after hearing an interview.

More than that, though, the bookstores, which are also footing part of this bill by ordering extra copies, putting on more staff, and making room for the author, are also taking out ads in local papers and circulars, maybe some radio spots of their own, and of course, sending the information to their special customers in their newsletters.

Those ads also bring in a few sales. Multiply those increased sales by twelve days, and it might equal an extra thousand to ten thousand sales in a short period of time—enough to goose a book onto a list, which then provides even more advertising.

And by a list, I don't mean an Amazon bestseller list that's drilled down to the tiniest sub-genre. (Mystery/mystery novels/detectives/amateur detective/cozy/series/dogs.) I mean one of the big lists that "Our Sort," pays attention to, like *The New York Times* or *USA Today* or *Publishers Weekly*.

Can you do this on your own? I suppose you can try. It will take tens of thousands of dollars and somehow you'll have to convince booksellers, media bookers, and local venues to give you some of their time and space.

Chances are it won't happen. It doesn't always happen when a publicist from one of the Big Five publishing companies calls: if the bookseller, talk show host, theater owner doesn't want (or hasn't heard of) an author, they're not going to give that author expensive time and space in their venue just because someone asked. Certainly not because the author asked.

Yes, your local bookseller(s) may hold a charity signing for you. Yes, you might even have a mutually beneficial local event. But it won't make any real difference to your book sales, and it certainly won't be worth your time.

Long-term booksellers know that. They know that only certain authors draw readers to a store. These booksellers are also respectful of the author's time, realizing that well-known authors generally don't have an afternoon to give to sitting in a bookstore. And I do mean "give." Writers don't get paid for those appearances, and the sales don't make up for the lost hours of work.

Most traditionally published writers get paid a percentage of each book sold, earning as little as $2 per hardcover sale, and sometimes as little as 50 cents on each paperback sale. That money might not reach an author's pocket for six months or more (if ever). So, sitting in a bookstore for two hours and selling even twenty hardcovers is only worth $40 to the author—six months from now. And if the writer had to drive to the signing, and had to get a hotel room (on her dime) and had to buy her own meals, well, she lost money.

Big name writers do get appearance fees for speaking at libraries and auditoriums. And many big name authors (most, in fact) donate those speaking fees (minus expenses) to charity.

But it's still something they charge for so that they're not running around, giving free speeches, in the hopes of boosting their book sales—like so many beginning authors do.

The book tour is geared toward velocity, not toward building an established readership. How many times have you, gentle reader, bought a book at a signing because the author looked so uncomfortable or because no one had bought a book yet and the bookseller asked you to break the ice? Have you read those books?

When should a writer go on a book tour? When it's being paid for by someone else (preferably your traditional publisher) and it has a realistic chance of boosting book sale velocity to a bestseller list. So many of professional writers (me included) have gone on book tours only to discover the idiot Big Five publisher did not inform its sales team that the signing would happen. Therefore, the publisher did not distribute the books to the bookstores.

At first, I thought this only happened to me. Then I became friends with one of the biggest independent bookstore owners in the United States, and found out it happened more often than not. It certainly doesn't endear those publishers to anyone, and it shows just how haphazard traditional book marketing really is.

Book Signings

Are worthwhile sometimes. But not for the reasons you think. They're not there for discoverability. I think I can probably count on one hand the number of people who bought a book of mine at a book signing because the book looked interesting. I'm sure there are many more people who bought a book because they felt sorry for me sitting there all by myself or because someone else made them buy the book.

I have watched at countless signings as writers guilt potential readers into buying a book. Unless the reader has a small budget and reads everything he buys, I can guarantee that the guilt-book never gets read, and will not create new fans.

This is why traditional publishers cringe when a writer goes on her own book-signing binge. I personally know several writers who spent thousands of dollars going on those binges, and sold a lot of guilt-books. The problem is that those sales do not repeat when the next book comes out, so the sales figures for writers who spend that money go *down*.

In indie publishing, it's only a ding to the ego. In traditional publishing, messing up your numbers with an unsanctioned book signing tour can make the difference between selling your next novel and not selling your next novel to a publisher. Most of the writers I know who did the guilt-tour did not sell their next novel—at least not under the same name.

So when are signings worth it? They're worthwhile if you're already giving a speech or attending a convention. Readers who also happen to be your fans want their books signed. They often won't buy the new books at the event. Sometimes just the cost of attending eats up the book budget. But they get to meet you and have their books personalized.

A lot of book dealers will want a signature for their books. I've seen authors refuse to do that, forgetting that book dealers can be your best friend. Even if the dealer never reads a word of your fiction, the dealer can hand-sell your books and often does just by mentioning that you're a nice person.

If you're going to do a signing, however, that will increase your reader base, however, only do mass signings. I attended only one in 2014, at Powell's Cedar Hill Crossing in Beaverton, Oregon.

I have participated in Powell's mass signing for years now. I sell more copies of my books there than I do at other mass signings I've been a part of because the event is targeted: it's genre-specific, and none of the names are small. Everyone at the Powell's signing either had an established fan base or was already on the bestseller list or both.

The customers who came to that signing had money to spend, and boy, did they. They bought books they hadn't heard of, books they had always wanted, and books someone else recommended.

The amount of money I earned on book sales at Powell's probably wasn't worth the gas I spent to get to the event, but I wasn't doing it for the money. I wasn't even doing it to increase the reader base. Really, it was old home week. Of the thirty-plus attendees, twenty-five or so were friends. We didn't get a lot of time to visit, but we could at least say hello.

So, if you do a signing, don't do it to be discovered. Do it at a venue where your fans can get their books signed. They're the ones who support you, after all. They're the ones who spread news of your work to their friends. They're the ones in charge of word of mouth.

Sign their books graciously. Your readers owe you nothing. They have given up their money and time to support your work. You can smile at them and sign the book. If that's too much to ask of you, then don't go out in public. Period.

Finally, a side note on signing. I sign books by mail, if the sender includes packaging and return postage. I don't travel as much as I used to due to my health, so I'm happy to spend some time putting my signature on a page. Again, the readers support me. It takes so little of my time to give back to them.

Consider it, the next time someone asks you to sign a book.

Media Interviews

C-SPAN has a channel called Book TV. Every time I surf past that station, I'm struck by one thing: Writers generally make for *terrible* television. They can't read their own work in an interesting fashion. They're terrified of questions. They don't dress well. Mostly, they wait for others to help them.

For the most part, writers are introverts who should never be asked to perform in public. Yet traditional publishers have demanded that their writers do radio and television appearances to promote books in that high-stakes velocity period.

Some writers do well. They're relaxed, they're funny, they're wise. George R.R. Martin gives a good interview when he feels like it. George used to work in television and isn't intimidated by the people behind it or the lights or the fact that he's suddenly talking to a huge audience.

Most television hosts haven't read a book, let alone the book they're doing the interview about. In fact, most people who do the booking for television shows will ask the interviewee—in this case, the writer—for questions to ask about the work.

Very few such interviews do anyone any good. I've known a lot of writers who are more interesting in person than their work ever is, and even more writers who are dull as dishwater in person while their work is lively as ever.

But an interview is free advertising, and a good interviewer will hold up a book for a good ten seconds or so, to promote it. Does that sell books? Who knows? Most of the television interviews you see with bestselling writers occur in the same week as the Big Release from their traditional publisher. That publisher is doing everything in its (uneducated) power to get the word out about that book.

That same week, there are book signings all over the country (or region), paid advertising, reviews, and more. It's hard to tell which is more effective. I liken it to a movie opening. Lots of people might attend a movie on opening weekend, particularly if the film is heavily promoted. But after that, it's up to the film's quality to deliver the audience.

How many publishers have sponsored major tours, and signings, and events, and not seen much increase in sales at all?

The answer is more than you'd think.

Just like the fact that television interviews don't move books. How do I know that? From writers who aren't in the middle of a big publicity push, yet who end up on television a lot. If they do an interview, and the host holds up the book, the writers don't usually see a blip in sales.

The key to discoverability isn't one appearance on the *Today* show. Discoverability is really about ubiquitousness—those weeks when you can't avoid the name of that book or that author. So an appearance here and there doesn't work. It has to be in concert with everything else.

That said, having a television series made from your book, even a bad series, will increase sales. *As long as your name is attached to the show.* Too many writers, happy with the idea that they might have sold something to Hollywood, don't pay attention to things like credits.

"Based on the novel by" needs to be in the front of the show, along with the actors' names and the name of the director. You don't want your name in the end credits since, in the US, at least, the end credits go by at high speed and are so tiny that they're unreadable. That's not marketing. That's contractual obligation done poorly.

But you can't guarantee a movie sale or a TV deal at the right time for your novel. And you probably can't get a television interview with the *Today* show as an indie writer—hell, most publishers can't get their big names on television; you're certainly not going to do it either.

Not that it matters. Television isn't something you should do if you're not witty and outgoing and a little bit fearless.

Radio's a bit more forgiving. For one thing, the listeners don't see you. Radio's intimate as well. You're usually in a booth with one person, having a conversation. Properly miked, any writer will sound good.

A good radio interview might sell a few copies of your book. But only a few.

Radio is primarily local, even today with satellite stations, etc. Traditional publishers get past the local stigma by forcing their writers to do a "radio tour" usually from some sound studio somewhere or barring that, on the phone, with radio stations all over the country.

The author sits and answers the same questions from different interviewers in the space of a few hours. It's repetitive and difficult and often at the wrong time of day for wit. If you can move five books per interview, then that series of interviews might sell a few hundred copies of your books.

Max.

And that's if you're a good talker. Most writers aren't.

Very few programs move a lot of copies. One of them is *Fresh Air* on NPR. Terry Gross is good at making even the dullest writer interesting; she reads the books, asks hard questions, and can move a couple hundred copies all by herself.

But to get booked on *Fresh Air*, the book needs a hook. It's not enough that you published it. Heck, Stephen King isn't on every single time he releases a book. When I initially posted this chapter on my website in late 2013, I went to *Fresh Air's* website to see who the most recent author interviews were. They were Delia Ephron, Matthew Hart, Ben Bradlee Jr., and James Tobin.

Who? you might ask. Well, novelist Delia Ephron is a two-fer. Her more famous sister, Nora, died in 2012 (sob) and in 2013, a collection of Nora's works appeared, as did an autobiographical book of essays by Delia. The other three interviewees are nonfiction writers whose topics are much more interesting than they are. The topics are South African gold and crime, Ted Williams, and FDR.

In other words, the long form interviews have a good hook, one that the listener will want to hear.

I used to schedule long-form radio interviews on local topics when I was the news director of a radio station. We turned down a lot more people than we ever brought in. The main reason? The person who wanted an interview was dull.

If you want to do a lot of interviews, do them because they're fun. They won't sell books, but they might get your name out there. Remember that traditional publishers set these interviews up as a velocity package and for every writer who gets an interview, dozens of other traditionally published *bestsellers* get turned down.

Also, interviews are extremely time-consuming. Apply the WIBBOW test to each and every one of them. Ask yourself why you're doing this. If the answer is to sell books, then you're wasting your time.

Stock Signings

I recently spoke to a dear friend who had gone on a big tour for her traditionally published novel. She was shocked that her publisher insisted on stock signings. Because, whenever she went into a bookstore, there was very little stock to sign.

Stock signings were once the heart of any book tour. Bookstores and distributors would have dozens, maybe hundreds, of copies of a writer's book, and the writer would spend an hour or more signing those copies. Once the copies were signed, they wouldn't be returned for credit. In fact, they would remain on the shelf with an "autographed" sticker on them.

In the 1980s, the romance writers started going to regional distributors and to meet the truckers who put out the books, and sign, usually bringing coffee and donuts as a favor to the people who took care of their books.

It worked. The signed copies would go on store shelves, and the truckers would place the romance writer's new title in a position of prominence in grocery stores and truck stops.

Regional distributors disappeared in the late 1990s and chain bookstores stopped the practice of keeping signed books about six years ago. In the last few years, the American Booksellers Association has made a concentrated effort to bring the independent bookseller into the computer age.

This means that independent booksellers generally don't carry a lot of stock. They keep one copy on the shelf, and if the book is in high demand, one or two copies in the back. When a copy sells, the bookseller immediately reorders and the copy is replenished within a day or two.

That's why my friend didn't have copies to sign when she arrived for the publisher-scheduled stock signings. The bookstores had become efficient in their ordering. They keep very few copies in the store.

Stock signings are no longer of any importance. They don't benefit the writer or the bookseller. It actually shows how out of touch traditional publishers' marketing departments are when they have their poor touring writer drop in at a bookstore for a stock signing (which are usually unscheduled). Because there no longer is stock to sign.

Reviews

Good, bad, or indifferent, reviews are your friend—if they're in the right venues. If you want to be discovered, then you need to be in the tried-and-true venue for your genre. *RT Book Reviews* for genre books (particularly romance), *Mystery Scene* for mystery novels, *Locus* for science fiction, just to name a few. Industry bibles *Publishers Weekly* and *Library Journal* inform their respective markets that novels are coming out. Good or bad, the review doesn't matter, because it's *advertising*. It tells the bookseller (or the librarian) that a book is on the way.

Is it worth your time to get into the "self-published ebook" part of *Publishers Weekly*? No, of course not. Because *Publishers Weekly* goes to *bookstores*, and most bookstores don't carry ebooks.

A lot of reviews at the right time are like little ads. If you're indie published and mange to get a review in these venues, you'll see an uptick in *paper* book orders through extended distribution in Createspace or whatever print-on-demand company you use. You probably won't see any difference at all in ebook sales.

Traditional publishers use these review venues as pre-publication advertising. The traditional publishers also invite major booksellers to do their own reviews of upcoming titles. But, since every traditional publisher does this, booksellers get inundated in free books—and rarely read them.

Again, it's not worth your time unless you know how to do it right. Doing it right often means having a real publisher behind you, a real ad budget (since some of these publications won't review books if your publisher hasn't placed an ad in that publication), and real advance reading copies.

However, of all the things that traditional publishers do, the one to emulate is getting reviews in traditional venues like the book publications, newspapers, magazines, and book review programs like those on NPR.

Decades of training have conditioned booksellers, readers, and librarians to glance at reviews and order from them. All three groups use reviews as information—not as to whether or not the book is worth their time—just as a way of knowing a book exists.

Pull Quotes

Since we're dealing with reviews, let's discuss "pull quotes." Pull quotes are those bits of reviews that publishers use to entice the reader into buying a book. There are rules about pull quotes.

Don't take the quotes out of context. If the reviewer said "A great example of how horrible a romance novel can be," don't pull "A great... romance novel" and attribute that quote to the reviewer/publication. You're participating in false advertising. Believe it or not, this practice was litigated in California against (unsurprisingly) the movie companies, and the movie companies lost. You can't change the tenor of a review.

You can pull a single sentence out so long as it represents the review as a whole.

Do reviews make a difference to readers? I don't know. I know that I will scan pull quotes in the front of a novel to see if I'm interested. But I'm also looking at where the quotes came from. If they come from "An Amazon Review" or "Writer's Family Member," then I'm not interested. If they come someplace like *The New York Times* or *Publishers Weekly*, I'm much more apt to buy.

I'm less apt to buy if the pull quotes come from other writers. Even if the writers are big names. A friend just recently showed me a popular history nonfiction book that both of us *wouldn't* have bought even though we were interested in the subject matter. Why? Because *all* of the pull quotes came from talking heads who specialized in politics, in specific, politics that my friend and I disagreed with.

Had those pull quotes come from reputable historians who also doubled as talking heads, we would have been interested.

Remember, advertising can backlash. So be careful how you use it, even with something as small as pull quotes.

The other thing to remember about pull quotes? Usually they're just a design feature. They're put on a paper book to balance the back cover copy or to provide interest across the art. If you don't need the design feature, you don't need the pull quote. It's that simple.

Bookmarks, Posters, Promotional Materials

Worked for a handful of writers in the early 1990s. Debbie Macomber started this trend (and probably regrets it). When she did it, no one else was doing it. Then everyone started. Now I have so many bookmarks littering my office that I can throw a dozen of them out and still have enough for my books.

Ask yourself. Have you ever bought a book because you saw a cool bookmark? No?

What about a cool poster? No? Then why the hell are you wasting your hard-earned dollars on that crap?Particularly when bookstores and other retailers simply throw the things out. (Or give them to visiting readers, like me.)

Blog Tours

The last part of the Old Ways includes something that I would have thought of as a New Way just a few years ago. The blog tour.

So many publishers are now forcing their writers to go on a blog tour. What is that, really? It's writing ad copy or an article or *something* for a blog geared toward readers.Old-timers like me were stunned the first time we got asked to do a blog tour. Write *for free*? We didn't write for free. But that was the blog culture, and this was advertising.

I did my first blog tour for Sourcebooks several years ago, and I did it because I was new to them. I figured I'd give this tour thing a shot. I had no way to measure if it worked, but the bloggers were grateful. I put it in the same category as attending a convention on my own dime.

The next time Sourcebooks asked, I had a way to measure the blog tour's impact. WMG Publishing had published several of my Grayson novels, and I had access to the numbers. Sourcebooks was publishing a Grayson novel as well. For a month, my blog tour articles appeared on various blogs—and didn't cause a single blip in my sales. Not anything.

Maybe I was doing it wrong. I figured that was possible. So I asked my hybrid writer friends who also were doing traditionally publisher mandated blog tours if they saw any change in their indie numbers.

None of them did. Not a one.

Anecdotal, I know. But this is where the WIBBOW test comes in.

I continued to do the blog tour for my Sourcebooks titles because I had started the tradition, and I didn't want to insult the bloggers. I appreciated—and still appreciate—their support.

However, on my final release from Sourcebooks, *A Spy To Die For*, I kept track of my word count for the blog tour.

7,500 words of *free* blogging. With no return at all.

That was in July.

In June, *Asimov's Science Fiction* magazine published the origin story for my character Skye from *A Spy To Die For*, "Skylight." *Asimov's* mentioned my DeLake pen name, but the story was published under Rusch.

Dozens of readers have read "Skylight" and asked me personally if *A Spy To Die For* continues Skye's story. "Skylight" is 8,000 words long.

Gee, write a short story that I get paid for, and which shows results (and can be repackaged in a variety of forms, including as a stand-alone ebook) or write blog posts that can only be used once, and really do little to promote the book…which do I want to do?

If you also under that publications like *Asimov's* charge $1,000 per page for an interior ad,[5] and a story takes up *several* pages, then you realize that you're getting paid not only your word rate for the story, but $1,000 per page in which that story runs. Because your story *is an ad*.

Not everyone can get published in the traditional magazines, primarily because most writers never try. These days, no word is wasted. If your stories don't sell to traditional markets, then put the stories up as ebooks—which also will provide more for your book's marketing than any blog tour ever will.

And guess what? Writing a story passes the WIBBOW test because (*hello!*) you *are* writing.

The old ways work for a handful of books that have a set purpose. If those books need to sell a lot of copies in a short period of time, then the old ways *might* work. Remember, you can't make consumers buy something they don't want, even if that something is advertised repeatedly.

Apply the WIBBOW test. Chances are, you'll always be better off writing.

11

WHEN THE OLD WAYS WORK

Yeah, yeah, I was pretty disparaging of the old ways to promote books in the previous chapters. And there's a good reason to disparage the way Things Have Always Been Done.

But here's the catch: The old ways work.

Occasionally.

Sometimes.

When done right.

They usually aren't done right. In fact, most places—including traditional publishers—use all the old methods because that's what they've always done, not because it's good business.

What are the old ways?

Reviews in major publications. Prominent placement in catalogs. Advertising. Display advertising (risers, book dumps). Billboards or signage in subways or on buses. Banner ads. Bestseller lists. Library placement. Paid placement in bookstores. Interviews with major publications, websites, and radio personalities.

All of those things cost time and money. All of those things are things you as a small publisher—an indie publisher—can do, given the time, the planning, and the willingness to work hard on your publishing business.

These things do not work if you're ebook only. Nor do they work if you're one-person publishing house. You'll need a receptionist/secretary/assistant, just for starters. And you'll need an actual publishing company, with a different name from yours, real ISBNs (as opposed to those that say the name of your print-on-demand publisher), a different address for the business, a different phone number, and different email addresses. A website for the business itself, with a good design.

In other words, you'll need to be running at least two businesses if you want to use the old ways—your writing business and your publishing business. You'll need contracts between your writing business and your publishing business. You'll need different bank accounts. You'll need to think like a publisher when you've got your publishing hat on and like a writer when you're creating.

It's a lot of work.

Why in heaven's name would I tell you to do all this? Because having a publishing company pays huge dividends in the long run. If you're successful, having a company other than your writing business allows you to spread out your pre-tax dollars (you Americans), gives you the opportunity to participate in things that are for publishers only, and gives you the legitimacy your writer-owned business will never achieve.

But a real publishing company will take time to set up properly, it will take some business savvy (which you can learn. If I did, anyone can.), and it will take a willingness to take the long view of your work, rather than a short-term *I want it now!* view.

Because if you take the long view, you'll make more money, you'll have two solid businesses, and you'll have something that will definitely live beyond you—particularly if you set up your estate properly.

Okay, that's all a very short way of dealing with a huge topic. If you want to run a business like a publishing company, here are some books I would recommend: My *Freelancer's Survival Guide* covers everything you need to think about to run a small business (it also applies to writing alone). Dean Wesley Smith's *Think Like a Publisher. The Copyright Handbook* from Nolo Press, so that you understand exactly what you're marketing and why. There are other books, but I haven't fully vetted them. These are the three I'm sure of.

When you buy books to help you set up your publishing company, buy business-focused books, not writing-focused books.

I've started two publishing companies, and advised several others. It's not as hard as it sounds. It is more work than you might think, however. And the learning curve is always there, because the industry is changing.

Why would you want to do all that work?

Depending on who you listen to and which statistics you believe, ebooks are now 20 to 30% of all book purchases in the United States.

What that means is this: 70 to 80% of all book purchases are still in paper.

This is where traditional publishing gets its hooks into indie writers, by telling them that their books can't reach bookstores without a traditional publisher's imprint. And that's just not true.

There are dozens of ways your books will end up in bookstores. I'll deal with some in future chapters. For example, if you price your paper books correctly (and you *are* doing a paper edition, right?), the books will get into bookstores without you contacting the stores at all.

But the books might not be noticed.

So, how do bookstores "discover" books?

Using the old ways.

Sure, booksellers look online. Booksellers have their favorite writers too, and booksellers keep up on what those writers are doing. Not all of those favorite writers are bestsellers. Many are midlist writers the bookseller discovered on their own and/or writers whose work the bookseller encountered in other ways.

All of those discovery tools we'll examine in upcoming chapters work with booksellers. But the best way, the very best way, to get a bookseller interested in your book is to use the old methods.

Yes, booksellers order books when a customer requests them.

But you want the bookseller to order your book as soon as the book sees print. The only way to do that is using the old methods.

What can you do?

First, let me tell you what not to do. Don't contact the bookseller directly unless the bookseller is a friend.

I tell you this because of the way that publishing operated over the last fifty years. Generally speaking, in the past, the only writers who contacted booksellers directly were vanity press writers and clueless newbies.

The reason booksellers ignore you these days when you come into their bookstore, offering to "let" the bookseller carry your work, is because 99% of the writers who asked this before you—from about 1960 onward—were total blithering idiots who couldn't write their way out of a paper bag.

Seriously. And they were the kind of idiot who never took no for an answer.

You want to put yourself in a box with those people, be my guest. But if you really want to be taken seriously as a writer, then stop going to bookstores with your cartons of books and begging the bookseller to carry a few copies.

Here's what you actually do—after (and only after) you set up a real traditional publishing company of your own.

First, you pick a publication date. It must be at least five months away from the actual date the book is completed. Why? Because you'll need reviews—and reviews in the big venues, not on a blogging site.

You will need to produce an advance reading copy (ARC) —in paper, because many review publications still want paper copies. That advance reading copy had better look like one produced out of the Big Five. That means you'll need to find some advance reading copies and look at them.

How do you find advance reading copies?

If you know reviewers, get them to show you a few recent advanced reading copies.

If you are friends with booksellers, have them share some with you. If you lack those connections, go to eBay. Even though ARCs are marked Not For Sale, booksellers and reviewers sell them all the time. (Traditional publishers cut booksellers and reviewers off the ARC list if they get caught selling the ARC before the book comes out. That still doesn't stop people.) Put Advance Reading Copy in the search engine, and you'll be surprised at what you find. Buy a few that were produced in the last twelve months, so you can see how it's done. Then copy that format on your own ARC. Make sure you understand the jargon of the ARC, what kind of promotions are listed and what the jargon words mean, before you say that you will be doing such things.

Write a cover letter to go with the ARC that is all sales material. Reviewers will crib off that letter, so make sure the letter is positive and accurate. Have your assistant sign the letter, not you.

The letter needs to come from your publishing company—you need a street address on it, a publisher email, and a publisher phone number. Some traditional review sites will call those numbers, so make certain that your traditional publishing company has professional voicemail and a trained person answering the phone.

Follow the rules that each publication has for review copies. If you don't follow the rules, all your money and time will be wasted. If you don't follow the rules, the publication will toss out your ARC.

Some publications want paper ARCs. Some want eARCs. Some want paper ARCs for certain genres, and eARCs for other genres. Follow the rules to the letter.

Particularly pay attention to the rules governing how far in advance the publication needs the ARC. *RT Book Reviews* needs its copy five months ahead. *Publishers Weekly* needs its copy about four months ahead. Other publications have different rules.

Just because you send an ARC doesn't mean your book will be reviewed. And just because you send an ARC doesn't mean your book will get a *good* review. Take your writer hat off, and put your publisher hat on.

You're doing the reviews in traditional publications to let booksellers know that the book exists. Most booksellers don't care if the book got a starred review from *Booklist*. Booksellers are notoriously opinionated people, like most readers, and will make up their own minds. However, booksellers will use the reviews—good or bad—to figure out which books to order for the storefront, not just to have on their website.

Three other caveats. First, if you're going to all the trouble to send out ARCs, then make sure your publisher website lists all your books. Make sure that the publisher website also has dealer discounts for booksellers. Here's the dealer discount schedule that WMG Publishing uses. I took this directly off their website:[1]

All titles published as paperbacks on this website can be ordered direct from WMG Publishing. All orders must be prepaid.

Discount Schedule
> *2-4 assorted books, 40% discount + shipping.*
> *5-9 assorted books, 45% discount + shipping.*
> *10 or more assorted books, 50% discount, free domestic U.S. shipping.*

The booksellers will probably never order direct from your publisher, but they want the option. Besides, they'll also want to know that the publisher is legit—and to them, the publisher is not legit unless it offers booksellers a way to order direct.

The second caveat deals with the traditional sites themselves. *RT* will review books, provided the publisher takes out an ad in the magazine at least once per year. This has been *RT*'s policy for more than thirty years, and is one reason the publication still exists. (It's also the reason that *RT*'s content shows a bias toward traditional publishers versus indie writers. Traditional publishers pay the bills at *RT*.)

Buy a publisher's ad, not a writer ad, with them. Because...you've got a publishing company, remember?

An ad does not guarantee a review, nor does it guarantee a good review. But you have no hope of getting a review at all without buying an ad.

If you've set up a traditional publishing company, don't send your ARCs or eARCs to *Publishers Weekly Select* or the other review sites that traditional review publications have set up for ebooks.

Why? Well, you're trying to get into bookstores with your paper books. Booksellers don't read *Select* and those other publications because they're not for paper books. (And those publications have a whiff of that vanity press thing. Booksellers are very snobby about that.)

So if you're trying for booksellers, spend your advertising/discovery dollars where the booksellers actually look to discover books.

The final caveat is this: there are services like Net Galley that will, for a *very* large fee, make your eARC available to people who are a "reviewer, blogger, journalist, librarian, bookseller, educator, or in the media."

Traditional publishers use Net Galley (and other services like it) but *never* on the books they really want reviewed or covered. This is a place that traditional publishers use as an afterthought. If you see an ARC from a traditional publisher and it says "ARCs available through Net Galley," it usually means that's all the promotion the traditional publisher is doing on that title.

Avoid places like Net Galley.

Go direct.

Review and review copies are the cheapest thing I'm going to mention in this post. The other things are expensive and only available to traditional publishers.

One of those other things is the American Booksellers Association.

To join the ABA as a "publishing partner,"[2] your publishing company needs to have "at least five titles currently in print [in paper] and readily available for booksellers to order either direct [from the publisher] or from wholesalers [such as Ingrams or Baker & Taylor]."

If you meet those qualifications, then you must pay the $350 annual fee (with a $25 handling fee) to join. What do you get if you join?

Lots of direct opportunity to contact ABA member bookstores. The ABA has a list of member bookstores on its website. I suggest you look at it, and think about the direct mail opportunities presented here.

Let me give you two examples of direct marketing through the publishing partner program.

The Red Box (which is actually a white box with a red sticker) goes to 1,100 member bookstores. Publishers can include catalogs, notifications of special books, flyers, posters, all kinds of promotional material for a partic-ular book—except the ARC. To include these items costs an additional fee, and you have to follow certain rules. But the ABA sends out twelve of these boxes every year, and booksellers do comb through them.

The White Box goes to 750 select bookstores (following ABA rules) and includes galleys, ARCs, and finished paper copies of a book. It costs anywhere from $1.50 to $2.50 per item to be included (minimum 450 items) so it can cost you as little as $675 or as much as $1,875 (not counting your production cost for each book).

Booksellers do read the books or at least look at them. If your book is badly produced—or if you send a romance novel to a noir mystery store—then the bookseller will give the book away or toss it.

In other words, the bookseller will behave just like everyone does with advertising. We only look at the stuff we're interested in.

There are other great advertising programs through the ABA. The best part about these? They're legitimate, unlike schlepping your books to a store and having the owner think you're an idiot for even trying. You get to reach booksellers the way that writers/publishers always have, using direct methods.

Here's the secret, folks. If you set up a traditional publishing company, you can do everything that the Big Five can do.

Everything.

What does it take? Money and know-how.

You can buy ads in book-oriented publications like *The New York Times Book Review* or the *Los Angeles Times Book Section*. (Booksellers read those.) You can send your employees to trade shows like Book Expo in New York or the dozens of local book-oriented trade shows across the country. (There are huge trade shows worldwide: you can send your employees to those, too, if you have money to burn.)

You, the writer, should never man that table, because you're "the talent." (Although you can be on panels.) Like anything else to do with discover-ability at this level, just because you spent the money doesn't mean you'll get a good return. You can give away hundreds of free copies at the New Atlantic Independent Booksellers Association meeting next fall, but that doesn't mean the booksellers who get the copies will read them or order them for their stores.

It's a risk. Like all advertising is.

The ABA isn't the only group that will put you directly in front of a bookseller or librarian. Baker & Taylor will as well. They have huge publisher participation programs, with an entire downloadable flyer[3] that explains all of their services—kinda. Many of these promotion services start at $10,000 and go up from there. Big publishers use these things all the time.

I suggest you scan through the offerings, just to see what kind of things are available. Some things that are available won't be listed in a flyer that goes to everyone.

For those things, you'll have to talk to a rep directly—and even then, after you've spent some time and money.

These programs exist on all levels of retail. How do you think certain products get placed up front in a grocery store? The supplier pays for that position.

When you're dealing with books, book distributors, and bookstores, you're dealing in good old-fashioned retail. And retail has a lot of paid-for positions that are advertising positions.

Do you want your book on a bestseller list? Many of those in-store lists are purchased positions. You have to work with a distributor's ad rep (usually) to buy—say—the #10 position for books in the Safeway grocery store chain. (No, I have no idea how much that costs. But it's in the tens of thousands.)

Are you offended that bestseller lists like that are bought? Think it through. Bestseller list positions are always bought. Even indie writers buy their place on a list, often by reducing the price or restricting distribution to one outlet only.

To get on any paper bestseller list, a book must be widely distributed at minimum. Most of those lists (even the in-house B&N list) are paid for by the publisher. To get on the non-paid-for list, like *The New York Times*, takes a knowledge of velocity, the ability to distribute (and promote) the book widely, and sometimes a sideways bit of know-how. Every year or two, some reporter discovers that someone bought a place on a reputable bestseller list. In 2013, Jeffrey A. Trachtenberg of *The Wall Street Journal* found a company that put at least two books on bestseller lists by gaming the system.[4]

All that articles like this prove is that with enough money and know-how, everything in publishing can be done—with or without the Big Five.

I don't expect you to hire a company that claims it can make your book a success. In fact, I would hope you stay away from them. Too many writers get scammed on this one thing alone. Marketing scams are the biggest business scams in existence. Don't fall for them.

However, you can pay to have your product—a book—placed at the checkout stand of some non-bookstore like a grocery store or a discount retailer. Book publishers do that all the time. It takes money. Will that payment translate into sales? Sometimes. But not always.

The way you can tell a marketing scammer, by the way, is that they will *guarantee* sales. None of these other programs do. They will gladly take your money in exchange for product placement. That's all. It's up to the product to sell itself.

So...really, what it takes to get all of the benefits that a traditional publisher can bring you and more, in all aspects of publishing, is that you start a traditional publishing company of your own. I know. It's easy to say, and hard to do. But all of those things that you the writer want a traditional company to do are the things your company can do for you.

Think I'm spinning you a line? Think no one has tried it? People have done this from the beginning of publishing. Dean and I did it with Pulphouse Publishing before ebooks existed.

Ten years ago, author Helen A. Rich, one of the heirs to the Wrigley fortune, decided to start Medallion Publishing. It caused quite a kerfuffle in the industry. People claimed she was starting a large vanity press, that she was only doing this because she was rich. Medallion did things that big publishers did—buying the cover of *Publishers Weekly* to advertise books, buying expo space at BEA, and so on.

More importantly, Medallion didn't go away. It's still around, has a rather large staff, and has published a lot of writers. I've heard good and bad things about the company. I've never worked with them, so I have no idea how good they are to their authors (and honestly, I don't want to know—that's not the point of this piece).

Medallion is now a "media group" that has its fingers in publishing, music, and movies. I will tell you one thing about people and their money: they don't keep throwing good money after bad if the experiment doesn't work. Financially, then, Medallion is working.

Medallion is just one such publishing company that started from one person's vision and has grown larger. Sourcebooks is another. Dominique Raccah made a $17,000 investment seventeen years ago, and has grown Sourcebooks into a major player in a variety of genres.

Both of these companies, and many much smaller companies, do the advertising things I've mentioned, and do all the work that the Big Five publishers do to attract booksellers. These two publishers have played with the Big Boys from the beginning.

Anyone can do this, with some savvy and a willingness to spend on the right project. You don't have to do all of it. If you want to attract booksellers, really, you only need to do a little of it.

But you need to plan how you're going to go after this much larger world.

And you'll know how to plan by the time you finish this book.

PASSIVE MARKETING

12

BRANDING

Passive Marketing is exactly that. These things are things you do *once*, and then can forget about for years at a time if you wish. They are extremely effective.

In fact, they're necessary if you want to sell a lot of books.

But they don't feel like *marketing*, because the effort involved isn't all hype and screaming.

Passive marketing in particular is the main reason I told you at the beginning of this volume that you need to have published many books before most of the suggestions here will help you.

If you've published only one or two books, the next several chapters will help you plan your future. If you've published many books, you'll probably see an uptick in sales after doing the items in the next few chapters.

The problem with passive marketing is that much of it requires a huge learning curve. It's a learning curve you'll need to do if you're going to publish your own work.

The other problem with much of this passive marketing is that traditionally published writers cannot do most of it. Those writers rely on their publishers for this stuff.

But hybrid authors can do it for the books they control, and indie authors can do all of it for all of their titles.

Traditional business has a very firm definition of the word "brand," some of which applies to what we're doing and some of which does not. So,

I'm not going to send you to business pages or business blogs here, because I don't want to confuse you. If you research the words used in this piece, you'll find more on the topic of branding.

Definitions

Branding is a means of *identifying* a product. Traditional businesses think of branding this way. (Experienced business readers, please cut me some slack since I'm being very general here.)

First, there's the brand itself. That's the product (or products) that we want to lump together.

Then there are greater and greater levels of recognition for the brand. We'll deal with just a few of these.

1. **Brand awareness**—that's mostly what we're talking about in this book. Brand awareness makes sure customers know the brand exists.

2. **Brand experience**—that's just what it sounds like. That's the customer's experience with the brand. The brand experience, which is often an emotional reaction, can also be called brand image. That's what the customer thinks of when they hear the brand's name. Obviously, customers need brand awareness before they have some kind of reaction to that brand.

3. **Brand recognition**—that's a widely known brand *within its target audience*. For example, I mentioned Beyoncé in an earlier chapter. All of my readers knew who she was, but not all of you had experience with her brand. She not only has a brand (her name) but she also has brand recognition—people with no brand experience might still know who she is. (And might have an opinion about her brand, which some would say fits in brand experience.)

4. **Brand franchise**—this one's tricky. This is where a customer might recognize a brand based on images or some element of the brand without a mention of the brand's name. For example, if you show an image of a bubbling dark soft drink in parts of the American South, people might identify that drink (regardless of what it is) as a Coke. A tissue might be called a Kleenex, even if it's not. Those two brands are brand franchises.

Branding 101 for Writers

Readers identify these things as brands (in no particular order): Characters, Worlds, Series, and Writers. Readers rarely (almost never) consider a publisher a brand. There are exceptions—Harlequin has done a fantastic job branding its fiction. But most traditional publishers have not.

In fact, traditional publishers seem to have very little idea what branding is at all. They do branding on bestsellers, almost accidentally. Generally, the book's designers have no idea how to brand anything. A few years back, Putnam decided to brand Nora Robert's work, and the publishing trades made a big deal out of it.

But if you're traditionally published, chances are your work has no individual branding—meaning, the branding is not tied to your writer name. The branding is tied to something else if branding exists at all.

Traditionally published writers of long-standing, like me, have books that look like mishmash of stuff, even if the books are in the same genre and same series. The lack of branding has hurt us.

Branding is not an area where you, as indie publishers, should look to traditional publishing. You need to think outside their narrow little box.

You want your readers to identify your work as quickly as possible. You want them to find you easily. Hybrid writers who understand this are actually changing the industry. Their traditional publishers are starting to ask who the hybrid writers have hired as cover artists, and are copying the self-published designs of the hybrid writer, rather than the other way around. (Sad, isn't it?)

Traditional publishers tend to brand 99% of their books in one way—by genre. Indie writers need to do this as well, because readers expect it.

Genre Branding

Don't tell me you don't know what I mean. Every time you see a muscular woman with her back to the viewer, looking over her shoulder while brandishing a weapon, you know you're looking at an urban fantasy novel. Genre branding is so ubiquitous that in some genres, it becomes cliché. Then some traditional publisher changes up the genre branding, and everyone follows suit.

I'm not telling you that you need to put that sexy mean babe on your urban fantasy novel. But…

As an independent publisher, you must make decisions within your publishing house about branding. On this matter, your publishing company needs both a name that's different from yours and it needs a logo. Keep the logo simple and small, so that it can fit on the lower spine of a *paper* book.

Then you must decide how your publishing house will distinguish between the genres you write. If you only write in one genre, and you only write a series, then it's pretty simple. We'll discuss that in a moment.

But if you're a writer who writes in more than one genre, like I do, then you will need different branding for each genre you write in.

In other words, your stand-alone romance novel cannot look the same as your stand-alone mystery novel which should not look the same as your stand-alone fantasy novel.

I'll be using a lot of my covers as examples here because I'm most familiar with them, and because Allyson Longueira at WMG Publishing is fantastic at branding. I'm not going to discuss all the elements she puts into the covers. But I will say this: she uses different font families for different genres, as well as different kinds of art for each genre as well.

When I did this chapter as a blog post, I was able to include covers from all of the books that I mention here. But because ebook formatting is different than web formatting, and because I don't have permission to use any covers other than my own in this format, the best way to see the examples is to click here or go to my website at kristinekathrynrusch.com and click on the Business Resources drop down menu, hit Discoverability series, and then click on the link marked "Branding: Discoverability Part 6." You'll be able to see all of the examples.

You must brand by genre. Readers expect it. They want to know what they're picking up. For example, many romance readers read the genre to escape the difficulties in their lives. They have enough tribulations; they don't want those in their fiction. They would be horrified if they picked up *Sins of the Blood*, without some clue that it's a horror novel, not a sweet romance like one of my other novels, *The Death of Davy Moss*.

You want to be discovered? Being discovered by genre is a fine way to do so. Make sure your listings on the various bookstores are correct as well. If you don't know genre—and most writers don't (even though they think they do)—then learn it. WMG Publishing offers a genre structure class that will help you learn what genre is.[1]

Don't mess up genre. It'll anger your readers.

For example, I recently downloaded a free ebook that was marked romance, and seemed right up my alley. It was even marked "Sweet." And it opened with our supposed hero in bed with three women. The sex act was graphically described—and he was treating all three women badly.

That's not a sweet romance. It's some kind of erotica. I didn't read far enough to find out.

But I can guarantee you that I'll never download another ebook from that author again. There's no way to know what I'll be getting.

When you identify by genre, you're going for brand identification. A reader likes romance, so she'll pick up a romance novel by someone she's never heard of. What you want from your genre-identified book is for it to move to the brand experience (and brand identification) from the *genre* to the *author*.

And that's our next step.

Author Branding

If you write under different names, then you'll want a different look for each name. In the past, changing names was the only real way that an author could control her branding.

As a traditionally published author, I chose to have pen names not to hide my work, but to make a clear line between my graphic horror novels or the brutal realities of some of my science fiction works, and the sweet romances I wrote. (There were other marketing reasons for the pen names, which I've discussed before, that are not relevant to this chapter.)

Savvy writers knew that different pen names in different genres would get a different branding on the books—branding that would not confuse the reader. I'm glad I did this for the reasons I used, but it leaves me with a problem now that the market has changed, and *I* control my author branding.

I'm many writers, not just one, and each writer has her own following. I've chosen to continue some of my pen names for that reason, rather than publish everything under Rusch.

If I were a beginning writer in today's marketplace, I would probably use Rusch for everything, and Let The Reader Beware.

But I would still make things easier for the reader by branding by genre, like I mentioned above. That way, the reader would know *just from the cover design* that *Sins of the Blood* is a very different book from *Spree*, but that there are elements that a lover of one of those books might like in the other.

When you brand by author, you develop a specific design that reflects that author. Note the way my name is on all three books mentioned above. It's at the top of the book, with the title below.

But if you look at *The Perfect Man*, a romantic suspense novel written under my pen name Kristine Dexter, you'll see its design is slightly different from my contemporary romance, *Davy Moss*: The placement of the name is different, and there are other subtle (and not so subtle) differences. The font family, however, is the romance font that WMG uses, so the eye recognizes that font.

As I mentioned, Putnam has gone to great lengths to brand Nora Roberts. They have little circle near her name (called a "bug"), an NR logo that long-time Roberts readers know means this title is brand new. (Her books have been reissued so many times, that readers actually complained about being unable to distinguish new from old, so the readers forced the publisher [or, rather, Nora did] to identify the new books.)

I do not have permission to put Nora's covers (or indeed, any author's covers) in this book, so you'll have to go to this blog post on my website to see these covers. Again, click here, or go to my website at kristinekathrynrusch.com and click on the Business Resources drop down menu, hit Discoverability series, and then click on the link marked "Branding: Discoverability Part 6." You'll be able to see all of the examples, because on my site, I include links to the books themselves, so that you can purchase them, something I can't do here.

However, note the very different branding on her J.D. Robb pen name. Same person, but different look for a completely different kind of book.

You want your readers to identify *your* books by their covers. You get to decide how you want to brand your author name.

This is particularly important when you write cross-genre novels, like Dean Wesley Smith's *Against Time*. The romance font is suggested on *Against Time* because it has a heavy romance element. But it's not the same font that WMG uses for its other romances.

The look of the book is very, very different than the look of my books, because Dean is a different writer. This was a tricky design, because the book is SF too. So Allyson hinted at both romance and sf. (Told you she's good.) She blended the genres in the entire design, from fonts to art to placement. Not to mention Dean's author branding.

Allyson did something similarly cross-genre for my Kristine Grayson books, such as *Simply Irresistible*. They're sweet romances, but they're paranormals and because I wrote them, they're heavy on the fantasy. WMG decided to put covers on those books that would intrigue fantasy readers as well as romance readers. So the look is unique to Kristine Grayson.

Your author brand should have similarities throughout your titles (name placement, etc.), so that readers know how to find your work. They know at a glance what your books look like, and they'll pick those books up.

What you want to do, through your *storytelling*, is move your readers from brand experience (they liked one of your books) to brand recognition (Hey! Look! There's another book by one of my favorite authors!).

They can make that move without your constant tweeting, promotion, ads, and everything else *if you've figured out how to brand your books by author.*

Series Branding

This is something that traditional publishing stumbled into, and doesn't always manage to do. When St. Martin's Press published my Smokey Dalton series, they never branded the covers. Each book looks *very* different from all the other books, which is death to a mystery series. (Yes, pun intended.)

However, Roc books does a lovely job in general with series branding, and they did a good job with branding my Retrieval Artist novels. If only they had left the previous books in print when the new book came out...

Please forgive that personal moment of ennui.

When WMG Publishing published both series, the company took care to brand each series. But that means that my traditionally published first editions look very different from the current editions. You can buy each book in the new format, although Amazon doesn't always show it that way.

This happens with all authors who are traditionally published. If they have jumped publishers in the middle of a series, then that series lacks a uniform look. Go to my site to look at Robert Crais' first novel in his Elvis Cole series, *The Monkey's Raincoat,* as published by Bantam.

Then look at a mid-series novel, *Voodoo River,* published by Hyperion.

And finally, look at *Taken,* to see how the series is being branded now by Berkeley.

Bob's books have never gone out of print, so his series is scattered between several publishing companies, which hurts the branding of the series. Readers still find them, but it's better to be branded uniformly by series.

Compare to George R.R. Martin's Song of Fire and Ice series, which most of you know as the Game of Thrones series. It's been with the same traditional publisher from the beginning.

You'll have to go to my site to see these examples. But look at how the book is currently being branded. The titles all mention the HBO series, and use one dominant image.

Initially, though, the publisher had no idea how to brand the first book, and tried several looks. You can see all of them, if you look at the oldest (and most expensive) copies of *Game of Thrones.* I've posted tiny versions of the first hardcover (the silver thing) and the first paperback (with the horse) on my site.

Even though George has been with the same publisher, the books have gone through at least three different looks. But the entire series gets rebranded every time the look changes.)

WMG is working hard at branding my various series. The Smokey Dalton series has a dark historical look.

My Diving series has one SF look. And my Retrieval Artist another SF look.

They share some of the same font family though, and some other subtle things that Allyson does with sf design.

Allyson brands across different series as well. I write Christmas novellas as Kristine Grayson (including *Visions of Sugar Plums*), and they have a slightly different look than the Grayson book above because they're in a different series.

Allyson brought that look into *Fiction River* (which has its own branding) when I edited a Christmas anthology under my Kristine Grayson name, *Christmas Ghosts*. In other words, she combined *two* series brands so that readers would recognize both.

That's high art. Allyson has degrees in design, is an award-winning designer, and has worked in graphic design for years. She's also studied branding. She's focused on this, and you'll see more of these branding things on my work as time goes on.

Using the Brands

In 2012 and 2013, Allyson redesigned all of WMG's books so that they would have the proper look by genre, author, and series. In 2014, she's been taking that design into the websites. You'll see changes on the websites as we brand it. Kristine Grayson's website will reflect the book designs, as well the websites for the Retrieval Artist and the Diving series.

The brands you design can cross into other forms of advertising as well —print ads, visual ads, etc. But you must design the look first, so that you move into brand recognition—and maybe brand franchise. Only one author I've mentioned in this piece has achieved brand franchise, and that's George. He didn't do it himself; the HBO miniseries did, and that's why his books look so professional now.

The traditional publisher mimicked what HBO did. (All of The Game of Thrones merchandise uses that branding.)

You know that HBO knows branding. Just think of that sound that starts every single HBO program. It's brand franchising. The sound makes you think of HBO before you even see the logo.

Branding Bonus

Branding helps new readers discover you (genre branding) and it helps regular readers find new works (author branding/series branding). It will sell your work without you doing anything after you've finished with your cover design.

For a few years, at least.

The Bad News

Think you're done after you've branded all of your work? You are...for five to ten years. And then you need to modernize the brand's look—particularly if you're only doing genre branding.

At some point, the dominant look will become stale. (Yes, I'm using produce terms.) I'm already tired of that muscle-bound woman on urban fantasy covers. I'm usually right on the cusp of trends like that. If I'm not happy, then other readers aren't, either. They'll pass over that woman, thinking the contents are as stale as the cover. Or, that they've already read the book.

After five to ten years (and I can't tell you specifically when), you will have to redesign the book's cover to make it more reflective of a newly published book.

Think of it this way. The three-year-old you see now might, twenty years from now, be the perfect reader for your urban fantasy novel. Twenty years ago, the term "urban fantasy" did not exist, although the book type did. Twenty years from now, that term might be dated. She might look at your muscle-bound woman cover and think she's seeing something that won't interest her because it's *old*.

Design a new cover for a new generation of readers.

That will mean a redesign of all your urban fantasy books. And if they're in a series, then you'll have to do a series redesign—from the ground up.

You might want to redesign to refresh, like Berkley is doing with Nora Robert's very first book. Berkley acquired the rights years ago, and has done a couple of reissues. Silhouette initially published the novel.

Go to my website to see the 1981 Silhouette edition, and the way that

Berkley repackaged it in 2012 to match Robert's other contemporary romances.

Refreshed and redesigned for a new generation.

Or you might want to redesign because of some new cultural phenomenon. William Morrow did that with Phillip Rock's books to capture the readers who watch *Downton Abbey*. My site has the original 1979 cover of *The Passing Bells*, as well as the *Downton Abbey* fan's cover from 2012.

Branding. It's truly an art. But it's an art that aids discoverability. If you like Downton Abbey, then you should pick up Rock's book. The branding tells you that, even if you've never heard of him. *The Passing Bells* is part of a trilogy, so all three books have a similar look. That's brand recognition.

How to Brand

You don't have to get a degree in design, like Allyson has. You can hire a designer, and help that person along with examples and explanations. If you can't afford to hire someone with experience, then do something simple. (Again, WMG has some online classes and short lectures on cover design, taught by the marvelous Allyson.[2])

Make sure your genre covers look like other covers in the genre. Have a clinch on your romance; a gun on your mystery. Make your series books have similar covers.

You don't have to learn branding from us, but you should learn it. You are in charge of your own publishing company, after all. You might not do the design. (I certainly don't [and the world is grateful!].) But you need to know terminology and know what you're asking for. You need to know what's right when you see it, and what's wrong.

Once you have your branding set, though, your sales will go up because you've made it easier for your readers to find you.

And that's what discoverability is all about.

13

PRICING

When I initially wrote this chapter, which ended up as a two-part blog post on my site, I dreaded it. Because I knew I would get excoriated by people who treat price like a religion. Whether that price is free, a 99-cent ebook, or a $45 hardcover, writers seem to "know" what price is too much and what the market will bear. They base this knowledge, not on a study of pricing, but on their gut or their friends or their own price prejudices.

After I wrote this chapter, I wrote Chapter Seven: Types of Readers to try to explain even more clearly why some prices work for some people and don't work for others.

So, before you read this chapter, please review (or read) Chapter Seven. I want us to be using the same terms. And as you read Chapter Seven, think about what type of *reader* you are. Because the type of reader you are affects your gut instincts about pricing.

Remember that readers are different, and often the same person is a different type of reader for different types of books.

Those are very important concepts when discussing price.

Realize, too, that most of the "wars" you've been seeing between giant retailers like Wal-Mart, Barnes & Noble, and Amazon, and their suppliers, such as the Big Five publishers, are over price.

The suppliers want to set a price and have the retailers stick to that price. The retailers want to set a different price based on the way that the retailers define their own businesses, and want the freedom to discount or *increase* prices accordingly.

Price is important, and it's not as simple as "My friends do this" or "I want that." Pricing is not something you do by gut instinct or what your best friend tells you or how the people on your Facebook page react to the price you set. Nor is it something you should just trust to your friends on writer boards.

Pricing is a major field of study in both economics and in business. There have been more scientific studies on price and the impact of price on the consumer (on the business, on an industry) than anything else in retail. Price is extremely complicated, and people's reaction to it even more so.

Remember, price is at the heart of the Department of Justice case against Apple and the traditional publishers. Price is important enough that parts of it are regulated, and regulated differently in different industries, and in different countries.

If you don't believe me, just go to Wikipedia and start down the "price" rabbit hole. If you read all the links related to pricing just on Wikipedia's site, not the footnotes, you'll lose the better part of an evening.

With that in mind, I'm going to discuss only those aspects of price that will bring *more* consumers to your work. I'm going to do this without linking because of the rabbit holes and because this information is out there. Much of it is basic economics.

If you're in business, and you don't understand basic economics, that's like being a writer who has never read a book, but believes they know everything there is to know about storytelling.

Forget your economics classes from college. If they were anything like mine, the professors were hired after a search for the dullest lecturer possible. Economics truly isn't dull, and believe it or not, neither is pricing. Go forth, read. Learn.

I've included pricing in the passive marketing section because you can set a price for your book and then not think about price ever again. You can also change prices weekly, as an active marketing strategy, but that's usually not as effective.

It's better to set a standard retail price—a baseline, if you will—and work from there. I'll explain that later in this chapter.

The best way to handle pricing for all of your writing *products* (and remember, we're discussing products in this book; the art is finished) is this:

Make initial decisions, and occasional changes, but for the most part, once you make your decisions for your business, you are done until something major happens.

That said, here we go on pricing and *discoverability*.

Here's how you get discovered:

Set the Right Price for Your Work

As I mentioned above, this is harder than it looks.

If you're traditionally published, this has little to do with you—except that you need to remember this: the longer your book, the higher the purchase price will be. If you want an affordable mass market paperback for your readers, then write three 70,000 word novels instead of one 210,000 word novel.

Yes, your readers will pay more in the end than they would if they only bought the big honkin' book.

But price is a factor only at the cash register (virtual or otherwise).

Which means this: a consumer will hesitate before buying a fat fantasy priced at $12.99 in mass market paperback, but won't hesitate to buy a single mass market one-third the size at $7.99.

Once the purchase is complete, and the reader is hooked on the novel, she'll buy the next two at $7.99, because she wants them. Which means she will spend more in the end than if she hadn't balked at the $12.99 mass market (which, you can now see, was an actual bargain).

Remember this:

Price is most important to the consumer at the moment of purchase. I'm not just referring to high prices. I'm also referring to low prices.

If a price is too high, you limit the number of consumers who will buy your book. Some might find value in that perceived high price, but most will not.

If the price is too low, the consumer believes something is wrong with the product. In fact, low-priced items get returned more and receive more complaints from consumers than overpriced items.

The price has to be just right. It's the Goldilocks rule, and believe it or not, it's not individual.

Prices work on three levels:

1. The industry level (the standard prices for everyone in the field; the prices the consumer expects)

2. The market level (the prices that competing works or similar works have in the same market)

3. The transactional level (the discounts on one particular product or with one kind of consumer, which generally occur at the moment of purchase)

Too many indie writers operate only on the transactional level, ignoring the first two.

Traditional publishers work on the market level, ignoring the other two levels.

In book publishing, the industry level is always there, but never really discussed.

So, let's begin with the industry level. You need to know how traditional publishers price their books. Like it or not, consumers have a price expectation on books, and that expectation is set by traditional publishing. Hardcovers can and do cost $25–35; trade papers generally run $15–20; and mass markets $7–10. These prices have remained relatively stable for the past ten years.

The problem in pricing has come from electronic books, not because indie publishers made things cheap, but because consumers are smarter than everyone realizes. Consumers know that a paper book has costs. They hold that paper book in their hands, feel the pages and the ridged letters on the spine. They know that item had materials.

They also know that the book was *written* by someone, and edited, and formatted in some way. But consumers also know that once a book is formatted and uploaded onto various electronic devices, there is not a *massive* per-unit cost, like there is with paper. There is a per-unit cost, more like a rental space, for the digital files, but it didn't cost trees and printing and binding and shipping and shelf space.

So, consumers balked at paying $20 for an ebook at the same time as the hardcover. However, as this new side of industry has stabilized, consumers have shown a willingness to pay more than $10 for an electronic book, as long as that electronic book is two things: 1) the cheapest edition available and 2) a brand-new title. Once the title is older, then the price needs to go lower than $10, but not significantly lower than $10.

In other words, electronic book prices have started to stabilize *for novels* between $5–10 for backlist and $8–12 for front list.

As I prepare this chapter, the fight between Amazon and Hachette over electronic book prices has gone public. Even if you lived in a cave in the summer of 2014, you heard about this fight, generally from Hachette's point of view, because the mainstream media is based in New York and because many of the media outlets are owned by the conglomerates that also own the Big Five publishing companies.

Hachette, like the other Big Five Publishers, wants ebook prices for new releases to be $14.99 to $19.99, to protect hardcover sales. Amazon believes that ebooks, with some exceptions, should be priced at $9.99.

These companies are discussing *industry standard*, and as I mentioned above, industry standard is something you as an indie writer need to pay attention to. By the time most of you read this book, the Hachette/Amazon feud will be resolved in one way or another, and a new industry standard will exist.

Industry standard is something you as an indie writer need to pay attention to. You don't want your possible consumer to ask who the hell you think you are when you charge more than $15 for an electronic book, nor do you want that consumer to ask what's wrong with the content when your electronic book's normal price is under $5.

Now, remember, not all consumers are the same. When we discuss reader reaction in general, we're discussing the Sometimes Buys New readers, which, for most of us, are the bulk of our readers. The True Fans will ignore price, if possible, and the brand-loyal readers will buy according to their pocketbooks (if they can buy the expensive edition, they will; otherwise they'll buy when the book reaches a price they can afford).

Industry standard on paper books has remained stable for nearly a decade. You need to produce paper books to aid in discoverability. Those paper books *must* be priced properly. You need to make at least $2 on your paper book, and possibly more.

If you want your book to go to traditional bookstores, such as Barnes & Noble and Powell's, you need to price that book the way traditional publishers do. *Not* to be like those publishers, but so that everyone else in your supply chain makes their usual (small) profit off the books.

I've noticed that many independent booksellers buy an occasional underpriced indie paper book from their distributors, and then *raise* the price of that indie book so that the bookseller can make its usual profit. Independent booksellers try to stock what their customers want.

Barnes & Noble, and other chain bookstores, won't put anything on its store shelves if the book is underpriced.

Here's something most indie writers don't know: If you click extended distribution in Createspace and fill out the proper forms on other POD sites (*not* anything marked deep discounting), then you will get into the catalogues offered by traditional distributors like Ingrams and Baker &

Taylor *automatically*. Traditional bookstores order 99% of their books through these venues.

However, if your prices are too low, Ingrams and B&T won't put your book into their catalogs at all, even if you clicked extended distribution.

Why?

Because Ingrams and Baker & Taylor can't make their usual percentage profit on the book. If they can't make their usual percentage, then they can't sell the book at a discount to bookstores.

Bookstores need to buy books at a discount so that they can then sell the books to readers at the book's suggested retail price. If there is no profit margin on that book for the bookstore, then the bookstore won't carry your book either.

So, when you hear indie writers complain that they have POD books through the various POD printers' distribution programs, but those books never show up on bookstore shelves, you have to look at a few things.

Does that book have a good cover, blurb, and story?

If so, is the price too low? Because the low price, more than almost anything, will keep a book off bookstore shelves.

Now, a sidebar, thanks to the comments from my blog's readers. I wasn't clear on these points when I initially wrote this section as a blog post. So let me be clear here:

When I tell you that you will get on bookstore shelves if you price your paper books correctly (which means at least $2 profit to you in extended distribution—not $1.50, not $1.68, but $2), I don't mean you'll get on *all* bookstore shelves. Nor do I mean *actual shelves*.

Here's the hard truth about bookstores: *No* bookstore carries every book published that week, let alone that month or that year. When I was travelling by air in January 2014, I stopped in bookstore after bookstore, from Hudson News to Powell's to some other indies whose names my tired brain can't remember, and *none* of them had one of my favorite mystery author's latest book.

This writer is a *New York Times* bestseller. His latest book had been released *the day I left* on my trip. I had special-ordered a copy from our local independent bookseller, and figured I would regret that special order, because I'd see the book everywhere. Instead, I saw it nowhere.

In the past, I would have seen the book in every store.

These days, most books never reach the *actual* shelves, not even new releases by *New York Times* bestsellers. Hell, that April, I couldn't find megaseller Nora Roberts's newest hardcover on any bookstore shelf. That one shocked me.

You'd think Nora would get shelf space. But she wasn't.

Why aren't books showing up on the physical shelves?

Because bookstores now have virtual catalogs, and the authors their customers buy less frequently aren't on the physical shelf, but in the virtual catalog.

Which is where you will *not* be if you price your books incorrectly.

And you need to be. Because, another factor in reader behavior that I didn't discuss in Chapter Seven is political attitudes. Some readers *never* buy through chains, but want to buy online. And those readers will buy from their local independent bookseller, off that bookseller's website.

For an example, go to the website for Mysterious Galaxy[1], a major California genre independent bookseller.

Mysterious Galaxy carries many of my Kristine Kathryn Rusch books, from WMG Publishing and from traditional publishers. Yet neither I nor WMG ever contacted Mysterious Galaxy directly about taking a book.

So, how did they get these books? Through Indie Bound, the program that the Independent Booksellers Association runs (which helps bookstores build websites, by the way). Indie Bound took the books after a few stores requested them (again, not instigated by me or WMG), and supplies the books through one of the distributors (either Ingrams or Baker & Taylor).

That's what I mean. You don't have to lift a finger. Someone just has to ask for a paper copy of your book at an independent bookseller, and that bookseller has to order the copy (and pay for it). Voila! Your book will be warehoused with a distributor (who generally orders more than one copy). Then, your book will be in that distributor's catalog, which is a good thing. It's another way to be discovered.

When I posted this clarification on my website in the pricing blog sections, many indie writers who had paper books in the genres that Mysterious Galaxy sells looked for their titles and discovered them—all without the indie writer lifting a finger. The comments are still there. If you want to see them, go to the comments section of the Pricing Blog Part Two in the Discoverability section (under the Business Resources tab).[2]

So, back to pricing paper books.

Why do you want to be on a bookstore shelf (virtual or physical)?

Because more than 80% of all readers buy paper books. So, if you're not putting your books into paper, you're cutting out 80% of the market.

And if you price your books wrong, you're still cutting out 80% of the market. Got that?

After you've done all the production, uploading, design, storytelling, and everything else right, price is the next most important thing to set in order to sell your book.

Set a price range for your publishing company. Hardcovers should run between x and y, depending on size; the same with trade papers. Ebooks should have a price range as well. The best thing to do is to use industry standard pricing for the *suggested retail price* of your book. It's easiest.

Note I use the term "suggested retail price." It's not firm. Amazon will discount you, so will Barnes & Noble. If you're lucky enough to get into some other chains like Wal-Mart, they will discount you as well.

But they'll discount off *the suggested retail price*. You need some give there.

(And for God's sake, don't complain about standard retail practice. That's how business works.)

Here's the other things you need to do on setting the right price:

1. Your newest book should have the *highest* price. The demand will be highest for the new work, so charge at the top of your price range for it.

2. Have a standard price for backlist. Use that price for works that are not new.

3. When your next book comes out, decrease the price of your most recent book to that standard backlist price. In other words, when you've released Book J, reduce the price of Book I to the same price as Book H.

4. Make sure your hardcover costs more than your trade paper, your trade paper more than your ebook. (Of course, most indie writers *under* price, so I have no idea why I'm even putting that here.)

5. If the industry makes price shifts, make sure your prices reflect those shifts. Usually, the shifts are in an upwards direction. Even if it feels bad, raise the price on newer titles only to reflect the shift.

6. *Do not underprice your books*.

Let me repeat that louder: ***DO NOT UNDERPRICE YOUR BOOKS***.

I'm still talking about suggested retail price here. The reason I am is because if you price your books *too low*, you'll appeal to the Discount Readers and no one else. You want your fans or potential fans to buy your books. They will judge by *perceived value*. If you price too low on your suggested retail price, they'll wonder what's wrong—or think your newest book is a backlist title.

Do not set your *suggested retail price* for *a novel* in ebook format at $2.99. Do *not* do it.

If you look at what has become industry standard, $2.99 is the price that most traditional publishers are charging for *short fiction*, and most consumers (outside of the tight world of indie writers) are paying that price.

I am *not* talking about specials here or discounts or anything. I am talking about the *suggested retail price* for the book. Or what most people call *full price*. Currently, industry standard suggested retail price (for indies as well as savvy traditional publishers) is $6 for a novel in ebook. *Minimum.*

The worst thing you can do as a *businessperson* is underprice your product. Perceived value goes way down, for one thing. Your profits do as well. In the middle of its Hachette fight, Amazon developed a nifty price calculator. The next time you upload a book on Kindle, use the price guide that Amazon provides on the set-your-price page. If you track up or down, you'll see the correlation between price and profit.

It's a handy tool, and Amazon itself used it in one of its press releases during the Hachette mess.[3]

> *It's also important to understand that e-books are highly price-elastic. This means that when the price goes up, customers buy much less. We've quantified the price elasticity of e-books from repeated measurements across many titles. For every copy an e-book would sell at $14.99, it would sell 1.74 copies if priced at $9.99. So, for example, if customers would buy 100,000 copies of a particular e-book at $14.99, then customers would buy 174,000 copies of that same e-book at $9.99. Total revenue at $14.99 would be $1,499,000. Total revenue at $9.99 is $1,738,000.*
>
> *The important thing to note here is that at the lower price, total revenue increases 16%....*
>
> *Is it Amazon's position that all e-books should be $9.99 or less? No, we accept that there will be legitimate reasons for a small number of specialized titles to be above $9.99.*

What Amazon does not say here, because this point was irrelevant to Amazon's fight with Hachette, was that if the price was too low (99 cents for an e-novel), sales would go up, but profits would go *down*.

In other words, industry standard should be set at the sweet spot that maximizes profit *and* readership.

Hachette wanted its readers to buy hardcovers (where it makes the most profit). Amazon wanted the pricing in the sweet spot for ebooks regardless of the hardcover price.

As I said, industry standard evolves. But you need to pay attention to it.

As I write this, industry standard for a book-length title, published as an ebook, is between $5.99 and $9.99.

Industry standard for a book-length title, published in paper formats, vary by format. Those industry standard prices are between $24.99 to $34.99 for hardcovers, $14.99 to $19.99 for trade papers, and $6.99 to $9.99 for mass-market paperbacks.

If you underprice your paper books, your book doesn't get into most retail markets.

If you underprice your ebook, then you can't offer the kind of discount pricing that makes a book attractive to a consumer.

Discounts

Discounts aren't something you do willy-nilly or because it seemed like a good idea at the time.

In fact, *you don't offer a discount to get someone to **buy** your book.*

Got that? The discount exists for other purposes. The fact that the consumer buys your book at discount is a *side effect* of your promotion, rather than the reason for the promotion itself.

The only exception to this rule in discounting is when a retail store has ordered too much inventory, and wants to get rid of it. Then they discount that inventory that isn't selling *to get it out of the store forever.*

Consumers know this: that's why they don't pay a lot of attention to discounted items (unless they need that particular item, and even then, they might not buy something discounted).

Realize that for this section, I'm talking about the majority of consumers. I'm not talking about those consumers who *only* buy discounted stuff—the folks I call Discount Readers. I'll discuss them below.

So, why would you use discounts to promote your book?

Here are just a few reasons:

1. You want to build readership for all of your books.

2. You want to build readership for a particular series.

3. You just released a new title, and you want readers to sample your older work so that they will then buy the new title at full price.

4. There's a *real world* reason to run a promotion at this particular time. For example, it's Black History Month and your protagonists are African-American and/or your books are set in the Harlem Renaissance.

Downton Abbey just premiered so you discounted your World War I historical. See? Stuff like that.

5. It's the slow season (summer, for example) and you want to goose all of your sales just a little.

And so on.

You need a strategy, every time you discount.

But, before you discount, you need to do several things.

You need to...

1. Have more than one book published. You discount book one in your series so that people will buy the rest of the series at full price.

If you do not have any other books, then write more. Once you have at least three books, then you can start contemplating a discount on the first book.

But only then.

Because if readers like your discounted book, they will often buy more. But readers don't remember author names if they encounter that name only once. *Even if they have read one book by that author.*

So asking the reader to wait and *remember* doesn't work.

2. Place a time limit on the discount.

One day, one week, one month—but nothing more than that.

In fact, one month might be too long, except in something like the Black History Month promotion. Offering your book at a discount is one of the very few times when you work off the old publishing model of velocity.

Actually, it's the *Buy Now! Before It's Too Late!* model of retailing.

3. You do *not* offer the same discount again for several months.

Because it hurts #2. Think about it.

4. Offer a good discount.

That means you need an industry-standard suggested retail price. The bigger the discount, the more likely the average reader is to buy—except in one area.

Free.

Free has its own problems and pitfalls, which I will discuss later. Right now, I'm not discussing Free. I'm talking discounting from full price to half price or more.

If you don't believe me about having a proper suggested retail price and then offering a good discount, then go to BookBub's website, and look at a post from December 2013 titled "Does Discount Size Matter For eBook Promotion?"[4]

Like Amazon, BookBub has empirical evidence on this topic. (Of course, so does every single business book about pricing, but I know most writers ignore that stuff. [Yes, your sarcasm detector just went off.])

The anonymous BookBub blogger wrote [the parts in bold were their emphasis, not mine]:

> ...we ultimately found that **the size of the discount does make a difference.**
>
> Average subscriber response rates in recent months show that books reduced by at least 65 percent resulted in click-through rates **over 20 percent** higher than titles discounted by a smaller amount. And the average click-through rate for books discounted by at least 85 percent was over **40 percent higher**....
>
> The effect was magnified when we isolated our analysis to titles that had all been reduced to $0.99. The only price difference between these books was the original price, and of course a title that is marked down from $7.99 is more steeply discounted than one that typically sells for $5.99. Once again, the data suggests that readers may respond better to titles that are more steeply discounted, even if the deal price is the same....

They have lovely charts and graphs and everything else.

What's fascinating to me about BookBub's site is that in their marketing posts, they assume that book publishers don't want to offer discounts—and you know what, they're right.

Because most places understand that discounting is a weapon that should be used sparingly, with lots and lots of forethought.

You need a marketing plan whenever you offer a discount. And then you need to test that discount.

What do I mean?

In 2013, WMG Publishing and Sourcebooks tried various book discounts on several of my series titles. WMG always used the first book in one of my series. Sourcebooks seemed to just randomly use old backlist titles, without a care as to what they were.

Most discount promotions through a major retailer (like Amazon or Kobo) really didn't have much effect.

Big discount promotions done directly to readers, like BookBub, had a strong effect—so strong, in fact, that I could see the wave of readers flow through the rest of the series like a mouse being digested by a snake. I'll be discussing these kinds of promotions more in later chapters, but here's the takeaway on the price side:

When you experiment with a discount, make sure you then watch to see if the discount had *long-term* effect on sales—not just of the title you discounted, but of the other titles related to it (either in a series or under the same pen name or in the same genre).

Remember Chapter Four: How To Measure Success. Test your promotions. Just because you goose the sale of one book for a weekend doesn't mean the discount worked.

Again, *you don't offer a discount to get someone to **buy** your book.*

You offer the discount as part of a marketing plan that should have an impact on your entire business.

Put another way, if your entire business is one book—and that book is *fiction*—then your discount hurt your profit margin and gained you nothing. (This technique works better for nonfiction, which we are not discussing here.)

If your business includes several books, then the discount might actually *improve* your profit margin.

Ack! I know. I just discussed profit margin at the same time as discoverability.

Most writers never think in those terms. They want readers to read their one book, logic be damned. I want writers to build long-time readership, to become an automatic buy for readers, so that the new book, priced higher than the older books, gets *pre-ordered* no matter what the price. (Yes, we'll discuss pre-orders later.)

Discount Readers

As I mentioned above, when I initially posted the blogs on pricing, I had not written the section on different types of readers. So many writers who had success discounting every book they published wrote back and told me I was wrong or stupid. (Look at the comments. I let through the polite ones; you should have seen the impolite ones.)

What those writers had done inadvertently was sell their books *only* to the discount readership.

The discount readership isn't as small as you would imagine. Writers can, and do, make a good living selling discount only.

Dean and I recently bought back a retail store that we built and owned before the recession. We hired a man to run the store who had spent years running a discount chain bookstore in the local mall. That store closed (because of a decision made by the mall, not the chain's owners). Our new employee was most worried about his regular customers, some of whom showed up every week to see what was in the store.

Those Discount Readers bought books regularly, but only those books available at the cheapest possible price. (And, sadly, books in those stores from traditional publishers do *not* pay any royalties to the traditionally published authors of those titles.)

Discount Readers rarely venture out of the discount bookshops (or the virtual discount sections of Amazon and other e-tailers). You can build a loyal readership from Discount Readers.

But why would you do that?

Because if you refer back to Chapter Seven, you'll see that the majority of readers are *not* Discount Readers. They buy occasionally based on price—often when they're testing a writer—but usually they'll pay full price.

Remember that sweet spot between profitability and readership. You want to maximize both.

The best way to do that is to offer the *occasional* discount, and let the Discount Reader buy your work when it's on sale. Discounts also allow your regular readers a price break or to buy a book as a gift for a friend.

Go into the Discount market, but use it to *maximize* your readership, not *minimize* it.

A Final Word on Discounting

When I initially posted the section on Discounting, many of the blog readers worried that Amazon (or B&N or some indie bookstore) would discount their book upon receiving it, and advertise it for the low price. Some writers even lower their prices to prevent that, proving that the writers have no idea how bookstores work.

Amazon will discount your price and, depending on the terms and conditions they have with you and your company, you might get a percentage of the discounted price, or you'll get your percentage of the full price. These things vary according to the type of book you're publishing, how you're doing it, who you're doing it through, and how the percentage gets paid to you. I can't tell you if your book will end up paying you a full royalty or not.

Accept standard business practices.

Amazon discounts *everyone*. If you don't like the policy, don't do business with Amazon. It's that simple.

If you want your prices to look low, and you want your customers to have choices, here's how to do it without lowering any of your prices. Have a paper edition.

For example, the listing for the Kindle edition of my novel *Snipers* lists the print suggested retail price of $18.99.

Then Amazon lists the Kindle suggested retail price of $7.99

And then, Amazon kindly tells you how much you'll save if you buy the Kindle edition: $11.00.

The Kindle book looks like a hell of a good deal for cost-conscious readers.

Amazon has done this for years, and readers will compare across formats because many, many readers like both paper and ebooks, and will base their purchases on price. (If the prices are close, then the reader is more likely to buy paper, wait until a new edition appears, or wait until the price drops.)

Free

When used properly, "free" is a strategy that works.

The problem is that most writers have no idea what "properly" means. Unfortunately, in the early days of self-publishing, "free" worked, even when it was misused. Amazon's algorithms took a book on the Top 100 Free Bestselling Books, and for 12–24 hours after the book's price got restored, that book would shoot up on the Top 100 Paid Bestselling Books.

Shortly after Amazon established Kindle Select, that strategy stopped working. Why? Because every writer discounted their books to nothing, and the Top 100 Paid got cluttered with books that really weren't selling. Those books were given away.

"Free" no longer works that way. If you've read advice telling you to market your book for free so that book will make an Amazon bestseller list for paid titles, then you're reading advice that is either five years old or based on advice that's five years old.

And yet, here I am, telling you that "free" works sometimes—when used properly. The best term for "free" isn't "free book" but "loss leader."

According to The Business Dictionary,[5] a loss leader is:

Good or service advertised and sold at below cost price. Its purpose is to bring in (lead) customers in the retail store (usually a supermarket) on the assumption that, once inside the store, the customers will be stimulated to buy full priced items as well.

You aren't running a grocery store, but you are running a business. And the moment you offer a loss leader, you are using a *retail strategy*. You're discounting a book not to sell the book. You're discounting the book to lead a customer to other products.

Entire marketing classes exist on the use of loss leaders. And marketing professors write entire scholarly papers on the effectiveness of loss leaders. Not to mention the fact that different schools of economic thought believe completely different things about whether or not to ever use loss leaders.

When loss leaders are used in physical retail environments, like grocery stores, the stores do many things that we as writers cannot do. For example, the stores put the free item at the back, so you have to wade through aisles of product to get to the free thing. That will increase sales of fully priced goods.

We don't have that placement option in an e-shop.

An effective loss leader displays the full price, so that the consumer knows what a great deal they're getting. With luck, that consumer will already buy other items like the loss leader, so that price knowledge exists deep in the consumer's subconscious.

Back in the day when traditional publishing ruled the world, we all knew that a book cost anywhere from $5 to $25. So a free book was worth at least $5 (mass market) or $25 (hardcover). Now, with so many people offering books for free, that special feeling you get from receiving a free book has pretty much disappeared, particularly with ebooks.

All business books recommend that you should limit the number of loss leaders you offer. In other words, if you're giving away television sets to get people into your Best Buy, you better have no more than a hundred television sets in stock, so that deal item vanishes fairly quickly.

Those of you who shop major sales, such as Black Friday sales, will recognize one other thing about those loss leader sales. The advertising about those free television sets will be limited to a hundred televisions, and no more. Customers who arrive after the sets are gone will have no chance of ever getting their hands on a free TV. But chances are those customers will shop in the store anyway.

We can't limit the number of free ebooks offered on a retail site that we do not own. What we can do is limit the time of the free giveaway.

So free for one day is better than free for one week and free for one week is better than free for one month. Perma-free defeats the point of a loss leader entirely. (I will discuss perma-free below.)

Loss leaders should be *scarce*, to prevent stockpiling. This is where "free" has lost its power.

With so many writers offering so many books for free, readers have stockpiled books. If I read every free book on my ereader, I wouldn't have to buy books for a year. (Don't tell Dean that.) Fortunately for you all, I do buy books anyway.

Honestly, the best loss leaders are high-priced items that have been discounted to an obscenely low price. Not *free*. In books, for example, Nora Roberts' Donovan Series sells as a collection on Kindle for $25. If you want to make that a loss leader, then you would discount the collection to $5 for one day only. That's a hell of a savings, and it would introduce readers to Roberts' work (for those ten people who've never read anything by her).

Time that loss leader with the next release of her latest novel, and hope that the loss leader means you will sell more copies of the new book.

In other words, whenever you're offering a loss leader, you're taking a deliberate loss with the hope of later gain.

The loss-leader strategy works as intended only if you have more than one product, and generally more than ten.

So, if you offer one of your books for free, then you are gambling (and I mean gambling) that readers will then flock to your other books and pay full price for them.

The more books you've published, the better this strategy works. If you've published five sf books, three romances, and two mysteries, then offer your loss leader in sf, because that gives you the greatest chance of recouping the loss you've taken on discounting your price to nothing.

The best use of the "free" strategy, however, is to give away the first book in a series for a limited time only. Make sure you have at least two more books in that series, or the math will not work.

What is the math? The sales on Books Two and Three have to increase enough to make up for the loss of the income on Book One.

For example, let's assume Book One sells ten copies per month, Book Two sells ten copies per month, and Book Three sells ten copies per month. All three books make you $5 per sale. That's $150 per month.

You decide to offer Book One for free for a month. If the sales of Two and Three go up to twelve copies each, you have *lost* money, no matter how many people have downloaded your free book. You will have made $120 instead of $150, a $30 loss.

The new readers might eventually come to your series, but they might not. You might have attracted Discount Readers, and they won't continue the series.

For your free promotion to *break even*, Books Two and Three must sell fifteen copies each in that month. And there's no guarantee that readers who "buy" free will ever pay for a book.

Sometimes "free" works, and Books Two and Three sell significantly more. Sometimes "free" fails, and Books Two and Three don't sell more than fifteen copies each.

That's a strategy and a gamble. If readers don't like Book One, they won't move to Book Two, no matter what they paid (or didn't pay) for Book One.

In those instances, "free" doesn't work at all.

There are two other reasons that "free" is a gamble, even as a loss leader. The first is that most people who take the free product, whatever it is— perfume, a show ticket, a song, or a book—toss that product away or never look at it. When we were in Vegas in January 2014, I was offered free moisturizer (twice), free show tickets, free meals, and a free lighter. I took everything but the moisturizer (I'm allergic to perfume; didn't want to touch the stuff), and tossed every free item away before I left.

Everyone I traveled with received something free on that trip, and to my knowledge, none of us used the free item. In fact, as I type this now, months later, I can't remember the names of the companies giving me the free promotions.

So not only did those companies lose money on me, they didn't get me to remember them either.

That's the risk you take. If you have a thousand free downloads of your novel, be happy if 10% read the book, and be ecstatic if 5% buy another book of yours.

Most people download a lot of free at various points in their ebook reading career, and most people usually stop doing so after the newness of the ereader wears off.

The other big risk of offering a book for free?

The increase in negative reviews. Everyone who has ever offered a book for free has experienced this. Reviewers who wouldn't normally buy a book based on title, subject matter, and genre feel obligated to comment on that book.

Often, you'll see reviews of romance novels that slam the happy ending or the fact that the book focused on a relationship, reviews of mystery novels that are "too bloody" for the reviewer's taste—or not a rehash of Agatha Christie, and so on. All because the Discount Readers didn't understand the conventions of the genre.

Most readers who come to the book after the free promotion won't bother to read those reviews that say "I don't normally read this type of book, but…" and will only see that your book has a hundred reviews, and half are negative.

Those negative reviews (particularly a cluster of one-stars) will drive away some regular readers willing to pay full price away.

When you offer a loss leader to everyone, then a good percentage of the recipients will not like the product. You have to factor that into the success rate of your "free" campaign.

There are better ways to use "free" than a blanket offering across all platforms.

Here are a few:

1. Offer a book for free to your dedicated fans if they sign up for your newsletter.

What do you get out of this? You get names for your newsletter, email addresses, and a chance for positive reviews because these folks are already your fans.

2. Offer the first book in a series for free when the latest book the series appears.

What do you get out of this? Theoretically, you'll get new fans who will then flock to the next books in the series, including the latest book. If you let people know on social media that the first book is free because the new book is out, you're doing double-duty advertising: your fans will become aware that your latest book has just appeared—and if they really like your work, they'll tell a friend about the free book. This strategy starts word-of-mouth on both the series and the latest project.

3. If you sell books on your website, set up a buy-two-get-one-free offer. Buy two full-price books, and get the third book free.

What do you get out of this? Well, you don't have to set the book for free on any of the online retailers. Again, you're getting names for your newsletter. If you set your prices right, you get more money when you sell off your website, so you can afford to discount all three books (which is, effectively, what you're doing).

Those are just three free strategies. There are a million others.

I do mean a million.

But…think twice before you use *this* strategy that has become really common among indie booksellers.

Do not pay to give away your book for free.

Places like BookBub and other advertising newsletters will list free books, but you have to pay to buy an ad with those companies. The only way to recoup that ad money is to have many books published, preferably in the same series.

Remember, though, that most people don't read their free books. So you're losing money on your BookBub ad, at least in the foreseeable future.

It's okay to discount to a lower price (not free) for those ads—again, if you have a strategy in place (and more than one book published)—because you will probably recoup the cost of your ad.

But advertising a product for free is something you should do only if you have deep pockets and money to burn. And a lot of other published books. Even then, I don't recommend it.

Why? See the math for the free promotion above. You've just added the cost of your BookBub ad to the halo effect of your free promotion. Instead of selling fifteen copies each of Books Two and Three to recoup your losses, now you'll need to sell fifty or a hundred copies each of those books (depending on price) to pay for that ad.

Always have a strategy for your free books. Always. Then measure that strategy and see if it actually succeeded. Often, these strategies do not. Or they succeed on the free title, and not other titles.

Perma-Free

I know a lot of writers are having success with this strategy in 2014. I have my doubts about it. I even invited writers on my blog to share their numbers from the perma-free promotion, to show how well the perma-free book increased the sales of their other titles.

Only one or two writers were able to show an actual *related* increase. The rest just told me how many copies of their permanently free book they're giving away.

The only way I can see a perma-free book working is for that book to be the first in a series. And even then, you're appealing only to the Discount Readers. So many people search only for free books, and they'll never buy other books in the series, unless those books are for sale.

Most book buyers, in truth, are more comfortable paying for books. It's weird, I know, but three books on the Amazon Paid Bestseller List when I initially wrote this chapter prove my point.

The first book was *Twelve Years a Slave* by Solomon Northup, which is in the public domain and has been for about a century. In January 2014, the movie tie-in edition sold as a $6.99 paperback. When I wrote this chapter, that tie-in edition was #75 on Amazon's paid bestseller list even though there were many free paper editions available.

The second book was *The Catcher in the Rye*. That week in January, PBS aired a documentary on J.D. Salinger. Because of that documentary, *The Catcher in the Rye*, a $5.99 paperback, rose to #4 out of the top paid 100 on Amazon in books despite the fact you could get the book used for less than a dollar at any used bookstore in the country. (Or free and battered, since so many schools made the novel required reading.)

And finally, nearly a year after the movie came out, a $9 paperback of *The Great Gatsby* was #39 on the Amazon paid bestseller list even though *Gatsby* also exists in a million editions, many free or as low as 99 cents.

Readers don't care about free. They buy a book because they want it, not because it's on sale.

Free, Perma-Free, and Discoverability

Remember, this series is on discoverability.

"Free" is not your best tool for discoverability. Why? Because, let's be honest, free books are everywhere.

Don't believe me? Then walk into your public library (Americans). For the price of signing up for a library card, and a time limit on how long you can enjoy the book, you can walk out with any title in that library for absolutely nothing.

Writers, you want to increase your visibility? Get into libraries. It's not as easy as it sounds, especially with paper books. You can't give your books to a library; they'll put the book in the library book sale, not on the shelf. They have to purchase the book through library distributors (which is too complex a process to describe here).

However, if your ebooks are available through Overdrive or if you've clicked library distribution on Smashwords, then your ebooks are in most libraries' databases and can be checked out.

Perma-free—at no cost to you.

Also, if your marketing plans work and the libraries hear of you, they'll order the paper copies through Ingrams or Baker & Taylor—without ever contacting you. As of this writing, my novel *Snipers* has multiple copies in every library in the Salt Lake County Library System. I live in Oregon, and have never had contact with anyone in Salt Lake County.

What happened was that someone read a copy of *Snipers*, and nominated it for the Salt Lake County Library System's Readers Choice Award. All of the patrons of the library system get to vote on that award, so not only is the book in the system (without me doing anything or WMG doing anything), but it's prominently displayed.

That's word of mouth, which we'll deal with in Chapter Twenty.

If the word of mouth on your book is good, your book will show up in bookstores and libraries, because *customers* have asked for it.

One final thing on pricing that didn't used to be an issue in the old days, but is now:

Set the Right Price for Your Work Overseas

You need to take into account currency fluctuations and pricing prejudices in other markets. The ebook markets have ways to help you price properly.

When Amazon first started to go into non-US markets, we only had one choice on pricing. We set our price in the States, and then Amazon would mark the book overseas at whatever the equivalent price was in pounds or euros. That led to ebooks being priced at things like 1.17 Euros and weird stuff like that, which of course, made consumers balk.

Kobo, iBooks, and Amazon now allow you to set your price *per country*, and I suggest you do so, using the same rules as in point one. Each country has different price prejudices, and honestly, life's too short to learn them all.

But at least you can price your books in the same way that other publishers do, rather than some weird-looking price that automatically makes the consumer aware of price instead of clicking the "buy" button.

Yes, changing the price to reflect other currencies will often *raise* the price of your book. Ah, well. Consumers will pay for those books anyway. Since WMG changed its prices on my work to reflect various currencies, my overseas sales have *increased*. Yours will too.

One Final Point

Please remember that every time you price your books, you must do so with a strategy in mind. That strategy should not be "become a bestseller" or "sell as many books as Famous Author John Doe," but an actual business plan, which you should have for your books.

Pricing is both a tool and a weapon. The tool should be used properly. The weapon should be used sparingly.

Good luck.

14

MORE PASSIVE MARKETING

In the first week of February 2014, Hugh Howey put a funny post on his website. Titled "One-Man Operation,"[1] Hugh's post profiles—if you want to call it that—the man who runs Nautilus Publishing in Taiwan. Nautilus publishes Hugh, and according to the post, has existed since 2010, and has done two books per year. They're always bestsellers. Hugh says his book has sold 50,000 copies in Taiwan alone.

Apparently, the publisher at Nautilus works alone. Hugh wanted to know how the man did it all, what made his books such a success. The answer?

> *"The blurb," he says. "The synopsis. You have to grab the reader with the synopsis."*
>
> *C'mon. He's pulling my leg. It's not that easy.*
>
> *"Oh, and a good cover."*
>
> *Whatever. He's not telling me. My guess is a deal with the devil. I mean, the guy bats 1,000 in an industry where the whiffs are more common than contact. And he's doing it alone.*

Nautilus also does its own translations, and apparently finds great stories to translate. After all, Hugh hit bestseller lists as a mostly one-man operation as well. That happens when the books are good, even if there's no promotion.

Hugh clearly doesn't believe his publisher, but I do. What the publisher of Nautilus Publishing in Taiwan told Hugh is what I always tell you: Passive marketing works. Good covers, good stories, and a good sales-oriented blurb (written in active voice).

That's enough.

But we writers all want to do more, and we all want readers to discover our work. There are ways to augment the good cover/good blurb/good story trifecta. Not supplant it. You absolutely need those things. But you can add to them, which is what this book is all about.

For the purpose of this chapter, I'm going to use the word metadata to mean "descriptive metadata." I'm too lazy to use both words throughout. I know, I know, there are many other kinds of metadata, even in book publishing, which will give you all kinds of information about sales, readership, etc.—on whatever site provides the data in whatever way they want to give it to you.

I'm not going to talk about that, because to track that when you have more than one or two titles on more than one or two sites, you'll need a dedicated employee to handle the information or you'll need to hire a service. I don't recommend either at the moment, unless you're very, very rich. Tracking that kind of metadata is like hugging a train. It's also not worthwhile if you've only published one or two things.

Let's move back to descriptive metadata, shall we? This is the kind of metadata that helps readers find you. Yes, there's an entire science to it. And honestly, keeping track of all that metadata when you've published as many things as I have is a game of whack-a-mole.

I often have to deal with metadata issues. In February 2014, the Amazon links to my trade paper Nelscott books from WMG Publishing disappeared. Again. The poor staff at WMG has asked Amazon several times to repair those links. The links get repaired. And then, for reasons unknown, the links slip off the books again.

Discoverability becomes harder when that happens. And it's not just Amazon. That same week, as I prepared for the book bundle I was in with Mike Resnick, Kevin J. Anderson, Robert J. Sawyer, and several other wonderful writers, I looked at the Barnes & Noble listing for the book I was entering in the bundle, *Alien Influences*, and discovered that the trade paper listing was missing a cover.

I have no idea why. It got fixed. But I'm sure there are other metadata breaches that need addressing. And once they're resolved, then others will crop up.

Virtual whack-a-mole. And those moles need to be whacked, because metadata is basic passive promotion.

These little glitches are common. One of the many reasons that WMG Publishing went direct with Kobo was that Smashwords never updated the metadata. Often Smashwords titles on Kobo lacked covers or any description at all. You can't sell a book that way.

So once you have your cover and your sales-oriented blurb (and your really good story), here are some metadata things you need to do right.

Genre

Most writers don't know what genre they write in. They think they have it, and they're wrong. Don't feel bad. Unless you've made a study of genre and the conventions of that genre, then you have only a vague sense of what the genre is.

For example, if *Romeo and Juliet* were published today, what genre would it be marketed as?

Most of you would answer "romance," because that's what we learned in school. *Romeo and Juliet* is "romantic." Actually, it's tragic.

The hallmark of the modern romance genre is *a happy ending*. And *Romeo and Juliet* both *die* at the end of their story.

Not a modern romance.

Literary fiction, yes. Modern romance, no.

Just because your book has a romance in it doesn't make that book *romance*. Any more than a contemporary fantasy novel set in the New England countryside with a strong female protagonist is urban fantasy. Note one word in the name of that subgenre—"urban."

Urban fantasy has to take place *in a city*.

Like price, genre suffers because everyone thinks they understand it, when they do not.

Assume you don't know anything about genre, and take some classes in it. WMG Publishing offers a genre structure class, as well as some lectures on genre.[2] Take those, do a lot of reading on what genre is—particularly the *endings* of genre novels—and then ask reader friends what part of the bookstore they would look for your book in.

You'll be surprised at their responses. And believe me when I tell you that their responses will be more accurate than your initial thoughts on the genre you're writing.

Writers never see their own work clearly, which does hamper marketing efforts on occasion. You need to ask for help, particularly when it comes to genre.

Because, if you do not know what genre you're writing in, that's a serious, serious problem for you. It has an impact on your branding, on your pricing, and on the ways you will interact with your readers.

Genre is such a large topic that all I can do is recommend you take the genre structure class listed here. The homework alone will show you how to study genre, so you can understand it. Please, please, please learn genre. Please.

Keywords

If you don't know genre, you can't do keywords properly. Keywords, for those of you who don't know, are part of online metadata. If your book is in any online store, whether in paper or in ebook, your book will have keywords associated to it.

The very first keyword it should have is its genre. And then its subgenre. And then its sub-subgenre. I'd write an entire post on keywords if M. Louisa Locke hadn't already done so, and so thoroughly that I don't have to.

I'm not going to write in-depth about keywords and setting categories because in the short time between this chapter's original existence as a blog post and the publication of this book, the entire way that keywords work has changed.

I'm pretty sure that by the time some of you read this chapter, it will change again.

So I'm going to default to M. Louisa Locke's blog posts on keywords. She links to the previous information in her post, "How to Get your books into the right Categories and Sub-categories: Readers to Books/Books to Readers—Part Three," from December, 2013. I'd poke around her website and see if she's updated those posts by the time you read this chapter.[3]

The short of it all is this:

Amazon, for example, allows keywords that help readers find your books using the search function. Readers who know you will search by your name or a series name or a book title. But if the reader is browsing, they might be looking for other reasons. This is where keywords help. As Locke writes in her second post:[4]

Just as authors have no control over which books vendors display in the front windows and on the display tables of their physical bookstores, so authors have little control over what books Amazon displays on the main Kindle Store Page. The one part of this first page that authors do have some influence over, however, is the search bar (found at the top of the screen.) Since many consumers have been trained by their use of Google and other web search engines to search for stuff using keywords, this is probably the most important place to start if you want to maximize a book's discoverability.

She has a lot of suggestions on how to find the proper keywords. Please read her three posts and the comments, because she has done such a thorough job that I would only be duplicating it here. Go there, and learn.

Websites

You need a functional website as a writer, one that advertises you and your work. Which all sounds well and good, but most writers don't do that.

I discovered this one night as I was writing the introductions to stories for *Fiction River*. Most of the writers did not provide me with any information such as when their next book was coming out, so I went to their websites to find that information.

And I couldn't.

I discovered that even bestselling writers have suckizoid websites. For example, for all of the writers I dealt with last night, I couldn't find their latest release (despite poking around for at least five minutes), nor could I find the series books in order. In one case, I couldn't find any books listed at all, even though the author had published a dozen.

This is a case of do what I say not what I do. If you come across this book in the early fall of 2014, you'll see that my website is much improved over the website of 2013, but it's still not the best it can be. I'm working on that all through 2015.

So, with that in mind, let me show you three different websites (none of them mine) and tell you what you can learn from them.

First, *New York Times* bestselling romance writer Stephanie Laurens' site,[5] which is easy to find because you type her name and a dot-com into the web browser, and the site comes right up.

Stephanie's website is pretty, it's professional, and it answers questions easily. (Note the nifty thing she's doing with branding as well.) Please go look. It's searchable. There are two different places on the front page to get a newsletter or join an email list if you want to. (You don't have to.)

It also easily answers questions about her series and series characters.

And new releases are on the first page of the website, so the hardcore fan can find what's out right now.

The website also seems appropriate for a romance writer. So romance readers see the subtle genre branding right from the start.

Second, mystery writer Dana Stabenow.[6] Her website, which you can find by typing in her last name plus dot-com, is very different from Stephanie's. Not as slick, a little older, but still it does what it needs to do.

Dana's website is more blog oriented, which is appropriate, since Dana is also a travel writer (and that writing informs her fiction). You can find out information on her series by clicking the header, but there's even more information at the footer. You can join the newsletter if you scroll down the side of the home page.

This is an active website, one that the writer maintains almost daily with blog posts, etc., as opposed to Stephanie's which is more static. But again, it gives the information that all levels of readers—from first-time readers to fans—need.

Finally, take a peek at Hugh Howey's website,[7] which you can find by typing in Hugh's name and adding dot-com. (Are you noticing a trend here? Get the website in your name or pen name whenever possible.) Hugh's website is a little loud for me, but it's appropriate for a science fiction writer. It has a techy feel.

This website combines the static side of website design with the active blog. You can find recent releases and, importantly, what's coming next. You can order off the site, which is just great, particularly for an indie writer. You can follow the blog if you want to.

It's a fan-based website, that's interactive and fun.

Notice that all three websites reflect the writers behind them. All three make it easy to sign up for newsletters—if the reader wants to do so. All three answer the basic questions:

1. What has this author written?
2. What order should I read in (if any)?
3. What's new?
4. How can I learn about new books (if I want to)?

Some websites need even more data. When you're writing in a series, you might want to list how many books the series will/does have, when the next book is coming out, and how long you plan to continue the series. Get a sense of what the fans want to know, and provide those answers in your FAQ.

Newsletters

Newsletters are effective, if used properly.

In other words, don't overdo it. And make certain that *you* write your newsletter. Readers know when someone else is writing it for you. Your voice is unique. The best newsletters sound like a letter from a friend (the author) rather than something written by the PR Department of a publisher.

You don't need a newsletter, if that sounds like too much work for you.

However, you should have a mailing list—an email list, preferably (it's cheaper)—so that you can notify the fans who sign up when your latest release is coming.

In other words, you don't have to do something fancy. Just a nice email saying, "Hey, my new novel That Book You've Been Waiting For, will appear on Tuesday in all formats on all sites. Thanks for your continued support." That's it.

And don't spam your list. I have new works being reissued every week, and if I emailed every time something new happened, people would get a daily Kris email.

Don't do that. Figure out how to do it right.

The best way to do it? Let readers sign up, and do something whenever you need the reader support.

Upcoming Titles

Build some anticipation. Let people know it's on the way, even if it doesn't have a title yet. Some writers, like Hugh Howey, keep track on their site of their various projects in the works. Others just mention the publication dates of upcoming titles. Whatever works for you as a writer. Let your readers know something is coming, though.

Preorders

The minute you let your fans know that there's an upcoming book, they're going to want to know how they can get it. Indie writers don't have the same preorder options that traditional publishers do. For example, at the moment, it's very hard (if not impossible) to get Barnes & Noble or Amazon to allow a paper preorder if you're not a traditional publisher.

So what? You can still offer preorders. Amazon's publishing program (KDP), Kobo, Omnilit, and iTunes offer ebook preorders with a minimum of fuss.

In the United States, if your book has an ISBN with your publisher name on it, and your book has received reviews in major channels (like the real *Publishers Weekly*, not that pay-for-play thingie), then distributors will put that ISBN into their system, take orders for the book from bookstores, and then order copies of the book the moment it becomes available. How do I know this? Because it happens over and over again with WMG titles.

In other words, distributors will do preorders for you, and you won't even know it's happening.

Finally, you can and should do the preorders yourself. Dean and I learned this a million years ago when we were running Pulphouse Publishing. If you can't get into the system (and then, we weren't doing large enough press runs to go into traditional distribution channels), you can offer preorders yourself that you ship.

At Pulphouse, we did it with a paper catalogue, but now, you can do it on your website. Offer the paper book, signed, as a preorder at a good price. Remember to include shipping, because you're going to have to ship copies to your place, before shipping them out yourself.

Once you announce the book's upcoming publication, make sure you have a preorder page on your website. Use the various options for payment, like PayPal or Amazon Pay, and then take the order.

Before the book's release, order your copies, sign them, and mail them to the fans who signed up. As a relatively new writer, you won't get many preorders at all. If you're a hybrid writer, you might get more than you want to handle, so enlist the help of friends and family to aid with shipping.

If you're doing the right kind of series, by the way, you can also do subscriptions. *Fiction River* does. Dean does to his *Smith's Monthly Magazine*. Just remember, subscriptions should give the subscriber a break for paying up front. So price accordingly.

It doesn't take a lot of work to set up preorders. You should do so.

Remember, however, that on the print editions, if you do a preorder on your website, those book sales will *not* count toward any bestseller list. Just like some ebook sales won't either (Omnilit, for example).

Oh, well. What would you rather have? A good Amazon ranking or a lot of books sold to hardcore fans?

I know the answer for me.

Bio

If someone in publishing asks for your bio and/or you put a bio on your website, think about this.

No one cares if you were born in Upstate New York to a math professor and a homemaker. They don't care if you're the youngest of four children or that you're happily married. They don't really care if you are childless, but spend your time with cats. They don't care if you live on the Oregon Coast.

They don't.

They want to know how many books you've published, how long you've written, if you've won any awards, been on any bestseller lists, how many copies of your books are in print, and if you're working on other books.

Seriously.

I went to writer website after writer website after writer website last night as I wrote story introductions for *Fiction River* and got to find out people's personal lives (sometimes too much—if I want to steal your identity, people, thanks for giving me the keys) but nothing on the writing and the books.

I have a bio on my website, but it's not the one I give to magazines who request it or to the media. I have a variety of bios, all of them focused on my career. I have one for Kristine Grayson, one for Kris Nelscott, one for my mysteries (under both Rusch and Nelscott), for my sf, for my short stories, for my mainstream work, and so on. I even have a catchall.

Also, update your bio on Wikipedia. On one of the Hollywood projects I'm currently working on, the producer went to Wikipedia first to write his promotion material, only to find that *I* hadn't updated my Wikipedia page in a long time.

I fixed that quickly, because, as he mentioned, *everyone* uses Wikipedia. He's right.

Remember, no one cares that your Great-Aunt Mildred forced you to take elocution lessons in the fifth grade. Readers care about the next book you're planning to publish. Or the one you just published.

Think about it.

Frequency of Publication

One of the most important passive discovery tools you have is frequency of publication. It took me a while to get past my Midwestern reticence on this. Plus I had the crap beaten out of me verbally and critically for two decades for being a fast writer.

(I was unfortunate enough to start in science fiction, where one book per year was considered fast [back in the day] rather than romance where five books per year was scarcely noticed.)

So I spent a lot of time hiding my speed. I still have trouble mentioning it at times.

However, this modern publishing world has finally caught up to most romance writers and writers like me. Readers like to have a lot of choices. And as I read through a 2010 Sisters in Crime Survey,[8] I found this under a category called Points to Ponder:

> *James Patterson appears at the top of lists of popular authors cited by both younger and older readers, suggesting the frequency of publication may contribute to name recognition.*

Realize this survey was completed in the last few days of the Dark Ages of Publishing, before ebooks really took off, and it became clear to industry watchers that frequency of publication really does make readers notice a writer—in a good way.

The more you publish, the more readers will notice.

Note that they will not buy everything or even anything, but they will recognize your name, which will put you in the conversation.

In other words, it really and truly will help with discoverability.

There are a variety of ways to do frequency of publication.

For example, I use one method on my website. I publish—without missing—a short story every Monday. You folks know you can rely on that. I've run the short story—which is free—since November of 2010 (and have yet to repeat a story!). I take the free story down the following week, so you only have one week to read it on the site.

For five years, I also ran a free nonfiction blog (with the donate button) every Thursday. I got tired, and am now occasionally running a free nonfiction feature.

Because of those two things, my profile as both a nonfiction writer and as a short story writer has gone up tremendously. I can see the difference in the sales of my work on the various sites because of these two things.

I've also been concentrating on getting my backlist out, which means there's new material almost weekly from me in ebook, and monthly from me in trade paper and/or audio. I'm selling hundreds of titles each month, not counting the individual sales of each title.

Readers have choices not only of format—ebook, paper book, audio book—but also of genre, and type of story.

What's most fascinating to me is I'm beginning to see segments of my readership coalesce—readers who buy this kind of book buy the latest version of that kind of book—without me doing any active promotion at all.

And my readership has grown steadily over the past several years.

Enough so that I can finally hire someone to help me with active promotion, leaving me more time to write (see Chapter One). For me, the latter half of 2014, and the first six months of 2015 will be an experiment in a wide variety of active promotion techniques, some of which I will blog about.

However, I've been doing the ones that I mention the rest of this book, all by my little self, without help from an employee.

You can do those things too.

Just turn the page for active marketing ideas.

ACTIVE MARKETING

15

BLOGS AND INTERVIEWS

I promised you that I would move from passive discoverability tools to more active ones. By active, I mean techniques that will take a lot of time from your writing by forcing you to write something other than your normal worlds or by repeatedly taking writing time to do something that is not writing. Other active techniques will cost you a lot of money, as well. I'll be discussing all of these.

And yes, I know, the passive techniques mentioned in the previous chapters also take time and sometimes take money, but usually they're a one-and-done project. (Once you've designed your cover, you don't need to redo it every week—unless you're repeatedly screwing up.)

So everything I'm going to be discussing from here on out needs to be factored against Scott William Carter's WIBBOW test. Ask yourself the question: **Would I Be Better Off Writing?** If your answer is yes, then stop whatever marketing you're doing and get back to the keyboard.

It doesn't matter if your best friend's answer is different from yours or if your editor wants you to do tons of promotion. If it doesn't pass your personal WIBBOW test, then for heaven's sake, don't do it.

I'm going to start with the active marketing that traditional publishers have been requiring of their writers for the past five years now. A lot of indie writers are doing the same things that traditional writers are doing, and in similar ways.

Websites/Blogging

A few years back, a dear friend of mine sold the first novel in her urban fantasy series. Her then-publisher (a big traditional publisher) paid to have her website revamped and linked with their website.

The publisher insisted that she blog. Her blogs needed to be about her books, the publisher said, or about something related to her books. Think about that: the blog had to be about her one and only book or nothing at all.

I'm not telling you who this is because not only did she leave the publisher, but she took back her website. The publisher-designed site was impossible to use from both the front and back end. And the publisher's stricture on how to blog was ridiculous.

We discussed websites in Chapter Fourteen, but we didn't discuss blogging. Blogging on your own site is up to you (not your publisher), as are the topics you choose to write about.

If you are only writing fiction, however, blogging about writing is a very bad idea. First of all, millions of people blog about writing and publishing. Secondly, except for writing about your own process or your own work, you won't have a lot to add to what the chorus of writers has already written—particularly if you're a newer writer.

So, if you feel the need to blog, do it creatively. For example, writer Kelly McCullough blogs about his cats every Friday.[1] But he doesn't write cute stories about them. Instead, he posts nifty pictures with great captions.

I read Kelly's fiction before I ever went to his website, but I discovered his cat blogs almost a year ago, and honestly, I try not to miss them. (I have cats too. I understand.) His website is clear, and it's easy to find information about his work. He also has a book cover on the sidebar, so it's easy to discover his writing from the cat blog. You can also see the upcoming titles, right below that cover.

Most readers are not writers. Most readers want to know what the next book is or something interesting about the writer, *not* a how-to guide.

Because I write nonfiction as well as fiction, I stumbled into nonfiction blogging. It started as business blogging (*The Freelancer's Survival Guide*) and eventually morphed into a business blog about publishing. But that's not all I do on my website.

Every Monday, I post a free short story that stays up for one week only. The free fiction started as a gift to my established fans because I figured that they'd be the ones who find my website. Turns out that a lot of the nonfiction readers clicked on the free fiction just because they wanted to see who was nattering at them and if she really could write.

When I was doing the nonfiction blog weekly as well, that blog and the free fiction blog get about the same number of hits, but if you drilled down into the numbers, you'd see that the unique visitors are very different. Both features of my site attracted a different group (with some crossover).

Initially—and I mean about seven years ago—I designed the site to be like a magazine with a variety of different features. The only features that have survived are the free fiction and the monthly recommended reading list. The recommended reading list gets yet another group of people to visit. I'm not sure about the crossover there.

Dean's taken a different tack with his blogging. He's blogging about his daily word count and his life.[2] Kind of a slow-motion reality show. I thought of it as writer-only, and then it became clear that his readers like reading about his day-to-day activities as well. Since he started the daily blog, his daily unique visitors have tripled. Those folks buy his books.

It works for him.

Other writers have a static website, and spend little (or no) time blogging. It's a passive choice versus an active choice. If you're a slow writer or someone with a day job and young kids, daily blogging (or even weekly blogging) might not be for you.

With blogging, you have to do two things:

1) Be consistent

2) Provide good content

Like anything else, it takes time to build an audience for your blog, but an audience will come, particularly if you follow those two rules.

You are balancing something, though: you're balancing discoverability for your *blog* with discoverability for your *published works*. And those things aren't always one and the same. So do follow your website numbers (and your sales) over time to see if your blogging is worthwhile.

Of course, if you enjoy doing it, then continue no matter how it impacts your writing. But if you hate it, *don't do it.*

That's the rule of thumb for all of these active marketing techniques.

Remember, they are not one-size-fits all.

Blog Tours

My rule of thumb with my traditional publishers has always been to give their marketing a try. When I started publishing romance, I was excited about doing what the publishers asked, because the romance genre is well known for its marketing savvy, and for being on the cutting edge of various marketing techniques.

What I didn't realize at the time was that the romance *writers* were always on the cutting edge; the romance *publishers* usually were behind the times.

Still, publishing romance gave me the chance to experiment with a variety of techniques, some of which I'll discuss in future chapters.

I have published romance under five different names. (One is a pen name I don't disclose.) The reason I have five different names is that I started in traditional publishing, and I couldn't use the name Rusch for most of my romance. I finally did publish a romance as Rusch (*The Death of Davy Moss*) but that was after I started indie publishing.

Two of my pen names have gone on publisher-mandated blog tours. Sourcebooks, who published *Wickedly Charming* (under my Kristine Grayson pen name) in 2011, asked me to do a blog tour. Sourcebooks' publicist set it up, and boy, did she do a lot of work.

A blog tour, for those of you who've never done it, is a press tour in the blogosphere. A writer writes a guest blog for a well-known book blogging site. Usually the guest blog also involves a book giveaway.

The Sourcebooks publicist contacted the bloggers, set up the giveaways, gave me deadlines and word counts, and then forwarded everything I wrote to the blogger. The blog would go up, and I was supposed to comment on the site or answer questions if I could.

Each blog tour lasted one month and usually involved a dozen different blogs. The publicist made certain the writers who were blog-touring did not write the same blog for each blogger. (That would be a disaster!)

The writers use the bloggers to promote the books, and the bloggers use the writers' names (and giveaways) to promote the website.

Blog Interviews

Sometimes a blog tour includes interviews and sometimes it doesn't. Often, a blogger will ask to interview a writer about the writer's work. This happens after you've had a modicum of fame. It's also something you can trade with your writing/blogging friends, if you so choose.

The interviews seem pretty straightforward. The blogger sends you a series of questions via email, and then you respond via email. Sometimes those questions run for pages. Sometimes there are only two or three.

Like the guest blog, the interview promotes the writer, but it also promotes the blogger and the blogger's website.

Once again, if you choose to participate in something like this, then you cannot just cut and paste your answers from previous questionnaires. The Internet lives forever, and nothing goes away. Fans who follow your work will see that you've answered the same question the same way before, and that will defeat the purpose of doing this kind of promotion.

What is the purpose?

Well, that's the question, isn't it? And I'll get to it below. After one more thing.

Giveaways

Bloggers often ask for giveaways: free stuff that they'll give to one lucky commenter or reader. Usually the giveaway is a copy of the book you're promoting. Sometimes it's an advance copy. Sometimes it's something more elaborate.

If your publisher doesn't provide material for the giveaway, then the giveaway comes out of your pocket, and it costs you money.

Is that worth the promotion on the website? Well, let's examine this, shall we?

The Point

When I was doing blog tours for Sourcebooks, I initially did the tours as an experiment, to see if they were worth my time. After saying yes the first time, though, I really didn't want to insult bloggers by saying no the next several times.

The entire tour was a catch-22 for me, set up by Sourcebooks. Before they had even asked me to tour, they had contacted the bloggers to see if they wanted me to guest blog. The bloggers had said yes. So, instead of saying no to my publicist, I would have been canceling existing blog tour posts—which, in my personal opinion, would have been a bad thing.

Here's what I learned on my blog tours. I wrote about 10,000 words of free blog posts each time I did a blog tour, not counting responding in the comments (if I remembered. Sometimes I was traveling, and simply couldn't respond.). The bloggers provided space, and did promotion to their readers. Sourcebooks provided the giveaways.

There is no way to know if the people who read my blog posts—with the topics often determined by the bloggers themselves (not me)—actually bought my books. I have no idea if the sales of the books went up because of the blog tours, because the blog tours, like so much in traditional publishing, occurred in the first month of publication.

So were my sales goosed by the tours? Or did the tours make no difference at all?

In talking with other romance authors who set up their own blog tours, I suspect the tours made very little day-to-day sales difference. There was never really a spike after visiting a single blogger's site, even if that site had tens of thousands of readers.

But, remember, discoverability isn't just about a single blog post or a single encounter with an author/book. Advertising—and that's what a blog tour is—is more effective if your name/book title are everywhere at once. People see the name mentioned a lot and eventually, they'll at least look at the book (if, indeed, it sounds interesting to them).

So, with that caveat in mind, a blog tour might be a way to raise your profile shortly after your book is published. If you can set it up yourself (or your publisher's publicist does) and if you have the 10,000 words of writing to spare. And, if you're doing it yourself, you want to foot the bill for the free giveaways, with no actual and obvious return.

There are other places for free giveaways that we'll discuss later that might be more effective than doing so here.

Some book blogs get tens of thousands of unique visitors every month. Others only get four to five hundred unique visitors. Those visitors might be passionate, but you have to weigh the visibility you'd get among the blog's regular readers against your time.

Again, a blog tour is your choice. It might get you favorable reviews from a blogger. But the book bloggers pride themselves on honest opinions. You might write a blog for a site only to find your post side-by-side with a negative review of your book.

That's a risk you take when you do things like this.

Interviews seem easier at first because the questions are there for you. But I find that interviews take me a lot longer than a four- to five-hundred-word guest blog. I've gotten very picky about doing email interviews, and will turn down those of more than ten questions. (Even ten is difficult these days.) Much as I like supporting my fellow bloggers, I simply do not have the time to spend three hours answering questions for someone else's blog.

I say no more than I say yes. Although I admit, I still do the occasional short interview. I did one on the afternoon I originally wrote this chapter.

That was a four-question interview and it took me fifteen minutes. Will I get any book sales from it? I have no idea and I have no way to measure it.

Generally speaking, I'm doing the interviews as a favor to my fellow bloggers.

Now that I'm no longer published with Sourcebooks, I will probably stop doing guest blogs. They aren't worth my writing time. I have other uses for that time that will aid discoverability. I'll get to that in a future post.

One last thing: Because I write a blog and the recommended reading list, my website shows up on a lot of writer/reviewer blog lists. Two or three times per week, some hapless writer asks me via email if they can write a guest blog on my site to promote their work. I now have a standard guest blog rejection letter for these people.

Clearly, they don't come to my site and have no idea what I do here, because if they did, they would realize that I do not have guest blogs, and I don't review new material. I just recommend what I happen upon within a month.

I'm not offended by the writers who do this, because I've edited off and on for decades. I know that writers rarely if ever look at the markets they're submitting to.

But if you're going to ask someone if you can guest blog on their site, you need to make sure that they accept guest blogs, that they actually have a large audience interested in your genre of writing, and if they will review the books by the writers who guest blog. Be aware that you might get a negative review from that site. It's part of the process.

Do I recommend guest blogging for fiction writers? If you're doing it to goose your sales, no. If you're doing it to get your name out there in the month of release on your books, maybe. If you're doing it for the ego-boost, please, find another way to get your ego stroked.

I can see guest blogging/interviews only as a way to aid discoverability —and certainly not the best way. It's work intensive with little return.

That said, I'm going to add a small caveat for the nonfiction writers. Guest blogging works for nonfiction writers, especially those with active websites. It is something to keep in mind.

And honestly, if I were Kelly McCullough and a cat website asked me to guest blog, I'd do it. Because it's different and interesting and might bring a whole different audience to my website and writing. The same if a cat site asks me to guest blog because of all the cat short stories that I write. It's an unexpected place to guest blog, and it's the kind of advertising that you wouldn't normally get. Would I ask a cat site to let me guest blog? No.

I often participate in *SF Signal's* Mind Meld blog.[3] Mind Meld's interview is a single question that I can answer with a modicum of ease. It's readable. Lots of authors participate and all of them have something interesting to say. It's not the same-old, same-old. And because of that, it gets a lot of targeted readers.

That said, I don't do it to increase my own readership. (I'm sure I piss off as many people as I intrigue.) I participate because it's fun.

If the stuff you do around your writing isn't fun, then don't do it. No matter how many people tell you it's a very good idea.

Take the WIBBOW test with all of this discoverability stuff. And answer it honestly. Because ultimately, it's your writing—and your career.

16

SOCIAL MEDIA

As I got ready to revise the social media blog posts into a chapter for this *Discoverability* volume, I worried that the posts would be horribly out of date. I've already cut some things from various blog posts in previous chapters because those things no longer work or apply.

The industry is changing so fast that six months can be forever. And since I'm trying to keep this book as useful as possible, I worried that I would have recommended a site that had gone away or failed to point to one that hadn't been developed yet.

Then I got to the posts and remember: I got excoriated when I wrote them for being "vague," and not telling every writer the "secret" of my social media success—even though I did tell them.

Everyone wanted to be told to go to Instagram or somewhere and do x, y, and z, and automatically get zillions of sales.

It doesn't work that way. I wish social media did work that way, but nothing does. No promotion will guarantee sales, ever.

And frankly, if you're going to social media for promotion only, you're doing it wrong.

I'll explain.

Traditionally published writers and indie writers alike are told that they must be on social media to promote their works. Some traditionally published writers are given marching orders by their editor—tweet at least three times per day, make Facebook posts, hit at least five social media sites per week, mention your book, mention your book, mention your book—and so on.

A month before I started compiling this book, I got an email from Sourcebooks telling me that I don't promote enough or in the proper way. Consider this: I had left the publisher two years earlier. Even though I still have several books in print from their company, I do not promote those books at all. I want the rights to revert to me, so I don't put any effort behind promoting the Sourcebooks editions.

Even if I did, all of Sourcebooks' commands—not suggestions, by the way. Commands—were the antithesis of what I'm going to tell you now.

Social media is to the modern writer what going to book signings and genre conventions was to writers ten years ago. Back then, publishers often demanded that a writer show up at major conventions—on her own dime, of course—and perform "well" on panels.

Not every writer does well in public, sitting on a panel in the middle of the afternoon, trying to be coherent. Nor does every writer do well on social media.

How valuable is social media? It depends on who you talk to, and what studies you believe. Does it sell your books? Again, it depends on who you talk to and what studies you believe. I can move hundreds of copies of whatever I'm pushing in a day on my various social media sites, and that's nothing compared to Neil Gaiman who can create whole new worlds with a single tweet. (Okay, that's not really true, but it feels true.)

Those of us who can actually inspire people to action with our social media sites have an obligation to use this power for good. Or at least, not to use this power terribly often. And there are other tricks to it as well.

I will get to the ways to use social media below, but first, I want to give you my opinion about its value.

In Chapter Fourteen: More Passive Marketing, I mentioned an old Sisters in Crime consumer book buying report[1] that I actually learned about through a comment on a blog post. (Thanks to Elise M. Stone for pointing this out to me.)

The Sisters in Crime report dates from 2010, which was the end of the Dark Ages of Publishing. Much of the information in there about ebooks, etc., is probably not relevant at all. I was looking at the report with an eye toward discoverability, though, and some of that information does not change.

And as I was drilling down, I noticed a generational gap.

That generational gap is always present when we discuss books and reading and trying new things. For example, in one of the discoverability blog post comments, someone hypothesized that the "current" generation might well react the way the generation raised in the Great Depression did when it comes to spending money.

My parents were raised in the Great Depression. My mother's father died in the 1920s, in fact, and my mother grew up in terrible poverty. My father's father worked as a postman and made a great deal of money for the time. My father never missed a meal in his life. My mother remembered missing several. My parents clashed about money constantly because my mother would use a towel until it was threadbare, and my father would spend money without thought to tomorrow.

This is a long way of saying that I realize every generation has its overall characteristics, but within that generation there is a wide variation (sometimes in the same household).

However, I agree with the commenter's premise: the generation that grew up in the Great Recession will handle money differently than other generations.

The differences aren't just in spending habits. They also exist in comfort with technology and in the methods of doing things. Every generation is special, and has things that it's comfortable with.

While I was writing this chapter, I was reading *Careless People* by Sarah Churchwell. That book is about the year 1922, and the way that the younger generation in 1922 looked at technology—which is very similar to the way that the current teenagers look at technology. Ways of thinking change, and what's strange to one group will be normal to another.

That shows up the most in Section 3 of the Sisters in Crime report, titled "What Influences Mystery Book Sales."[2] The designers of the report gave an overall result, then broke it down by age group. The groups differed widely. The survey found, for example, that "younger buyers are more likely to be prompted [to purchase] by a lower price."[3]

According to this study, age also factors into discoverability. The summary[4] states this:

The majority of mystery buyers over 45 are not influenced by online marketing. The majority of mystery buyers under the age of 40 can be influenced by online marketing.

I hope that someday someone updates this study, because I'll wager that some of these trends will have continued. If you are major reader who has for decades discovered your books by bestseller lists, major reviews, bookstore displays, and print marketing campaigns, I'll wager those things still influence your buying habits.

If you're a younger reader who never really developed those habits, then other things will influence your buying habits, such as book reader discussion sites, reviews in blogs and online forums, and social media. Start looking at page 24 of the Sisters in Crime survey and you'll see how discoverability varies according to age group.

I suspect that discoverability difference is the same now—or perhaps the divide is a bit wider.

So, when you're reading about how to get your book discovered and you see that, anecdotally, all of your friends and/or the blogger's friends find books using a certain method, realize that the advice might be spot-on—for a particular group. But it might not be right for another group.

In the years since the Sisters in Crime survey has appeared, social media sites have grown and changed. We've all heard the stories about how teenagers colonized Facebook, then moved away from it when Gramma and Grampa joined, only to colonize some place else.

But those generalizations don't help when you're deciding on a social media marketing campaign. They only give you the outlines of the campaign. You have to understand how your readership for your books uses social media.

For example, a fascinating interview with writer Danah Boyd in *Fast Company* outlines how teenagers use social media as I wrote the initial blog in early 2014.[5] Boyd, who just published a book called *It's Complicated: The Social Lives of Networked Teens* (based on ten years of research), tells the magazine:

> [Teens] are also more likely to have protected accounts, and use it to talk to a small group of their actual friends. To them Facebook is everyone they ever knew, and Twitter is something they've locked down to just a handful of people they care about—which is often the opposite of how adults use them....A lot of the teens I talk to, they'll have like 30 followers. It's a small world for them, as opposed to trying to grow large followings. ... There are also a lot of teens who use Twitter around interests. An obsession with One Direction, and just talking to other One Direction people. That becomes Twitter, and then they'll use Instagram with another group of friends. This one girl I talked to said, 'Yeah, if you're not into the things that I'm into, don't follow me on Twitter.'

You've seen the hashtag viral videos. Those refer to the way teens are using social media. (My favorite is the Fallon/Timberlake spoof from fall of 2013.[6])

Adults link to things. In fact, a Pew study from 2013[7] shows that about half of Facebook and Twitter users get news from those sites. (That includes me.) The news includes links to books and new projects. But that's an adult usage of the sites.

So, if you're a YA writer, you're going to reach fewer of your potential readers by using a conventional adult approach of linking on Facebook and Twitter. In fact, you're probably going to want to figure out your own social media marketing campaign on sites where teens actually hang out—and don't mind adult involvement.

Because here's something else that Boyd said that really resonated with me:[8]

What's interesting is that as a lot of young people are running away from their parents into a variety of apps, they're also running away from marketers. That will be an interesting battleground in the next couple of years, because that creates monetization issues for the app creators. Because you make this too markety, and guess what? It's one of those weird things where I think that people want to treat social media like Times Square, where there's advertising everywhere on it, and that just makes it as unappealing as Times Square.

That can also be your social media accounts. If you're constantly tweeting and talking about marketing, rather than just being a person, you're screwing up. People will stop following you.

So, before you use social media for marketing, know who your reader-ship is. If you're trying to attract teens on Facebook, you're doing it wrong. If you're going after romance readers on Vine, you'd probably be better off with your own YouTube Channel.

Think it through. And again, only use social media because you enjoy it, not because someone told you to.

When I initially came up with the idea to write this chapter, I started collecting good brand usage of social media. Then, I found a link on Hoot-suite's blog[9] that led me to some of the brand usage links that I mention later in the chapter. (I use Hootsuite for Twitter, mostly, but some people use it to compile all their social media.)

Remember that those links are the Hootsuite's bloggers' opinion of how big marketing companies are effectively using social media sites. Okay?

These aren't my opinions, but they're good examples of straight advertising being done in a creative way on these sites.

One thing to add before you look. Remember that people actively run away from ads—they fast-forward through them on the DVR (or cut them entirely), block pop-ups, and try hard not to see something directly marketed. So when a consumer voluntarily shares a viral video like the Spock/Audi commercial,[10] someone in marketing has done something right.

So, by showing you these links below, I'm telling you that someone repulsive has succeeded in catching people's attention. I'm not telling you to be repulsive. I'm saying here's something so entertaining that they've risen above the problems with direct marketing and managed to capture people's interest despite the repulsive side of advertising.

First, Pinterest—which (full disclosure) I'm not on. According to a really cool 2012 marketing study from BlogHer,[11] 47% of online consumers have made a purchase based on a recommendation from Pinterest, as opposed to 31% on Twitter and 33% on Facebook. 61% of online purchases are made because of a recommendation by bloggers. Or were, in 2012. (Some of the online stuff we'll look at below didn't even exist in 2012.)

To see the Pinterest Top 5 brands as chosen by Hootsuite,[12] (indeed, all of the following information), click on the links included in the footnotes.

The publicist(s) in charge of the Pinterest marketing are developing different sites, and labeling them well. For example, Hootsuite cites Lowe's Pinterest campaign, and mentions its "Build It!" board filled with DIY projects. Brilliant.

I know some writers who place their research or their characters on separate Pinterest boards and if I only had the time, I would develop Moon shots for the Retrieval Artist, some space ship and art shots for my Diving series, and photos of Chicago and Memphis for the Smokey Dalton series. And I'd never sleep, either. But I can imagine it—and so can you, if you enjoy this sort of thing.

A lot of writers have YouTube channels. I started one for WMG Publishing[13] years ago, then abandoned it for time. I was thinking of uploading some of my research on it, and hoping to make some cool videos. Of course, I could do that or I could write. Since then, WMG has been using the channel for nifty book trailers. You'll note, though, that my updates, which are video blogs, have about 600 views, and the beautiful well-produced trailers have at most 100 views.

I need to note that the trailers, as good as they are, are straight advertising, and the blog is attempting to be entertainment.

A video blog needs a narrative voice and something to bring the viewers back, just like a regular written blog.

However, if you want to do something short and fun, there's Vine. Six-second videos, which at first I thought would be worthless. But they're not. Among the short videos that the Hootsuite blogger thinks work are two I like.[14] Oreos shows how to make sprinkles out of the cookies. General Electric has a six-second science series.

As of this writing, a lot of teenagers are using Vine, so if you want to attract them, go there. If you want adults, stick to YouTube or (ahem) blogging.

Here's the biggie, though. Twitter. Hootsuite's Top 5[15] would be in my top list as well. They include Oreo, again, and Taco Bell. Note all of them keep things fun and light. Or at least interesting.

When I first joined Twitter, I followed some of my favorite comedians and discovered most of them don't know how to use 140 characters. One of the best usages of Twitter comes from Jimmy Fallon,[16] whose people Tweet a hashtag suggestion every week, and fans answer. Those tweets often go viral.

The best viral marketing on Twitter, though, happened during the live broadcast of *The Sound of Music* in December. DiGiorno Pizza's marketer live-tweeted the event, and was funnier than hell. He/She/It went viral fast —and should have.[17] And the live-tweet of the night during the 2014 Grammys came from Arby's, as they played on the link between their logo and Pharrell's hat.[18]

Really, you can't buy that publicity. But it's the right place and the right time with the right voice kind of marketing. The tweets mentioned in Hootsuite's Top 5 are consistently good.

You don't have to be consistently funny to be on Twitter, but you should be consistently interesting.

By the time you read this, there will be newer trendier sites, newer trendier viral videos, newer trendier ways to promote. I can't foresee what they'll be, but I can tell you the things that link *all* social media sites.

I can also tell you behaviors that will help you on social media, new and old.

Boy, there are a lot of misconceptions among writers about social media.

The first thing you have to realize about all social media is that no one service is better than any other.

If you're going to do targeted social media postings, then don't be prejudiced about which services you use. Make a logical decision based on the points later in this piece. Yes, Facebook reaches everyone of all ages, and not in a very direct way. Yes, Google+ has a better interface and has better communities. Yes, Twitter has more young people (at the moment).

Realize those things, and then use the services. Don't let your own biases get in the way of using the best service for you.

Most people have a misconception about social media that I have to address right here:

Just because you have 3,000 Facebook "friends" or 10,000 people coming to your fan page, just because you have 25,000 Twitter followers or the biggest community on Google+, does not mean that all of those people see or even care about everything you do.

On Twitter, you see only the posts of people you follow and even then, you rarely see ones from a few hours ago. It's the same with the other social media sites.

On Facebook says, only a subset of the people who friend you will see your comments. This means exactly nothing. Same with the boosting of the posts (the Facebook wants you to pay for). So what if only a fraction of your Facebook friends see your post? That's how Facebook has *always* worked.

If you're good at Facebook, then one of your posts will go viral. (Yes, the posts that go viral are usually about cats, and not about your latest book. Deal with it.)

People will respond in large numbers (more than fifty) to your viral post and those people move into your feed subset, for a while anyway. The fact that Facebook has limited who can see your posts, based on "interest," is an algorithm, nothing more. In the past, the people who saw your posts were the people who either went to your page and looked at them, people with a small group of friends who saw everything, and the people who were online the moment you wrote the post.

Now, after the change and the "boost," who sees your post? The people who go to your page, the people with a small group of friends who see everything, and a subset of the people who were online the moment you write the post.

Really, not a lot of variation there. So stop worrying about it. If you're worrying about it, I would venture to say that you're using Facebook incorrectly.

That worry about Facebook's limitation of the posts? It comes from the misconception that you'll reach *all* of the people *all* of the time.

Not going to happen—no matter where you go.

Here's how I think of social media.

It's a party or a convention, depending on size. Treat it like a public gathering of some sort.

Going to the largest social media "convention," Facebook, and complaining that it limits who sees your posts is like going to San Diego Comic-Con and fretting that the room you're speaking in only holds 1,000 people. That means 129,000 people won't see you! Oh, no!!!!

It doesn't matter how big the convention you attend is in real life. I learned this long ago. Half the time, the fans who attend the World Science Fiction convention have no idea who the Guests of Honor are. Those are the people who theoretically the fans have come to see.

The theory isn't true, of course. The fans have come to the convention for a variety of reasons. Some fans arrive to play games, others to socialize with their friends in fandom, still others to go to the masquerade. A subset will come just to see the writer Guest of Honor, but only a subset.

Even the large media conventions like DragonCon won't get 100% of the attendees seeing the big media guests. 90% of the attendees probably don't even know who the guests are.

People go to social media for the same reason they attend conventions in real life. Some go to meet like-minded people. Some visit to see their friends. Others come for an education. A goodly portion come to promote something.

Even if you give away something at the convention—a T-shirt, a coupon, a free book—not everyone will see it. Of those who do see it, not everyone will take the free item. If you do flyers or a bookmark or a catalog, half the attendees (or more) will toss them away without even looking at them. And that's if the flyer/bookmark/catalog was in the goodie bag. If it was just on a table for giveaways, even fewer people will see what you've done.

So stop fretting about who sees what and how many people you reach.

If you're only on social media to promote, then stop now. Go back to your cave and write. Because you absolutely have to enjoy your social media platform to use it properly.

How do you use it properly? First, you stop thinking about all those tricks marketers tell you will boost your followers. Stop following stupid marketing rules. The tricks might help for a day or two, but mostly, they're annoying—and the users of social media can always tell when there's a new trend or someone is following an old marketing idea. I had three people just last week try to sell me something in the comments on my posts. Um, no. Stop now.

Kris's Rules of Social Media

1. Have fun.

If you hate parties, do you go to them? Back in the day when your publisher forced you to go to conventions, did you spend most of the time hiding in your room? Do you hate the way that Facebook works and get annoyed every time you go?

Then don't go.

It's as simple as that. Participating in social media is truly not required. Remember Scott William Carter's WIBBOW test. Would you rather be writing? Then write.

I really can't stress this enough.

In 2010, I interviewed a group of people who were using social media very well at that moment in time. I did it for the Online Networking section of *The Freelancer's Survival Guide*. While some of the information shows its four-year-old roots, other things stand out.

Everyone I interviewed stressed that they *enjoyed* what they were doing. Writer Neil Gaiman said it best:[19]

> I'm not sure if any [of what I do online] is networking. I mean, if it is, I never did it to Network. I did it because it was fun, and because writing can be a very lonely profession. It's fun to have people to talk to, fun to have people who talk to you, and great to have people who will answer your questions (even if they're wrong). I also feel that it levels the playing field, which I like.

It's pretty clear, if you follow Neil on Twitter, that he enjoys this stuff. In fact, when he does do a marketing post or something about himself, he gets a little cute for my tastes. He always puts *WARNING: Contains me* on the post. I would hope he posts about himself. That's one reason I follow him.

The other reason? His tweets are always interesting—and clearly were four years ago as well.

I go on Twitter several times per day—not because I feel the need to or because I'm trying to hit a quota, but because I now use it as a news source and a way of seeing friends. Often, I don't Tweet at all. Twitter is my favorite social media site.

Many of my blog readers mentioned Google+ and Pinterest as favorites. I personally like Google+ and am afraid of Pinterest as a time-sink, so I avoid it. Those are my preferences.

Those are the parties I want to go to, with the people I want to see.

I have *fun* there, so I visit out of enjoyment.

2. Remember that you're in public.

Every week, some idiot celebrity hits the news for a stupid comment they made on their Twitter or Instagram account. Every week. Then they have their accounts taken down, or handlers take over the account (and it gets boring).

Before you type or pin or post anything, think this:

Would I say this at a convention? Would I show this picture on a panel?

If the answer is no, take your fingers off the key, delete the photo, and go elsewhere until the urge to overshare disappears.

This sort of thing can happen in the comment section on someone else's blog or in a listserve that has Internet access. Since the dawn of the public Internet (and I've been doing this that long—remember CompuServe?), someone has typed something stupid online in a place that they think is private, a place anyone can access, and that stupidity causes a shitstorm. It's happening as I type this in one community I'm in—no, wait. Two communities I'm in. No. Make that three. Ooops, I think it might be four.

Since I don't follow shitstorms or get upset by them, I can't keep track. Mostly, I shake my head and move on. I never get involved—because—I remember that whole party-in-public atmosphere. If I take a side in public, that side might haunt me forever.

Which brings us to the next point:

3. No politics or religion in your public, professional posts.

I am very politically active. I write a lot about politics and history. If you want to know what my politics are, then read my novels. It's pretty clear.

But I don't blog about current events, I don't comment on current events, I don't retweet most of what's in the news.

Why am I telling you not to mention your most deeply held beliefs? Because you're a fiction writer. People of all political and religious stripes will find your work and will love it for different reasons. Let them. Don't be in their face about the things you both would disagree about.

Let me give you two examples. First, when I was young, I found a bunch of books by a writer who shall remain nameless. They were wonderful adventure stories. I loved those things.

Then my father introduced me to this writer's nonfiction. It was strident and on a different side of the fence than I was comfortable with. From that moment on, I stopped telling my friends I read this guy's fiction. My friends hated him, and I didn't want them to think I agreed with the guy. Yes, I kept reading him—but look at the title of this book. *Discoverability*. In no way was I going to tell anyone about his books, much as I loved them.

His political beliefs shut off a small faucet of discoverability—the mouthy young Kristine Kathryn Rusch.

Later, as I got older, I realized this writer's beliefs *were* in the novels and I glossed over them because I attributed the beliefs to the character, not to the writer.

The second example is much more recent, and truly can be applied to more than one person in my life. When I joined Twitter four years ago, I followed as many of the fiction writers whose work I loved as I could find.

One fiction writer turned out to be bombastically political. Offensively so, calling anyone who disagreed with him an idiot or arguing them into tiny puddles of mush. I unfollowed him within two days. I had a new book of his on my shelf, and four years later, I have yet to read it.

Not because he was an asshole. I follow a lot of assholes on Twitter. (Okay, that sentence is just wrong, but you know what I mean.) I stopped following him because his politics were in my face the way that TV cable news is in your face. I don't watch that stuff. If I were at a party and this guy was yelling and sticking his finger in someone's chest over in the corner, I'd never venture into that corner.

The same with hot-button issues. You have an opinion. I have an opinion. We might agree. We might disagree. But let's keep our entertainment a hot-button-free zone. I don't need you to harangue me and I don't want to harangue you.

Even the friends I agree with can get vehemently nasty on social media. I unfriended a real friend on Facebook because of his continual in-your-face political opinions which, ironically enough, I agree with.

So...you write political thrillers. Can't you talk politics on social media?

No. Let your fiction do the talking. Please.

The same for those of you who believe strongly in your religion (or who are atheists). Leave it out of your social media platform. Even if you're a religious fiction writer. Make sure your posts follow the tenets of your religion without proselytizing.

Even within the large religions, there are huge variations. You might write Christian fiction, but you might be a Roman Catholic. Half your readership might be Southern Baptist. And I have enough friends of both persuasions to know that often each can anger the other with a glance.

So politics and religion. Off-limits.

Please. Remember. Party. Convention. No one likes to go near the argumentative loudmouth or the person who wants to convert you to their opinion all the time. Don't be the person people run away from.

Which brings us back to…

4. Entertainment and fun.

Who the most popular guest is always depends on the party. A witty raconteur might hold court at a large party and might be the best person in the room at a convention, but in a small gathering of five or ten, that person often dominates the conversation in a truly unpleasant way.

If the get-together is about research or learning, then the most knowledgeable or experienced person in the room—even if that person is soft-spoken and self-effacing—will be the one everyone listens to. If fans have come to see the person who wrote their favorite novel, then they really don't want to hear from someone who wrote something "just like" that book.

I know I'm talking in metaphor here, but you understand me.

People don't follow you on Twitter because you're famous. There are well-known Tweeps who are simply fun to read, and who have never published anything.

Remember, people are on these sites because they *enjoy* the sites. So if you're doing something to get in the way of their enjoyment, you're doing it wrong.

5. Actual promotion.

Last June, Dean and I missed the last episode of *The Voice* due to a power outage. When the power came back on, we decided to watch that episode of *The Voice* online.

Every five minutes—and I'm not kidding—a commercial came on. You couldn't click away from it. And if you tried, you'd have to watch it all over again. Any time you skipped to another section, you had to watch two minutes of commercials for five minutes of content.

As interested as we were (we had, after all, invested an entire season into the competition), we stopped watching. It wasn't entertaining. It was annoying.

We expected some ads—it was a commercial site, after all—but not so many that it interfered with our enjoyment.

When you go to see your favorite musician in concert, that musician will tell you what album a song is from before or after singing it. That musician might also tell you that T-shirts are available in the lobby. I went to a concert in Vegas in 2014 where a scroll ran on a TV screen while we were waiting for the event to start. The scroll advertised everything that the artist was currently doing.

I didn't mind. I was a fan who had come to see that artist, and I learned about things that I had missed along the way.

I've been to talks where the presenter spends a small portion of the talk plugging her work. Fine. I don't mind. I'm there to see that person, and I'm happy to learn about those things.

However, we've all been to convention panels where the least famous person on the podium litters the table with upright book cover stands and dominates the conversation about his latest novel. The fans had come to see the Truly Famous Person (say, George R.R. Martin), who will often mention what's coming next, but doesn't do heavy promotion.

The fans will not be happy with that least famous person at all, and will mention it to anyone who listens. At a party, at a convention, you don't want to be the person people are avoiding. Remember that.

Social media—that party/convention—is the same way. About once per day, I'll see Neil Gaiman mention something he's doing with a link that you can purchase from. And that's about it.

We expect to be informed of books, movies, video games. We don't expect to be bludgeoned by the news.

So keep your ratio of promotion to entertainment low. You want just a little promotion with a lot of conversation/entertainment/facts.

Be interesting, not annoying, no matter what site you're on.

6. Kindness and snark.

This is my personal preference showing here, okay? But I've noticed that the people who have the most followers—and have had them for some time

—are often kind. Yes, the snarky people will get followers, but those followers tend to pick fights. They also will leave the moment they get offended.

Respect the people you find your various social media sites. If you don't like them or they're nasty to you, don't engage. Unfriend/unfollow/block if necessary.

Also, it only takes a moment to thank someone for doing something kind for you.

All those kindergarten skills come in handy in social media: Please. Thank you. Excuse me. I'm sorry.

Use them. And be nice to people. Maybe they were rude to you because their best friend just died. Or maybe they're rude to everyone, in which case you should block them.

There are trolls in the world. If one gloms onto you, block that person. Report them if it becomes offensive. And move on. Life's too short to spend any time on them.

And snark will only make your point in the moment. Individuals will remember your kindness more.

Be known for what you do, not how funny and mean your words can be.

7. Test drives.

The day I started blogging about social media in early 2014, Facebook bought WhatsApp. Most people over a certain age (and in the US) have no idea what WhatsApp is. The news coverage was confused—why would Facebook pay so much for something so unknown?

You can research all of that yourself. The point I'm going to make here is that the day I started blogging about social media, a goodly chunk of the adult US population heard about a new social media site. (You can group chat on WhatsApp, which makes it social media, IMHO.)

And next week, there will probably be another new social media site, and then another and another.

If you discover a new site and it sounds intriguing to you, then take it for a test drive. Figure out if you like it, if it's fun, or if it seems like work to you. Apply the WIBBOW test.

If you end up enjoying the site, see if it is better for you and your career and your party/convention time than the other sites you're on. Move, and go have fun.

And here's the place for my one caveat:

. . .

Caveat

I personally believe that everyone should have a Facebook page that they check once per week. Even if you don't post. I've gotten so much paying work through Facebook that if someone asked me to leave now, I'd be truly reluctant.

Most of that work has come from overseas or from video companies or from film companies. Almost all of it has been subrights sales that agents will tell you only they can do.

Um, wrong.

I do the subrights sales myself, get more money, and often get the initial contact via Facebook. (My blog is inaccessible in some countries—so is yours, probably. Facebook often isn't.)

The expectation is that everyone is on Facebook, so if you're not on Facebook, then you're some kind of Luddite. That's more true than not. This advice might change next year—there might be a site that everyone has moved to. But I doubt it.

Facebook has become ubiquitous, like the telephone. You might not like it, you might not use it much, but you probably should have one in case someone needs to reach you.

8. Target your marketing to what you enjoy.

Once you've taken a bunch of sites for a test drive, use those sites properly. Find out what the main audience is for your favorite site and then do some targeted posts to that audience.

Some of this you will know intuitively because you like the site as well. If you do, then do what you've found effective on that site. Don't treat Instagram like Facebook or Twitter like Pinterest.

Make sure you're marketing—what little you do—is site-appropriate.

9. Watch your time.

You will often hear that social media is a time sink. You hear this from two very diverse groups of people—the people who are told they have to do marketing on social media (and hate it) and the people who love, love, love social media.

We've already dealt with the first part—don't do this if you don't like it—so let's deal with the second.

You like it. You really, really like it.

You're going to have to limit your access. There are apps like SelfControl[20] (Mac only) that will block the distractions on your writing computer. I'm embarrassed to say that I have only one blacklisted site on my writing computer, and that's Twitter. I will read something cool as I'm online to quickly research something, hit a "share on Twitter" button, and suddenly I'm down the rabbit hole of links and cat videos and funny interactions with friends.

I love Twitter. I love discovering things, so I'm always thinking of adding, sharing, looking. And, like you, I need to write.

So I can access Twitter only on my Internet computer (three flights and a whole house away from here) and on my iPad (which mostly lives in the kitchen).

The time sink comes when you love something too much. When you'd rather talk with your best friend than write the difficult scene in your novel. When you'd rather clean the refrigerator than write the difficult scene in your novel.

When you discover a social media site you love, you've discovered a time sink. You'll need to figure out how to control it—for you. No Pinterest until you've finished your writing for the day, or something like that.

Final Thoughts

If social media is like a party or a convention, why do it? How does it aid discoverability?

Because consumers like to support businesses and brands that they have a connection to, people they "know."

They'll test your work because your social media presence is fun. Or they'll follow you to find out what you're doing next, then be the first to tell their friends about it.

My biggest measurable source of discoverability for individual projects comes from social media. In other words, if I mention on my three main sites that something is new, then the people online at that moment will check things out.

If something discoverable lasts for a long time—a month, say—I'll mention it a few times, never more than once per week. If the promotion is only a day long, I'll only mention it once.

If it's a new release—once. Why? Because I'm not going to harangue anyone. They'll find the books on their own.

Trust your readers. Be kind to your fans. Have a social media presence only if you like interacting that way.

Because life's too short otherwise.

17

WITH A LITTLE HELP FROM YOUR FRIENDS

When we set up the anthology workshop that we held at the end of February 2014, Dean told everyone that they would have a great opportunity to network. After all, fifty professional writers whose work runs the gamut of the fiction genres would be there from all over the world.

A few of the new attendees worried about that admonition because, as introverts, being in a new setting with that large a crowd (however sympathetic) was difficult.

But Dean's comment wasn't about the usual meet-and-greet stuff. Most writers are not good at that glad-handing hail-fellow-well-met thing that happens at most conferences.

Dean was referring to the fact that throughout the week, writers would meet fellow writers with similar interests, similar tastes, and similar problems. Even the most reclusive introvert could find a friend at the workshop.

We spent a lot of time talking about stories, filling anthologies, and discussing business. But we also had unscheduled down time. Writers either slept or walked on the beach with new friends or made plans. Several books will come out of this workshop, and so did some discoverability plans, from guest blogging to group websites.

Plus we had fun. The writer/editors had fun as well. We invited John Helfers, Kerrie L. Hughes, Kevin J. Anderson, and Rebecca Moesta because we liked their editing skills, yes, but also because we knew that their reading tastes were different than ours—and because we like them.

I don't know where the synergy started with the six editors. We've all known each other for a long, long time. But I do know that introvert-me met Kevin (less of an introvert) at a creative writing class at the University of Wisconsin–Madison. We have been friends ever since.

Over the years, we have written novels together, planned parties together, stood up for each other at weddings, helped each other in times of need, and oh, yeah, boosted each other up in our writing careers.

I met Dean (even less of an introvert) at a workshop as well, then introduced him to Kevin. Kevin introduced us to Rebecca.

We met John when Martin H. Greenberg hired him to work at Tekno Books, and were friends damn near from hello. Then he introduced us to Kerrie. And all six of us, in combination and separately, came up with some truly fantastic ideas at this workshop as well.

I could go on like this about the whole workshop because writer networking leads to great projects. It also leads to discoverability.

At the workshop, we introduced Kevin and Rebecca to the great writers who are part of our writing network (formed through our Coast Workshops). They have introduced us to great writers through their Superstars network.

Writer networking also happens online. Sometimes it happens in forums, and other times it happens on websites. The Business Rusch blog became a small community that shares information, which I hope will continue as I move from weekly blogs to occasional blogs. Some writers share via the comments. Others send me emails. And still others donate to support the blog, keeping the information going.

Dean's blog has a different community. In fact, every major blogger has attracted a community to his/her work. It's networking at both its best and its worst. (Best when the information is shared through thoughtful discussion; worst when those networks turn into paranoid sound vacuums. See Chapter Sixteen about politics and religion and blogging.)

There are a variety of networks. Some are informal, like the blog communities. Others are formal. The formal networks have contractual agreements that the members have to sign before they join. Some of these networks also have dues or volunteer time requirements.

One of the formal networks that I'm familiar with is Book View Café.[1] It's a cooperative publisher, which it defines thusly:

> Our members are authors across all genres, from science fiction to romance to
> historical to mainstream. We function as editors, copyeditors, ebook formatters, cover

artists, website maintainers and more. We offer both reprints and new titles, currently in ebook form, but we're looking at expanding to print...

Book View Café does not prevent its members from placing their ebooks in other stores, such as Amazon, B&N, or iTunes. But it does prefer to sell the books through its website.

How all this works, aside from the fact that there are legal documents governing the relationship, is not something I'm really privy to. Some of the answers can be found on their FAQ.[2] I know some others, because I know members, but I have no idea what information is private or not.

I mention them here, not because they're the only cooperative publisher I know of, but because I spoke via email with friends from the café for this piece. Also, BVC has been around almost as long as this ebook revolution, so they're very well informed about what works and what does not.

They have a fluid business model, which adapts to the changes in the industry—in a smart way, as far as I can tell.

Less formal networks exist in all sorts of ways, which I will list below.

I will say this: If you're forming a network, and that network involves financial transactions and/or expectations of work, then you absolutely *need* a legal agreement.

Too many lawsuits occur because someone handled money incorrectly or feelings got hurt over volunteer work. I used to work for a nonprofit staffed by volunteers, and believe me, we had the most difficulty when there was no legal contract governing the relationship.

So, if you're setting up a network, and someone handles money—even on one project—make certain you have a contract between all parties involved.

That said, networks are a generally a good thing. Yes, they can get toxic and yes, there's always going to be someone who pisses in the pool.

If no finances or division of labor is involved, make sure the network is run by one person who decides which direction it goes. If there are finances or expected division of labor, you need that contract to get rid of the troublemakers. (And you will never be able to predict in advance who those troublemakers will be.)

For the purposes of this blog, we'll talk only about the way networks aid discoverability. Networks can be invaluable in helping writers get discovered. There are a million ways to do it.

I asked a few of my writer friends who were very good at discoverability in 2014 how they or their organization did the work.

In no particular order, here's how networks can aid discoverability:

Call-to-Arms

I put this one first because it's the one everyone thinks of. It's the obvious way to use a network. You give the network members information, then ask them to use their social media/bookstore connections to promote your work.

Honestly, I rarely do a call-to-arms. When I do, I don't do it for my work. I do it for a charity or a good cause. Once, Dean and I did a call-to-arms for a friend's business being badly misrepresented on a recommendation site. We asked anyone who had direct personal experience with the friend's business to write about that experience. Dozens of people did, and the problem got resolved.

A call-to-arms is different than a notification. A notification is a single post or tweet or message letting your fans know that something new is available. A call-to-arms directly asks people to retweet, tell their friends, or do some kind of action for you. The more you do it, the less your network pays attention—and the less people outside the network pay attention.

Fantasy, historical, and mystery writer Pati Nagle, who publishes her work through Book View Café, says that group learned this the hard way.

In an email,[3] she wrote,

> One thing we've learned from past experience is that just having everyone share and retweet each other's book posts isn't all that effective—especially when we have friends in common and they start seeing the same post multiple times. That gets regarded as spam.

A call-to-arms is huge, easily misused weapon. Do this rarely, if at all.

Bundling

In the past year, I've been in ten time-limited book bundles with other authors. In March 2014, I was in a bundle curated by Kevin through Story-bundle.com. Kevin asked me to be part of that bundle, not just because we're buds, but because I had a series that fit with it. (He's done other bundles without me. [pout])

The March bundle offered nine books. I put in the first book in my Fey series. Kevin included a book, of course, and so did David Farland, James A.

Owen, Peter Wacks & Mark Ryan, Peter David, Brandon Sanderson, Tracy Hickman, and Neil Gaiman.

Readers set their own price for the bundle (no lower than $3), and some of the money went to a charitable cause dear to all of us, The Challenger Center.[4] The bundle was available for only three weeks.

It sounds like a super-powered bundle, and it was, but I urge you to go to the site to see how it came about. Go to the archives at Storybundle.com and click on the link for the Truly Epic Fantasy Bundle.[5] If you click on the book covers you find there, you'll see Kevin's curated comments. The comments are not about the books. Each one describes how Kevin met or knows the writers in question.

The comments go like this one for Neil:

> *How can I not have a soft spot for Neil Gaiman? Fans know him as a god among writers, one of the most successful authors working today. For me, though, I got to know Neil when his young son (now a successful doctor!) was a big fan of our Star Wars Young Jedi Knights series. OK, Neil, we'll let you in the StoryBundle... —Kevin J. Anderson*

If you read the curated comments all together, you'll see a network at work, and the center of that network is Kevin.

You'd think that this group doesn't need discoverability, but every writer is unknown to a vast majority of readers. In fact, when I told one of my best friends (an avid reader [not a writer] who also knows Kevin) that this bundle was starting, my friend asked, "Who's Neil Gaiman?"

My friend was serious. He has read some of the other writers, but Neil has somehow never crossed his radar. Even when I told my friend the name of Neil's books and the movies made from his work, my friend had *still* never heard of Neil. So, if my friend reads all the books in the bundle he bought when it was live, one of the authors he will discover will be Neil Gaiman.

Bundles like this one are run by a bundling company. The company brings its own newsletter to the table, plays host for the bundle and does the work getting the books ready for download, etc. For that, the company gets a percentage. The charity gets a set percentage. The curator gets a percentage. The rest is split with the authors.

And yes, absolutely, we have a contract.

Bundles like this, which are available for just a few weeks, only work when the writer-participants inform their own networks that the bundle exists. The pooled networks invite readers to try writers they've never heard of.

If the readers like that writer's work, then the readers will buy more of the work.

The magic doesn't happen quickly, and sometimes it doesn't happen at all. Readers will respond—good or bad—when they get the books. We writers are gambling that readers who buy the bundle will like at least one other writer in that bundle. (And if the reader's not one of our regular readers, then we're hoping the writer the reader likes is us.)

What I love best about the book bundles is that the power of the bundle lies entirely in the work itself. You're gambling that readers who have never seen your writing before will like it.

I did one bundle last summer with the first book of the Retrieval Artist series, and I watched the readers work their way through the rest of the series like a mouse through a snake. I thought it was done until my sales for the series went up last fall on sites that offer ebooks in multiple formats. Bundles like this attract readers who like those sites, who will then buy the remaining works through sites that don't require a particular ereader or proprietary technology.

But bundles don't have to be through a formal bundling site. There are other ways to do this.

At the anthology workshop that I mentioned above, six authors came up with a fascinating way to cross promote. The authors created a website called the Uncollected Anthology.[6] Every three months, they release short stories based on the same topic.

Here's what their website says about the concept:

Every three months, the authors pick a theme and write a short story for that theme. But instead of bundling the stories together, they each sell their own stories. No muss, no fuss—you can buy one story, or you can buy them all. (We'll be honest: we hope you buy them all!)

By the time you read this, the second anthology will have come out, featuring the work of all six authors: Dayle A. Dermatis, Michele Lang, Annie Reed, Phaedra Weldon, Leah Cutter, and Leslie Claire Walker. The stories have similar covers. The writers promote on each other's websites, and in the back of each other's books.

I'll be honest: the moment they had the website up, I signed up for their newsletter. As an editor, I've bought stories from all six of those women, and I *love* their work. This is a fun concept and one that I think will only grow more popular over time.

At that same anthology workshop, award-winning romance writer Anthea Lawson (who also writes fantasy as the bestselling Anthea Sharp) told me about a successful bundle that she has done.

I asked her to write it up for me for this book.

She got the idea from another group of writers in a collective called The Indie Voice,[7] which I had not heard of until Anthea emailed me after the workshop. I urge you to go to the Indie Voice's About page so that you see how writer networking can lead to Something Good.[8] Here's a sample:

Eight writers met, many for the first time, on a windy day at an all-inclusive hotel in Cancun, Mexico on February 22, 2013 in a big ass hot tub. What began as a mere spark of an idea to join together to promote and market literally exploded ... Needless to say, bonds were made, friendships were forged, and the moment everyone got home, big ideas did not disappear within hectic work schedules, but instead became reality amongst a deluge of Facebook comments and emails. In hopes of realizing widespread results, two more writers...were suckered into joining The Indie Voice, completing this unique partnership.

(And yes, this is one of those formal groups with a contract. It required everyone to put in up-front money.)

In March 2013, according to Anthea, these women started doing multi-author bundles that were very successful. Anthea did what any good businessperson does—she studied the model and tried to see how to adapt it to her own work.

She writes,[9]

While some authors were banding together to try and hit lists, I know that YA fantasy (without vampires/werewolves/fallen angels) is a soft market. My goal was to try and reach new readers within my genre and cross-pollinate and promote with [similar] authors. I also knew I wanted to position the bundle as a long-term loss leader if it ended up taking off.

She adds that having a large mailing list or bestseller status was not the point of including an author.

Having a good fae-fantasy YA book with a follow-on series was the baseline.

The plan included putting all the proceeds into advertising the bundle. They launched in June at $2.99, but over time, decided to lower the price to 99 cents.

> *By October, we were selling thousands of copies a month. Collectively, we decided to keep the .99 price point going. In December, we sold 15K copies of the bundle and at this point everyone's follow-on books in their series were taking off. Sales of my Feyland books more than quadrupled...*
>
> *As of now (March 2014) we have sold over 50K copies of the Faery Worlds bundle. Our ranking on Amazon has finally dropped out of the top 1,000 overall but we're still selling plenty of copies and reaching LOTS of new readers, not only on Amazon, but B&N and Kobo as well...*

This is how networking can work—with some smarts, targeted marketing, and set goals. If you want to see the bundle, it's called *Faery Worlds* and is, at this writing, still available for 99 cents.

Sidebar: Be Prepared

If you're going to tap into vast fan networks other than your own, you need to be prepared. At minimum, you'll need a newsletter. The staff at WMG Publishing worked really hard to have my Fey series website up and running properly before the March bundle hit. (Believe me, these folks worked their tails off!)

You want your site to be as professional as possible, even if it's a static site, so that people will find the information they're looking for and maybe give you their email address.

But if you don't want to do all the work of a bundle, then here's something less complicated, but which seems like fun:

Blog-Hopping

In March 2014, writer Esther Schindler tagged me on Facebook with this sentence:

> *I rather like this idea for fiction authors (and maybe us non-fiction authors): a blog hop.*

Then she sent me a link to two participants in a blog hop that occurred on December 21, 2013. To celebrate the longest night of the year (in the Western hemisphere), thirty-one writers "cast light into darkness." That was what they were supposed to blog about.

It was the blogging equivalent of a progressive dinner party (or safari supper, as you Brits call it) where you eat a different part of the meal at a different home. Readers start with the first blog, then "hop" to the next. All thirty-one were up that day, and readers could spend the long night reading about light.

The blog that intrigued me the most was Nicole Evelina's "What Lurks Beneath Glastonbury Abbey?"[10] but the others were interesting as well. Scroll to the bottom of Evelina's post and you'll find the entire list.

You'll note that the Uncollected Anthology is, in its way, a blog- and book-hop. Fun how things combine, isn't it?

Joint Giveaways

Kathryn Loch emailed me[11] in the middle of February 2014 to let me know that "a bunch of us romance authors get together and chip in for a Kindle giveaway or Amazon gift card." I don't have a link for you, but she tells me that she's gotten a lot of exposure and sales that way.

Finally...

Not all networks that aid discoverability need to be networks of fiction writers. Because of the blogging post I did (that became the chapter on blogs), Bonnie Koenig contacted me. Bonnie runs a site called The Cat Post Intelligencer,[12] which focuses on...you guessed it...cats. I had mentioned that I wouldn't mind blogging about cats and she gave me the opportunity —plus, completely unasked, she promoted my books. (Pleased me, I tell you.)

That one contact put me in touch with The Catblogosphere,[13] a website devoted to cat blogging. A number of cat bloggers now follow me on Twitter and Facebook and are retweeting my (almost weekly) cat pictures. I have no idea how many new readers this has brought to my books or website (if any), but it's a network I can tap, particularly for some animal-based charities that I have peripheral involvement with.

Links, Connections, Ideas, Discussions

It took me nearly a month to recover from the anthology workshop. While it went on, I agreed to some things, and worked on promotions—particularly for Fiction River—that would not have occurred without the workshop.

It was fun, but like everything to do with discoverability, it was also a time sink.

As you develop your own discoverability plan, remember that you will be using up some of your writing time for every project you agree to. Also remember, the most important thing you do is write.

If the things you do for discoverability interfere with that, then you need to clear the promotions and marketing out of your office and get back to work—writing the next story.

18

A SAMPLER OF SAMPLES

Every now and then, indie writers erupt into discussions of price. Writers remain convinced—no matter how much logic you show them—that readers won't buy a book written by a new writer unless that book is cheap.

If that statement were true, then traditional publishing would not exist. Traditional publishing—as long as it has been around—has sold books by new writers at the same price as books by established writers. There is no tiered pricing for new to old.

Honestly, tiered pricing has nothing to do with the arts. Tiered pricing is day-job thinking, believing that the writer's experience matters more than the piece of art itself.

People who work day jobs expect to start at a lower wage than people who've been in the job for a while.

If you think about things from a writer's point of view, day-job thinking kinda makes sense. You'd think that established writers should get paid more than writers who are brand new.

But even in the most corporate part of publishing, traditional publishing, tiered pricing does not exist. It doesn't even exist when it comes to advances paid by traditional publishers. If a traditional publisher believes that Brand New Writer's Very First Novel will be a worldwide bestseller, then that traditional publisher will pay an advance to Brand New Writer in the six or seven figures, while Established Writer with a long track record who has just released her fiftieth novel might get an advance in the five figures. If she's lucky.

Both books, by the way, will have the same suggested retail price on their covers.

Publishing isn't about the artist. It's about the art, the product, the item.

And for readers, it's about the story.

Does the reader want that story? Does the reader like reading that genre? Does the reader think that story will entertain them?

Readers do shop by price, but not in the way that writers think readers should. We've had that discussion. It's in Chapter Thirteen.

So, why am I mentioning it here? Because pricing and sampling are related. But not in the way you'd think.

The best way for a new writer to get discovered is in the company of established writers. Buy your favorite writer's newest story—and get another story as a bonus. If the reader enjoys the bonus story, she goes on to read more by the same author.

That's why bundles work. That's why networked blogs and other group activities also aid discoverability. (See Chapter Seventeen.)

The best way for *any* writer (new or established) to be discovered is to become familiar to the reader.

How can a new writer do that without lowering the price of her precious novel?

There are a variety of ways to do that. And many of them involve sampling.

Most indie writers think of sampling as that opening of the novel that etailers let you put up for your book. The first 10 or 20% absolutely needs to be available to the reader, so don't clutter up the opening of the ebook version of your novel with pull quotes or a table of contents. (In the ebook, put the table of contents in the back.) Let the opening of the book speak for itself.

But there's a lot more to sampling than simply having the opening of your book available to the readers.

The best way to let readers sample your work is through more of the work—not free copies given away on ebookstore sites—but as part of a larger whole.

The best way to sample? Write short stories.

I write a lot of short stories. I love them, which is one reason I write them. I also write short stories as a means to worldbuild my novels. I would much rather work out a story question while figuring out how part of my world works, than write some dry nonfiction piece for the book's bible that no one else will ever see.

Even if I'm not writing science fiction or fantasy, I write stories to worldbuild. I use short stories as practice. Writers so rarely think they need to practice, but we all do. Sometimes I practice a historic milieu. Sometimes I practice a character. Sometimes I practice a technique.

If the short story doesn't work, I'm out a few hours (or a week) of my time. If the novel doesn't work, then I'm out several months.

The best thing about short stories, though, is their versatility.

Let me give you an example.

In March 2014, my short story "Play like a Girl" was my Free Fiction Monday story on my website for one week only. I wrote the story by invitation for an anthology of short stories based on the songs of Janis Ian. The anthology, *Stars*, has just been reprinted through Lucky Bat Books. It also has a brand new audio edition through Audible. WMG Publishing has just published a standalone version of the story with a great cover.

So, during that week in March, readers had four ways to find that short story. Readers who came to my weekly free fiction post found "Play like a Girl" and maybe liked it well enough to buy some of the other slipstream stories or women's fiction that I write. Maybe they even picked up my novel, *Bleed Through*, which is also marketed as women's fiction (and which also has a new audio edition).

Readers who like women's fiction might discover the standalone short story through a search of new women's fiction on the e-tailing sites. Or readers might pick up the ebook because of the spectacular cover that Allyson Longueira at WMG designed.

But the best way for readers to discover me and my work through that short story is in the anthology *Stars*. Thirty different writers, including Janis Ian, have stories in that anthology. Fans of each of those writers might pick up the anthology. Fans who like more than one of the writers definitely will pick up the anthology.

If those fans are completist readers, like I am, they'll read the other stories in the volume. If they like "Play like a Girl," they'll flip to the bio I've put in which accompanies the story, and find my other work. Or they'll come to my website to see what else I'm doing. Or they'll do a search of my work on Amazon, Barnes & Noble, Kobo, or whatever online retailer they usually use.

The readers might not buy a full novel. They might buy a short story. They might sample some books before trying one. They might see a storybundle on the sidebar and order it, getting a bunch of books for less than the price of one.

They might take one of my novels out of the library. Or they might not remember my name at all—until they encounter another of my short stories somewhere, and then remember that they had liked "Play like a Girl."

The best part of discoverability via short stories, in my opinion, is that the *work* introduces the reader to other work by the author.

Plus the short story is advertising. Think about it. It costs a minimum of $600 for a half page (horizontal) to advertise one time in one of the Dell short fiction magazines.[1] It costs $1,000 for a full-page ad.

In the May 2014 of *Analog*, I have a short story that runs seven pages. To run seven pages of full-page advertising would cost me $7,000. Instead, I got paid for the short story—and readers get a chance to sample my work.

That's quite a financial swing in my favor.

And the story's not done doing its job. My contract with *Analog* allows me to reprint the story a few months after publication. I can reprint the story any way that I want to. Including in an ebook, which will allow more readers to find my work.

Analog has this lovely fact on their website:[2]

> *According to our reader survey, more than 80% purchase books by the authors they have been introduced to in our magazines. And about 33% read more than 15 science fiction novels per year!*

I write science fiction, so having an sf story in *Analog* puts my name in front of their 27,000 readers.

When I edited *The Magazine of Fantasy & Science Fiction*, we did a similar survey and got similar results. Unlike book publishers, magazines do survey their readers because a loss of circulation means that magazines can't charge as much for advertising. So magazines need to know what their readers want and how to make sure the magazine caters to those wants.

I have no idea how many people have bought/will buy the *Stars* anthology. But even if it's only 10,000 readers, those 10,000 readers might not have seen my work otherwise.

I publish stories in a wide variety of venues, from the major sf magazines to small literary magazines like *Rosebud*, which has a small but loyal readership of 2,500 to 5,000,[3] depending on the issue.

I can't measure how many readers cross over from the short stories to the novels, mostly because I haven't tried, but I do know that many, many fans tell me they encountered my short stories long before they bought my books.

I keep the short stories in the mail. I still submit to traditional short story markets all the time. I do so because writers never become "established" (despite what new writers believe.) There will always be new readers who have never heard of you.

As a writer, you will never, ever be able to rest on your laurels. New readers enter the book buying pool every day—and the vast majority of those readers have not heard of you. They haven't heard of Nora Roberts either.

They're *new*.

It's up to you to find ways to allow those readers to discover you.

I know what you're thinking: so many of you are going to tell me that you submitted five or fifteen or a hundred stories to the various magazines and got some rejections. [Shrug] I got three form rejections during the week I wrote this chapter as a blog.

Writers collect rejection slips—virtual or paper, it doesn't matter. Even big name writers get rejected.

Keep those stories in the mail (virtual or snail). It takes an average of six months to get a response from the literary and small magazines. Plan to keep your stories in the mail for a few years before taking them out of the traditional publishing markets. I've sold stories ten years after I've written them—all because I kept them in the mail.

Yes, I know, you can put them up online right away, and maybe you'll have your story in front of five pairs of eyeballs. But you can wait and sell them, and be in front of thousands of pairs of eyeballs.

Which is better? Thousands, in my opinion, particularly if you're a fast writer.

Chalk up each short story to practice, keep sending the stories to a market that might buy them, and write more short fiction. It's certainly better than spending your hard-earned dollars on display ads that won't work unless you do them right as we discussed way back in Chapter Eight.

What if you never sell to the major magazines? What if they don't like your voice or your quirkiness or whatever? What if you've been around for a long time as a short fiction writer and never gotten traction?

Think about the stuff you just learned in Chapter Seventeen. Put together an e-anthology of your own. Make certain that you have the rights from your fellow contributors to do so, and make sure that you have a contract and a way to do the accounting if you're going to charge for it.

Book View Café does anthologies of its members on a regular basis. So, on the traditional side, does The Mystery Writers of America.

And if you don't play nice with others, what then?

One week, or one month, or something regular, put a story free on your website only. The idea is to drive traffic to your site and build readership. The nifty thing about my Free Fiction Monday short stories is that so many readers make a point of coming to the website every Monday.

I have no idea how many of these readers buy my work. Honestly, I don't care. What these readers do is become a resource for other readers. Almost daily, someone recommends my work on Twitter to someone else. The week I wrote this, the discussion on Twitter has been about female science fiction writers, and someone linked to my work. Previous weeks, the discussions have been things like paranormal romances or noir fiction.

I don't initiate these discussions. I see them only because someone has looped me in. But often, that looping includes a link to that week's free story.

It takes time to establish an audience for the free fiction—several months of regular posting, in fact. But that audience will become loyal.

I don't offer fiction for free in online bookstores. Only on my website. And only for one week.

It works.

It probably would work better if I made an announcement every week to the various websites that track free fiction. But I'd rather be writing, so I don't do all of the things that I "should" when it comes to discoverability.

Short stories aid discoverability. So, logically, it would seem that nonfiction does too.

If you're a nonfiction writer, then articles and blogs will help.

But think about this from a reader's point of view. Readers are very smart people. They know that fiction writers and nonfiction writers use different skills. A nonfiction writer venturing into novels? Readers are skeptical.

So if they sample and like your nonfiction, they'll search for more of your nonfiction, not your fiction. And readers really don't care about writing or publishing. They have their own lives and their own careers. They're trying to escape from those things with a few hours of adventure or romance. They don't want to read business stuff about an industry that's not their own.

Are there exceptions that make nonfiction writing/blogging aid the discoverability of your novels?

Very few, and they have to be creative.

If you write historical novels, then articles in various journals on the difference between the way the time period is presented in fiction versus nonfiction might help. Or an article about the cool stuff you discovered on the way to something else.

For example, a mystery writer friend of mine who is researching women in World War II for a novel sent me an email with this tidbit: Bea Arthur (*Maude, Golden Girls*) served in the United States Marine Corps during that war.[4] Which makes sense, honestly, but it's also cool.

An article based on found tidbits might lead readers to a writer's fiction. Or it might give that writer a big nonfiction readership for the tidbits.

You want readers to sample your fiction if you're writing fiction. Remember that.

A lot of systems enable sampling. Writers really need to stop bitching about libraries and used bookstores. Think of those places as a location for readers to get free samples. (And no, I'm not going to get into how to get into libraries right now. It's constantly changing. I repeat what I said in an earlier chapter: Libraries will order through normal book channels if there's enough interest in a book.)

Finally, one other great way to encourage sampling is to get your books into the book club circuit.

WMG Publishing ventured into the book club circuit with a targeted ad to African American book clubs in May 2014 (which cost all of $80) for my Smokey Dalton series. St. Martin's Press, which initially published the series, refused to let African American readers know about my African American detective because I'm white. (Yes, I know, there's no real logic there.)

So the targeted ad through a company that collects information on African American book clubs was a gamble, but an inexpensive one. And it paid off immediately. The sales of the series have gone up dramatically from that one ad, which surprised me. I expected it to take two or three or four (that familiarity thing).

There are other ways to promote to book clubs, some I haven't tried yet. I plan to do one with *Bleed Through.* Several book clubs have already used the title to spur discussion.

How do I plan to help with *Bleed Through*'s discoverability for book clubs? A book club edition. Traditional publishers do them. They have essays from the author, sample questions, and suggestions for other titles that might be useful in the book club.

I asked my sister, an avid reader and member of at least one book club, to help with resources for book clubs. She gave me a long list of the things her club uses.

I've decided not to share those lists. Because the websites and lists make it very clear that the websites are for readers. Writers might be invited to give an interview, but they have no place on those sites. Nor do publishers.

Most book club loops on the Internet are private. Many don't want authors there at all. The book club members want the freedom to discuss the writer's work without fear of insulting the writer.

Do a book club edition, mark it as a book club edition, with added material, and put that in your keywords. It'll help.

If you need assistance, then look at various book club editions. Some are marketed that way. Others have a marketing bug that's specific to a particular company. For example, Harper Perennial uses "P.S." with a section of the cover marked off to let readers know there are "extras." (You can see what I mean if you look at the front and back covers of the book club edition[5] of Michael Chabon's *Manhood For Amateurs*.)

Yes, you'll have to do another edition. Yes, you'll have to make sure that's got a separate title from the standard edition. Yes, it'll take some work.

Just like writing short stories will take work.

But this is the kind of work that writers are good at.

Writers write.

And if that writing makes the rest of your oeuvre easier to discover, then what's not to love? Give it a try

You'll have a lot of fun.

THE INVISIBLE CHAPTER

SURPRISE!

I stressed about this chapter from the moment I decided to put the blog posts into an actual book on *Discoverability*. Because when I did this as a blog post, I actually surprised my readers.

For five years, I posted my nonfiction business column on Thursdays. When this chapter was a blog post, it appeared on a Tuesday. And everyone *was* surprised.

I couldn't quite replicate that surprise in book form without driving my publisher nuts. So I decided to do the simplest thing.

I did not put this chapter in the numbering system or in the table of contents. You won't know it's here unless you scan through the book. (Or actually read it. Horrors!)

I wanted to catch you off-guard. In the blog, I broke the regular weekly schedule, and some readers noticed. The rest noticed on Thursday or the weekend, and weren't quite as surprised.

Those of you reading the book should be a bit startled. This chapter isn't quite the norm.

And that's on purpose.

I'm making a point.

The point is that when you do things the same way, day in and day out, the predictability actually helps. In something like a blog, it makes the readers show up as if they had an appointment, expecting that bit of entertainment or information. It's part of their routine.

When you shake up that routine, it's a bit uncomfortable, but it catches people's attention.

Which I did with that blog post.

Most of you read a lot of nonfiction, and you know how chapters work. You should be able to find things with the table of contents. But you can't here.

And that shook up a different sort of routine.

Like I just did with some of you.

Weirdly, the Tuesday of the blog post happened to also be April Fool's Day, and a lot of my regular readers scanned to see if I was pulling off an April Fool's Joke.

I wasn't.

The fact that this post landed on April Fool's Day was a bonus. I'd been planning the surprise post as the penultimate post in this series since December 2013.

Why December?

Because that's when I remembered just how marvelous surprise is.

December—or more specifically, the wee hours of Friday, December 13, is when Beyoncé slapped the music industry upside the head by releasing her latest album with a single announcement on Instagram.

I discussed this release in Chapter Six: The Most Important Thing a Writer Can Do. Beyoncé's move, the move of a secure, settled artist, was brilliant.

Her promotion campaign? Even more brilliant. That single post with an attached video[1] said simply, "Surprise!"

What she did dominated the worldwide entertainment conversation over the holidays, the worldwide music conversation for about a month, and the music industry—well, they're still discussing it.

Because what she did is impossible to repeat.

It came from her: her art, her brand, her desire to do something different. And yes, I know. She's so much more famous than everybody, of course she can do it.

Of course.

Anyone who is that famous can do it. Um, not. Not now. Because now, they'd be pulling a Beyoncé. She surprised us, and she owns method. It won't be as exciting if Billy Joel does it or if Taylor Swift decides to release her next album the same way. It won't be a surprise.

Surprises seem so obvious after the fact.

Of course, Beyoncé can do this. Because she's Beyoncé.

Of course, Beyoncé can do this. The album is stellar, just like we expected.

Of course, Beyoncé can do this. She has the fan base.

And on, and on, and on.

And yet, surprises—good surprises—catch our attention all the time. Sometimes they're serendipitous, like a spectacular Hail Mary basketball shot executed by a player on North Carolina's Bishop McGuinness boys' basketball team that made national news. CBS News has the video[2] (which you should watch), and explores the sweet narrative that adds to the surprise.

Sometimes good surprises are the result of something the owner/creator knew (or hoped) but no one else did. The *Veronica Mars* Kickstarter project,[3] which funded in eleven hours surprised even its creator in the speed of funding, but Rob Thomas knew that the defunct series had a lot of die-hard fans (called Marshmallows—don't ask).

The surprise was a pleasant one for him and the cast, but a difficult one because they now had to deliver a movie. They did so in March 2014, and that movie release included surprise at the box office—the film is still doing better than the studios expected, probably due to (ahem) word of mouth (see Chapter Twenty).

Those Kickstarter projects that came after *Veronica Mars*? They made some money, but didn't surprise the way the *Mars* Kickstarter did. In fact, they probably disappointed, because the creators expected a *Veronica Mars* effect. I know the media did.

I know someone is going to ask this, so here's how it would go if I were teaching this in person.

Student: So, how do you surprise?

Kris: Really? Seriously? You're asking me that—BOO!!!!!

But some of you are thinking it, so here goes.

Believe it or not, surprise takes a lot of thought. Sometimes it's serendipitous as in that basketball shot with the fantastic back story, but mostly, surprise is the result of good hard work.

For writers—and discoverability—surprise takes two forms.

First, you must surprise with your art. What does that mean exactly? It means if the reader knows how all of your books will end—or, if you're writing romance (or something else with a prescribed ending), the readers will know exactly how you get to the end.

The book must catch the reader off guard. Sometimes that off-guard is big, and sometimes it's just a different direction than the average writer would take the book.

In George R. R. Martin's Song of Ice and Fire book series, which everyone refers to as Game of Thrones, George included a major surprise in Book 3, *A Storm of Swords*. Readers were upset and intrigued in joint measure. Fans remembered this, of course, and if you go to the Westeros website discussion forum from a few years ago, the fans were trying to figure out when the HBO series would catch up to the book.

Because, the book fans (bless them) didn't want to ruin the surprise for the TV fans. But the book fans wanted to see the reactions of the TV fans, so they did what any good modern person does—they filmed their friends' reactions. I've linked to a video[4] of George on Conan O'Brien's show, discussing this, along with some clips of the surprised reactions. (If you are still spoilerific on Game of Thrones [and seriously, how can you be?], don't watch this.)

That's the kind of surprise that keeps readers reading, keeps viewers talking, and puts your work into the conversation. On March 23, 2014, the TV show *The Good Wife* had an even bigger surprise for its fans because no one except the people involved in the show knew it was coming.

The show had already earned the respect of fans with a fantastic game-changing episode in the fall—all of this in Season 5, when most shows run out of steam—and so when the show's previews said that the game-changer was really on March 23, fans tuned in, not wanting to hear discussion of the show the next day.

Was there a surprise? Oh. My. God. (Seriously, be nice to me. I'm still in recovery.)

The Good Wife is an even better example of artistic surprise for a couple of reasons. First, the producers received some very bad news in early 2013, and rather than let it derail the show, they used that news to make the show better. Second, the show has never been a highly rated series. However, because it's been consistently part of national entertainment dialogue for the past two years now (and because it wins awards), it has been renewed when other series with the same ratings haven't been.

On the other hand, one of *The Good Wife*'s Sunday night competition shows, *Revenge*, had so many surprises and so many twists and turns that the show got completely and utterly ridiculous. The surprises ceased to be a surprise and just became a single question: Do the writers know what they're doing? My guess, as a former fan, is no.

So surprise in art is something you use sparingly, but you must use that tool in your creative toolbox. And you need to use it in your promotion toolbox as well.

What, exactly, do I mean by that?

Well, almost everything writers believe they "need" to do to promote their books was something that originator of the promotion had done as a successful surprise.

Romance author Debbie Macomber is a promotions maven. I tried to Google the history of her promotions, but I couldn't quickly find anything, because she's been promoting her work for so long.

What I do know is this: She was the first romance author to make a concentrated effort to go to bookstores. She did flyers, she did bookmarks, she did a newsletter before anyone else. She gave away something with every book—and it was never the same thing, nor was it the same as something other authors were doing.

When the rest of the romance world heard what she was doing and started producing bookmarks, Debbie had given her best bookseller promoters aprons. She has done all kinds of intriguing promotional things. I'm being purposely vague because I followed what she was doing, saw a lot of it come through a bookstore (to a grumpy male bookseller who still took notice), and heard her speak more than once on the things she did.

She was always inventing something new, and is so far ahead of the game that when I Googled this, I found that her fans collect her promotional items. Which, after thirty-one years of publishing and promoting, makes complete sense.

Debbie enjoys doing this. She loves the fan interaction. She's good at it. I'm not saying you have to do it, but if you do promote and you want someone to notice what you do, then do something different.

Surprise us.

Stop doing what everyone else does. Do something that connects to one of your books, and make that something memorable. Make it original.

Think about it.

What would you like to see a YA writer do to promote her work? Or a romance writer? What really cool thing did you get from some non-book promotion that you could see easily translate to books?

What caught your attention in the last week with promotion, somewhere in the arts or in business? Can you do that? Should you do that?

Be creative, and be innovative.

But more important than that, be true to yourself. Don't do something that makes you uncomfortable, that feels like pandering, or is something you're doing only because someone else told you to.

Remember to write the next book.

Or write a column early.

Like this one.

GOALS AND PLANNING

19

PUBLICITY CAMPAIGNS

When I started writing this chapter on a Monday night two weeks before I posted the chapter as a blog, my Kris DeLake novel, *A Spy to Die For*, ranked #1 on two Amazon bestseller lists. Both are subgenre lists:

1. Kindle Store > Kindle eBooks > Romance > Science Fiction
2. Books > Romance > Science Fiction

And #6 in another:

Kindle Store > Kindle eBooks > Mystery, Thriller & Suspense > Thrillers > Espionage

To be perfectly honest, *Spy* doesn't belong in the mystery/thriller/espionage category at all. Some readers are going to be very disappointed.

I'm not responsible for the rankings (or the keywords). Sourcebooks, the novel's publisher, set up *A Spy to Die For*, as one of that Monday's Kindle Daily Deals. Unlike the Kindle Daily Deal that Sourcebooks had set up for one of my Grayson novels on the day after Christmas, this deal listed *Spy* on the front of the Daily Deal page, and on the email that got sent out.

It got a response.

I have no idea what the sales numbers are, because I won't see them for months (Sourcebooks being a traditional publisher). I also don't know how much Sourcebooks paid to be part of the promotion. I know they're doing a major investment in the Daily Deal, at least according to the email that I received announcing this one. At least one Sourcebooks novel daily was part of the Daily Deal for several days in March.

Let me be perfectly frank here:

I have no idea why Sourcebooks included *Spy* in this promotion. Yes, they have two of my DeLake books, both backlist now. (*Spy* came out in July 2013.) Sourcebooks and I jointly canceled the contract for the third, so there are no new Sourcebooks DeLake novels, and I personally am not going to get to any of my other series until I'm done with several other projects.

The Grayson novel that was part of December's deals was even older than *Spy*, and that promotion made a touch more sense to me. Sourcebooks has five backlist Grayson novels, and getting movement on them is a good idea. Kinda.

But from an investment point of view, why spend the money on an old book with no new books on the horizon? The entire staff at Sourcebooks knows that I'm not going to publish any more novels with the company. The promotion dollars are better spent on other writers with upcoming books.

All I can think is this: Sourcebooks has an in-house algorithm that flags backlist novels for promotion every few months or once a year or something. Once the novel gets placed in the promotion cycle, then the promotion goes ahead as planned, no matter what's happening with the author or the other books in the series.

I have to applaud Sourcebooks for marketing its backlist titles. Most traditional publishers don't market most of their backlist titles at all, except for their bestselling titles. Or they only market the most recent backlist novel when the next novel appears.

The fact that Sourcebooks invests continually in its backlist is one of the many reasons I chose to join the company in the first place. They're an innovative business that is constantly trying new things.

So I shouldn't complain—and I'm not, really. I'm just puzzled. Because it seems to me that Sourcebooks, as innovative as it is, is also practicing one-size-fits-all marketing.

You hear this all the time: writers have to do x, y, or z to make their books work. Suzy Q. lowered her book's price, so it's doing well. Or it isn't doing well. Susie X. spent $20,000 on advertising her latest, and hit *The New York Times* extended list. And so on.

The success of Kindle/*Spy* deal has little to do with the type of book or even its price. The novel was also $1.99 on Barnes & Noble on that Monday, and wasn't moving very many copies at all (as far as I could tell from B&N's algorithms).

The reason this particular sale is successful is that the book has a wonderful cover, and it was on the front page of the deal/email. When my Grayson novel was on page 12 or whatever of the deals, it didn't do nearly as well. In the past, when a novel of mine has been on the first deal page, it's done well, and when it's not been on that page, it has done...less well.

The halo effect is smaller too.

Kindle's deal email is targeted advertising. Readers have to sign up for it or be a member of Amazon Prime to get it. If the book gets on a bestseller list, even a subgenre bestseller list, like *Spy* was for nearly two weeks, the list acts as advertising.

In the spring of 2014, I was finishing up the discoverability blog series, and being routinely excoriated on the Kindle Boards (for indie writers) for never having a book in the top 100 of any Amazon list [Rusch pauses, shakes head, forces herself to continue].

While that Kindle Boards shouting went on, *Fiction River: Hex in the City* sat on top of three different subgenre lists. Dean and I are the series editors of *Fiction River*, although credit for that particular volume goes to the actual editor, Kerrie L. Hughes, and to the authors whose stories make that one of the most delightful issues we've done so far.

When *Hex* hit the subgenre lists—with no paid promotion from WMG, no Kindle Daily Deal, no reduction in price—the halo effect lasted for days. People saw the book on the list, then ordered it. The sales stayed high because of the list. The other *Fiction River* volumes rose in sales as well, just as you'd expect.

This is why traditional publishers buy slots on a bestseller list. As I mentioned in Chapter Eleven, many so-called bestseller "lists" are paid advertising positions. The Barnes & Noble list (inside the brick-and-mortar store) is paid advertising. So are the books that are marked 1–10 at your grocery store or at any non-bookstore, like Costco.

If you go into a chain bookstore or a chain store that carries books, and see a bestseller list that's in-house, it's probably paid for. If the bookstore and/or chain store labels the books as part of an outside bestseller list—like *The New York Times* bestseller list—then the books on that shelf labeled with the outside list are ranked in an unpaid list.

But if the shelf just says "Bestselling Titles," and lists the books numerically, that entire shelf is paid advertising.

Traditional publishers pay for all kinds of advertising. And we writers can too, if we set up our publishing business properly.

But, it is a lot of work.

The question is not *is this work worthwhile?*

The question is **when** *is this work worthwhile?*

As I've said all along in this book, the last thing you want to do is one-size-fits-all marketing.

Each book that you publish should have a different marketing campaign. That's not how the Big Boys of Publishing do it. They market books according to advance levels or expectation.

Did they pay more than a quarter of a million dollars as an advance on that book? Then it'll get the same kind of marketing that every other $250,000 and above (advance) book gets (regardless of genre).

Did they pay less than $10,000 as an advance on that book? Even if the book breaks out, gets great pre-publication reviews and a ton of pre-publication orders, the marketing remains the same as every other book in that publishing house that received $10,000 and below as an advance (regardless of genre).

Which is really stupid. And not something you want to repeat.

Here's what you want to do. You want to plan the campaigns for the right reasons, and in the right way for you.

Throughout this book, I have given you a ton of options on how to make your work visible. Now it's time to implement some of those options.

The Overall Decision

Are you marketing yourself or your books? Because there's a huge difference between being a famous writer and having written a well-known novel.

Some writers give speeches and travel everywhere. They're guests at every convention they can think of or they receive speaking fees. These writers become celebrities in their own right.

From the 1970s through the 1990s, a friend of mine graced the television talk shows and was well-known for espousing controversial opinions. That same friend made at least five figures for each public appearance (plus expenses). That friend, by the way, turned out almost no new material in those twenty years.

I'm currently watching two other friends do the same thing this year, and those friends are slowly discovering that writing time dwindles in the face of celebrity.

One of these friends has always flirted with celebrity, and will probably do more than flirt for the next few years. This friend travels the world, making public appearances on behalf of literacy, but hardly writes at all any more.

The other friend has always been a slow writer, and has become positively glacial in the face of convention appearances, magazine interviews, and TV guest shots.

You must choose between being a celebrity writer and the writer of a well-known book *before* you start promoting anything.

Because the path between writer of a well-known book bleeds into celebrity writer, and you might travel for years along the wrong path for you before you even realize you've moved from one category to the other.

You can probably tell my choice in my tone. I don't want to be a celebrity. I've been a major celebrity writer/editor inside my own genre.

I did a lot of conventions and traveling when I was editing *Pulphouse* and *The Magazine of Fantasy & Science Fiction*. My health made me cut back about the same time I stopped doing the editing (thank heavens), but I would have cut back anyway.

I'm an introvert, and I truly hate being recognized. In fact, back in the dark ages, I quit an on-air radio job because people recognized my voice in restaurants. I am good at the celebrity thing; I just don't enjoy it.

My celebrity friends make more money than I do, just on their appearances alone.

But the thing is: once they stop appearing places (like the friend who was famous in the last two decades of the 20th century), the money dries up as well.

If you keep writing, the money continues, even when you can't face a crowd.

If you decide to market yourself rather than market your work, you'll have to find your own path. The rest of this chapter won't help you.

But if you choose to market your work, then the tips that follow will make a difference.

To launch a publicity campaign (or campaigns), you need to plan, using all of the tools I've given you in this book.

Here are the things you need to plan:

1. Assess the work you've published.

Is each item worth promoting? I'm not talking about quality here. I'm discussing time versus earnings.

For example, for me, it's not worth promoting every single short story I publish. I'll let my fans and readers know that a new original story is out, but I've even stopped mentioning when WMG Publishing reprints my backlist shorts.

If someone discovers them, fine; if they remain undiscovered, fine. I have only a finite amount of time to promote my work, and I'll use that on projects that can have a halo effect.

When you're assessing, realize that each project is different. For the rest of this chapter, I'm going to discuss novels only.

If you've only published one novel, write the next one. That's the best discoverability you can do.

If you do too much at once, your readers will get tired of your promotion. A very well-known writer who has published more than I have sends me a newsletter listing every time something new comes out—which is often as much as three times per week.

Don't be that person. Remember your readers have a life as well, and want to pay attention to that as well.

You know what you have to promote. Then what?

2. Figure out your marketing budget.

By "marketing budget," I mean the budget in both money—and in time. In fact, time is the most important part of that budget, because you might recoup your financial losses, but you'll never recoup lost time.

3. Allocate your resources.

After you've figured out your time and money budget, you will most likely realize that you won't be able to promote everything.

And you definitely shouldn't, particularly all at once.

But from this point on, each publicity campaign becomes as personal as the novel that inspired it.

I'll give you my opinions and some suggestions, but what you can do with your scarce resources is ultimately up to you.

Opinions/Suggestions On Marketing Campaigns

Let's say you've published nine novels, three in one series, three in another series, one standalone, and two in the current series. You're about to publish the next novel in the current series. And you're almost done with another standalone novel. And this week, you've decided you are going to start promoting everything in your inventory.

I believe that each series should be viewed as one unit, one project. A single book in an uncompleted three-book series isn't worth promoting —yet.

But, according to our hypothetical, you have two finished series. If they're in the same genre, then they'll feed on each other. If they're in different genres, then they won't help each other at all.

Let's assume they're in different genres. So you must decide which series is worth your time at the moment. If you have a political fantasy series like Game of Thrones, then you might piggyback on the promotion as the new HBO season premieres.

Or you might decide to wait until fans have watched the current season, and are searching for something to fill the void.

You think about how to do this, and then you work on it. You *plan.*

Backlist, in particular, needs some creativity. Pay attention to the culture around you. If you have a novel set in 1865 at the end of the American Civil War, time your promotions to coincide with all the news articles that are going to appear at the 150th anniversary in 2015. You might even be able to promote in odd places—like take an ad in *Civil War Monitor,* or maybe see if you can write an article for them that perhaps mentions (or concerns) your book.

The same goes for location. If your book is set in Appomattox, then talk to the news outlets there for special promotion around the 2015 celebrations. It will give the newscasters a slightly different version of their story, and it'll get you some different promotion.

The key to backlist is this: It stays in print.

We writers never used to have this luxury, so we're not used to thinking about it in that way. We don't need to shove our backlist into the old promotion methods, and we don't need to ignore it, either. Nor should our backlist books be promoted the same way each and every time.

Think about each project, maybe schedule a time to promote it, and then don't worry about it. Maybe promote one backlist novel every quarter.

Or capitalize on promotional opportunities that come your way.

You don't always have to promote your latest novel. In fact, you probably don't want to. Scatter your promotions around. Readers discover different books in different ways; help them find the right book for them.

For example, I mentioned cat bloggers in Chapter Seventeen. That encouraged Bonnie Koenig to ask me to guest blog on her cat-oriented site, and she brought me to the attention of other cat bloggers.

That lead to a giveaway promotion sponsored by Layla Morgan Wilde of one of my short story collections, *Five Feline Fancies.* The giveaway promoted her blog Cat Wisdom 101, yes, but also to promote my cat-oriented fiction. (Thank you, Layla!) I didn't ask her to do this. She just did.

The collection, by the way, has been out since 2010. It gained new life in the spring of 2014, thanks to a connection made through a throwaway comment on my blog—and my willingness to do a few guest blogs in an area different from one I usually promote.

Similarly, the big fantasy storybundle that I mentioned in Chapter Seventeen got promoted to a variety of different places. Most of us writers in the bundle go directly to readers whom we know—and we tend to know the same readers/fan groups. But the Challenger Center, the charity that some of the funds from the bundle went to, also emailed their mailing list— which I know is very different from the lists that we writers have. We found new readers that way, and the readers get to sample our work.

When I initially posted the blogs that make up this book, I got a lot of pushback on the content of Chapter Eleven: When The Old Ways Work.

Most of the old ways—traditional publishing's way of doing things—is based on the Newer! Better! Stronger! method (okay, I watch way too much Jimmy Fallon [or listen to too much Daft Punk]).

Seriously, the old ways are based on this attitude: Buy this book now, before it spoils! Buy it before everyone else does! Be the first on your block to read this book!

That's because traditional publishers believe that books go out of fashion within weeks, if not months. All of this is based on an out-of-date attitude, something that was true just ten years ago—that books had a short shelf life in brick-and-mortar stores.

Even though books now stay in print indefinitely, most traditional publishers still base their promotions on the old-fashioned notion that a book is worthless when purchased six months after its initial release.

Most of the traditional promotion to bookstores is based on that books-will-spoil notion. This is why major review publications only review new releases, and why ARCs need to be completed six months in advance.

Bookstores do their ordering based on what's coming, not on what's available. Your book has to be in the what's-coming system.

When bookstores are ordering for the first time after the book came out, the bookstore is less likely to promote that book and less likely to put that book on the shelf. Instead, the bookseller will put the order behind the counter for the reader who did the special order.

If your upcoming trade paper release has been reviewed in major markets, booksellers will want to order in advance. If you announce a release date and have an ISBN, then the distributors will take orders for that book—even if the book isn't out yet. So your book is being preordered without you lifting a finger.

Because your book will have to wait six months from the moment it's finished to the moment it actually goes on sale, you'll want to use the old ways to market your work only on the most special project. Something standalone, perhaps, something that might be award-worthy (award nominations aid discoverability), something that might benefit from bookseller word of mouth.

Some genres work best with reviews and lots of lead time.

Most mystery fans, for example, buy more paper books than ebooks. Plus there are still a lot of mystery bookstores. (We're seeing that with our Fiction River series: the Crime issue has had the most paper sales upon release of any of our issues. We did a traditional promotion, with ARCs and press releases to mystery publications, with that edition of FR.)

So your mystery novel might benefit from the traditional approach.

Romance novels generally don't get a lot of traditional media coverage even when the novel is by a Big Name Author. Plus, a lot of romance readers prefer ebooks to paper books. (Or mass market paperbacks, which indie writers can't do yet.) So, a traditional push on a romance novel might not be time (or money) well spent.

Be strategic—and figure out your promotion campaign (if you're going to have one) before your finished novel comes out. Sometimes it'll be worth the six-month wait to do the ARC and all the traditional promotion. Sometimes it's simply a loss of six months of sales.

That's your decision—and one you should always think about when you're finishing standalone novels.

What about that hypothetical half-finished series I mentioned above? What about the third book in that series?

Promotion again depends on genre. It also depends on how the previous books in the series were promoted. Are you continuing a formerly traditionally published series out of your own press? Then use the marketing plan that the traditional publisher used (and improve on it).

Has the series been indie from the start? Then use indie techniques.

When you finish the series—after book three or book five or book six—then you do a major promotion on the entire series. You'll bundle the books together for easy purchasing (while keeping the individual novels in print) and you can do a post-publication ad buy in traditional markets for the entire series.

However, as you're releasing new books in that series, you want to focus your promotion on book one of the series.

The thing that traditional publishing has always done poorly is promote a series. In the past, book one was usually out of print before book three came out, so new readers could never jump on board.

Series often died because the readership didn't grow fast enough. (Traditional publishers don't see the contradiction here—they still take series books out of print, although now, they often do it only with the print version—you know, 80% of the market...)

Your series will remain in print, so your promotion on the new book in that series should have a two-pronged approach.

The first prong goes to long-established readers of the series. You blog about the new book, you send out a notice in your newsletter with the new book's publication date, letting everyone know the book is (or will be) available. Urge them to buy sooner rather than later, so you might have a shot on being on one of the various bestseller lists—even if it's a subgenre list. (It does add to the book's promotion.)

The second prong of your approach? Discount that first book in the series. Maybe buy a BookBub ad for it. Let your fans know that the first book is available for a lower price, so they can hook their friends on the series. Make sure the lower price is for a limited time only, because you want this promotion to be special. You want people to hurry to the first book, so they'll read through the series to get to the new book, and boost its numbers.

You promote that first book every single time you get a new book in the series.

If you permanently keep the price of the first book low, you can't do these promotions—and that will actually harm discoverability. So lower the price when the new books come out, then raise the price after the Discover-the-Series promotion is over.

You can always use that first book in other promotions—like group book bundles (which we discussed in Chapter Seventeen) or six months later, when the sales of the new book start to flag.

Remember, your promotions can happen at any point. Don't want to promote book one right now? Wait a few weeks and do it then. Or do it when the sales flag.

Promote your standalone titles in the proper season—a winter book in winter (promote in the US in December; Australia in June), a beach read in summer (reverse the above promotions). You have lots of choices—and they're all limited to your imagination...

...and your time...

...and your finances.

Remember, every moment you spend promoting a book is time you cannot spend on writing. You can find a million ways to promote, which means you can find a million ways to avoid writing.

In short, then:

Whenever you release a new book, have a publicity campaign planned for the book—even if the campaign is to not promote the book for a year or two or ever.

Think about what kind of promotion this new book should have, then *stick to your plan.*

Make sure each of your books has a different promotion plan from the other books. Treat the books like the individuals that they are.

You'll do so much better that way, and you won't waste your valuable time doing the same old thing that everyone has seen before.

Your publicity campaign should be a campaign, planned and executed accordingly. And then go back to the information in Chapter Four. Measure the success of that campaign before launching a new one.

Because your resources are finite. And you should be writing the next book.

Remember, publicity and promotion are ultimately your decision. Choose wisely and your promotions won't hurt your writing (much).

Do what everyone else does, and you're probably wasting your time.

Be yourself, and you'll probably benefit from the little bits of time you spend promoting your work.

20

WORD OF MOUTH

Let's be honest here. Why are we doing all this promotion stuff?

I'm sure everyone will have a different answer, but the real answer is this:

You want to inform readers that you've published a book.

It really is that simple. But, as we discussed previously, it takes repeat viewings for advertising to sink in. So we can either be the most annoying people on the planet, trying to get people to buy our work, or we can trust our readers.

Because once you've informed the reader, you want to build word of mouth.

So many writers say they want to build readers. As if readers are a collection. Writers seem to think that once you "own" a reader, they're yours for life.

Sorry. It isn't that way at all—and you the reader know it.

You the writer have just forgotten it.

If you want to build anything, you want to build *word of mouth.*

And to do that, you'll have to do something most promoting writers suck at.

You'll have to trust your readers.

To do that, you'll have to trust your inner reader.

Think about what you like, and work from there.

This came home to me as I initially wrote this chapter. I wrote it in

November 2013, just after I had realized that I was writing more than one book in my Retrieval Artist series.

I initially thought I was doing a trilogy inside the larger series. After I had finished the "last" book in that trilogy, I realized I hadn't addressed anything, and I had much bigger story to tell.

It ultimately took me six more books to tell it. The saga, called *The Anniversary Day Saga*, is eight books long. Six of those books will appear (or appeared, depending on when you read this) back to back in the front part of 2015.

Which WMG Publishing will/has promote(d) like crazy.

But when I initially wrote this chapter, I had just told the fans of the Retrieval Artist series that they wouldn't be getting a book in December like they had for the previous two years.

I knew, as a reader, that some of the remaining six books in that series would disappoint the readers if the books appeared one per year, but would excite the readers if the books appeared one per month. I knew this because I read reader responses to larger series when the annual novel focused on side characters rather than main characters.

I also knew this because I'm an avid reader myself.

I love series that go on for a long time. I love it when the books in that series stand alone (more or less). I know how much richer those books can be when they're read in order.

In September 2013, I read (and recommended) a novel by one of my favorite writers, Elizabeth George. She ended that book on a cliffhanger (more or less) involving three of my very favorite characters in her series. I immediately preordered the next book, *Just One Evil Act*.

Unlike many other books I preorder, I actually counted the days until that one arrived. When it arrived, I started it immediately—and ultimately included it in my December 2013 Recommended Reading List.

I didn't do any of that because I felt I owed Elizabeth George anything. She's bought two of my short stories for anthologies, and I'm greatly honored given how much I love her work, but I have never met her, and I feel no obligation to buy her next book.

Instead, I feel an obligation to Barbara Havers and her neighbor, young Hadiyyah. As far as I'm concerned, those two people (and Hadiyyah's father, Taymullah Azhar) are living, breathing human beings, not characters in a book series.

I need to know what's going to happen to them all. Right now.

In fact, I needed to know in September.

And had I read *Believing the Lie* when it came out in 2011, I would have needed to know two years ago.

Why do I believe in Havers, Hadiyyah, and Azhar? Because Elizabeth George is a fantastic writer, and if you love mysteries, I think you should read everything she's written.

I'm a fan, and I want you to be fans, too. Not to support Elizabeth George, much as I like her work. But because I want you to meet Havers, Lynley, and the others who live and breathe in those books.

By the way, my monthly recommended reading list isn't me as a writer trying to promote anything. It's me as a reader sharing reads with other readers in the hopes you find something you'll like.

I try to keep my fangirl side and my reader side in close proximity when I send my books to market. One of the greatest frustrations for me as a writer has been traditional publishing's unwillingness to acknowledge the power of readers.

Traditional publishers, as we have discussed many times, do not think of readers when they take books to market. They think about booksellers.

I adore booksellers, and for about a decade (from 1993 to 2003), they were the primary sellers of books in this country. When the regional and local distributors used to market books in places other than bookstores, such as truck stops and grocery stores, coffee shops and museum gift shops, collapsed in the late 1990s, only the bookstores were left standing—and in many places, only the chains.

Publishers got rid of their local sales reps around that time and they also refused to give good deals to indie bookstores, destroying the widespread availability of books. The problem then, in traditional publishing, was that publishers started selling books to the chain bookstore buyers—about ten people total—and if those people weren't interested, well, then, the lazy publishers thought, no one was.

(*Except the readers! Us! You know! Us!* [Sorry. Couldn't resist.])

When it became easier for writers to publish their own books, the thing that caught traditional publishing by surprise was that those books actually sold. They sold electronically because that was often the only way to finish a half-finished series that the ten buyers for the chain bookstores thought wasn't important.

Books by unknowns sold as well, often because they were in genres that the ten buyers for the chain bookstores believed no one read (like western and science fiction). What's more, the books by unknowns—those writers not vetted by traditional publishers—weren't one-shot wonders. Often, those books became series, and each book in the series sold more than the previous book in the series.

Because the unknown writers were great storytellers, and the fans wanted the next book.

Fans are the best advocates for books, not for writers.

Fans are the ones who determine word of mouth.

The movie studios learned this the hard way a few years ago. Before Twitter became popular, a well-advertised but terrible movie could often hit #1 at the box office for the first weekend. Sales would drop horribly by week two, because by then word of mouth would have hit.

Then Twitter arrived. Moviegoers who saw the first show of Terrible Well-Advertised Movie would tweet that the thing sucked. That meme would get picked up on Facebook and then, before going to the movie on Saturday, people would check with their friends who had seen the movie on Friday.

It took one entire year for the movie industry to realize that the expectation for Terrible Well-Advertised Movie to hit #1 at the box office had become—almost overnight—a false expectation.

Word of mouth now moved at the speed of the Internet, and a movie saw its box office revenue *fall* hourly as word got out.

So for a while, the studios tried to have fake Tweeters building up the movie. That didn't work. There weren't enough paid Tweeters to overcome the response of the real audience.

And so it is with books.

You the writer cannot start word of mouth. It must come spontaneously from your readers. A good blog on a marketing website called Artful Thinkers[1] says this about word of mouth:

> *Talkers are your most valuable source for marketing, if they can speak from first hand experience. You can buy fans. Buying fans does not create loyalty or truth telling. The best talkers are those that trust you will deliver your value... People talk about what they like, what they trust and what they value. All of these are earned markers of success in business. You earn them by doing a great job and exceeding expectations...*

The problem with writers is that they try to "buy fans." The writers do everything wrong, urging their readers at the end of books with things like, "If you liked this book, please leave a review on Amazon," or "please tweet about it." Or worse, the writers demand that their readers do such things, reminding their readers that the readers owe the writer.

Um, no. They don't.

Readers owe a writer nothing.

Readers who liked a book but aren't tweeters or hate being cajoled will think you desperate. The thing is, readers who like your book will do everything you want and more to promote your work without you ever asking.

The ironic thing is that most writers learned this bad behavior from traditional publishers. Traditional publishers try to force word of mouth while ignoring how it really works.

Because traditional publishers work on the produce method of publishing—they have titles on the shelf for only a few weeks before the titles "spoil" and new titles come out—the publishers have a limited time in which to sell the book.

So traditional publishers do a full-court press, and demand that their writers do the same. *Tweet about your book all the time,* the traditional publishers tell their writers. *Make sure you do a "blog tour" the week of publication. Do a book tour on your own dime. Or maybe on our dime.*

As we discussed in the Old Ways Section, these methods work only on select titles, if at all. And they rarely work in the produce model.

By the time word of mouth starts spreading about good traditionally published midlist books, those books are no longer on the shelves of brick-and-mortar bookstores. These days, bestsellers often don't stay on the shelves very long either. So if you hear about a good book, say, two years after some traditional publisher released it, you might be stuck buying a used copy or an ecopy because your preferred copy isn't available. And that sale? It won't be counted toward the produce/velocity sales that are all-important to a traditional publisher.

As an indie publisher (or self-published writer), you don't have to take books out of print. Your books don't have to sell in the week of release, either. You have time.

You can, and should, let word of mouth build on its own.

The *only* way to jumpstart word of mouth is to let readers know that you have a new book out. Or an older book that has a new cover. Or maybe is about an event in the news.

All of the discoverability tools in this book should be used with that gentle jumpstart idea in mind. Because if you use them any other way, you'll turn people *away* from your books, not toward them.

All readers want to know is this: When is the next book coming out?

The next book is a particular thing per reader. It might be the actual next book in Series A. It might be the next book in Series B. It might be a book that's been out for fifteen years, but the reader is new to a writer's work and hasn't found that book yet.

To that reader, that fifteen-year-old novel is the next book.

One tool you have to help with the next-book syndrome is a newsletter. Only the truest of true fans sign up for a newsletter. They're the ones who want to know the day, the second, a new book releases. They will buy it very quickly and then, if they like it, start spreading word of mouth— without being asked. That's the key.

Don't ask. Don't beg. Don't expect.

Inform, and then back off.

Building a fan base takes years. Keeping fans takes work, generally consistent work. By that, I mean that you publish more than one book every five years.

Readers like to read a lot by their favorite writers. All of us can read a book faster than we can write one. And that's true of all writers, which is why we can never write fast enough to overwhelm our readers.

Plus, readers are choosy. For example, some of my readers come to my site for the free nonfiction. Some come for the Monday free fiction. Some read my science fiction. Some read my mysteries. Some don't read my fiction at all.

I don't expect them to. I certainly don't demand that they should read everything.

What someone reads is *her* choice, and I respect that.

The hardest thing to learn about discoverability is this:

Once you have published your book, you have no control over what the readers do next. None.

You have given word of mouth over to your readers.

They might choose to help you. They might forget for months to tell anyone about the book. They might never share your book with anyone else.

And that's okay.

You owe your readers only two things:

1. *A really good story (available in as many markets as possible)*
2. *Information on previous and upcoming works.*

That's all.

And if you don't do the second, well, someone (probably a fan you've never had contact with) will do it for you on a variety of websites, most of which you will never see.

Here's what you have to remember—what traditional publishing has never known or forgotten:

Readers and writers have the exact same goal. We want to lose ourselves in story for a few hours. Readers like to share the story that allowed them to leave their life for a while. Writers do too.

If you do your job as a storyteller, then a reader you never met will tell another person you'll never meet about your book.

You won't know it happened. You won't even know if that sale you made last Thursday came from word-of-mouth by a reader.

You'll *never* know.

And you have to be okay with that if you're going to publish your work.

However, try to be respectful of your readers. As I mentioned above, I try to tap my inner reader all the time.

Most writers never think like readers, and I think that's a problem.

Because if writers thought like readers, then writers would know when readers are feeling impatient or uninformed.

Most readers wait patiently for the next book or the next installment of whatever. Most are silent about it, but not all.

But we writers who are also readers should understand the desire to read a book *right now*, this moment, immediately after we have finished the previous book.

Because that impulse, that desire, is what causes readers to spread word of mouth. *Hey, everyone! I loved this series so much I can't wait for the next book.*

Exactly.

Since I posted about the difficulties I'm having writing the next book of the Retrieval Artist series, my readers—the ones who come to the site regularly (and there are thousands who do not)—have been very gracious.

I'm glad they're being understanding. I'm trying to treat them the way that I would like to be treated.

However, if they weren't understanding, I'd still write the books my way.

I did not write the story to reader expectations. Nor did I hurry up because I imagined some reader would get mad at me for writing books slowly.

I wrote this large project as fast as I could to finish it in a cohesive fashion. Then, with WMG's help, I'm publishing the books the way that I as a reader would want the books published. One right after the other, and relatively fast in publishing terms.

I'm doing this to please me, and to keep the project's integrity. By having all of the books in this saga available, readers can then choose how or if they want to read all of them.

Some readers will get every book as they come out.

Other readers will spread the books out over months or years.

And some readers might think the saga too long and never get to it.

It's all about choice.

It's also about remembering the thing that traditional publishers have forgotten: The customers for our books aren't ten buyers for chain bookstores. The customers for our books are readers worldwide.

Individuals, who choose to spend their hard-earned money on our work.

Some of those readers move on to the next book they want to read.

Others become evangelists for the books they love.

You can't beg customers to promote for you. You can't expect them to buy the next book. You can't expect them to remember the book title.

You can't even expect them to remember your name.

Write the next book. Publish it well (with good covers and blurbs, in all markets). If you enjoy writing that book, someone out there will enjoy reading it.

Trust the process.

It works.

And your inner reader knows it.

NOTES

1. What Is Discoverability?

1. http://en.wikipedia.org/wiki/Marketing#Types_of_marketing
2. http://en.wikipedia.org/wiki/Marketing#Types_of_marketing
3. http://www.businessdictionary.com/definition/marketing.html
4. http://www.businessdictionary.com/definition/four-P-s-of-marketing.html

6. The Most Important Thing

1. "Why Beyoncé Doesn't Believe the Hype and Why You Shouldn't Either," Michael Roffman, *Consequences of Sound* [http://consequenceofsound.net/2013/12/why-beyonce-doesnt-believe-the-hype-and-you-shouldnt-either/]
2. http://instagram.com/p/h2YFO6Pw1d/
3. "What We Can Learn from Beyoncé," Judah Joseph, *The Huffington Post*, 12/23/2013. [http://www.huffingtonpost.com/judah-joseph/what-we-can-learn-from-be_b_4491175.html]
4. "Beyoncé surprises Wal-Mart customers by paying for holiday gifts," Renee Dawn, *Today Entertainment*, December 23, 2013. [http://www.today.com/entertainment/beyonce-surprises-wal-mart-customers-paying-holiday-gifts-2D11792420]
5. "Beyoncé's Game Change," Gerrick D. Kennedy, *Los Angeles Times*, December 13, 2013. [http://www.latimes.com/entertainment/music/posts/la-et-ms-beyonce-surprises-internet-with-secret-album-20131212-story.html#page=1]
6. "Why Beyoncé Doesn't Believe the Hype and Why You Shouldn't Either" by Michael Roffman, *Consequences of Sound* [http://consequenceofsound.net/2013/12/why-beyonce-doesnt-believe-the-hype-and-you-shouldnt-either/]
7. "Beyoncé Spends Second Week at No. 1 on Billboard 200 Chart," Keith Caulfield, *Billboard*, December 26, 2013. [http://www.billboard.com/articles/news/5847921/beyonce-spends-second-week-at-no-1-on-billboard-200-chart]

7. Types Of Readers

1. http://www.rwa.org/p/cm/ld/fid=582
2. http://kk.org/thetechnium/2008/03/1000-true-fans/

8. Advertising And Traditional Publishing

1. http://www.ew.com/ew/static/advertising/rates.html
2. http://www.rtbookreviews.com/magazine/print-advertising-rates
3. http://en.wikipedia.org/wiki/Romantic_Times
4. http://en.wikipedia.org/wiki/Entertainment_Weekly
5. http://locusmag.com/Magazine/RateCard.html
6. "Shatzkin: The Challenge and Opportunity of Self-Published Authors for Publishers,"

Jeremy Greenfield, Digital Book World, November 18, 2013. [http://www.digitalbook-world.com/2013/shatzkin-the-challenge-and-opportunity-of-self-published-authors-for-publishers/]

9. The Fierce Urgency Of Now

1. "Cyber Monday set record as shoppers sought online bargains" Tiffany Hsu, *Los Angeles Times*, December 3, 2013. [http://www.latimes.com/business/la-fi-cyber-monday-results-20131204-story.html]
2. "'Catching Fire,' 'Frozen' Are Hot at the Movies," Erich Schwartzel, *The Wall Street Journal*, December 1, 2013. [http://online.wsj.com/news/articles/SB10001424052702304355104579232291023007608]
3. "Summer Winners and Losers," *Entertainment Weekly*, September 13, 2013. [http://www.ew.com/ew/article/0,,20733755_4,00.html]
4. http://www.huffingtonpost.com/2013/11/28/walmart-fight-black-friday_n_4357939.html
5. "Bad Black Friday Deals," Kathy Kristof, CBS Moneywatch, November 28, 2013. [http://www.cbsnews.com/news/bad-black-friday-deals/]
6. http://en.wikipedia.org/wiki/Don%27t_Stop_Believing
7. "Summer Winners and Losers," *Entertainment Weekly*, September 13, 2013. [http://www.ew.com/ew/article/0,,20733755_4,00.html]
8. "Howard Changing Topics to His Space Trip – *The Big Bang Theory*." [https://www.youtube.com/watch?v=dkIEuyEsVgY]

10. The Old Ways

1. "James Patterson Inc.," Jonathan Mahler, *The New York Times Magazine*, January 20, 2010. [http://www.nytimes.com/2010/01/24/magazine/24patterson-t.html?pagewanted=all&_r=3&]
2. "James Patterson Inc." Jonathan Mahler, *The New York Times Magazine*, January 20, 2010. [http://www.nytimes.com/2010/01/24/magazine/24patterson-t.html?pagewanted=all&_r=3&]
3. *Hothouse: The Art of Survival and the Survival of Art at America's Most Celebrated Publishing House, Farrar, Straus, and Giroux*, Boris Kachka, Simon & Schuster, 2013. P. 211 in the hardcover edition.
4. "Dickens V America," Matthew Pearl, *More Intelligent Life*. [http://moreintelligentlife.com/story/dickens-vs-america]
5. 2014 Ad Rate Card, *Asimov's Magazine*, http://www.asimovs.com/pdfs/Sci-fi_2014rates.pdf.

11. When The Old Ways Work

1. http://www.wmgpublishinginc.com/booksellers/#sthash.5Qwv70Oq.dpuf
2. http://www.bookweb.org/aba-publisher-partner-program
3. http://www1.baker-taylor.com/PDFs/2014ProductMarketingGuide-LoF.pdf
4. "The Mystery of the Book Sales Spike," Jeffrey A. Trachtenberg, *The Wall Street Journal*, February 22, 2013. [http://online.wsj.com/news/articles/SB10001424127887323864304578316143623600544]

Notes

12. Branding

1. http://www.deanwesleysmith.com/online-workshops/
2. http://www.deanwesleysmith.com/online-workshops/

13. Pricing

1. http://www.mystgalaxy.com
2. http://kriswrites.com/2014/01/22/the-business-rusch-pricing-part-2-or-discoverability-part-7-continued/#sthash.rsBHeFgz.dpbs
3. "Update re: Amazon/Hachette Business Interruption," Amazon Kindle Forum, July 29, 2014. [http://www.amazon.com/forum/kindle/ref=cm_cd_tfp_ef_tft_tp?_encoding=UTF8&cdForum=Fx1D7SY3BVSESG&cdThread=Tx3J0JKSSUIRCMT]
4. "Does Discount Size Matter For Promotion?" *Unbound: Ebook Marketing Insights From BookBub*, December 4, 2013. [http://unbound.bookbub.com/post/68933121888/does-discount-size-matter-for-ebook-promotions]
5. "Loss Leader," Businessdictionary.com, [http://www.businessdictionary.com/definition/loss-leader.html#ixzz2rBxGOzqh]

14. More Passive Marketing

1. "A One-Man Operation," Hugh Howey, Hughhowey.com, February 4, 2014. [http://www.hughhowey.com/a-one-man-operation/#more-5143]
2. http://www.deanwesleysmith.com/online-workshops/
3. "How to Get your books into the right Categories and Sub-categories: Readers to Books/Books to Readers—Part Three," M. Louisa Locke, blog post on her website, December 16, 2013. [http://mlouisalocke.com/2013/12/16/how-to-get-your-books-into-the-right-categories-and-sub-categories-readers-to-booksbooks-to-readers-part-three/#more-1572]
4. "Readers to Books/Books to Readers-Part Two: How to Sell Books in the Kindle Store with the Search Bar," M. Louisa Locke, blog post on her website, November 21, 2013. [http://mlouisalocke.com/2013/11/21/readers-to-booksbooks-to-readers-part-two-how-to-sell-books-in-the-kindle-store-with-the-search-bar/]
5. http://www.stephanielaurens.com
6. http://www.stabenow.com
7. http://www.hughhowey.com
8. "The Mystery Book Consumer in the Digital Age," Sisters in Crime, 2010. P. 42. [http://www.sistersincrime.org/associations/10614/files/ConsumerBuyingBookReport.pdf]

15. Blogs And Interviews

1. http://kellymccullough.com/category/friday-cat-blogging/
2. http://www.deanwesleysmith.com
3. http://www.sfsignal.com/archives/category/interviews/mind-meld/

16. Social Media

1. *The Mystery Consumer in the Digital Age*, Sisters in Crime Report, 2010. [http://www.sistersincrime.org/associations/10614/files/ConsumerBuyingBookReport.pdf]

2. "What Influences Mystery Book Sales," *The Mystery Consumer in the Digital Age*, Sisters in Crime Report, 2010, page 16.
    [http://www.sistersincrime.org/associations/10614/files/ConsumerBuyingBookReport.pdf]

3. "What Influences Mystery Book Sales," *The Mystery Consumer in the Digital Age*, Sisters in Crime Report, 2010, page 18.
    [http://www.sistersincrime.org/associations/10614/files/ConsumerBuyingBookReport.pdf]

4. "What Influences Mystery Book Sales," *The Mystery Consumer in the Digital Age*, Sisters in Crime Report, 2010, page 29.
    [http://www.sistersincrime.org/associations/10614/files/ConsumerBuyingBookReport.pdf]

5. "What Your Teen Is Really Doing All Day On Twitter and Instagram," Evie Nagy, *Fast Company*, February 18, 2014.
    [http://www.fastcompany.com/3026499/most-creative-people/what-your-teen-is-really-doing-all-day-on-twitter-and-instagram]

6. https://www.youtube.com/watch?v=57dzaMaouXA

7. "News Use Across Social Media Platforms," by Jesse Holcomb, Jeffrey Gottfried, and Amy Mitchell, Pew Research Journalism Project, November 14, 2013. [http://www.journalism.org/2013/11/14/news-use-across-social-media-platforms/]

8. "What Your Teen Is Really Doing All Day on Twitter and Instagram," Evie Nagy, *Fast Company*, February 18, 2014.
    [http://www.fastcompany.com/3026499/most-creative-people/what-your-teen-is-really-doing-all-day-on-twitter-and-instagram]

9. "Why People Ignore Social Networks and How To Stay Engaged," by Evan LaPage, Hootsuite blog, February 2014. [http://blog.hootsuite.com/why-people-ignore-social-networks/]

10. Zachary Quinto vs. Leonard Nimoy: "The Challenge," Audi ad.
    [https://www.youtube.com/watch?v=UengULt6t7Q]

11. "Women and Social Media in 2012," BlogHer, Page 9. [http://www.blogher.com/files/2012-socialmediafinalv2-120314103327-phpapp02.pdf]

12. "These 5 Brands are Nailing It on Pinterest," Hannah Clark, Hootsuite blog, December 2013. [http://blog.hootsuite.com/5-brands-pinterest/]

13. https://www.youtube.com/channel/UC0iJLP8xA_Xhr0IABc1brgg

14. "5 Great Brands on Vine," by Evan LaPage, the Hootsuite blog, August 2013. [http://blog.hootsuite.com/5-great-brands-on-vine/]

15. "Brands Having Awesome Conversations on Twitter," Hannah Clark, Hootsuite blog, January, 2014. [http://blog.hootsuite.com/brands-awesome-conversations-twitter/]

16. https://twitter.com/jimmyfallon

17. "DiGiorno Pizza Live-Tweeted NBC's 'The Sound Of Music' in 'Unplanned Event' and It Was Amazing," Erica Futterman, *BuzzFeed*, December 5, 2013. [http://www.buzzfeed.com/ericafutterman/digiorno-pizza-live-tweeted-nbcs-the-sound-of-music-in-unpla]

18. Arby's Slayed the Grammys With This Tweet About Pharrell Williams' Hat," David Griner, Adfreak, January 27, 2014. [http://www.adweek.com/adfreak/arbys-slayed-grammys-tweet-about-pharrell-williams-hat-155237]

19. *Freelancer's Survival Guide*, Third Edition, Chapter 34: Networking Online.

20. http://selfcontrolapp.com

17. With A Little Help From Your Friends

1. http://bookviewcafe.com/bookstore/
2. http://bookviewcafe.com/bookstore/book-view-cafe-frequently-asked-questions/
3. Personal email to the author, March 2014.
4. http://www.challenger.org
5. https://storybundle.com/archives/truly-epic-fantasy-bundle
6. http://www.uncollectedanthology.com
7. http://theindievoice.com
8. http://theindievoice.com/about/
9. Personal email to the author, March, 2014.
10. http://nicoleevelina.com/2013/12/20/what-lurks-beneath-glastonbury-abbey/
11. Personal email to the author, February, 2014
12. http://www.mysiamese.com
13. http://www.blog.catblogosphere.com

18. A Sampler Of Samples

1. Ad Rate Card, Dell Magazines. [http://www.analogsf.com/pdfs/Sci-fi_2014rates.pdf]
2. *Analog* Mediakit, analogsf.com. [http://www.analogsf.com/mediakit.shtml]
3. http://www.pw.org/content/rosebud_magazine
4. http://en.wikipedia.org/wiki/Bea_Arthur
5. http://www.amazon.com/gp/product/0061490199/ref=olp_product_details?ie=UTF8&me=

The Invisible Chapter

1. Beyoncé's Instagram Page, December, 2013. [http://instagram.com/p/h2YFO6Pw1d/]
2. "N.C. teen's Hail Mary shot gets help from late friend," Steve Hartman, CBS News, March 21, 2014. http://www.cbsnews.com/news/north-carolina-teens-hail-mary-shot-gets-help-from-late-friend/
3. "The Veronica Mars Movie Project," Kickstarter.com [https://www.kickstarter.com/projects/559914737/the-veronica-mars-movie-project]
4. "George R. R. Martin Watches 'Red Wedding' Reaction Videos" – CONAN on TBS. [https://www.youtube.com/watch?v=azr99OfKLxk]

20. Word Of Mouth

1. "Growing Your Business By Word of Mouth," Jamie Glass, Artful Thinkers. [http://www.artfulthinkers.com/growing-your-business-by-word-of-mouth]

NEWSLETTER SIGN-UP

Be the first to know!

Please sign up for the Kristine Kathryn Rusch and Dean Wesley Smith newsletters, and receive exclusive content, keep up with the latest news, releases and so much more—even the occasional giveaway.

So, what are you waiting for?
To sign up for Kristine Kathryn Rusch's newsletter go to
kristinekathrynrusch.com.
To sign up for Dean Wesley Smith's newsletter go to deanwesleysmith.com

But wait! There's more. Sign up for the WMG Publishing newsletter, too, and get the latest news and releases from all of the WMG authors and lines, including Kristine Grayson, Kris Nelscott, Dean Wesley Smith, *Fiction River: An Original Anthology Magazine, Smith's Monthly, Pulphouse Fiction Magazine* and so much more.

To sign up go to wmgpublishing.com.

ABOUT THE AUTHOR

KRISTINE KATHRYN RUSCH

New York Times bestselling author Kristine Kathryn Rusch writes in almost every genre. Generally, she uses her real name (Rusch) for most of her writing. Under that name, she publishes bestselling science fiction and fantasy, award-winning mysteries, acclaimed mainstream fiction, controversial nonfiction, and the occasional romance. Her novels have made bestseller lists around the world and her short fiction has appeared in eighteen best of the year collections. She has won more than twenty-five awards for her fiction, including the Hugo, *Le Prix Imaginales*, the *Asimov's* Readers Choice award, and the *Ellery Queen Mystery Magazine* Readers Choice Award.

Publications from *The Chicago Tribune* to *Booklist* have included her Kris Nelscott mystery novels in their top-ten-best mystery novels of the year. The Nelscott books have received nominations for almost every award in the mystery field, including the best novel Edgar Award, and the Shamus Award.

She writes goofy romance novels as award-winner Kristine Grayson.

She also edits. Beginning with work at the innovative publishing company, Pulphouse, followed by her award-winning tenure at *The Magazine of Fantasy & Science Fiction*, she took fifteen years off before returning to editing with the original anthology series *Fiction River,* published by WMG Publishing. She acts as series editor with her husband, writer Dean Wesley Smith.

To keep up with everything she does, go to kriswrites.com and sign up for her newsletter. To track her many pen names and series, see their individual websites (krisnelscott.com, kristinegrayson.com, retrievalartist.com, divingintothewreck.com, fictionriver.com, pulphousemagazine.com).

ABOUT THE AUTHOR

DEAN WESLEY SMITH

Considered one of the most prolific writers working in modern fiction, *USA Today* bestselling writer Dean Wesley Smith published almost two hundred novels in forty years, and hundreds and hundreds of short stories across many genres.

At the moment he produces novels in several major series, including the time travel Thunder Mountain novels set in the Old West, the galaxy-spanning Seeders Universe series, the urban fantasy Ghost of a Chance series, a superhero series starring Poker Boy, and a mystery series featuring the retired detectives of the Cold Poker Gang.

His monthly magazine, *Smith's Monthly*, which consists of only his own fiction, premiered in October 2013 and offers readers more than 70,000 words per issue, including a new and original novel every month.

During his career, Dean also wrote a couple dozen *Star Trek* novels, the only two original *Men in Black* novels, Spider-Man and X-Men novels, plus novels set in gaming and television worlds. Writing with his wife Kristine Kathryn Rusch under the name Kathryn Wesley, he wrote the novel for the NBC miniseries The Tenth Kingdom and other books for *Hallmark Hall of Fame* movies.

He wrote novels under dozens of pen names in the worlds of comic books and movies, including novelizations of almost a dozen films, from *The Final Fantasy* to *Steel* to *Rundown*.

Dean also worked as a fiction editor off and on, starting at Pulphouse Publishing, then at *VB Tech Journal*, then Pocket Books, and now at WMG Publishing, where he and Kristine Kathryn Rusch serve as series editors for the acclaimed *Fiction River* anthology series, which launched in 2013. In 2018, WMG Publishing Inc. launched the first issue of the reincarnated *Pulphouse Fiction Magazine*, with Dean reprising his role as editor.

For more information about Dean's books and ongoing projects, please visit his website at www.deanwesleysmith.com and sign up for his newsletter.

Made in the USA
Columbia, SC
14 August 2020

16310375R00297